THE

ARYAN HOUSEHOLD

ITS STRUCTURE AND ITS DEVELOPMENT

AN INTRODUCTION TO

COMPARATIVE JURISPRUDENCE

BY

WILLIAM EDWARD HEARN, LL.D.

DEAN OF THE FACULTY OF LAW IN THE UNIVERSITY OF MELBOURNE

THE LAWBOOK EXCHANGE, LTD.
Clark, New Jersey

ISBN 978-1-58477-124-1

Lawbook Exchange edition 2002, 2026

The quality of this reprint is equivalent to the quality of the original work.

THE LAWBOOK EXCHANGE, LTD.
33 Terminal Avenue
Clark, New Jersey 07066-1321

Please see our website for a selection of our other publications and fine facsimile reprints of classic works of legal history:
www.lawbookexchange.com

Library of Congress Cataloging-in-Publication Data

Hearn, William Edward, 1826-1888.
The Aryan household: its structure, and its development: an introduction to comparative jurisprudence / by William Edward Hearn.
p. cm.
Originally published: London; New York: Longmans, Green, and Co., 1891.
Includes bibliographical references and index.
ISBN 1-58477-124-0 (cloth: acid-free paper)
1. Law, Indo-European. 2. Domestic relations—Europe—History—To 1500. 3. Domestic relations—Asia—History—To 1500. 4. Family—Europe—History—To 1500. 5. Family—Asia—History—To 1500. I. Title.

KL175 .H43 2000
346.01'5—dc21 00-056302

Printed in the United States of America on acid-free paper

THE

ARYAN HOUSEHOLD

ITS STRUCTURE AND ITS DEVELOPMENT

AN INTRODUCTION TO

COMPARATIVE JURISPRUDENCE

BY

WILLIAM EDWARD HEARN, LL.D.

DEAN OF THE FACULTY OF LAW IN THE UNIVERSITY OF MELBOURNE

LONDON AND NEW YORK
LONGMANS, GREEN, AND CO.

MELBOURNE SYDNEY AND ADELAIDE
GEORGE ROBERTSON AND COMPANY

1891

TABLE OF CONTENTS.

Chapter V. *The Clan.*

Chapter VI. *The System of Archaic Kinship.*

Chapter VII. *The Near Kin.*

Chapter VIII. *The Distinction of Ranks in the Clan.*

Chapter IX. *Community.*

Chapter X. *Immunity.*

Chapter XVI. *The Territory of the State.*

Chapter XVII. *Law and Custom.*

Chapter XVIII. *The Law and Custom of Property.*

Chapter XIX. *The Rise of Civil Jurisdiction.*

Chapter XX. *The Decadence of the Clan.*

INTRODUCTION.

I PROPOSE to describe the rise and the progress of the principal institutions that are common to the nations of the Aryan race. I shall endeavour to illustrate the social organization under which our remote forefathers lived. I shall, so far as I am able, trace the modes of thought and of feeling which, in their mutual relations, influenced their conduct. I shall indicate the germs of those institutions which have now attained so high a development; and I shall attempt to show the circumstances in which political society took its rise, and the steps by which, in Western Europe, it supplanted its ancient rival.

My subject is confined to the institutions of the Aryan race. I do not offer these pages as a contribution to the history of culture. I do not seek to propose or to support any system as to the origin or the evolution of man. With the theories that have been advocated on these subjects, I am not now concerned, and I express no opinion upon them. I neither affirm nor deny their truth. I seek to investigate the early history of the institutions of one family of the human race, and to follow that inquiry so far only as there is positive evidence for our guidance. Even within these limits the subject is wide enough and grand enough to warrant a separate discussion. That family of nations of which I write is confessedly the foremost in the world. It includes almost all the nations of Europe. It includes the Empire, once so great, of Persia, and the multitudinous tribes of Hindostan. Its history is more glorious, its renown is more diffused, its progress in science and in art is more advanced, its religion is more pure, its politics and its laws are more beneficent and more just, than those which prevail elsewhere upon earth. It, too, is that great mother of men by whose sons vast continents have been, and still are being, won from the wildness of nature, and converted to purposes of human use and human enjoyment. By their strong arms and their bold hearts the aspiration of Poseidon* has been fulfilled, and the Aryan name and the Aryan fame have been borne wherever Eos sheds her rays. The early history of such a race is worth an inquiry for itself. Except, therefore, when it is necessary to prove the present existence of some social force which has ceased to operate among ourselves, I have omitted all notice of non-Aryan peoples. If no conclusions be drawn wider than the premises, if the assertions made be limited to Aryan men, no reasonable objection can be taken to this course. We thereby sacrifice, indeed, much that is of interest, and detract much from the pretensions of our inquiry to scientific rank. Yet, if we lose in extent, we gain in accuracy. Our evidence as to early Aryan institutions is far superior to the evidence respecting the institutions of any other people, except the Hebrews. Most of our knowledge of other races rests upon the unsupported testimony of travellers or sojourners. Of these persons, many had little competency as observers. Even where the skill of the observer is undisputed, the difficulty of communication between men whose intellects are on a different level, the difficulty of explaining in a strange language strange and complicated customs, and the fact that the information thus

* *σὸν δ' ἤτοι κλέος ἔσται ὅσον τ' ἐπικίδναται ἠώς.*—Il., vii. 458.

acquired relates to contemporaneous matters only, and does not profess to explain preceding states of society, all tend to diminish the value of the evidence. In the case of such testimony, even though it be the best of its kind, we anxiously look for some corroboration. This corroboration is attained, in a special degree, in the case of the Aryan nations. For them, or at least for some of them, we possess trustworthy records, both direct and incidental, of their modes of life, their beliefs, and their manners, for a period extending backwards for 3,000 years. Not only are our materials richer, but they have been more thoroughly treated, and are more ready for use than those which exist in any other case. And for the Aryans alone, the recent sciences of Comparative Philology and of Comparative Mythology have thrown new and welcome lights upon the remote past. Further, the Aryans form a well-marked ethnologic division. Even if foreign elements sometimes present themselves, the main influencing forces are homogeneous. We can pursue our inquiries without being disturbed by the appearance of that unknown and immeasurable quantity termed race. When definite conclusions respecting the primitive Aryan culture have been established, these conclusions may hereafter receive—indeed, we may confidently anticipate will receive—a much wider extension. But, in the present condition of our knowledge, it is prudent to avoid all disturbing influences, and to trace as fully as we can those lines upon which the great edifice of Western civilization has, in fact, been built.

For these reasons, I have assumed as my starting point the earliest state of Aryan society of which we have any distinct historical proof. How that state began, or what were its antecedents, I do not inquire. Doubtless society had a beginning upon earth as well as life itself. Whether these beginnings are, or are not, discoverable, I do not pretend to say. But all of truth that the following pages contain will remain true in whatever way society began, or whatever may have been the antecedents of our race The other extreme, however, of our inquiry is more difficult to mark. The stream of history not only broadens and deepens, but also divides as it flows down. I do not say that a history of Aryan civilization, or even a general history of the Aryan race, is an impossibility; but it is a task which I have no intention to undertake. All that I propose is to examine the structure of our archaic society, and to indicate, if I cannot fully trace, the process of its development. That development has, of course, varied with the circumstances of each people. I can but illustrate its mother form, and note the rudiments of our present institutions. I have thus to describe, first, the clan system, which was the original type of Aryan society; and, next, the rise of political society, and its relation to the earlier system. With the complete establishment of the later form my task is done, and I leave to others the narration of the complex fortunes of the State.

In all its leading characteristics—political, legal, religious, economic—archaic society presents a complete contrast to that in which we live. There was in it no central government, and consequently there were no political organs. There was no law to make, and there was none to be executed. There were neither parliaments, nor courts of justice, nor executive officers. There was no national church. The great bulk of property, not only as to its tenure, but as to its enjoyment, was in the hands—not of individuals, but of corporate households. There were few contracts, and no wills. Men lived according to their customs. They received their property from their fathers, and transmitted it to their heirs. They were protected, or, if need were, avenged, by the help of their kinsmen. There was, in short, neither individual nor State. The clan, or some association founded upon the model of the clan, and its subdivisions, filled the whole of our forefathers' social life. Within its limits was their world. Beyond it, they could find no resting place. For the origin of this clan relation, we must ascend a long way in the history of the human mind. It is due neither to force nor to fraud, nor to any calculation of personal advantage. It has its source in the sentiment of religion. In archaic society, the one unfailing centripetal force was community of worship. As many as were forms of worship, so many were the associations of men. Where men were associated, there a special worship is found. The symbol of the common worship was a meal shared in honour of the Deity. Of these various worships, probably the oldest, and certainly the most persistent, was the worship of the Lares, or house spirits, or, in other words, deceased ancestors. These spirits, together with their living descendants—whether natural, or adoptive—in their several ranks formed collectively that corporate body which, though it is known by a variety of names, I have called the household. Over the household the House Father presided, with powers limited only by the custom of his race. He was generally the eldest male of the line. He represented the household in all external dealings. He was charged with the management of its property and with the celebration of its worship. Sooner or later, when the household became inconveniently large, it spontaneously divided into several households, all related to each other, but each having a separate existence, each holding distinct corporate property, and each maintaining its special worship. The continued increase of these related households gave rise to the clan, the form in which, historically, our ancestors first become apparent to us. This wider association, which naturally resembled, in many respects, the household of which it was the expansion, marked the boundary line of human sympathy in the archaic world. Within the clan there were the truest loyalty and devotion. Beyond the clan there was at best absolute indifference, and usually active hostility. The clan was settled upon land of which it, in its corporate character, had the exclusive ownership, and which it shared among its members according to certain customary rules. It possessed an organization sufficient for its ordinary wants, and was essentially autonomous. It had, too, its gradations of rank. Every clan contained nobles—that is, men of pure blood and of long descent, and free men whose blood, though good, was not maintained through the necessary number of generations. But it contained others besides the men of pure blood. These were dependents, varying in degree from the honoured guest to the mere slave. Some of these dependents, who were personally free, and were settled on the land, acquired, by a residence extending over three generations, rights of inheritance in the soil; and could not, according to general custom, be removed from their holdings so long as they performed their customary duties. But although property was thus generally held by corporate households, agencies were at work which tended to introduce separate interests. The old customs were inflexible. They admitted of no deviation, and of no extension. Accordingly, their rules of property applied only to certain specified objects. These objects, including generally the house and the land, with certain rights incident thereto, and the instruments of cultivation, descended from father to son. They were the *corpus*, so to speak, of the household estate, and were intended to be inalienable. But other kinds of property, otherwise acquired, were not within the custom. Two kinds of property seem thus to have grown up together, both of which, in regard to different objects, might co-exist in the same person. Thus, although all households had their respective shares in the common estate, one household might become much richer than another. In a time when there were few markets either for the sale of surplus produce or for the purchase of objects of desire, the larger part of any superfluous wealth was naturally expended in the maintenance of permanent retainers, or in the occasional supply of food and equipments. Thus we have two institutions —the village community, and by its side, in favourable conditions, the enlarged independent household under the absolute control of its head. Such apparently was the form of the society in which lived the common forefathers of the great nations of Western Europe. In their original home in Central Asia they lived much as the Rajpút clans now live, as the Highlanders lived two centuries ago, as the Romans lived under their kings, as the Athenians lived before the time of Solon. This was the germ—even yet in some places discernible in its original form—from which, by lineal descent, came the Empire of Rome and the Empire of Byzantium, the chivalry of the Latin nations, the restored sceptre of the united Fatherland, and the long glories of the British Crown.

These clans gave rise to new combinations. Sometimes they formed the model for other associations more or less lasting, which, although the motive for their establishment varied, always assumed the form and followed the rules of a brotherhood. Sometimes new and kindred clans arose in the ordinary course of evolution, and acknowledged an inter-gentile relation similar to the relation which existed between members of the same clan. Sometimes separate clans combined, either for temporary objects, or with the intention of a permanent alliance. One of these forms of union gave rise to what we call the State. Between the different coalescing bodies a true integration took place, and the aggregate acquired a life separate from the life of its several component parts, and ultimately superior to it. This union was at first, like all others, personal, but finally became territorial. The tie that held the society together was not the fact of a common descent, or even the fact of a common worship, but the fact of its occupation of a common country. Early political history consists mainly of the narrative of the relations between the clans and the new body to which they had given rise. The great example of this process is found in the history of Roman law, both because Rome was the earliest example on a large scale of a true State, and because the results of that process directly and largely influenced the history of modern Europe. I have therefore endeavoured to compare the two analogous social functions—Law and Custom; the one belonging to the State, the other holding a similar place in relation to the clan. I have sought to trace the early history of property, and the gradual growth of the supremacy of law; and I have followed the sinking fortunes of the clan until, all over the ancient world, the State shone forth sole regent of the social sky in the unclouded splendour of the Julian line.

The discovery that society may be organized otherwise than politically, and that our own political society includes among its antecedents such an organization, will ultimately lead to a reconsideration of some important departments of human knowledge. The earliest and the most conspicuous and the most extensive changes may be expected in history. The tale must be told over again, and from a different point of view. Narratives which pre-suppose the existence of a state of society similar to our own, and of similar motives, cannot be set right by a few notes or corrections. The stand-point must be changed, and the old materials must under the altered light be studied anew. Still more than in general history the necessity for reconstruction appears in the history of law. Law is a secondary phenomenon, and is itself the result of remoter antecedents. It follows, therefore, that, in the words of Sir H. S. Maine, "Nothing in law springs entirely from a sense of convenience."* In law, above all things, we must leave the streams and seek the sources. It is not long since it was thought to be a sufficient explanation of any legal peculiarity to refer it to the feudal system; and the feudal system has to answer for many an error, and much perplexity, in original inquiries into archaic society, and sometimes for more serious and practical inconveniences. It is now clear that we must go a long way behind feudalism, and that the so-called feudal analogies among (for example) the Rajpúts and the Afghans are altogether delusive. To these earlier social forms many branches of our law and our institutions may readily be traced. The development of the village, or assemblage of dwellings, gave the πόλις, or City State. The development of the arable mark gave the Indian and the Slav village communities. The development of the pastoral mark explains many peculiarities of the Keltic clan. The *Comitatus* is merely an enlargement of the household. The law of allegiance, the law of the precinct, the law of the peace, were all consequences of the *Comitatus*. They marked the authority of the House Father, whether personal, or local, or guaranteed. The various associations, whether for religious, or industrial, or professional purposes, pre-suppose and imitate the archaic forms of society. And these forms, and the modes of thought to which they give rise, alone explain the old disputes between the nobles and the plebeians, the nature of the tyrannies, and much else that is perplexing in the law and the government of antiquity.

* "Ancient Law," p. 233.

I may here notice a consequence of this view which throws some light on a once famous controversy. I mean the theory of the social contract. That society was based upon a contract few persons would now care to maintain. There is no evidence that any such contract was in fact made. It is in effect inconceivable that it should have been formed; it is scarcely less inconceivable, that having been formed, it should have been observed. But it is, I think, too much to say that no political society could have at least originated in contract. I suppose that, in the case of the United States, and in the case of the United Kingdom itself, we have examples of two great political societies of which contract is the foundation. Colonial governments, too, are formed, if not by contract, yet artificially by legislation. We shall see that the earliest political societies were in the nature of voluntary associations, the basis of which was community of worship. The controversy seems to have arisen from the failure to perceive that political society, although it is the highest, is not the only form of society; and that men have lived, and still live happily, without kings, and without parliaments, and without laws.

There are other matters, too, on which, under the penalty of serious error, we must not apply, to men under different conditions from ourselves, our ordinary standards of judgment. Much of the opposition to political economy has been due to the very natural, or at least very British, desire of some of its earlier teachers to generalize from British phenomena alone. This error has been corrected; but it is evident that there are some societies which the ordinary economic rules do not fit. I think that the reason is, that the conditions of political society alone furnish the postulates of political economy. I believe that political economy is a true science; that is, that its phenomena may be traced to ultimate laws of human nature. These laws are at all times the same, but the conditions necessary for their operation did not exist, or very imperfectly existed, in archaic society. Political economy requires competition, and is hopelessly embarrassed by custom. Competition implies free individual action, and such action is unknown under the clan *régime*. The conclusions of political economy are universally true, but only on the assumption that a certain state of society is present, and that certain beliefs and motives are absent. What can political economy do with a Chinaman, who, for the sake of posthumous worship of himself and his ancestors, is willing to be hanged for the sum of £33? "It is difficult," says Mr. Lyall,* "to deal with a holy man whose disciples are ready to bury themselves alive if the Government puts pressure on their master for land-taxes, and thus to bring down a curse upon the whole administration. This is the Hindu method of excommunication, very effective still in Rajpútána, and not to be faced with impunity by the most powerful chief."

Similar observations apply in the case of ethics. The principles of right and wrong are immutable, but their application in dealings with other persons is different in different ages. Among archaic men the clan, or other association like the clan, forms to each individual his world. Within it his duties lie, and are recognized. Without it he acknowledges no more obligation towards other men than he does towards the inhabitants of another planet. It is unreasonable to blame men for not conforming to a standard which they never accepted, and of which they never heard. The theory of utility would have been altogether incomprehensible to our archaic forefathers. The theory of the moral sense would have been intelligible,

* Ed. Rev., cxliv., 198.

provided that its operation was limited to a man's own kin. The recognition of the brotherhood of the human race has been a slow and painful lesson, and perhaps even yet some portions of it remain to be learned. We should not, therefore, be harsh in our condemnation of archaic men whose moral standard was different from our own, because they, without hesitation, did acts or observed forbearances which, among those who walk by a better light, would call forth merited reprobation.

One suggestion of a practical character I will, in this connection, venture to offer. One of the great difficulties that missionaries have experienced in dealing with those people whose society is archaic has been the ruinous social consequences of conversion. In such circumstances a convert must literally obey the precept of the Gospel, and, if he desire to follow his new Master, must leave all. He becomes an outcast from his own people and his father's house; but his new religion does not supply him with a new place in the world. A religion which has adapted itself to a system where the social unit is the individual, strangely misfits a convert who has never known any other form of society than that of the clan. Yet in its early days Christianity was formed upon the ancient type, and the Church was practically an all-receiving non-genealogic clan, in which every new comer found his appointed place and his fit society. To some such primitive form it will have to revert when it deals with people whose social state is imperfectly developed. Amongst them the Church must compete, as once among our own race it competed, with the household and the kin; and the mutual relations of Christian men must, under such conditions, be rendered far more intimate than for a thousand years they have been in Europe. I believe that, in India at least, some of the missionaries perceive this necessity. Villages have been formed of converts collected from a variety of districts. It is said that these persons readily fall into a "brotherhood,"* and assume the character of a genuine village community. The experiment is one of deep interest to those who observe social phenomena. To those who are occupied with higher concerns it may possibly prove a new and potent force.

If we cannot measure the Past by the Present, so it is vain to seek for the Present a standard in the Past. The structures of the two societies are radically different. Some persons have fancied that they can see in the Russian *Mir* the realization of their communistic dreams, just as the philosophers of the Porch once thought that they had found in the jurisdiction of the Prætor their long-sought Law of Nature. But the *Mir* is on a lower level of social structure than that of Western Europe; and the attempt on our part to imitate it is not more reasonable than would be an attempt to make men quadrupeds, or to convert mammals into birds. We cannot, while we remain what we are, restore the institutions of the past. The better adapted these institutions were to their original purpose, the less fit are they for the altered conditions of our present life. The land tenure of archaic times implied among the freemen an aristocracy of birth, and below the freemen a servile population. Our forefathers would have regarded the doctrine of the equality of man as folly, and the doctrine of the free transfer of land as impious. We cannot, then, hope to learn from the history of these lower forms any practical improvement in our social arrangements. But we can more or less distinctly trace the steps by which these arrangements in fact arose. We can see how much of them is permanent, and in what direction alteration is safe.

* Sir H. S. Maine, "Early History of Institutions," p. 238. See also Mr. Hunter's "Orissa," vol. ii., p. 143.

Most of all, early history suggests how slow, and difficult, and uncertain a process is national growth; how easily the oak that has stood for centuries may be cut down; how impossible it is to fill its place. There was true wisdom in the admonition of the Doric mother to her son, "*Spartam nactus es; hanc exorna.*" The study of the Past teaches us to be proud of the Present, although with no indiscriminating pride; and while it warns us that change is the law of social life, it also warns us that the character and the limits of that change are not arbitrary. Such will, I think, be the predominating sentiment in the mind of every one who, from the scattered fragments and faint memories of the Past, essays to—

> "Spell the record of his long descent,
> More largely conscious of the life that was."

CHAPTER I.

ARCHAIC WORSHIP.

Objects of archaic belief.

§ 1. THE truth or the falsity of any belief has a very different meaning in history from that which it has in physical science. In the latter case, it is the supreme question. The object of science is to ascertain whether certain facts do or do not bear certain relations to certain other facts; and a belief upon the subject is useful only when and so far as it agrees with the actual state of things. But in discussions relating to human conduct, the matter is often different. In these circumstances, the inquiry relates not to the character of the belief, but to its existence. We ask not whether such a belief be true or be false, but whether men have or have not entertained it and acted upon it. In this aspect, the quality of the belief is immaterial. It is not relevant to the purposes of the inquiry. The great problem of history is to trace the process by which the Present has been evolved from the Past. One main agent of that process is human beliefs; and human beliefs include—and in their early stages absolutely pre-suppose—human errors. We must not, therefore, turn with scorn from the simple theories by which our forefathers sought to account for the phenomena which they observed in themselves and in the external world. In the absence of any accumulated experience, of any extended observation, of any systematic knowledge, these theories were of necessity rude enough. They were, however, the best that the nature of the case admitted. On the assumption that they were true, the inferences deduced from them were for the most part reasonable and consistent. But no accuracy in reasoning could cure the original defect. That defect men were slow to discover; and when it was discovered, it was no easy matter to alter the practical arrangements to which it had given rise.

It is no part of my present purpose to narrate the history of primitive beliefs, either generally or even among the men of our own race, or to trace the circumstances which gave rise to the states of mind from which these beliefs proceeded. It is enough for me that, so far as the external world was concerned, men applied the sole standard which they possessed—namely, that which they found within themselves. That man is the measure of all things is a very ancient maxim. Hence the archaic man supposed that every force to which his attention was directed was similar to that which he recognized in himself, and either was or implied a like being. He was conscious, or thought that he was conscious, that he himself consisted of a soul and a body—of something substantial, and of something insubstantial; and he concluded that, in like manner, there were souls in things. The forces of Nature were generally more powerful than he, and were, or seemed to be, capable of doing him good or evil. They therefore appeared to him fit objects of supplication—beings whose favour he might procure, or whose wrath he might avert. Hence arose the whole system of Nature-worship, and all the myths of the Sun and of the Moon—of the Dawn, the Twilight, and the Night—of the Wind and the Storm—of Earth, and Sea, and Sky. The uncultured man, indeed, worships every force * that assists, or that obstructs him in his daily work. That worship is

* See Mr. Lyall, cited in Sir H. S. Maine's "Village Communities," p. 399 (2nd ed.).

his recognition of the existence of such a force, and of its connection—or, at least, its possible connection—with his own welfare. It is the method by which he accounts for phenomena which have casually attracted his attention, or affect his life. In other words, Mythology was the natural philosophy of the early world.

But there were other forces than those of external Nature that more nearly—and, therefore, more powerfully—affected men's minds. Explanations were needed, not only of physical, but of biological phenomena. Fearfully and wonderfully as man is made, his own structure and its functions, since they were independent of his volition, seemed to imply the interference of some external agency. The animals and the plants which surrounded him presented similar phenomena, and received a similar explanation. The Romans, at least, created a complete pantheon of natural history. It is, indeed, difficult, when we read the long and curious catalogue of that pantheon which St. Augustine * has preserved for us, to believe that the deities whom he describes were ever regarded as anything beyond mere names of certain physical forms and processes. However this may have been, other phenomena of our nature suggested —and more than suggested—some unseen, superhuman, power. Sleep and waking—birth, and life, and death—dreams, trances, and visions—madness and the varied forms of nervous disease — all these raised questions, some of which have not yet been answered. From these facts it was almost inevitable that the untrained and unassisted intellect should draw the conclusion that disembodied spirits bore no unimportant part in the economy of Nature, and that these spirits — terrible, because unseen — were capable of becoming friends or foes. The dwelling-place of the spirit

* "City of God" (Mr. Dod's translation), vol. i., pp. 144, 149, 249, 260.

was not unnaturally assumed to be the place where the body was laid. Men, therefore, sought to conciliate the spirit of some distinguished stranger whose last home was, or might be made, in the land of his votaries. Thus the Thebans and the Athenians disputed over the body of Œdipus, and the Argives and the Trojans fought for the bones of Orestes. Thus the Acanthians offered sacrifice to the gigantic Persian engineer who died amongst them, and the people of Amphipolis to the gallant Brasidas.* So, too, the Hindu of the present day adores the name of any prominent English official that happens to be buried near his village. Such worship was natural, according to archaic ideas; but far more natural, by the same standard, was the belief that the spirits of those whom men loved and honoured in their life continued after death their vigilance and their aid. The interests of men in the flesh were also their interests in the spirit, and the loves and the hates of this world followed the deceased to that world which lay beyond the grave.

Manes-worship, therefore, stands on the same base as the more picturesque worship of Olympos. As the latter is the explanation which the youth of the world offers of physical phenomena, so the former is its attempt to solve the mightier problems of human existence. The one is primitive physics, the other is primitive biology. But they agree in applying to these different classes of facts the same method, that method which we still observe in children and in uncultured races, that method so natural to man when he seems to himself the measure of all things. In both cases alike, the phenomena are interpreted by the presence and the action of some sentient being, feeling and thinking as man himself feels and thinks. Thus, primitive worship and that great

* Herodotus, vii., 117; Thucyd., v. 11.

train of consequences that it has transmitted to us depend, like primitive mythology, upon the state of our intelligence. It is, after all, the intellect that ultimately directs and determines the main current of the varying and tortuous stream of the world's history.

Early philosophy, then, and early religion were at first one. Such a union in later times tends indeed to produce, in the words of Lord Bacon, "an heretical religion and a fantastic philosophy." But, in an early stage of mental development, the combination is one which we are prepared to expect. Whether or not there may have been a still more rudimentary and homogeneous form than any with which we are acquainted, I am not now concerned to inquire. At all events, at the first dawn of our historical knowledge a differentiation is apparent, and we perceive two forms of this combination. In their philosophical aspect these forms represented, the one the natural philosophy, the other the biology of our forefathers. In their religious aspect, the one was the mythical, or heroic, or Olympian religion; the other was the domestic religion, the religion of the hearth and of daily life. It is of this latter religion—the earlier in point of time, the more effective in its moral element, and the more influential in determining the growth of institutions and the general course of events—that I now propose to treat.

The relations between the Divinity and the Worshipper.

§ 2. Nothing was farther from the minds of archaic men than the notion that all men were of one blood, and were the creatures of an All-Father in Heaven. The universal belief of the early world was, that men were of different bloods; that they each had fathers of their own; and that these fathers were not in Heaven, but beneath the earth. They had a strong and practical conviction that they lived under a Divine protection; that this protection extended to themselves and all the members of their households; and that its influence not only did not defend, but was usually hostile to others. Those others had in like manner their own gods, who naturally favoured and protected them, as household gods ought to do. Every aggregation of men, whether domestic or passing beyond that limit, had its tutelary spirit; and this spirit was the only known means of securing the permanency of the aggregation. The House Father of old cared little whether the universe had one author or many authors. His practical duty, his hopes and fears, centered upon his own hearth. Profoundly religious, indeed, he was; but his religion assumed a different form from that with which we are familiar. In its origin, its objects, and its results, it was entirely domestic.

Thus, in place of the uniform government of an impartial Creator, whose sun shines and whose rain falls alike upon the unjust and the just, the world presented itself to the archaic mind as governed by a vast variety of gods, acting each on his own principles, and each seeking the exclusive interest of his worshippers. Every assemblage of men had their own god, and regarded that god as their exclusive property. If they prospered, he prospered; if they were unfortunate, his worship suffered with them; if they were conquered, he was conquered too. They repudiated any obligation to any other deity. They resented any worship of him by any other persons. They even contemplated the possibility that he might be stolen from them or induced to abandon them. As they owed to him true and faithful allegiance, so they expected from him protection and support. If he was negligent or impotent, if he was unwilling or unable to help them in the time of need, they regarded the contract as dissolved, and renounced their allegiance to so useless a protector.

It is not easy to give strict proof of propositions which are not so much expressly stated by any early writer as implied and assumed throughout all ancient literature. But this conception of property in special deities, strange as it sounds in Christian ears, admits of illustrations ranging from the present day to the remotest records of our race. We know that, at this day, it is the first duty of a good Hindu * to worship his village god. The old Zend inscriptions make mention of similar divinities under the suggestive title of *Vithibis Bagaibis*, the Wick-Bogies.† It is needless to cite examples of the special cults of Hellas or of Italy; or to tell of the Argive Herê and Athene of Alalkomene; of the great goddess whom all Asia and the world worshipped; of the great Twin Brothers whose home was on the Eurotas; or of the less famous Jupiter of Anxur, and Jupiter of Lanuvium; of Feronia of Terracina; or of Anguitia Marsorum. We read of special gods of the Teutonic tribes, and of special gods of the Keltic tribes; of the worshippers of Hertha, and the worshippers of Woden; of the god of the Gadeni,‡ and the goddess of the Brigantes. In how special a light these deities were regarded we may infer from various incidental notices. Polyphemos § scorns the authority of Zeus, and recognizes no god but his father, Poseidon. In "The Suppliants" of Æschylus,|| an Egyptian herald tells the Argives, to whose land he has come, that he does not dread their gods, for that they did not rear him nor maintain him to old age. The gods around Neilos, indeed, he venerates, but to the gods of Argos he gives no heed. The Russian peasant of the present day draws, we are told,¶ a clear line between his own Damovoy and his

* Mr. Hunter's "Orissa," vol. i., p. 95.

† Mr. Spencer's "Sociology," vol. i., part i., Appendix A., *n.*

‡ Mr. Skene's "Celtic Scotland," vol. i., p. 71.

§ "Odyssee," ix., 275. || vv. 893, 922.

¶ Mr. Ralston, "Songs of Russia," p. 129.

neighbour's. The former is a benignant spirit, who will do him good even at the expense of others. The latter is a malevolent being, who will steal his hay and drive away his poultry for his neighbour's benefit. The disasters of their worshippers, too, extended to their gods. The "vanquished Penates" of the poet might, perhaps, if the expression stood alone, be regarded as a daring image; but both Cicero and the Digest confirm it in its most literal sense. The former tells us that victory made all the sacred things of the Syracusans profane.* The Digest very plainly lays down the rule of which the case of Syracuse was an example. It declares † that the tombs of our enemies (however holy in their eyes, or however holy our own tombs may be in our own estimation) are not holy to us. It also states ‡ that when places are taken by the enemy all things cease to be religious or sacred, just as if free men had come into a state of slavery; but that if they have been freed from this misfortune, they return by a sort of *Postliminium*, and are restored to their original condition.

The exclusive character of this religion is easily shown when a number of Hellenic clans united for a common object. The bond of their union was the worship of some common god; but, without their express invitation, no stranger to that worship could resort to their sacred feasts or participate in their games. The mere presence of a stranger at religious ceremonies, or even at any holy place, was intolerable. "And this woman," exclaimed Demosthenes,§ denouncing a gross case of sacrilegious fraud, "offered up the mysterious sacrifices for the welfare of the State, and saw what it was not right for her to see, being an alien; and notwithstanding what she was, entered places to which, out of the whole Athenian community, no

* In Verrem, lib. iv.

† xlvii., 12, 4.

‡ xi., 7, 36.

§ Against Neæra

one but the wife of the King-Archon is admitted." The prophet Helenus * warned Æneas to veil his head when he was performing sacrifices, lest the appearance of a stranger should intervene between the holy fires in honour of the gods, and disturb the omens. The Brahmins punished † those who happened to be near enough to hear the sound of their prayers or to witness their sacrifices. Even later, in the Middle Ages, men believed that in the celebration of the Mass ‡ the breath of one of evil deed polluted the sacred day, and that from his abhorred approach the holy things recoiled. There was, perhaps, another reason besides the mere dislike to interruption that led to this extreme privacy of worship. Men seem to have then lived in constant dread that their god should be stolen from them, or be seduced to abandon them. Thus Troy could not be taken before the theft of the Palladium. Hence, too, the name of the tutelary god of Rome was a profound state secret; for, without a knowledge of the name by which he ought to be addressed, the spell which was of power to compel the god to abandon his seat could not be spoken. The Romans had themselves a formula that is still preserved, by which they induced Juno to abandon Veii and transfer her residence to conquering Rome.§

Another curious consequence seems to have followed from this peculiar conception of property in a divinity. The relation was held to be terminable at the pleasure of the parties. The divinity, as we have seen, might neglect or even desert his worshippers; and in like manner the worshippers might abandon, and, in the old sense of the term, defy or withdraw their allegiance from their divinity.

* Virgil, Æn. iii., 405.

† Prof. Max Muller, "Chips," vol. iv., p. 254.

‡ See Sir Walter Scott's Scottish Ballads—"The Grey Friar."

§ See Mr. Tylor, "Early History of Mankind," p. 127. "La Cité Antique," pp. 179, 256.

If property may be abandoned, and if a divinity be property, the conclusion that the divinity might be abandoned was inevitable. Such a proceeding was, of course, a grave and dangerous step, but upon good grounds it was not infrequent. Even in the case of the domestic and kindred gods its admissibility was fully recognized. The theory and the practice of adoption implied, as we shall see, both the *detestatio sacrorum*, the solemn abjuration of a former worship, and the *transitio in sacra*, the equally solemn admission into a new worship. In other cases than those of kindred gods, in cases where some celestial patron had been voluntarily chosen, the difficulties of change were naturally even less formidable. The relations between the divine Patronus and his worshipper seem, as the name itself suggests, to have resembled those which we usually describe by the terms sovereignty and subjection. The subject owes obedience and service; the sovereign owes protection. In return for his adoration and his offerings, the tutelary spirit was bound to fight for and defend, both in the spirit world and against all enemies of the flesh, his servant and worshipper. People who had no conception of physical laws believed that the world was inhabited by spirits and by men; and as they had their alliances with the one, so they thought it necessary to form their alliances with the other. They seem, indeed, to have regarded the two alliances in a very similar aspect. As they would not have hesitated to leave an earthly protector with whom they were dissatisfied, so they had no scruple in abandoning a celestial patron who was unable or unwilling to defend them. We read of deities being taken or left according to the exigency of the time. Augustus is said* to have disestablished Neptune. The statue of the Cuman Apollo,†

* Suetonius, Aug., c. 16.

† St. Augustine, "City of God," vol. i., p. 101

in consequence of an ill-timed fit of weeping, had a narrow escape from being thrown into the sea. Fortunately, the better opinion prevailed, that his tears were for his old friends the Greeks, and not for his new friends the Romans. The conversion of Clovis was due to a prayer which he conceived to have been answered in the crisis of a battle. On the occurrence of a severe pestilence, as Bede * tells us, the people of Essex apostatized, and returned to their old faith until they were reconverted by Gearoman. When the question of Christianity against Paganism was debated in the council of King Edwin of Northumbria, Coifi, the pagan chief-priest, declared in favour of the new religion, because, as he with perfect *naïveté* said to the king,† "Not one of your people has applied himself more diligently to the worship of our gods than I have; and yet there are many who have received from you greater benefits and greater honours, and are more prosperous in all their undertakings: whereas, if the gods were good for anything, they would rather forward me, who have been so zealous to serve them." ‡

Even to this day, among uncultured people, practices similar to those of Coifi sometimes occur. A prince of Nepaul, in his rage at the death of a favourite wife, turned his artillery upon the temples of his gods, and, after six hours' heavy cannonading, effectually destroyed them. In like manner, a Portuguese Indian, the skipper of a craft from Goa, refused to light the usual lamp before the image of his patron saint, because the patron could not, or would not, give him fair weather; and threatened, if another squall came on, to throw his worthless image overboard and to take Santa Catterina in his stead. §

* Hist. Eccles., iii., 30.

† Bede, *ubi supra*, ii., 14.

‡ See also for Sweden, Milman's "History of Latin Christianity," vol. ii., p. 438. Dr. Dasent's "Burnt Njal," vol. i., p. xviii.

§ See Mr. Spencer's "Study of Sociology," pp. 302, 160.

So, too, the Finns do not hesitate, in time of need, to have recourse to the more powerful gods of the Russ. When Yumala* and the other Finnish deities do not do as they are desired, their worshippers apply for protection or assistance to the Madonna and the "Russian god." If their own traditional magic rites do not suffice to ward off evil influences, they naturally try the effect of crossing themselves, as the Russians do, in moments of danger. At the harvest festivals, Tchervash peasants have been known to pray, first to their own deities, and then to St. Nicholas, the miracle worker, the favourite saint of the Russian peasantry.

The relations between Co-worshippers.

§ 3. In the archaic world, society implied religious union. When any new household was formed, or when any combination of individuals, or any combination of clans, or any state, or any combination of states, or any subordinate association within a state, was established, a special form of worship was simultaneously set up. Community of worship was, indeed, the one mode by which, in early times, men were brought together and were kept together. Every form of worship, as I have already said, implied a special relation between the divinity and his worshipper. But when several persons joined in the worship of the same divinity, they naturally developed, as between themselves, new and special sympathies. Community of worship always implied both a fact and a symbol. The fact was the special and intimate relation that thereby arose between the co-worshippers. The symbol of that relation was the participation by them of a meal intentionally prepared and eaten in honour of the object of that worship.

That a community of worship established special relations between co-worshippers is a proposition on which the

* Mr. Wallace's "Russia," vol. i., p. 235.

following pages mainly depend. I hope to prove that, among at least the Aryan nations, and it may be over a much wider area, the original basis of human association was religion. In the early world, it was not the tie of blood, or of family habit, or of superior physical force, that held men together, but the far more potent bond of a common worship. Those who worshipped the same gods were relatives, although no drop of common blood flowed in their veins. Those who did not worship common gods were not relatives, although, according to the flesh, they were brother and brother, or parent and child. When a man was adopted, he formally renounced his original *sacra*, and passed over into the *sacra* of his adoptive father. He thereby ceased to be of kin to his natural father and his natural brothers. He could not inherit from them, nor they from him. It was not his duty to assist them, or to avenge their deaths; nor were they bound to notice his fate more than that of any stranger. All his duties and all his rights were attached to the family which he had joined. Towards the members of that family he stood in precisely the same relation in which he would have stood if he had been born a son of their blood.

The proximity of kinship, too, was measured by the same standard. The Hindu made to his ancestors, within a certain degree, offerings of cake; to those beyond that degree, offerings of water. Those persons* who made to a common ancestor offerings of cake were termed Sapindas, or fellow cake-men. Those who made to a common ancestor offerings of water were termed Samanodocas, or fellow water-givers. But those who were not connected by either of these modes of worship were simply strangers, and stood to each other in no recognized relation. So, too,

* Laws of Menu, v. 60.

when a contest arose in the courts at Athens upon a question of inheritance, we find* that the proper legal evidence to establish kinship was the proof that the alleged ancestor and the alleged heir observed a common worship and shared in the same repast in honour of the dead.

For this theory of archaic relationship there is abundant proof. Natural love and affection was not its cause. I say nothing now of the difference between the agnates and the cognates, the relatives by the male line and the relatives by the female line. But mere birth was not the basis of relationship even between agnates. If two brothers, being slaves, were emancipated, they ought, on the principle of birth and natural affection, to have had reciprocal rights of succession. Yet the Roman law† did not regard them as agnates; and, upon the death of one of them, his property went not to his surviving brother, but to his patron. The father's superiority of physical strength was not the foundation of his power. Old blind Appius Claudius, or old Cato the Censor, was not stronger than the young men who were in his *manus;* and yet both of them ruled their respective households with absolute sway. Nor can we rely upon the force of habit arising from long years of undisputed authority during infancy. The same force is in operation in the modern no less than in the antique world; yet, parental authority and its consequences are far from being the same. Further, this explanation will not account for the obedience of an arrogated son, an adult man, who voluntarily accepted the *potestas* of another. On the other side, in support of the theory I have stated, there are—in addition to all the considerations that I have mentioned, and shall hereafter

* See Becker's "Charicles," p. 394, and the authorities there cited.

† Inst. iii., 7.

mention—the express words of Menu and of Plato. The former defines the character of the nearer and the more remote relatives of the Hindu, according to the character of their ancestral worship. The latter says distinctly that relationship is the community of the same domestic gods.

The symbol of community of worship was the Common Meal.

§ 4. Of this community of worship and its resulting bond, there was a well-understood symbol. That symbol was the partaking in common of a meal prepared in honour of the object of the worship. The common meal prepared upon the altar was the outward visible sign of the spiritual communion between the divinity and his worshippers. The connection between this meal and the religious ceremony is constant. We never hear of any public worship without a common meal. In domestic life every meal was a sacrifice; that is, it was eaten in honour of the house spirits, and, as it was thought, in their presence. Other examples abound in all the earlier books. In the Iliad the King of Men is constantly engaged in the sacrifice of an ox, fat, five years old, to the all-powerful Son of Kronos. In the Odyssee, King Alkinoos offers a sacrifice when he gives a feast to his people. In the Greek language—and the same remark * may be made in the case of some tribes in Northern India—the same word is used to express the act of killing and the act of sacrificing. In Virgil, we find King Latinus and King Evander holding their sacrificial feasts after the manner of the Homeric kings. Feasts in honour of the dead, in which the kinsmen shared, were habitually celebrated in India, in Hellas, in Rome, in England, in Scandinavia. They are so celebrated in Russia up to the present day. The names of the kin in their several degrees, the Sapindas and Samanodocas of India, the Ὁμογάλακτες

* Mr. Tylor's "Primitive Culture," vol. ii., p. 359.

and 'Οργεῶνες of Greece, the Confarrei of Rome, express in themselves the community of eating and drinking as forming the basis of their relation. And as a share in a common worship was legal evidence of kinship between any two persons, so the participation in a common sacrificial meal was legal evidence of that community of worship.

The most striking evidence of the belief that a tie, and a tie of no common efficacy, was formed by such a participation, not only between the co-worshippers, but between each worshipper and the object of his worship, is found in a remarkable passage * of St. Paul. The Apostle is writing on the evil of Christians being in any way concerned with the sacrificial feasts of the heathen; and he asks, as though the answer to his question were self-evident—"Are not they who eat of the sacrifices communicants of the altar?" Although his immediate subject is Jewish sacrifice, yet he appears to select the familiar Jewish rites merely as illustrative of the more general question. Accordingly, he proceeds to declare that a sacrifice to devils—that is, to the heathen gods—makes him who takes part in the sacrifice "a communicant of devils." It was this belief that rendered the early Christians so uncompromising upon the question of meats offered to idols; a question, at that day, of the most practical and urgent importance; but of which, in the altered circumstances of modern times, we can hardly even appreciate the difficulty.

The Common Meal implies both act and intent.

§ 5. It is not enough to say that the common meal was the symbol of worship. Something more than the mere fact of the meal was required. It must be a meal specially prepared for, and offered to, the object of the worship. Sometimes the nature of the meal, the mode of its prepara-

* 1 Cor. x. 18-20. And see Dean Stanley's Commentary.

tion, and the form of its presentation, were rigorously prescribed. But, in all cases, the intention was essential. The characteristic difference of a sacrificial meal, as compared with an ordinary meal, was, that it was eaten with a religious intent. The spirits were not supposed to come unbidden. They did not help themselves. The offering must be made to them, their presence invited, and their share set apart. Then, and then only, would they participate in the meal; and then, and then only, did their worshippers enjoy the benefits which their presence, their favour, and their guidance conferred.

We can thus understand the nature of certain difficulties to which I have already referred as having beset the early Christian Church, and the solution of those difficulties which the Fathers of the Church, with their characteristic common sense, supplied.* So numerous, at the time of the Empire, had the public religious festivals in the great cities become, that it was no easy matter to avoid, in ordinary consumption, the use of meats that had been offered to idols. Not only were these meats necessarily used on all occasions when the people made holyday, but they formed a principal source of supply to the retail butchers. But to eat such meat appeared to scrupulous minds to be the actual establishment of a communion between the Christian consumer and the false spirit and his votaries. In these circumstances, it was decided—first, that any wilful participation in any idolatrous meal was a breach of Christian duty; second, that a Christian was not under any obligation to ask any question regarding any meat that he might purchase, or that might at any private entertainment, be set before him; third, that if his attention were called to the fact that such meat had been idolatrous, he ought not to use it. The ground of this

* See Dean Stanley's "Epistles of St. Paul to the Corinthians," 131 *et seq.*

last-mentioned prohibition was expedience only, and not duty. The Christian abstained from meat respecting which he had notice, not because any spiritual communion was, by the use of such meat, established between him and the false spirit—for he did not eat the meat with that intent—but because he desired to avoid the scandal and the misconception which might arise from the fact of a Christian knowingly eating meat that had been offered to some idol. The fact would, to many persons, be evidence of the intent. The same difficulties continued, long after the decision of St. Paul, to vex the souls of Christian missionaries. It was one of the subjects with which Gregory the Great* had to deal on the evangelization of England. The Penitential of Theodore has a long chapter upon the heathen practices of communicants and their appropriate penances.† Among these offences a conspicuous place is occupied by sacrificing to demons, eating and drinking near heathen temples in honour of the god of the place, eating what has been sacrificed to demons, and celebrating festal meals in the abominable places of the heathen. These demons were the ancient gods; and the belief on which their rites were founded, and the practical difficulties thence resulting, were the same in Northumbria as, six centuries before, they had been in Corinth. So, too, we find that, in dealing with their Norse converts, the Christian missionaries had to struggle against three leading abominations.‡ They insisted that all Christian men should abstain from three things—first, they must not worship idols; second, they must not expose their children; third, they must not eat horseflesh. Why the Church should trouble itself on the last point, or why, if such abstinence were desired, it should be placed on

* Bede, Hist. Eccles., i., 30.

† Kemble's "Saxons in England," vol. i., p. 524.

‡ Dr. Dasent's "Burnt Njal," vol. i., p. xxvi.

a level with the two preceding requirements, are questions that to our modern notions are hard to answer. When, however, we remember that horses were habitually offered at the Norse sacrifices, we perceive at once the true explanation. The prohibition of horseflesh meant the prohibition of meats offered to idols. It is probable that the prejudice which still prevails against the use of a meat that is otherwise unobjectionable is a survival of the days when the horse was sacrificed to Odin, and when Angstur and his companions ceased not to warn their disciples against those sacrificial meats, from which, as the Apostles once said, "If ye keep yourselves, ye shall do well."

§ 6. It thus appears that a close connection existed between common worship and common meals. Meals were an essential part of religious ceremonies. Wherever we read of such ceremonies, we hear of such meals. Wherever we read of public meals, we always find that they formed part of some religious celebration. We find the Greek terms for kinsmen and for feasters used as synonyms. We find that the right to partake of a common meal was regarded as the proper legal proof of a community of worship. We find, too, that the common worship and the common meal were universal among the Aryan nations. Among them, at least, and probably among many other races, it is not too much to say* that "the earliest religious act seems to have been the eating of a meal prepared on an altar." The question, however, still remains, How are we to account for these facts? What were the beliefs which led to the universal adoption of this particular symbol, and to the establishment of these peculiar relations? Such an inquiry is necessarily difficult. We cannot enter into the thoughts and the

The theory of this symbol.

* M. De Coulanges' "La Cité Antique," p. 182.

feelings of men upon a much lower level of culture than our own. We have little definite information on the subject, partly because men are habitually reticent on such matters, and partly because there was no need to treat of subjects that to the readers of that time were perfectly well known. The ideas themselves, too, were from their very nature more or less vague. Finally, these ideas must be distinguished from other and similar, though probably later, ideas. With this distinction I must preface my remarks.

The idea of sacrifice implies either a benefit to the recipient or a loss to the giver, or partly the one and partly the other. In the first case, the benefit may consist either in actual assistance, or in some gratification, or in merely a mark of attention and respect. In the second case, it consists in the costliness of the gift, a costliness which is measured either by the rarity of the object, or by the pain with which the donor yields it. Sometimes these motives are blended. But these complex motives generally relate to the attempts made to propitiate external and unknown forces. They thus belong rather to the class of Nature-worship than to the simpler and older rites of domestic religion. *Parva petunt Lares:* the Household worship sought no costly sacrifice. Men thought that the disembodied spirit retained similar feelings, and similar needs, to those that he had in the flesh. It was thus equally a duty and a pleasure to share with him the customary meal, and to pay to him the wonted respect. But there was something more than this. The common meal was the sole means by which a communication could be maintained between the spirit-world and the earth. The spirits were not perceptible to human senses; but the offering of food and of drink formed a sort of middle term by which the spiritual and the earthy could be brought together. Every object, whether animate or inanimate, was supposed to consist of two parts—of a substance and of a shadow, of a soul and of a body, of something immaterial as well as of something material. The articles of food and of drink possessed this nature. It was upon the immaterial part of the offerings that the spirits fed, while the earthly parts were left for men. Thus both the spirit and the worshipper lived on the same nourishment. That which supported and strengthened after its kind the human frame, supported and strengthened by its spiritual force the spirit to whom it was presented. Nor did the worshippers doubt that at every such meal their Divine Head sat present, though unseen, among them.

Each of these propositions is fully supported by abundant evidence. We know that Animism—that is, the belief in the souls of objects—both did exist in primitive times and does at the present day exist among the races of lower culture. That the spirits retain in the spirit-world some semblance of the interests and the pursuits of the present life is a familiar belief. We need but recall, for its illustration, the classical descriptions of the shadowy heroes pursuing the hostile shades, or chasing the phantom deer. Even to this day, among races of lower culture, the distinction between the spirit of the sacrificial victim and its flesh is well understood, and is distinctly stated. "When," says Sir John Lubbock,* "it is observed that meat-offerings are not consumed, it is supposed that the spirit eats the spiritual part of the victim and leaves the meat to the worshipper." Thus the Limboos, near Darjiling, say—"The life-blood to the gods, the flesh to ourselves." "By that time," says Marco Polo,† writing of feasts in certain Indian temples, "they say the spirit of the idol has consumed the substance of the food; so they remove the

* "Origin of Civilization," p. 237. † Vol. ii. (Col. Yule's ed.), p. 282.

viands to be eaten by themselves with great jollity." "The Chinese," says Mr. Doolittle,* "entertain the idea that the spirits of the dead partake of the essential and immaterial elements of the food and the wine. What the living consume at the conclusion of the ceremony is only the coarse and material portions, which the dead leave untouched." For further evidence it is enough to refer to the numerous facts accumulated by Mr. Tylor.† Nor does this belief sound wholly strange to those who remember the frequent mention that Homer makes of the savour of the sacrifices being wafted to the gods.

We can also see that, in the state of mind of which we speak, the belief exists that the gods and their worshippers form one community. They are, literally, in the old phrase which Aristotle cites respecting the primitive family-groups of the Hellenic tribes, of the same meal-bin and the same hearth. They have a common descent, common interests, common property, common sympathies, common enjoyments. Plato‡ speaks of the kinship and communion of the kindred gods that have the nature of the same blood as their worshippers. He says that a man, if he honour and venerate the kindred and the communion of his kindred gods, that have the nature of the same blood as he has, may reasonably expect from them the blessing of children. Pollux,§ a later writer, but of high authority, who apparently expresses the views of Aristotle, uses, as terms of apparently the like meaning, words denoting respectively blood relations or kinsmen—men who make a common offering, and men who partake of a common feast.

I shall frequently have occasion to notice the strength of this sentiment towards the Household gods. It is to them,

* "Social Life of the Chinese," vol. ii., p. 48.

† "Primitive Culture," vol. i., p. 435.

‡ "Laws," v. 729.

§ viii., 9, 111.

indeed, much more than to any patron saint, as we might term him, that their feelings were specially directed. We may trace among uncultured people the operation of a similar sentiment even at this day. The Chinese describe certain feasts in honour of their deceased ancestors by the expressive name, "keeping company with the gods." In Fiji too, we find a singular illustration of these old beliefs. The term *Veita uvu* means sprung from the same root, and denotes people who worship the same god, who may swear at each other and take each other's property. This privilege of swearing is explained by the belief that the god invoked cannot, or will not, injure the person cursed, because he belongs to him. But, when one cursed a stranger, the wrath of the god thus invoked may be expected to fall upon the person cursed, in whom he has no interest, and who has offended one of that god's people.*

It may have been that the primitive view of this matter is that which I have thus endeavoured to describe, and nothing more. It may have been that our forefathers regarded their gods as members of their clan; invisible, indeed, and with greater and more varied powers than those of any mortal clansman, but still presenting essentially the same relation. But it may also have been otherwise. There is another and a less obvious explanation. It is, at least, conceivable that the religious relation was based upon a more mystic idea. A belief—vague, indeed, but not on that account less intense—may have prevailed that, by the eating of the holy food, a portion of the divine essence entered into and became incorporated with the worshipper. A savage will eat his enemy, in the belief that he thereby appropriates that enemy's strength and skill and courage.

* Mr. Thurston's "Memorandum on Ownership of Land in Fiji," in Report of Commodore Goodenough and Mr. Consul Layard, "On the Colony of Fiji," presented to House of Commons, July, 1874.

The strange blending of the identity of the father with that of the son formed, as we shall see, a prominent part of the primitive theory of life and of society. In some such manner it may have been thought* that the common food produced some kind of interchange between its participants, whether human or divine; that, in cases where a patron saint had been chosen, the Divine Father and his adopted sons had become identified; that the Divine essence dwelt in the man, and the human essence dwelt in the Divinity; and that the worshippers were alike animated by the same indwelling Divine Spirit. Whether views of this kind were actually entertained, and if they were entertained, whether they formed part of the primitive beliefs of our race or were the addition of a fantastic philosophy upon the old creed, are questions which I do not underta to determine. Whichever explanation be correct, it will account for the general acceptance of that creed and for its symbolism in the common meal.

* See Mr. Spencer's "Sociology," vol. i., p. 299.

CHAPTER II.

THE HOUSE SPIRIT.

§ 1. THE belief which guided the conduct of our forefathers was the same as that which seems to have prevailed among most other of the first-born children of the earth. That belief was the spirit-rule of deceased ancestors. The simple minds of uncultured men unhesitatingly believed that the spirit of the departed House Father hovered round the place he loved in life; and, with powers both for good and evil supernaturally exalted, still exercised, although unseen, the functions which in his life-time he had performed. He still, in his spirit state, needed the shadow-food and drink such as spirits enjoy; and he still continued sensible both of the reverence and the neglect of his descendants. To him, therefore, were daily made, at the commencement of every meal, libations and offerings, not merely as tokens and pledges of honour and affection, but as his share of the property of the household. To this share he was entitled as of right, and its possession was essential for his happiness in the spirit-world. Consequently, the due performance of the sacred rites was to him a source of constant satisfaction. "Whatever a man endued with strong faith," says Menu,* "piously offers as the law has directed, becomes a perpetual, unperishable gratification to

Nature of House Worship.

* iii., 275.

his ancestors in the other world." On the other hand, the spirit to whom no such offerings were made was supposed to suffer the pangs of eternal hunger. If, therefore, the proper libations were made by the proper person, in the proper place, and at the proper time, the spirit would graciously guard and assist his sons. But the case was far otherwise, when, from neglect of his duties of piety (such was the technical expression among the Romans), a man destroyed his happiness and caused the misery of all his forefathers. The offended spirits did not perish. They were changed from faithful friends into deadly enemies. The benignant Lares became the dreaded Larvæ. Those powers which formerly were used for the offender's benefit were now turned to his destruction. The impious man, the man who neglected his filial duty, or violated the customary laws of the household, had not to dread any human punishment. He was given over to his own tormentors. His gods were against him; and every former blessing became a curse.

The difference between our mental state and that of our forefathers is so wide, that it costs no ordinary effort to realize those forms of belief, once so potent and so widespread, which I have endeavoured to describe. But this difficulty rests with ourselves only, and is no proof against the existence of that belief. It is not more difficult to comprehend that our ancestors found their Providence in their fathers' tombs, than it is to comprehend that a hundred million subjects of Queen Victoria believe that Ganges or Nerbudda is not merely the seat or the emblem of a god, but is itself a very god. If we doubt whether House worship be an actual existence, and not a dream of idle speculators, we should remember that, at this day, in China, three hundred millions of orderly, industrious, and intelligent men live and die in this faith. So powerfully does it act upon the Chinese mind,* that it is easy to obtain, for about £33, a man who will consent to be put to death. To such a sacrifice posthumous honour is attached. The family is rescued from poverty, and enters on the possession of comparative wealth; and thus provision is made for the constant performance of the offerings to the Manes. Nor is this belief confined to the Chinese empire. Numerous other nations in all parts of the world hold similar opinions. "In our time," says Mr. Tylor,† "the dead still receive worship from far the larger half of mankind; and it may have been much the same ever since the remote periods of primitive culture, in which the religion of the Manes probably took its rise."

The Worship of Deceased Ancestors an Aryan institution.

§ 2. It is thus certain that the worship of deceased ancestors is a *vera causa*, and not a mere hypothesis. It has, however, been questioned whether this cause, although it may have been elsewhere operative, was influential among the Aryan nations. I proceed, therefore, to state briefly the evidence for the proposition that this worship once existed in every branch of our race. Among the Hindus, the Vedas distinctly recognize the ancient religion of the Pitris, or Fathers. The Rig Veda relates‡ to the worship of the gods; but the Sama Veda relates to the worship of the Manes of the ancestors. "The Pitris," says Professor Max Müller,§ "are invoked almost like gods; oblations are offered to them, and they are believed to enjoy, in company with the gods, a life of never-ending felicity." The offering of cakes and water is the sacrament of the Manes, one of the five great ceremonies which Menu || enjoins. "An oblation by

* Sir John Bowring, *Fort. Rev.*, vol. i., p. 563.
† "Primitive Culture," vol. ii., p. 112.
‡ Menu, iv., 124. § "Chips," vol. ii., p. 46.
|| iii., 70.

Brahmins to their ancestors," says the same authority,* "transcends an oblation to the deities, because that to the deities is considered as the opening and completion of that to the ancestors." In this case the offering to the deities is merely incidental, and is intended to be "preservative † of the oblation to the Pitris;" or, in other words, to secure to them the quiet enjoyment of their sacrifices, without disturbance from their greedy and more powerful neighbours.

Among the Iranians a similar belief prevailed. They worshipped the Fravashis, or spirits of the dead, and especially those of their own ancestors. "There cannot be any doubt," says Spiegel,‡ "that the worship of the Fravashis played an important part with the Iranians, though, perhaps, more in private than in public. It would appear that there were two different sorts of it. General, certainly, was the hero-worship, the veneration of 'the pious men before the law.' With this, in some ages, perhaps, the worship of Fravashis of the royal family was combined. The ancestor-worship, on the other hand, was of a strictly private character." The Khordah Avesta § tells us that, when water is drawn from the celestial sea, Vouru-Kasha, those of the bold Fravashis of the pure who come down to earth "bring water, each of them to his kinsfolk, his clan, his confederacy, his region, saying thus: 'It is our own region,' to further it, to increase it. Then if there is an Overseer, a Ruler of a region, provided with like kingdom, he always invokes them, the bold Fravashis of the pure, against the tormenting foes. They come to his assistance if they are not tormented by him, made contented without revenge, unoffended: they bring him forward like as if a man were

* iii., 203. † *Ib.*, 205.

‡ See Mr. Spencer's "Sociology," vol. i., appendix A, p. 0.

§ Spiegel's "Avesta," by Bleeck, vol. iii., p. 88.

a well-feathered bird. They are his weapons, his defence, his support, his wall."

It is needless to enlarge upon the domestic worship of Hellas and of Italy. The facts are sufficiently well known, and they have been recently discussed with conspicuous ability in his "La Cité Antique"—a work to which I gladly acknowledge my great obligations—by M. De Coulanges. I will merely recall some of the familiar names. The Hellenic House Spirits were known by many designations. They were directly called *δαίμονες* and *ἥρωες*. They were the *θεοὶ ἐφέστιοι*, or the Gods of the Hearth; *θεοὶ μύχιοι*, or Penates; *θεοὶ πατρῷοι, ἐγγενεῖς, ὁμόγνιοι, σύναιμοι*, or Gods of the Fathers, of the kin, of the same race, of a common blood. The Latin language contains a variety of similar names. We meet with the Genius, Lares, Manes, Penates, Vesta. Of these words, Genius is generally taken to mean the spirit, or guardian angel, of a living man. The Manes, whether the word means the good people, or, as some suppose, the little people, are the dead generally. Vesta is the hearth, with its holy flame. But the Lares and the Penates are the true House Spirits, the souls of deceased progenitors that dwell in the interior of the house, and, along with the holy fire, collectively form its protecting deity. Of all the worships of Rome, as Mommsen * has observed, the worship of these House Spirits had the deepest hold; and of all those worships, as we know, it was the one which lasted the longest. In the other European nations, the Slavs, the Teutons, and the Kelts, the House Spirit appears with less distinctness. We have no early books of these peoples, like the Vedas and the Avesta, and the literature of Greece and of Rome. The influence, too, of Christianity has passed with varying force over each of these nations as we know them. Our

* "History of Rome," vol. i., p. 173.

acquaintance, therefore, with their domestic condition is derived mainly from writers to whom the House Spirit was an abomination, and who were anxious to bury in total oblivion all that related to the most formidable of their enemies. Thus the House Spirit presents himself in these countries to us merely as a survival, and we have no direct knowledge of his earlier worship. Yet the existence of that worship does not admit of doubt. The traces of it are seen clearly among the Slavonian peoples. Although Christianity has changed the Lar Familiaris into an uncouth shaggy demon, and has substituted the holy Eicons for the ancestral spirits, the old belief is preserved better among them than in any part of Western Europe. The Slavonian peasant holds that "each house* ought to have its familiar spirit, and that it is the soul of the founder of the homestead that appears in this capacity." To this belief many of their customs are due, in the building of their houses, in the changing their residence, and in many details of ordinary life. Mr. Ralston has collected a number of curious and interesting illustrations of this primitive belief. "There is no doubt," he says,† in reference to the old Slavonians, "about their belief that the souls of the fathers watched over their children, and their children's children; and that, therefore, departed spirits, and especially those of ancestors, ought always to be regarded with pious veneration, and sometimes solaced by prayer and sacrifice. It is clear, moreover, that the cultus of the dead was among them, as among so many other peoples, closely connected with that of the fire burning on the domestic hearth—a fact which accounts for the stove of modern Russia having come to be considered to be the special haunt of the Damovoy, or House Spirit, whose position in the esteem of

* Mr. Ralston's "Songs of Russia," p. 126. † *Ib.*, p. 119.

the people is looked upon as a trace of the ancestor-worship of olden days."

Among the people of Western and Northern Europe the House Spirit is reduced, even more plainly than his brother in the East, to the condition of a mere survival. Yet, notwithstanding all hostile influences, the Teutonic Haus-geist has left many traces of his individuality. He is known as the Husing or Stetigot, the House God or Lar Familiaris. He is also Ingoumo—a guardian of the inner part of the house—a term exactly equivalent to the Latin *Penas* and the *θεὸς μύχιος* of the Greeks. "We can often trace in them," says Grimm,* "a special relation to the hearth of the house, from beneath which they often come forth, and where the door of their subterranean dwelling seems to have been; they are peculiarly hearth gods." In this sense the Greeks would have called them *θεοὶ ἑστιοῦχοι*. The House Spirits had a multitude of other names which it is needless here to enumerate, but all of which are more or less expressive of their friendly relations with man. They always dwell in or about the house, and are, if they are well treated, always friendly and helpful in the house and in the yard. "The Kobold," says Grimm,† writing of them under one of these names, "is thus a useful, industrious spirit, who takes delight in helping the men and maids in the housework, and secretly doing a part of it. He grooms the horses, combs out their manes, gives their fodder to the cattle, draws water from the well, and cleans out the stable. His presence brings luck and success to the house, his departure withdraws them." The name of Kobold ‡ appears in Normandy, and hence probably in England under the familiar form of Goblin. In the latter country he has

* "Deutsche Mythologie," vol. i., p. 468. † *Ib.*, p. 478.

‡ See Keightley, "Fairy Mythology," pp. 208, 358, 171, 139, 140, 239, 476. Grimm's "Deutsche Mythologie," vol. i., p. 468, *et seq.*

many names. He is the Brownie, or as in Yorkshire he is called the Bogart, or Hob Goblin, or Robin Goodfellow. By whatever style he is described, his fee is white bread and milk; and overnight he does all the household work. In Scotland this same Brownie is well known. He is usually described as attached to particular families, with whom he has been known to reside for centuries, threshing the corn, cleaning the house, and performing similar household tasks. His favourite gratification was milk and honey. In the Orkney Islands a writer in the beginning of the eighteenth century states that "not above forty or fifty years ago almost every family had a Brownie, or evil spirit so called, which served them, to whom they gave a sacrifice for its service; and when they churned their milk, they took a part thereof and sprinkled every corner of the house for Brownie's use. Likewise when they brewed they had a stone wherein there was a little hole, into which they poured some wort as a sacrifice for Brownie." Among the Scandinavian nations there is, as we might expect, a similar House Spirit. In Denmark and Norway he is called Nisse God-dreng, or Good-fellow. The Swedes call him Tompt-Gabbe, the Toft-Gaffer, or old man of the house and its surroundings. I may add that the Nis, like his brother in Russia, the Damovoy, often cribs corn from the neighbours for the use of his household's horses; so that this spirit, although he is good to those who are under his protection, does not hesitate to injure, for their sakes, strangers. I am not aware that the House Spirit has left many traces of his existence among the Keltic peoples. His Irish representative is said to be the Cluricaun. A more trustworthy analogue is found in the Hebrides. In those islands at the present day, "The Gael* call their evil spirits Boduchs

* "Lewsiana," by W. Anderson Smith, p. 199.

(Boddus), while the word still retains its ancient secondary signification of old man, head of the family." It may, perhaps, be thought that the history of the word has been, in this passage, inverted; and that, as in other cases, the old man of the house had his usual and honourable designation, until the clergy banished him to the bottomless pit.

House Worship a veritable religion.

§ 3. The worship of these House Spirits was a veritable religion. It was something entirely different from that mythology which sought to explain the various phenomena of external nature. The Aryan, doubtless, like his European or his Indian descendant, acknowledged the might of the sea or of the storm, heard the voice of God in the thunder, and adored the bright sun-god as he ran his daily course. But these elemental powers were not his gods. He recognized their might, and deprecated their wrath; but it was not to them that he owed allegiance, or that he looked for help. They lived, indeed, but they did not care for man. In their wild caprice, they might benefit or they might ruin him. But God, even his own God, a very present help in trouble, the Divine and Gracious Protector who cared, and cared exclusively, for him and his; whose welfare depended upon his services; of whose divine company he would in the course of nature become a part; this Father, in the very fullest and most literal sense of the term, dwelt always at his hearth. To this Father the King of Men, when he returned victorious to his native Argos, first rendered thanks. So, too, Electra prays to the murdered Agamemnon *—" Have mercy upon me and my brother Orestes. Bring him home to his country. O my Father, hear my prayer, and receive my libation. Give me a heart

* "Choephoræ," 122, 135.

more chaste than my mother's, and purer hands." In Rome,* the elder Cato tells us that it was the first duty of the House Father, on his return home, to pay his devotions at the altar of the Lares. Virgil describes Æneas as adoring the spirit of his father Anchises, and seeking from it protection and aid. If a man be neither forsworn, nor mean, it is to the propitious Lares—as Horace † tells us—that his thanks are due.

In this aspect we can appreciate a notable function of the Lares. The House Spirits were directly charged with the preservation of the property of the household. They were, as Horace tells us, the guardians against thieves. They were, in the words of Tibullus, ‡ "the guardians of the land." They repelled the thief, so Ovid § assures us, and scared the enemy, and warned the trespasser. This duty was not limited to the house, but was extended ‖ to every part of the household's property. Their functions, however, seem to have been gradually specialized. With the Latins, the Garden Spirit was known as Hercules; and before the guardian of the boundary was confounded with his Hellenic namesake, the wandering son of Alkmene, he enjoyed under this name a high place in the Roman Pantheon. In Athens, these tutelary functions were assigned to Hermes, and we read of the more general expression, *θεοὶ ὅριοι*. Our Teutonic forefathers worshipped Freya, as the guardian of their boundaries. Throughout all antiquity, indeed, the landmark seems to have been invariably held sacred. It is noteworthy that both the Latins ¶ and the Greeks recognized divinities for the house and its precinct, for the cultivated field, and for the woodland. All these

* See Mommsen, "History of Rome," vol. i., p. 173.

† "Satires," ii. 3, 164.

‡ I., i. 23.

§ "Fasti," v. 141, xi. 677.

‖ Cicero, "De Leg.," ii. 11.

¶ Mommsen, "History of Rome," vol. i., pp. 173, 174.

deities seem to be included under the general description of Lares,* and their separate titles afford evidence for the existence among those peoples of the usual form of cantonal settlement.

§ 4. Of this tutelary spirit, or company of spirits—the Lar Familiaris, or Man of the Household, as the Romans called him; the Hero in the House, as he was known to the Greeks; the Husing of the Teutons; the Damovoy, or Angel in the House, of the Russian peasant at the present day—the hearth was the altar. There the holy fire ever burned, and there the gross corporeal substance of the food was purged away, and its spiritual essence was rendered fit for the acceptance of the spirit. On this hearth, where, in his lifetime, he had himself so often sacrificed, the departed House Father received at the hands of his successor his share of every meal, and heard from his lips, in his own honour, those familiar words of prayer and praise that were the heirlooms of his race. Every meal was in effect a sacrifice, and the Aryan House Father, when he reverently asked a blessing upon his humble board, felt that he was not only seeking a continuance of the divine protection, but that he was securing the happiness of those who were literally his fathers and his gods.

The Worship on the Hearth.

The hearth was thus, so to speak, the organ through which the living maintained their intercourse with the dead. This relation is expressly stated in the "Rig Veda," † "Thou, O Agni Gatavedas, hast carried, when implored, the offerings which thou hast rendered sweet; thou hast given them to the Fathers: they fed on their share. Eat thou, O God, the proffered oblation. Our Fathers who are here and

* "Religio Larum posita in fundi villæque conspectu." Cic., *ubi supra.*

† Professor Max Müller, "Rig Veda," p. 24.

those who are not here, our Fathers whom we know and those whom we do not know, thou knowest how many they are: O Gatavedas, accept the well-made sacrifice, with the sacrificial portions. They who, whether burnt by fire or not burnt by fire, rejoice in their offering in the midst of heaven, give to them, O King, that life and thy (their) own body, according to thy will."

We have abundant evidence to prove both the early worship of the hearth and its connection with the worship of deceased ancestors:—"*Tu quœ loca prima tenes*" are the words* in which Vesta was invoked; and Vesta, as we are expressly told, was neither more nor less than the living flame. So, too, Cicero † tells us that every prayer and every sacrifice concludes with Vesta. In India the same word ‡ (Vastya) occurs in Sanscrit, but is there used in the sense of house, while the holy fire is worshipped under the name of Agni. Under this latter name (Agôn or Ogôn), the Latin Ignis, the Russian peasant § still worships his domestic hearth. The ancient Scythians, an Aryan though probably long extinct people, used, as Herodotus ‖ tells us, to reverence ἑστίη under the name of Tabiti. He adds that they reverenced her beyond all the other gods. In Hellas, too, we read ¶ in the Homeric Hymns that Ἑστίη is to be invoked beyond all other gods. In the historical times we know that in every sacrifice to Zeus and Athene Ἑστίη was always first adored. Not less emphatic is the language of the Vedas**:—"Before all other gods we must invoke Agni. We will pronounce his revered name before that of

* Ovid, "Fasti," vi., 291, 304. † "De Nat. Deo.," ii., 27.

‡ Pictet, "Les Origines Indo-Europeennes," vol. ii., pp. 238, 259, 262.

§ Mr. Ralston, "Songs of Russia," p. 86.

‖ iv., c. 59. See Canon Rawlinson's "Herodotus," vol. iii., p. 166.

¶ "La Cité Antique," p. 26. Smith's "Dictionary Biography and Mythology," *s. v.*, ἑστίη.

** "La Cité Antique," p. 26.

the other immortals. O Agni, whosoever be the god that we honour, ever to thee be addressed the holocaust." Nor ought we to omit the Teutonic word, *heimath*, the exact equivalent for that "*pro aris et focis*" of the Romans which has become with us the synonym and epitome of all that is dear to man.

There is also a curious Keltic analogy. Among the Irish, the expression, 'the breaking of cinders,' "means* to charge and confirm guilt on a man at his own hearth, so that his fire, which represents his honour, is broken up into cinders. The trampling of a man's cinders was one of the greatest insults which could be offered to him, as it conveyed the idea of guilt, and not only on the individual himself, but also on his family and household." We may well believe that we have here a memorial of the time when the hearth was the centre and the shrine of the family, and when the fortunes of its head brought a like fortune to every member of the household.

As to the connection of the hearth and the House Spirit, we know that the Greeks called their House Spirits ἐφέστιοι or ἑστιοῦχοι, the sitters at, or the guardians of, the hearth. The Vedas constantly speak of Agni as a domestic deity. He is the lord of the village, of the clan, of the Sib; the household one, the member of the Sib.† In the Avesta,‡ Asha-Vahista, the genius of fire, is designated as "the house-companion of living beings." The Latin writers use hearth and lar as synonymous. Virgil § uses the term Lares and Penates indifferently, as his verse happens to require, and habitually associates these House Spirits with the fire on the hearth and the "*canæ penetralia Vestæ*."

* "Dr. Sullivan's Introduction, O'Curry's Lectures," I., cclxxviii.

† "La Cité Antique," p. 35. Pictet, vol. ii., p. 678.

‡ Spiegel's "Avesta," by Bleeck, vol. iii., p. 181.

§ See Æn., v., 743, ix., 259.

When the Russian peasant* changes his house, the fire from the old stove is raked into a jar and is brought into the new house, where its arrival is greeted with the significant salutation, "Welcome, grandfather." If the fire cannot be brought, a fire-shovel, or some other object connected with the hearth, takes its place, and is welcomed in the like manner. In the minds of these peasants the Agon and the Damovoy are the same. So, too, both Hector and Æneas † thought, when, in that vision on the night of Ilion's ruin, the spectre of the Trojan prince, in his country's name, committed to the protection of the Goddess-born the *sacra* and the Penates of Troy, and accordingly delivered to him the fillets, and the potent Vesta, and the ever-burning fire from the inmost shrines.

House Worship and House Burial.

§ 5. But the fact that the hearth is the seat of the fire, and that the fire is the instrument by which the sacrifice is conveyed to the spirit, is not the only connection between the worship of the ancestors and the worship of the hearth. There seems to be a still closer relation. The hearth was the seat, not of the fire only, but of the spirit himself. In earlier times, it appears that the bodies of the deceased ancestors were actually buried within their dwellings. In later times, although the bodies were removed to some sepulchre outside the house but within the grounds, they were first brought into the house, and there laid out for some time. This formal interment seems to have satisfied the old feeling, and the veneration for the hearth remained undisturbed. The adequacy of this explanation, if its truth can be shown, is, when we bear in mind the views of uncultured races about tombs and the presence there of spirits, sufficiently plain. That house-burial is a *vera causa*

* Mr. Ralston, "Songs of Russia," pp. 120, 138.

† Æn., ii., 292.

is proved by the fact that it is practised at the present day by multitudes among the inferior races. It exists among many tribes* of South America. It is also found † among the Fantees, the Dahomans, the Assins, and other tribes of Western Africa. Among the Aryan nations the practice has long since disappeared, and its very existence has been disputed. There is, however, direct evidence that at some remote period our ancestors were accustomed to dispose in this manner of their dead. Plato ‡ tells us that in early times the dead were buried in the house. Servius,§ an antiquarian of considerable ability, who wrote under the early Emperors, says—"Among our ancestors, all persons used to be buried in their respective houses, whence has arisen the domestic worship of the Lares; whence, also, we call the shades Larvæ: for the Dii Penates are different." In another place || he says—"Amongst our ancestors, wheresoever any one died, he used to be carried back to his own house, and there he remained seven days; on the eighth he was burned, and on the ninth he was buried. It is to be known that they were buried in their own house, whence arose the custom that the Dii Penates should be worshipped in houses." It is also a suggestive fact, ¶ that, in the case of colonies, which were established with ceremonies similar to those used in the foundation of new households, the Founder, or original House Father of the new settlement was buried in the Forum. A vestige of the same custom is preserved by Athenæus.** He says, that at Tarentum the dead were buried within the walls, each family having within their house tombstones with the names of the deceased, where funeral sacrifices were performed. There is a passage, too,

* Mr. Spencer's "Principles of Sociology," i., 273.

† "Through Fanteeland to Coomassie," by Fred. Boyle, p. 209.

‡ "Minos," p. 315. § In Æn., vi., 151. || In Æn., v., 64.

¶ Hermann, "Grecian Antiquities," p. 138, *n.* (3.)

** xii., 522. Müller's "Dorians," vol. ii., p. 404.

in the Rig Veda,* which seems to suggest something of the same kind. The Pitris or Manes are there called "Gharma Sád," that is, dwelling in the abode of Yama—*i.e.*, the harmya or oven.

We may, then, sum up the substance of this contention as follows. The primitive religion was domestic. This domestic religion was composed of two closely-related parts: the worship of deceased ancestors, and the worship of the hearth. The latter form was subsidiary to, and consequent upon, the former. The deceased ancestor, or his ashes, was either actually buried, or assumed to be buried, beneath the hearth. Here, therefore, according to the primitive belief, his spirit was supposed to dwell; and here it received those daily offerings which were its rightful dues, and were essential to its happiness. The fire which burned on the hearth rendered these offerings fit for the finer organs of the spirit world, and transmitted them to him for whom they were designed. Thus the worship of the Lares was the foundation and the support of the adoration of the hearth, which was in effect its altar, and of the holy fire which for ever burned there.

Ritual of House Worship.

§ 6. This domestic worship had, like every other worship, its own ceremonies and its peculiar celebrants. But while the celebrants were defined by an unvarying rule, there was no uniformity in the ceremonies. Each household had its own ritual.† It had its own festivals, its own forms of hymns and of prayers. So far from sharing the forms adopted by others, every household regarded its special forms as its own peculiar birthright. They were a precious secret, carefully guarded and never divulged. In the Rig Veda ‡ the Indian says—"I am strong against my foes

* Prof. Max Müller, "Rig Veda," pp. 205-207.

† Cicero, "De Leg," ii., 11.

‡ "La Cité Antique," p. 36.

by reason of the hymns that I hold from my family and that my father has transmitted to me." Menu makes frequent reference to the peculiar rites of each family. Ovid * tells us that the Lares have *sua verba*, their appropriate modes of address. The rule of Roman law is explicit —"*Suo quisque ritu sacrificia faciat.*" There are many passages in the Greek classics † which, in describing the reception of suppliants, illustrate both the sanctity of the hearth and the force of special forms of adjuration. One—not the least interesting of them—is the account which Thucydides gives of the flight of Themistokles. The great Athenian, close followed by his enemies, reached during the absence of its master the house of Admetor, the King of the Molossians, in Epeiros. The wife of Admetor instructed the fugitive in the proper form of address, and he accordingly, with the child of Admetor in his arms, sat down by the holy hearth. "And this," says the historian, "was the most powerful form of supplication." In a still earlier time we find the shipwrecked Odysseus receiving instructions in the proper mode of supplicating King Alkinoos, both from the king's daughter Nausikaê, and from the bright-eyed Athenê herself. In pursuance of these directions the hero, after he had declared his name and implored relief, sat down amid the ashes on the hearth.

I have said that the celebrants of this worship were defined by a strict and fundamental rule. All members of the household joined in it, and were, so to speak, bound together and confederated by this communion; but it was the son, the House Father for the time being, that was specially charged with its maintenance, and was responsible for its continuance. A daughter, as we shall see more fully, could not maintain, because she could not continue, the

* "Fasti," ii., 542.

† See Grote's "History of Greece," vol. ii., p. 109 (note).

household sacred rites. When she married, she was initiated into a different cult, and the gods of her husband became her gods and those of her children. It is, therefore, for sons that the ancient world habitually craves. "Oh! may that man be born in our line"—it is thus that in Hindu belief the Manes pray without ceasing—"who may give us milky food, with honey and pure butter, both on the thirteenth of the moon, and when the shadow of an elephant falls to the east." * If sons were denied to a House Father in the course of nature, he acquired them by adoption or some other recognized method. But we never hear—at least in any pure genealogic clan—of the adoption of a daughter; and the reason is, that an adopted daughter would have been useless to a man for the purposes that he required. It was the son alone who could continue the household. He was its visible representative and head, and he was bound not only to administer its temporal affairs, but especially to perform its *sacra*, and to maintain the purity of its ritual.

Persistence of House Worship.

§ 7. There are few facts in history more remarkable than the wonderful persistency of the worship of the House Spirit. We meet with it at the earliest period of recorded time; its traces linger among us even still. Such persistency is in itself sufficient evidence both of the antiquity of this worship, and of its hold upon the human heart. We have, however, positive evidence on these points. That must have been no feeble growth which Buddhism was obliged to recognize; which was unharmed by the spread of the nature-worship of Olympos; which was the last of the forms of the old religion to give way before Christianity; which, when proscribed both by Church and by State, yet

* Menu, iii., 274.

for centuries was not extinguished; which even at this day is the belief of the Russian peasant, and defies in China * the utmost efforts of the missionaries. Nor can we regard as modern that system which Menu tells us was, even when he wrote, the oldest religion among men. It is, as we have seen, mentioned in the Rig Veda, and consequently it existed when mythology had not commenced. Men worshipped the House Spirit on the hearth at a time when they perfectly understood that Dyaus meant the bright sky, and that Varuna or Ouranos was the arch of heaven. Centuries after the common apartment of the primitive house had disappeared, and separate rooms were assigned in spacious mansions for the various purposes of domestic life, the old altar,† the symbol of the holy hearth, survived, as the houses of Pompeii still show, undisturbed, in the *Atrium*. All the changes in thought and feeling which marked the rise of the empire were impotent against the Lar. Horace, Ovid, Petronius,‡ free-thinkers in principle and sensualists in practice, duly celebrated the worship of their hearths. Even among the early Christians themselves, the suggestive letters "D.M." upon their tombs § preserved for many a year the memory of the time when these tombs were avowedly consecrated to the Dii Manes.

We may, perhaps, trace some of the causes by which, during so many ages, the Lar maintained his peaceful existence beneath "the drums and tramplings" of repeated conquests. Sometimes other deities were added to the sacrificial list, and a double worship was maintained, cumulative, but distinct. Sometimes a different course was

* See Doolittle's "Social Life of the Chinese," vol. ii., pp. 424-5.

† Smith's "Dict. Ant.," *s. v.*, Focus.

‡ "La Cité Antique," p. 24.

Mr. Tylor's "Primitive Culture," vol. ii., p. 110.

adopted, and the names of the new deities were given to the old familiar friends. Sometimes the old worship was proscribed, and the House Spirit was not, indeed, abolished, but degraded. Of the first of these methods an example is found in India. I have already observed that Menu * directs that separate offerings be made to the gods and to the Manes: the oblation to the former always, as a matter of precaution, both preceding and following the oblation to the latter. Of the transfer of the names of the new religion to the old, we have many instances in both Greece and Rome. We read of Ζεὺς πατρῷος and of Ἀπόλλων πατρῷος, of Ζευς ἐφέστιος and Ζευς ἑρκεῖος; † of Ζευς ὁμόγνιος and Ζευς σύναιμος; of Ζευς φράτριος and Ζευς ὁμόφυλος. Medea swears by Hekate, "My mistress to whom I pray, and who dwells at the sanctuary of my hearth." Athene Ἀπατουρία presided ‡ over the πάτραι or clans at Athens and at Trœzen. Callimachus § identifies Hermes with the House Spirit, rising from the hearth to frighten a naughty child. I need not collect cases of Gentile gods—of Apollo,|| the founder of the Dorians, and Heracles their Genarch; of the Demeter of the Eumolpids, and of the Athene of the Butadæ. So too among the Romans we meet Jupiter Familiaris and Jupiter Penetralis, the recognized equivalents of Ζευς ἐφέστιος and Ζευς ἕρκειος.¶ Hercules belonged to the Potitii, and appears as one of the Penates of Evander.** The Nautii had their Minerva, and probably the Julii their Venus. In later times the same custom was continued, and even by individual

* iii., 205.

† See Odys., xxii., 335; Soph. Antig., 487; Herodotus, vi., 68.

‡ Müller's "Dorians," vol. i., p. 95.

§ Hymn to Artemis, 70.

|| Müller's "Dorians," vol. i., pp. 278, 425.

¶ Herceus Juppiter intra conseptum domus cujusque colebatur quem etiam deum penetralem appellabant.—Festus, *s. v.*, Herceus. So the Greeks translate the Roman Penates by Ἑρκεῖοι.

** Virgil, Æn., viii., 543.

citizens the Genius of the Emperor* was by a sort of adoption constituted an additional Lar. The Emperor was *pater patriæ,* and would consequently be entitled after death to a place in the public lararium, and to the proper offerings. But even during his life the admiration for conspicuous success secured him, as a patron saint, a place in many a Roman household.

These expedients, however, could not be adopted in the case of Christianity. The God of the Christians is in truth a jealous God. His worship is both exclusive and aggressive. The Church, and the State under the influence of the Church, were little inclined to make any terms with idolatry. A century after Christianity had become the established religion of the Empire, Theodosius prohibited, under extreme penalties, as well the other forms of Paganism as also the exercise of the worship of the Lares. Yet no positive law could wholly sever the ties which for countless generations had bound the people to the guardians of their hearths. The disestablished Lar became an evil spirit, as the Churchmen held; but to the people he was a friendly ministering genius, deserving kind treatment, and readily appreciating it. There is hardly a country in Europe, as I have already said, where some trace of this once widespread belief does not survive. I have already mentioned some of the most notable instances of this survival in Slavonic, Teutonic, and Keltic nations. Among the Latin nations the survival, though in somewhat different form, is not less marked. The patron saint, the guardian of the house, of the street, of the bridge, of the ship, is not unfamiliar in Southern Europe. So, too, in regard to a

* Te multa prece te prosequitur mero
Defuso pateris: et Laribus tuum
Miscet nomen uti Græcia Castoris
Et magni memor Herculis.—*Horace,* Odes, iv., 5, 33.

cognate but somewhat wider subject, the Church has accepted what it could not prevent, and sanctified the sentiment which had for its object the general worship of the dead. Even as the good Pope Gregory the Great permitted the newly converted English to retain their old temples, and their accustomed rites, attaching, however, to them another purpose, and a new meaning, so his successors found means to utilize the simple beliefs of early animism. Long and vainly the Church struggled against this irresistible sentiment. Fifteen centuries ago, it was charged against the Christians of that day that they appeased the shades of the dead with feasts like the Gentiles. In the Penitentials we find the prohibition of burning grains where a man had died. In the "*Indiculus superstitionum et paganiarum*,"* among the Saxons complaint is made of the too ready canonization of the dead; and the Church seems to have been much troubled to keep within reasonable bounds this tendency to indiscriminate apotheosis. At length a compromise was effected, and the Feast of All Souls converted to pious uses that wealth of sentiment which previously was lavished on the dead. Amongst the Slavic peoples, we are told,† the custom prevails of holding an annual feast for the dead. At this feast, which is not meant for any special person, but for the dead generally, they believe that the souls are personally present. Silently, little bits of food are thrown for them under the tables. People believed that they heard them rustle, and saw them feed upon the smell and vapour of the food. Among the peasants ‡ of the Tyrol, old Bavaria, the Upper Palatinate, and German Bohemia, special preparation is made, as All-Saints' Day approaches, for the reception of their disembodied visitants.

* "Canciani Leg. Barb.," iii., 76, 106.

† See Mr. Spencer's "Sociology," vol. i., Appendix A., p. 1.

‡ *Ib.*, vol. i., p. 322, and the authorities there cited.

"In every house a light is kept burning all night. The lamp is no longer filled with oil, but with fat. A door, or at least a window, remains open, and the supper is left on the table, even with some additions: people go to bed earlier—all to let the little angels enter without being disturbed." In Italy,* the day is given to feasting and drinking, in honour of the dead; while skulls and skeletons, in sugar and paste, form appropriate children's toys. In the simple villages of Brittany,† "the crowd pours into the churchyard at evening, to kneel, bareheaded, at the graves of dead kinsfolk, to fill the hollow of the tombstone with holy water, or to pour libations of milk upon it. All night the church bells clang, and sometimes a solemn procession of the clergy goes round to bless the graves. In no household that night is the cloth removed, for the supper must be left for the souls to come and take their part; nor must the fire be out where they will come to warm themselves. And, at last, as the inmates retire to rest, there is heard at the door a doleful chant—it is the souls, who, borrowing the voices of the parish poor, have come to ask the prayers of the living."

It is strange to turn from this vivid picture of the simple and tender superstitions of our own day, and to listen to the distant cry of the Fravashis of Irân,‡ when, at the close of the year, on the intercalary days added to it, they assembled for ten days upon earth in quest of their wonted worship. "Who will praise us, who will offer to us, who will make us his own—who will bless us, who will receive us, with hand provided with flesh, provided with clothes, with prayer which desires purity? Whose name of us will one utter here, to whose soul of you offer, to which of us here give gifts, so that there may be to him there-for

* Mr. Tylor's "Primitive Culture," vol. ii., p. 34. † *Ib.*

‡ Spiegel's "Avesta," by Bleeck, vol. iii., p. 87.

eatable food, imperishable, of eatable things for evermore?" And when the flesh, and the clothes, and the pious prayers have been offered, the strong Fravashis of the pure—contented, not revengeful, not offended—bless him, and declare that "in this dwelling shall be the fulness of cattle and men; there shall be swift horses and a firm chariot; the man shall be esteemed, the head of a congregation." Thus every Parsee who still makes, after the manner of his fathers, the yearly feast, and offers the usual clothing for the souls of the departed, every Spaniard who, on the anniversary of his bereavement, brings to the tomb of the lost one his offering of bread and of wine, every Parisian who, with loving hand, lays upon the grave the garland of immortelles—unconsciously continues the tradition of the times when Zeus, and Jupiter, and Indra were not; when there was neither Persian, nor Goth, nor Kelt; but when, on the plains of Bokhara, or on the rich pastures of high Pamîr, the common progenitors of our race did homage to the dwellers in the spirit-world, and, above all, offered their daily orisons to their own forefathers upon the holy hearth.

CHAPTER III.

THE HOUSEHOLD.

The Corporate character of the Household.

§ 1. ONE of the chief difficulties in the study of history is the tendency to judge early men and early institutions by the standard and the lights of our own day. This tendency is indefinitely strengthened if we use the same name for both the ancient and the modern institution. There is, for example, little hope that we shall understand the nature of the archaic family if we permit ourselves to call it by that name. It is not only that the word family, or Familia, is hopelessly ambiguous,* but also that the archaic Household is essentially different from the family, as we understand the term. Beyond the external resemblances that exist from the very nature of the case, that Household had little likeness to anything that is found in modern society. It rested upon a theory abhorrent to our beliefs. It aimed at an object which we can with difficulty comprehend. It used a machinery which we have long outgrown. The theory upon which it rested was the paramount and continuous obligation of ancestral worship. The practical object at which it aimed was the regular and proper performance of the *sacra*—that is, of the worship peculiar to the Household. The machinery by which the *sacra* were maintained was the corporate character of the Household, and the perpetual succession of the House Father.

* See for the various meanings of Familia, Dig. L., xvi., 195.

At the present day, the word family, or Household, denotes in English law no jural personality, but merely certain relations of individuals. These relations give rise to some simple general duties of forbearance, and to certain obligations. Except marriage, they are transient. The duties arising from the parental relation last only until the children have attained a specified age. During its continuance, the parental authority is subject to the control of the sovereign, whenever such interference appears to be beneficial to the children. The relation of the master to his servants rests entirely upon contract: his relation to his guests or other inmates has the same foundation. Marriage alone retains the character of a status. Even as regards succession, it is only in the absence of any disposition to the contrary that parents and children have towards each other any legal rights. Collateral relatives, although they have in their degree similar rights of succession, are not now regarded as belonging to the family at all. We may then say that the modern family has no separate legal existence, but is merely a collective name for certain definite individuals; is limited in its duration; has no present property, but only expectations, which may be defeated by the caprice of its master; and extends to lineal descendants alone.

From such a family the archaic Household was in every respect different. It formed an organized permanent body, distinct from its individual members, owning property, and having other rights and duties of its own. In it all its members, whatever might be their position, had interests according to their rank. Over it the House Father presided with absolute power, not as owner in his own right, but as the officer and representative of the corporation. With his discretion no external authority was competent to interfere; and the interest of the corporate body, not that of any individual member, was the sole object of regard. The tie between the members was neither blood nor contract, but community of domestic worship. Contract, indeed, between members of the same Household was impossible. Even when an artificial group was formed, the contract in which it commenced immediately merged, as in the case of a modern marriage, in the status to which it gave rise. The termination of the Household was not only not expected, but was regarded as both a public and a private calamity. Further, the Household, if no separation had taken place, extended not only to lineal but to collateral relatives. It included servants and dependents. It included children by adoption. It excluded children who were emancipated. Its one great aim was the perpetuation of the *sacra*. The *sacra* were essential both to the unity and the continuity of the Household. If they ceased, the Household was gone. The existence of a Household without *sacra* was inconceivable. Each term connoted the other. But the *sacra* could be performed only in a particular way. It was a worship of males by males, of past Fathers by present Fathers. After his death, not less than during his life, the *Pater* represented in the Spirit-world all those who on earth had been under his Hand, and required that the offerings due to him should be made by his successor and representative alone. Thus the House Father for the time being was the visible representative and head of the Household; and was bound not only to administer its temporal affairs, but to perform the ceremonies of its religion, and to maintain the purity of its ritual.

These principles serve to mark, both positively and negatively, the Household and its limits. All those persons who were under the authority of the same House Father were members of the Household. Every member of a

Household shared in that Household's *sacra*, and was under the protection of its House Spirits. No person who was not, either in consequence of his birth or by special favour, brought under the House Father's authority, was included in the Household, or could participate in its *sacra*. Thus the Household was not the result either of birth or of natural affection. It might contain a son who was such merely by adoption. It must exclude the most dearly-loved daughter who had become a wife, or the son who had been emancipated. Its foundation was neither consanguinity nor love, but religion. Its test was the community of *sacra*, as evidenced by the subjection to a common authority. Every person who was in the Hand of the same Father was a member of the Household, and offered his vows at the same hearth and at the common tomb.

The Household was thus an association formed upon religious belief, and contemplating religious objects. But it was something more. It was a permanent association. It was not intended to pass away and be re-formed like the generations of men. It was constructed, and was meant, to endure for ever. It was, in our technical language, a corporation. It had perpetual succession. It included in its members both the living and the dead. These members had various degrees of rank; but the whole number, taken collectively, formed one well-defined and distinct individuality. Of this corporate entity the House Father for the time being was the head, or, as we might say, the managing director. As against the living members of his Household, his authority was absolute. But he held himself responsible for his conduct to his divine predecessors, whose servant and interpreter he was. He held, if I may so speak, the property of the Household in usufruct, but not in dominion. When he died, his pre-appointed successor at once stepped into his place. There was no devolution, but, to use the language of the Roman law,* there was a continuation of ownership. That which is now the prerogative of Royalty was then the rule in every House. The House Father never died. In the order of nature he was removed, indeed, to join his predecessors; but, simultaneously with his removal, his place was filled by his heir. That heir retained, of course, all the Household's Property, which it was his special function to administer.

§ 2. It is not easy to give a succinct and orderly proof of the statement that the Household was a corporate body. Such a statement is, in truth, only a summary of many particular facts; and the generalization is, in our authorities, implied rather than expressly stated. I shall, too, have occasion to state the evidence in some detail, both in dealing with some of those particular facts, and also when we consider the nature of that joint undivided family which has survived to our own day. Still, I am reluctant to make, even provisionally, any large assertion without supporting it by proper historical evidence; and the principle in question is so important that I may be pardoned for a little repetition. I will endeavour, then, to minimize this unavoidable inconvenience by, in this place, citing, not the original authorities, but the conclusions of modern writers of repute.

Historical examples of this Corporate character.

Thus, in reference to the Hindu family, Sir H. S. Maine † says that "although the modern law of India gives such facilities for its dissolution that it is one of the most unstable of social compounds, and rarely lasts beyond a couple of generations, still, so long as it lasts it has a legal corporate existence." Of the Teutons the same

* Dig., xxxviii., 2, 11.
† "Early Hist. of Inst.," p. 78.

writer * says, "All the Germanic immigrants seem to have recognized a corporate union of the family under the *mund*, or authority of a patriarchal chief; but his powers are obviously only the relics of a decayed *patria potestas*." Of the Slav family, M. de Laveleye † thus writes—"The ties of the family have preserved among the Russians, as among the Slavs of the Danube and the Balkans, a power that they have lost elsewhere. The family is a kind of corporation which perpetuates itself, and is governed with an authority almost absolute by the chief called the Elder. All their property rests in common. There is in general neither inheritance nor partition." If we look to the western extremity of Europe, we find a similar state of things among the ancient Irish. The learned editor of the third volume of the "Ancient Laws of Ireland," ‡ observes that "the several families who formed a tribe, although possessing common property, and united defensively as against their neighbour, occupied, *inter sese*, the position of independent communities: there existed no sovereign bound to see that justice was done, no common tribunal to which an appeal might be had." In a subsequent passage,§ the same very able writer remarks that, "in the early Irish, as in other archaic societies, the *nexus* of the family was not marriage, but acknowledged actual descent from a common ancestor, and participation in the common duties and property of the family."

The corporate character of the Household, both in Greece and in Rome, is so well known, that little illustration of the subject is needed. "At Sparta," says K. O. Müller,‖ "the family, together with the estate, formed an individual whole, under the control of one head, who was privileged by

* "Anc. Law," p. 143.
† "De la Propriété," p. 23.
‡ Introduction, p. lxxix.
§ *Ib.*, p. cxliv.
‖ "Dorians," vol. ii., p. 204.

his birth." Of Roman law, M. Ortolan * says:—"The family, considered with reference to the *jus privatum,* was the aggregation in which property, the effects of obligation, the right of inheritance and of succession—that is to say, the right of taking and of continuing in the State the *persona* of the deceased—all centred." The last authority which I shall cite is valuable, not merely as that of a very careful and cautious writer, but as showing the extent to which these views as to the Household are now generalized and accepted. Mr. Justice Markby † says:—"According to the first notion of society—certainly, according to the first Aryan notion—ownership was not individual, but corporate. Property belonged, not to an individual, or a determinate set of individuals, but to an aggregate of indeterminate persons, such as a family or tribe."

§ 3. The first step in the formation of a Household was marriage. The *τέλειος ἀνὴρ,* the finished man, of the Greeks, meant what we should call a family-man. The δόμος ἡμιτελὴς ‡ that adds a new pain to the sad tale of the gallant Protesilaos, meant a marriage, of which the wished-for fruit had not been, and never could be, attained. "Then only," says Menu,§ "is a man perfect, when he consists of three persons united, his wife, himself, and his son." To our remote ancestors marriage presented itself in a very different light from that with which we are familiar. It was sought, not as in itself a good, but as a means to an end. That end was the birth of a son. It was the son alone who could continue the Household. It is for sons, therefore, that the Indian Pitris in their spirit-home continually do cry. It is the son by whose birth, as Menu ‖ teaches, the father discharges his

The foundation of the Household was marriage.

* "Hist. of Roman Law," p. 577.
† "Elements of Law," sec. 549.
‡ Il., ii., 70.
§ x., 45.
‖ ix., 106, 107.

duty to his progenitors, and by whom he attains immortality. It is the son who, in the words of Æschylus, is the saviour of the hearth of his fathers. But it was not every son that was sufficient to continue the Household. It must be a son born of a woman whom his father might lawfully marry, and whom in fact he had married. It must, too, be such a son, begotten for the express purpose,* and with the distinct intent of his assuming, in due time, his father's place. An illegitimate son was not only not acknowledged, but was excluded from the Household. "Those animals," says Menu,† "begotten by adulterers, destroy, both in this world and in the next, the food presented to them by such as make oblations to the gods and to the Manes." The rule of Attic law ‡ was clear, "*νόθῳ μὴ ἀγχιστέιαν ἔιναι μήθ' ἱερῶν μήθ' ὁσίων.*" Neither in the worship of the Household nor in its property had the bastard any place. An illegitimate son was, by the Roman law, not in *patria potestate*, and consequently was not a member of the Household. The German rule was exactly similar. "Illegitimate children," says Grimm,§ "were considered to be neither in true *sippe*, nor in the father's power." The old Norse law in reference to a Bæsingr, declares ‖ "That child, also, is not entitled to inheritance." So the illegitimate son of an Irish woman ¶ by a stranger, unless he were begotten with the assent and the knowledge of the tribe of the mother, would have no status in either the family or the tribe of the mother, and would be considered by them as a stranger and a trespasser. A legitimate son, therefore, every House Father must have; and as he could not have a legitimate son without having a wife, he took a wife, not for his own pleasure, but in

* Menu, ix., 107, 147. † iii., 175.

‡ Demos. against Makartatos, 1067.

§ "Deutsche Rechts Alterthumer," p. 475.

‖ "Cleasby-Vigfusson, Icelandic Dict.," p. 92.

¶ "Ancient Laws of Ireland," vol. iii., Introd. p. 146.

fulfilment of a sacred obligation. He married for duty, not for pleasure. The Roman bridegroom swore * that he married *liberorum quærendorum causa.* The Greek's single aim † in wedded life was παίδων ἐπ' ἀρότῳ γνησίων. "Mistresses," says Demosthenes,‡ "we keep for pleasure, concubines for daily attendance upon our persons, wives to bear us legitimate children and to be our faithful housekeepers." The man who intends to marry for the sake of having issue is one of the nine classes that Menu § recognizes as virtuous mendicants.

The personal motives, therefore, which led to marriage were, in the early world, very strong. The popular sentiment is emphatically expressed by Isaios ‖ when he says, "No man who knows he must die can have so little regard for himself as to leave his family without descendants, for then there would be no one to render him the worship due to the dead." A remarkable illustration of this sentiment occurs on a memorable occasion in Grecian history. When Leonidas arrived at the scene of his desperate defence of Thermopylæ, he was accompanied, says the historian,¶ "by the three hundred men which the law assigned him, whom he had himself chosen from among the citizens, and who were all of them fathers with sons living." According to modern notions, a forlorn hope would naturally be composed of men who had not given hostages to fortune. Such, however, was not the light in which the matter presented itself to the Greek mind. The human plant had flowered. The continuance of the House was secure. It was, therefore, comparatively of little moment what befel the man whose duty to his ancestors had been fulfilled. In the aspect of the case now before us, the fact that a man married, or

* Becker's "Gallus," p. 172.

† Becker's "Charicles," p. 474.

‡ Against Neæra.

§ xi., 1, 2.

‖ vii. 30.

¶ "Herodotus," vii., 205.

that he remained single, was not a matter which affected himself alone. The condition of his ancestors, the permanence of his Household, depended upon his conduct. We cannot, therefore, doubt that celibacy was regarded as a deadly sin. Even the State, although it was slow to interfere in matters merely *privati juris*, lent its aid to enforce this primary duty. Solon * prohibited celibacy. The laws of the Dorians,† the most conservative of the Hellenes, contained similar provisions. Criminal proceedings might be taken, both at Athens and at Sparta, against those who married too late in life, against those who married beneath them, and against those who did not marry at all. There is evidence that a prohibition to the same effect existed in early Rome; and Cicero ‡ notices, as a part of the duty of the Censors, the imposition of a tax upon unmarried men. In the laws of Menu,§ too, the marriage of the younger brother before the elder, and the neglect of the elder brother to marry before the younger, are regarded as crimes of the third degree.

The Rite of Initiation.

§ 4. It follows from this corporate character that a child is not born into the Household. The infant does not by the mere fact of birth become a member of the corporation. It must be duly admitted. It must be formally accepted by the House Father, and be by him initiated into the domestic worship. This rule of special admission, which, as we shall presently see, was applied to all persons, had a special reason in the case of sons. Such a son as the Household required was not any spurious offspring, or even any son that the House Father might

* See Becker's "Charicles," p. 475, and the authorities there cited.

† Müller's "Dorians," vol. ii., p. 307.

‡ "De Leg.," iii., 3.

§ xi., 61.

happen to beget. He must be a genuine or kindly son, *παῖς γνήσιος*, one born in lawful marriage, and even begotten with a special intent. Accordingly it was among all the Aryan nations necessary * that when a child was born it should be forthwith presented for acceptance to the House Father. It rested with him to recognize its claims to admission or to reject them. In the former case the new-comer was initiated into the domestic worship; in the latter it was either at once killed or was exposed. But if the least morsel of food or the least particle of drink † had touched the child's lips, the discretion was at an end, and the child was held to have shared in the meal, and so to be duly recognized. It is probable that the paternal recognition was followed by other ceremonies. At Athens, at least, a special festival ‡ was held on the fifth day, it is said, after the birth. There the child was carried round the sacred hearth, and was presented, in the sight of all its relatives, to the Spirits of the House and to the Household. Its name was then given to it, and of this presentation and this name the guests then assembled were witnesses. At Rome a similar ceremony was performed on the eighth or ninth day. A lustration was celebrated, and the prænomen was given.

The rule which governed the admission of children applied to persons less closely connected. Even in the case of slaves || some introductory ceremony appears to have been observed. When any suppliant or guest sought the protection of the hearth, a formal recognition of his claim was needed. It was in the discretion of the House Father, subject only to his own sense of religious duty towards the

* Grimm's "Deutsche Rechts Alt.," p. 455; Grote's "Hist. Greece," vol. iii., p. 136.

† See Grimm, *ubi supra*, p. 458.

‡ Smith, "Dict. Ant." *s. v.* Αμφιδρόμια.

M. de Coulanges' "La Cité Antique," p. 131.

House Spirit, whose protection was invoked, to accept or to refuse the appeal. If, however, he once gave his consent, the suppliant ceased to be a stranger, and was, like the other members of the Household, initiated, at least to a certain extent, into the Household cult, and placed under the protection of the benignant Lares.

The Property of the Household.

§ 5. The corporate character of the Household enables us to understand its rules of property. Over all movables, over the family and the stock, over the produce of the land, and the labour of his subjects, the power of the House Father was absolute. Although, in the cultivation of his land, he was bound by the customary rules of his community, he could determine to what use he would apply the produce. But he could not sell or charge the land itself. The land belonged to the Household; and the continuance of the Household depended upon the maintenance of the hearth and of the tomb, and of the offerings at them, which formed the first charge upon the common property. Of this primitive inalienability of land there is little doubt. In India * every such transfer is permissible only in case of extreme necessity, or with the consent of the collective communities. "Among the Rajpúts," says Colonel Tod,† "no length of time or absence can affect the claim to the *bapota* (*i.e.*, hereditary land); and so sacred is the right of absentees, that land will lie sterile and unproductive from the penalty which Menu denounces on all who interfere with their neighbours' rights." In the earliest Sclavonic ‡ laws it is a fundamental principle that the property of families cannot be divided for a perpetuity. Among the Teutons § the sale of the alod seems to have been

* Sir H. S. Maine, "Early Hist. Inst.," p. 109.

† "Rajasthan," vol. i., p. 526.

‡ Sir H. S. Maine, "Anc. Law," p. 268.

§ See M. de Laveleye, "De la Propriété," p. 168.

unknown until they had become acquainted with the Roman law. In Greece, Aristotle * tells us that "formerly, in some states, no one was allowed to sell his original lot of land;" and he elsewhere † specifies the Locrians and the Leucadians as having this law. A like restriction was in force in Sparta. It was there considered ‡ to be discreditable to sell any land; but to sell any part of the hereditary lot was absolutely forbidden. Among the Irish § the tribe land "could not be sold or alienated, or given to pay for crimes or contracts." So, too, Sir H. S. Maine || observes that the rule requiring the consent of the collective brotherhood to alienation, which is found in the Brehon law, constantly formed part of the customs of Indian and of Russian village communities.

The Welsh law on this subject is worth transcribing in full. ¶ "The father is not to deteriorate nor dispose of the rights of his son for land and soil, except during his own life; neither is the son to deprive his father, during his life, of land and soil; in like manner the father is not to deprive the son of land; and though he may deprive him, it will be recoverable, except in one case, where there shall be an agreement between father, brothers, cousins, second cousins, and the lord, to yield the land as blood-land; and that the son cannot recover, for peace was brought to the son by that as well as to the father; for these persons are grades without whose consent land cannot be assigned. And though such a person have no land, he is not an 'alltud' nevertheless, but an innate 'boneddig.'" This passage illustrates several points in archaic usages:—First, the inheritance of the land was, as a general rule, inalienable,

* "Politics," vi. 4. † *Ib.*, ii. 7.

‡ Grote's "Hist. of Greece," vol. ii., p. 553, *note*.

§ "Ancient Laws of Ireland," vol. ii., p. 283.

|| "Early Hist. Inst.," p. 109.

¶ "Ancient Laws of Wales," vol. i., p. 177.

but the House Father might part with his life-estate; second, the exception to this general rule was where the land was given as compensation for a blood-feud, in which case the benefit attained by the sale extended alike to all the parties liable to bear the feud; third, such a transfer required the consent of all the parties interested—that is, of the male relatives up to and including second cousins, and of the lord where such a person existed; fourth, the second cousin marks the limit of the Household, or Familia, or Mæg, or near kin, by whatever name they be described; fifth, the rank of the individual was determined by his birth, and not by his possession of land, since the ex-landowner, even after the loss of his hereditary estate, remained "an innate boneddig," that is, a gentleman by birth, a member of his Household and of his kin.

In Roman law we have no such direct proof, because in this case, as in so many others, the earliest customs of Rome are hopelessly lost. But we can trace various changes in that law which seem to be modifications of the original rule, and can readily be explained upon the assumption of its existence, although not by any other mode. Thus, by early Roman law, a magistrate gave execution, not against a man's property, but against his person.* Thus, the Twelve Tables provided that the tomb must remain with the Household, even though the surrounding land be sold. So, too, Cicero † notices the rule that the principle of usucapion, or, as we should call it, prescription, should not apply to the tomb or its vestibule.

That danger to the Household which could not be caused directly, could not be incurred indirectly. Thus, the mortgage of land, in the sense with which we are familiar, was unknown, nor was the land regarded as assets in the

* Mr. Hunter's "Roman Law," p. 807.

† "De Leg.," ii., 24.

payment of debts. It was, indeed, easier to deprive a man of his liberty than of his interest in his land. His labour might, at least, be mortgaged during his life, but the land was never regarded as his individual property. It belonged to his Household, and no act of his could permanently affect their rights. Nor could a House Father, of his own mere motion, devise his property to strangers, or even alter its devolution among his children. He was the officer of his corporation, the steward or manager of the property, with all the powers needed for the efficient discharge of his duties, but in no sense its absolute owner. "It is doubtful," says Sir Henry Maine,* "whether a true power of testation was known to any original society except the Roman." This opinion seems to be too cautiously expressed; and even in Rome that form of the testament from which the modern will is descended was certainly of comparatively recent date. "*Testamenti factio* † *non privati sed publici juris est.*" It is not upon the custom of the kin, but upon the law of the State, that the power of testation depends. It is, therefore, only where the State has become developed that wills are found. A curious trace of the old custom has been noticed by Niebuhr,‡ in the customary law on the extreme border of Germany. "In the island of Fehmern, he who belongs to a sept, if he makes a will, must pay the sept a certain sum of money. This is clearly a compensation for the right of inheritance; and the like custom would have been introduced at Rome, had not the gens been included in other more comprehensive bodies." Perhaps there is no fuller statement of the feelings of the ancient world upon this subject than the dialogue which Plato § supposes to take place between a Citizen and the Legislator. It marks, of course, a time when the old rules no longer commanded

* "Anc. Law," p. 196.

† "Dig.," xxviii., 1, 3.

‡ "Hist. of Rome," vol. ii., p. 338.

§ "Laws," xi., 923.

an unmurmuring obedience, and when the predominance of the State was established; but still it shows the sentiments which, even at the close of the great career of Athens, retained their effective power. The old rule was so far relaxed, that Plato would consent to give the power of nominating the heir from among the children. But his Legislator sternly represses the claim for uncontrolled testamentary power, and declares that "neither you nor this property belong to yourselves, but to your entire kin, as well that which was before as that which is to come after;" and, in a still greater degree, he adds, "the whole kin and the property belong to the city."

We may thus, perhaps, explain a distinction which Gaius * makes, and which otherwise is somewhat obscure. He is describing the different classes of Things, and after distributing "*res divini juris*" into "*res sacræ et religiosæ*," he defines these terms in the following words:—"*Sacræ sunt quæ Diis superis consecratæ sunt: religiosæ, quæ Diis manibus relictæ sunt.*" It is not at once apparent what distinction is intended between "*consecratæ*" and "*relictæ*." The form of the sentence suggests a contrast, and Gaius, when writing on a technical subject, was not likely to use words at random. I understand the passage to mean that "*res sacræ*" required a special act of dedication, which, as Justinian † tells us, was performed "*rite et per pontifices*," in the form prescribed by law, and by proper officers authorized thereto. No such positive and formal act was required in the case of "*res religiosæ*." They were simply left for the Manes. That is, the Manes and their living descendants were—as Plato, in the passage I have above cited, describes them—joint owners of the property of the Household. So much of this property as they required for their own use, the living men took. So

* ii., 4. † "Inst.," ii., 1, 8.

much as they did not use, they left, as their rightful share, to the Manes.

§ 6. Between the property of the Household and the performance of its *sacra* there was an indissoluble connection. The two things always went together. The one supplied the means for the accomplishment of the other. The person who was charged with the performance of the *sacra* was the heir. The heir was the person who was bound to perform the *sacra*. "The funeral cake," says Menu,* "follows the family and the estate." "The person who inherits," says the same authority, "whosoever it be, is bound to make the offerings on the tomb." Cicero,† in equally distinct terms, tells us that the obligations of the *sacra* devolve upon those who inherit the family estates. So, too, Gaius,‡ when commenting on the rule which made an inheritance an exception to the necessity of *bonâ fide* possession for the purposes of a succession, explains that "the motive for permitting at all so unscrupulous an acquisition was the wish of the ancient legislator to accelerate the acceptance of successions, and thus provide persons to perform the sacred rites to which in those days the highest importance was attached." In Athens the rule was not less explicit. The heir was, in the language of Plato,§ the successor to his ancestor's gods. To this day, "among the Hindus‖ the right to inherit a dead man's property is exactly co-extensive with the duty of performing his obsequies. If the rites are not properly performed, or not performed by the proper person, no relation is considered as established between the deceased and anybody surviving him." The question, therefore, arises, Who is the proper person to perform the *sacra*, and conse-

The Succession.

* ix., 142.
† "De Leg.," ii., 19.
‡ ii., 55.
§ "Laws," v., 740.
‖ Sir H. S. Maine, "Anc. Law," p. 191.

quently to hold the property? On this matter there is little room for doubt. From what I have already said, it is apparent that, under the primitive custom, a daughter could never inherit. She might, in certain circumstances, bring a son who would, in contemplation of law, be regarded as though he were the actual son of his maternal grandfather; but she herself could never fill the place of the head of the Household. The son, therefore, was the *heres suus et necessarius,* the person who continued upon earth his father's existence after that father had joined the House Spirits. But which of the sons, if there were more than one? To this question Menu* again supplies the answer: "By the eldest, at the moment of his birth, the father, having begotten a son, discharges his debt to his own progenitors; the eldest son, therefore, ought, before partition, to manage the whole patrimony." So, too, the same authority † tells us that "a man must regard his elder brother as equal to his father." That the eldest son was in ancient times the heir among the Teutons appears from the exception that Tacitus ‡ notes in the case of the Tencteri. He says, in effect, that in this tribe, which was especially famed for its cavalry, horses were regarded as objects of inheritance; and that, while all things else went to the eldest son, the heir of the horse was the bravest soldier. Among our immediate ancestors, Bede § tells us that parents were accustomed to recognize the eldest son as the head of the family, and to give him the preference in the division of the inheritance.

In the cases of Greece and of Rome our evidence is less obvious. Sir H. S. Maine,|| indeed, asserts that the privilege of the eldest son was unknown both to the Hellenic and to the Roman world. But this proposition, so

* ix., 106. † iv., 184. ix., 108.
‡ "Germania," c. 32. § "Vita, S. Ben.," ii.
|| "Early Hist. Inst.," p. 198.

far at least as regards the former, cannot be supported. The older Greek customs, if they do not in express terms state the rule, recognize it by necessary implication. There was a constant effort of the Hellenic conservative party in Sparta, in Thebes, in Corinth, and other cities, to revert to the old practice of a determinate number of lots or hereditary properties in each city; or, as it is sometimes expressed, of having only a given number of families. Such an attempt shows that the right of the eldest had existed, and that it was at that time in a state of decay. If we do not find similar evidence in the history of Rome, we must remember that our knowledge of Roman law commences at a comparatively late period of its development.

When the original Household separated into several related but independent Households, the reason of the rule as to the succession of the eldest ceased, and consequently the rule itself was disused. If there were several sons, each of whom became a House Father, and was therefore charged with the care of the *sacra* of the House, the performance of their separate *sacra* necessitated the division of the property. We are, therefore, prepared to find that in societies where the division of the Household was habitual, the custom of the succession of all the sons should have been established. Yet even in these cases we find vestiges of the archaic system. The eldest son has usually some advantage in the distribution. Among these advantages we sometimes meet with one that is especially significant. He retains the holy hearth. Thus in India, Menu * directs that the eldest son, on a partition of the inheritance, shall have a double share. The Greeks had a special word (πρεσβεῖα) to denote the privileges of the elder. At Athens,† this privilege consisted in his retention, as

* ix., 117. † See "La Cité Antique," p. 92.

an extra share, of the paternal house. In the Sclavonic family we can trace a similar rule. "On the death of the House Father," says M. de Laveleye,* "the authority and the administration pass to the eldest of the house; in some districts to the eldest son, in others to the eldest brother of the deceased, provided that he dwells in the same house." The House must in all circumstances be maintained. In the Keltic nations † the rule is still more explicit. In Wales, the brothers divided the paternal inheritance; the youngest, however, who, as we shall presently see, was there the heir, took the principal place, *Tydden*—literally, a residence, or house, with the buildings belonging to it, and a certain amount of land, probably the precinct or court-yard. In Ireland, the cattle and the land were equally divided; but the house and offices with their appliances went, in addition to his share, to the eldest son. He was regarded as "the stem of the family," and had, as such, certain responsibilities. There is, in England, a remarkable custom, which seems exceptional, but the exception belongs to that class that proves the rule. According to the Kentish gavelkind, and the custom known as Borough English, one son, indeed, is secured in the succession to the hearth and forty feet round it. This son, however, is not the eldest, but the youngest. We have just seen that a similar custom existed in Wales. It was in general use ‡ among the Frisons. Under the name of Mainеté, or the succession of the *minor natu*, it prevailed in Picardy and Artois. It can be traced § in several parts of Germany. It exists at this day || among

* "De la Propriété," p. 24.

† "Sullivan's Introduction to O'Curry's Lectures," clxxix., *et seq.*

‡ Robertson, "Early Kings of Scotland," vol. ii., p. 266.

§ Grimm, "Deutsche Rechts Alt.," p. 475.

|| Sir H. S. Maine, "The Nineteenth Century," vol. ii., p. 809.

some of the Southern Slavs. Various explanations, all more or less fantastic, of this singular custom may be found in Blackstone. Blackstone himself seems, although he was not acquainted with all the facts, to have perceived its true nature. As the elder brothers grew up they were initiated into the community. They thereby, in the words of Tacitus,* ceased to be "*pars domûs*" and became "*pars reipublicæ.*" In this capacity they acquired a right to an allotment of the public land. Thus the youngest remained with his father, and in his *mund* or hand. He was the person who was to carry on the paternal Household, and he was the heir of the family. Of him it might be literally said, "Son, thou art ever with me, and all that I have is thine." "The prevalence," † says Mr. Robertson, "of such a custom amongst a numerous class evidently implies the pre-existence of a state of society in which the eldest-born, as they attained manhood, became 'members of the state' and were provided for accordingly—in other words, the existence of a 'community.'"

It must, however, be borne in mind that this succession of the eldest, or, as the case might be, of the youngest, was something altogether different, both in its nature and its origin, from that which we now call primogeniture. The latter form is of comparatively modern date, and probably was due to feudal arrangements. In archaic days the heir did not take the property for his own use: he merely acquired the defined and well-understood position of manager of the common property. He succeeded to an office, and not to an estate. The Household with its property, upon the demise of its chief, remained as it was before. A new chief succeeded to the position of his father, and that was all.

* "Germ.," c. 13. † *Ubi supra*, p. 269, *note*.

CHAPTER IV.

THE DISTINCTION OF RANKS IN THE HOUSEHOLD.

The House Father.

§ 1. EVERY organism implies a distinction and correlation of parts. The extent to which this process is carried determines the relative position of the organism. We may, therefore, expect to find in the Household, as the elementary form of the social organism, a certain degree of differentiation and subordination, even though that degree be but limited. The description of the various members of the Household, and of their mutual relations, is sufficiently familiar. On its visible and external part, the House Father stands conspicuous and supreme. His authority, however, is exercised under a constant sense of his responsibility to his House Spirits, and is checked and regulated thereby. By his side stands the House Mother, the functionary charged with the care of the holy hearth—the natural head, subject to her husband's command, of the internal economy of the family; and, above all, the mother of the House Father to be. Then follow the sons, the hopes of the House; and after them, but on a lower footing, the daughters. If nature have denied the gift of sons, expedients may be adopted to supply the want; and the adopted, or otherwise recognized son, is accepted as fully as though he were natural-born. In the lowest place stand the slaves, and those outsiders who, while they more or less depend upon the Household, are not full members of it, but are associated with it for some particular purpose or some temporary object. Of each of these classes I propose in the present chapter to treat.

The word father was, in its original sense, a title of dignity. It denotes not a physical relation, but an office. So clearly was this conception marked, even in the full development of the Roman law, that, as Ulpian * tells us, a childless man, or even a ward, might be a *pater familias.* The office of father implies the exercise of two leading functions. One of these functions was spiritual; the other was temporal. One related to that portion of the affairs of the Household which concerned the dead; the other, to that which concerned the living. The House Father had, on the one hand, the charge of the *sacra;* on the other hand, the general administration and control of the corporate body of which the performance of these *sacra* was the object and the bond. The nature of the former function I have already considered. The House Father was responsible for the due performance of his *sacra* and for the purity of his ritual. He had, accordingly, full control over the property of the Household, and over the acts of all its members. He was charged with the duty of determining, subject to the customs of the Household, what persons should be admitted to membership, and so should be initiated into the *sacra.* He was bound to provide for the continuance of his office, and to give to the Household, either by birth, or, in default of birth, by adoption, or some other recognized means, a proper successor. Thus his authority in his own house was supreme; and all the subordinate members of the Household were, to use the expressive phrase that seems to have been common to most of the Aryan races, in his Hand. But the origin of the authority was, as I have already observed, religion, and not either natural affection or superiority of physical

* "Dig.," L., 16, 195.

strength. Whatever might have been the degree of affection between a married pair, or whatever might have been their relative strength, the wife did not come under the Hand of her husband unless and until she had, by the proper form, been initiated in the Household worship. A concubine or an illegitimate son was not, as such, a member of the Household, or within the regular scope of the paternal power. A grown-up son, even after his own marriage, remained until his formal emancipation as subject to his father as if he were still a child. We can perceive the aspect in which the Roman regarded this power by the name *potestas* which they applied to it. This term means an office or delegated authority, and is rarely used to express independent or physical power. The *patria potestas* was, in the Roman mind, analogous to the *potestas consularis* or the *potestas tribunitia.* It was created by law, and it was limited by law. That law indeed was not one which proceeded from the State, or with which the State had any direct concern. But the authority came from without, and was in its nature jural. Its foundation was something much more secure and much more exalted than the caprice of scarcely developed sentiment, or the brutality of force. It rested on that which is the basis of all political legitimacy *—reason, justice, and right. It is true that our views of what is reasonable, just, and right, differ in many cases from those of our forefathers; but, at least, there is at the bottom one common sentiment, the submission of the will to an authority that it believes to be its superior, and the sacrifice of personal desires and personal interests to the prevailing, though it may be mistaken, sense of duty.

The House Mother.

§ 2. The history of the word mother resembles in some respects that of father. Like father, it marks an office.

* See Guizot, "Hist. of Civilization," vol. i., p. 48.

Like father, it was used as a title of dignity. It occurs in the Rig Veda, in conjunction with the equivalent for *genetrix*. It is applied by the Greek poets to virgin goddesses, such as Athene and Artemis. The later Roman law declares that *mater familias* may even be an unmarried woman. In one notable particular, however, "mother" differs from its correlative term. Father, as I have said, is simply a title of dignity, and has no procreative signification. But mother is both a title, and also a word of procreation. Its root is *ma*, to fashion; for the main function of the mother is to bring a son to the Household. Her title, therefore, was not the wife, not the mistress, but the mother. Apart, however, from this primary duty, she exercised in the administration of the Household certain independent functions. It was her duty to keep, or cause to be kept, the fire ever burning upon the holy hearth. Of necessity, too, she directed the duties of the female children and dependents, and controlled the domestic arrangements. The importance of her position, and the necessity that she should be duly qualified to fill it, appears from Menu.* He is speaking of a Brahmin who has married a wife from the Sudras, or inferior population. "His sacrifices to the gods, his oblations to the manes, and his hospitable attentions to strangers, must be supplied principally by her; but the gods and manes will not eat such offerings, nor can heaven be attained by such hospitality."

In all the principal Aryan countries,† of which evidence as to the primitive form of marriage remains to us—in India, in Athens, and in Rome—the ceremony of marriage seems to have consisted of three essential parts. The first was in substance the abandonment of, or at least the agreement to abandon, his authority by the House Father of the

* iii., 18.

† See M. de Coulanges' "La Cité Antique," p. 44, *et seq.*

bride. The second was the formal delivery of the bride to the bridegroom. The third was the presentation of the bride to the House Spirits in her new home. Just as the Chinese bride at the present day worships in company with her husband his ancestors, so the Aryan bride did homage to the gods of the House to which she was introduced, and entered into formal communion with them. To this end she was presented, upon her entrance into the house, with the holy fire and the lustral water, and partook along with her husband, in the presence of the Lares, of the symbolic meal. So essential was this part of the ceremony that, at Rome, it gave its name, *confarreatio*, to the whole proceeding. By these means the new House Mother was installed in her office; and, thereupon, she passed into her husband's Hand, with all the consequences, both as to person and to property, of that position. From this ceremony, as I have thus described it, several important consequences followed as to the status of the wife. In the first place, she left* her own Household. She ceased to be a member of her father's house, and to worship her father's gods. This result was an inevitable consequence of the exclusive character of the domestic worship. No person could have two Households. He must cleave to the one, and leave the other. A woman, therefore, on going forth from her father's house, renounced her former gods, and was admitted to another and a different worship. She thus entered another family, but in a sense very different from that in which we at this day use the expression. She ceased to be a member of the one corporation, and she became a member of another and a different corporation. In the second

* 'Ου γαρ ἔτι τῶν πατριωτικῶν ἱερῶν ἔιχε κοινωνίαν ἡ δοθἔισα ἀλλ' ἐις τὴν τοῦ λάβοντος ἀυτὴν συντέλει πάτραν.

Dicæarchus in Steph. Byzant. in *v.* πάτρα.

See also Sophocles Fragm., *Tereus.*

place, when she was admitted to the new Household, the bride came under the Hand of the Father of that Household. She was in the Hand of her husband—not because he was her husband, but because he was, if indeed he was, the House Father. If an unemancipated son married during his father's lifetime, the wife came not into his Hand but into the Hand of his father. If, on the other hand, the House Father died, his widow, like every other member of the Household, came into the Hand of the new House Father. That this new House Father was her own son did not alter the case. He was his father's successor, and continued that father's authority. The corporation remained as before, although its management was changed. Thirdly, we can thus understand some rules of early law that are otherwise perplexing. A wife is not related to her own nearest kin. She is a mere stranger to her father and her mother, her sister and her brother. She cannot inherit from them, and they cannot inherit from her. The original tie was, as I have said, not blood but religion; and a nun in a Roman Catholic country is not more dead to her family now than in old times was every married daughter. Again, a widow is sometimes described as having been, in contemplation of law, the daughter of her own son. This is merely a forcible mode of stating the doctrine that a woman was always in the Hand of some House Father, whether he was father, or husband, or son, or some remoter kinsman. The widow was "*filiæ loco*"—that is, she ranked as a daughter; not that she was really regarded in every sense as a daughter, but that she was subject to Hand in the same way as a daughter or any other member of the Household was subject.

A marriage formed for such objects, and with such solemnities, could not easily be dissolved. For any misconduct on the part of the wife, she was answerable in *foro* *domestico*, and not elsewhere. But while she continued free from blame, she was a member of the Household, was under the protection of the House Spirits—to whose service she in a special manner administered—and could not be displaced without deep guilt on the part of him who abandoned her. We are told that a process did exist at Rome by which divorce could be effected, but that it involved ceremonies of a frightful character. Probably in early times, and it is of those times only that I write, divorce was unknown for any other cause than either gross misconduct or sterility. That the barren wife was put away or superseded we cannot doubt. She was wanted for a specific purpose, and, if she failed to fulfil that purpose, it was not likely that any concern for her feelings would prevent the accomplishment of that which was essential for the well-being of the collective Household. We find, both in Greece and Rome, occasional notices of divorce upon this ground. In Menu* there is distinct evidence upon the point. It is there provided that the barren wife may be superseded in the eighth year; the mother of children who have died, in the tenth year; and the mother of daughters only, in the eleventh year. On the other hand, when a married man died without children, his brother, or the next agnate who succeeded to the inheritance, succeeded also to his wife. The death of the former *pater familias* made no change in the form of the Household. His pre-appointed successor stepped instantly into his place, that he might raise up seed unto his brother. So absolute was this rule of succession that the succeeding agnate, if he were already married, was compelled to leave his own wife, and to take the *mater* † who, so to speak, ran with the inheritance. Personal feelings and personal interests could never compete with the welfare of the

* ix., 81.

† See Smith, "Dict. Ant.," *s. v.* ἐπίκληρος.

Household. Its continuity must at any cost be maintained, and the marriages of its subordinate members must give way to the higher duty of providing a representative of the deceased House Father in the right line. For that purpose a woman had been duly chosen and admitted into office, and she was not to be displaced so long as there was a reasonable prospect that she might fulfil her mission.

The Children.

§ 3. "The heir, as long as he is a child, differeth nothing from a servant, though he be lord of all." This statement —addressed, I may observe, to a people among whom the *patria potestas* was exceptionally* recognized—was at one time true, even without the limitation which the apostle attaches to it. No difference existed, or indeed could exist, between the position of the various classes of persons under the Hand of a House Father. The description of their condition consists entirely of disqualifications. The reason is that "Hand," in its technical sense, is equivalent to sovereignty in its fullest meaning, and that sovereignty in that meaning does not admit of degrees. What I have already said respecting the authority of the House Father, and the position towards him of the wife, renders any description of the condition of the son almost superfluous. We may, however, illustrate that condition from the Roman law,† where the primitive rigour of the doctrine of the Hand longest lingered. The House Father had the *jus vitæ necisque*—the power of life and death over his children. He could remove them from the family, either without further provision or by way of sale. In matters of property, whatever the son acquired was held for his father's use. If a legacy were left to him, the father received it. If he made a contract, the benefit of that contract,

* See "Gaius," i., 55.

† See Mr. Poste's "Gaius," p. 65.

but not its burthen, enured to the father. The son was bound to marry at his father's command, but his wife and children were not in his own Hand. They, like himself, were subject to the all-pervading rule of the father. Whatever the son had that he called his own, he held on the same terms as a slave held his property—that is, by the consent of the House Father and during his pleasure. In a word, the son had no remedy, either civil or criminal, against his father for any act, forbearance, or omission of any kind whatever. Such were the provisions of the early Roman law, which, though gradually modified, continued during many centuries to colour family life at Rome. It has been sometimes thought, from a misconception of a passage in Gaius,* that this remarkable system was peculiar to Roman jurisprudence. But we have evidence of its general prevalence. "Of the exposure of children," says Grimm,† "all the sagas are full, not only Teutonic, but Grecian, Roman, and Eastern. There can be no doubt that, in the early days of Heathenism, this horrible practice was lawful." The Hindu House Fathers appear ‡ to claim, and, so far as they dare, exercise the full paternal power, although such claims have never, of course, been recognized by the British Government. The early Greeks did not hesitate either to expose or to sell their children. Cæsar tells us that the Kelts exercised a similar power. In England, even as late as the end of the seventh century, and after Christianity had been established for nearly one hundred years, Mr. Kemble § cites from the ecclesiastical books of discipline very distinct and clear recognitions of this right. Among the continental

* "Gaius," p. 55.

† "Rechts Alt.," p. 455.

‡ Sir H. S. Maine, "Vill. Com.," pp. 113, 115.

§ "Saxons in England," vol. i., p. 199.

Teutons,* even late in the middle ages, the father's power of sale, in case of necessity—but not that of the mother—is recognized, although the exercise of the power seems to have become obsolete. Among the Russians, the power of the House Father is without any check. "The House Father," we are told,† "makes a match for his son, without consulting him, and mainly with a view to his own convenience. The bride lives under the common roof and the common rule. She is, in fact, a servant to the old man. Her husband does not venture to protect her as against his father. A patriarch is lord in his own house and family, and no person has a right to interfere with him; not even the village elder and the Imperial judge. He stands above oral and written law. His cabin is not only a castle, but a church; and every act of his, done within that cabin, is supposed to be private and divine." Generally, it may be said, ‡ that agnatic relationship implies the existence of the paternal power, and that agnatic relationship is discoverable everywhere. That, indeed, such a power must in early times have existed, we may infer upon general grounds. There was no person who was entitled to interfere with the acts of the House Father. The State was not then organized; and, when it was organized, it was not, as we shall hereafter see, disposed to interfere on behalf of persons whom it did not recognize as its members. The duty of vengeance rested upon the next of kin, that is, in the case supposed, upon the House Father himself. In a word, the House Father was sovereign, and, consequently, possessed over his subjects all the powers of sovereignty. And such is the meaning of Plutarch,§ when, in relating how, in a season of trouble,

* Grimm, "Deutsche Rechts Alt.," p. 461.
† Mr. Dixon's "Free Russia," vol. ii., p. 40.
‡ Sir H. S. Maine, "Ancient Law," p. 150.
§ Solon, c. 13.

many persons were compelled to sell even their own children, he adds the emphatic words, "for there was no law to prevent them."

The preceding remarks apply to all the sons during the life of the House Father. There was, in this respect, no difference either between themselves or between them and any other subordinate member of the Household. It was upon the death of the House Father, when the question of succession arose, that differences in the condition of the sons both as between themselves and as against their former fellow subjects began, as we shall presently see, to arise. The description, therefore, of *manus*, includes both sons—without distinction of age—and daughters. In dealing with the latter, the House Father probably allowed himself a little more latitude than with the former. The sale of daughters seems not to have been uncommon in early times. In the Odyssee * we read that Eurykleia had been purchased by Laertes from her father in her childhood, although the names of both her father and her grandfather are mentioned in the usual form in cases of noble birth. Solon prohibited the sale of daughters, a prohibition which, as Mr. Grote † remarks, is strong evidence of the prevalence of the antecedent practice. At Rome we find a similar prohibition, but limited to the case of the eldest daughter. No hesitation seems in either country to have been felt in exposing an infant daughter, for no other reason than that her presence was not desired. Among the Kelts we read, in the "Life of St. Bridget," ‡ that that saint was carried away by her father for sale as a slave to grind at the quern, because he was displeased at the amount of her charities.

* i., 429.

† "History of Greece," vol. iii., p. 188.

‡ Dr. Sullivan's "Introduction to O'Curry's Lectures," p. ccclxi.

Further, a daughter could not inherit the Household estate, or succeed to the paternal power. She could take neither *familiam* nor *pecuniam*. It was a son whom the Manes required, and the sacrifices offered by a daughter would have been ineffectual and absurd; consequently, since the property went with the *sacra*, and since the *sacra* could not be performed by a daughter, the daughter could not hold the property. For the same reason she must be always under power. If she were not under power, she must be the head of the Household. But that was from the nature of the case impossible. If, therefore, she were married, she was in the Hand of her husband or of his House Father. If she were not married, she remained in the Hand of the House Father for the time being of her former Household. If she were a widow, she was in the Hand of her husband's successor. She could not, like her brothers, be emancipated on her father's death, because she could not perform *sacra* of her own. But she was, nevertheless, a member of the Household, and was therefore entitled to her share in its property. It was the duty of the House Father to make provision for her maintenance; and, if she married, to provide her with a suitable dowry. In the case of a sole surviving daughter, the next agnate, on accepting the inheritance, was required to marry the heiress who ran with it. With this object he must, if it were necessary, divorce his own wife. If he failed to marry her, he was bound to provide a dowry, but upon such a scale, at least in Athens, as to indicate the intention of the legislature that the heir should derive no pecuniary benefit from his want of appreciation.

The incapacity of women to inherit the property of the Household or any part of it, and their liability to perpetual tutelage, are, in effect, consequences of the same principle; and the proof of the one assists to establish the proof of the other. Of their incapacity I shall, in a subsequent chapter, have occasion to treat at large. Of their liability to tutelage, well known though it be, it is fitting that I should here present briefly some of the leading proofs. "In childhood," says Menu,* "must a female be dependent upon her father; in youth, on her husband; her lord being dead, on her sons. A woman must never seek independence." These words might be applied without change to the position of women at Rome—"According to the old law,"† says a recent writer on the subject, "a woman never had legal independence. If she was not under the *potestas* she was under *manus* or *tutela*. Between the *potestas, manus*, or *tutela*, women were never legally their own masters." There was thus a specific name for each class of the relation; but the Roman woman, like the Hindu woman, whether maid, wife, or widow, "must never seek independence." So, too, it was with the Hellenic women—"Women‡ were, in fact, throughout their life in a state of nonage, and could not be parties to any act of importance without the concurrence of their guardians, whose place the husband naturally supplied during his lifetime." The laws of the Langobards, of the Alemanni, and of the Saxons declare, in the most distinct terms, the permanent disability of women. "It shall not be lawful," says the first of these codes, "for any free woman, who lives according to the law of the Langobards,§ to live under her own power—that is, in her own *mund;* but she must always live under the power of men, or at least of the king. Nor shall she have the power of alienating any property, movable or immovable, by gift or otherwise, without the consent of the person in whose *mund* she is."

* v., 148.

† Mr. Hunter's "Roman Law," p. 548.

‡ Hermann, "Grec. Ant.," p. 238.

§ Canciani, "Leg. Barb.," iii., 51.

The checks upon Paternal Power.

§ 4. The House Father, as I have said, was supreme within his own House. What he did there was no matter of concern to any person outside. He was amenable to no earthly tribunal. No authority, either public or private, could stay his hand, or punish his severity. He might divorce his wife or kill his son, and no person could question his conduct. The loss would fall upon himself alone, and upon his Household; and his neighbours were no more concerned in it than they were in the burning of his dwelling or the loss of his cattle. Yet we should greatly err in our conception of archaic life, if we were to suppose that the power of the House Father was the mere caprice of a despot. He governed—perhaps according to settled and general customs—certainly under the strictest sense of responsibility to his House Spirits. For any cruel or improper exercise of the paternal authority, either the offended House Spirit exacted punishment, or the offender was liable to the vengeance of the spirit of the person whom he had wronged. A House Father had the power of exposing his children after their birth; but, although the law did not interfere to prevent or to punish him, he was held to be accursed if he exposed any son unless the child were deformed, or his daughter if she were the eldest. A House Father might sell his son, but he who did so was accursed if the son were married. A House Father could kill his wife, but he must first, under penalty of the curse, establish her guilt in the domestic tribunal; * and must execute its sentence in the presence, and with the consent, of its members. The House Father might wring the last farthing from his dependent, but, although the law refused to interfere, the vengeance of the House Spirit did not sleep. So Menu † declares, that "when females are

* Grimm, "Deutsche Rechts Alterthümer," p. 450.

† iii., 56, 57.

honoured, then the deities are pleased; but when they are dishonoured, then all religious acts become fruitless." And he proceeds to describe the calamities that befall the House Father when female relatives are made miserable. Thus, in Hellas the Erinyes visited with prompt and terrible punishment the misdeeds of men in their own house. When Orestes killed his mother, Klytemnestra, the community was powerless to reach him, and the kin of the murdered woman were not entitled to avenge one who had passed out of their Household. The act of Orestes was lawful, whether we regard him as the avenger of blood for his father, or as himself the House Father. But the Erinyes of his mother, nevertheless, avenged an act, shocking to natural feeling, although done in obedience to what seemed a higher, and yet a conflicting, duty. A striking illustration of the House Father's power may be gathered from the tragic story that Herodotus * tells of Periander and Melissa. With the details of that tragedy I am not concerned. It is enough to say that Periander, the Tyrannos of Corinth, murdered his wife. No popular indignation, much less any legal retribution, followed this act. His position may, perhaps, have shielded him. But what I desire to notice is, that his wife's father, Prokles, the Tyrannos of Epidauros, seems both to have resented the deed, and to have been unable to punish it. The utmost that he could do was to suggest the truth to his grandsons when they visited his court. Thus the husband must be assumed to have had the right, however cruelly he may have exercised it. There is no trace of the blood-feud, for the wife had passed out of her father's Hand, and was no longer a member of his kin. The natural sentiment, indeed, remained, but its existence only serves to illustrate

* iii., 50.

the absence of all legal, and even customary, protection to the wife. If any such protection had existed, her father was both from his position able to defend his daughter; and, if he had the right, was willing to enforce it. But neither the State nor the wife's kin was entitled to interpose, and the conscience of the House Father was a law unto himself.

It seems, however, that the House Father, in the exercise of his authority, was expected to act in a judicial capacity. He was not to follow his own caprice, but he was the administrator of the customs of his clan. He usually acted with the advice and consent of a *forum domesticum*, or family council. Even when he proceeded in a summary manner, as in the case of offending slaves, the severer punishments—if, at least, we accept the elder Cato's practice * as evidence of the general sentiment—were not capriciously inflicted; but sentence was pronounced and executed after a semi-judicial investigation. But in the case of any serious offence by the wife or the children, the House Father acted—or, rather, perhaps, was expected to act—with the aid of his family council—that is, of his near relatives. We know little of the council, and less of its procedure. But at Rome L. Antonius was, by the censors, removed from the senate † because he had repudiated his wife, "*nullo amicorum in concilium adhibito.*" In the well-known case of Sp. Carvilius Ruga,‡ the divorce is said to have taken place "*de amicorum sententia.*" In a case mentioned by Tacitus,§ Plautius, according to ancient custom, in the presence of his near relatives, tried for her life his wife, Pomponia Græcina, a woman of rank, who was accused

* See Mommsen's "Hist. of Rome," vol. ii., p. 405.

† "Val. Max.," ii., 9, 2.

‡ "Au. Gell.," xvii., 2.

§ "Annals," xiii., 32.

"*superstitionis externæ*," and found her not guilty. Seneca * calls the *pater familias* "*judex domesticus*" and "*magistratus domesticus*." In a case † where a father, who had a good cause of complaint against his son, killed him when they were out hunting, the Emperor Hadrian declared that the father had killed his son by the right not of a father, but of a brigand, and sentenced him to deportation. The son may have been guilty, and the punishment may have been not excessive; but the deliberate severity of justice is a different thing from assassination. At a much earlier period of Roman history, we meet with an incident which seems to illustrate this regulated exercise of the paternal power. After the famous combat of the Horatii and the Curiatii, the victor, exasperated by her lament for her fallen lover, killed his sister. For this deed he was brought to trial; and his father ‡ contended on his behalf that he (the father) adjudged that his daughter was rightfully slain: had it been otherwise, that he, by a father's right, would have punished his son. Thus the *pater familias*, although he does not speak of a council, claims to pronounce a formal judicial sentence. He claims also, as of course, the power of life and death over his son. It is remarkable that, notwithstanding this protest, the State proceeded to try the offender whose act had shocked public morality; and yet the force of this plea to the jurisdiction was so strongly felt that, partly from this cause, and partly from a sense of his recent service, the offender, though the fact was undisputed, was acquitted.

It is probable that we meet in Athens with a trace of the same domestic tribunal, when it is said that a man ought not

* Mr. Hunter, "Rom. Law," p. 45.

† "Dig.," xlviii., 9, 5.

‡ "Moti homines sunt in eo judicio maxime Publio Horatio patre proclamante se filiam jure cæsam judicare: ni ita esset, patrio jure in filium animadversurum fuisse." Livy, i., 26.

to have recourse to the ἀποκήρυξις, or public declaration of disherison, without having previously consulted with his friends. Among the Teutons, Tacitus * tells us that the husband was required to inflict punishment upon the unfaithful wife *coram propinquis*—that is, with the concurrence of his family council. But the neglect of the House Father to convene this council did not render his act unlawful, or expose him to any legal penalties for its commission. In the case of L. Antonius, which I have mentioned, the proceeding of the censor was not a legal penalty, but merely an official mark of moral disapprobation. The true sanction, in these cases, was the religious one. The offender was, by the Romans, termed *sacer*—that is, he was regarded as under the curse of his angry gods. It is noteworthy that all the cases to which this curse was applied were breaches of domestic duty. No legal consequences seem to have followed from it. But as Mommsen † observes —"the pious, popular faith on which that curse was based would, in earlier times, have power even over natures frivolous and wicked; and the civilizing agency of religion must have exercised an influence deeper and purer, precisely because it was not contaminated by any appeal to the secular arm."

Tacitus ‡ tells us that among the Germans it was regarded as a public scandal (*flagitium*) to limit the number of their children or to put to death any of a man's agnates; and in that country, he adds, good customs are of more avail than good laws elsewhere. In this brief description we can trace with sufficient clearness both the existence of the House Father's power, or perhaps we should rather say, of his exemption from any legal restraint, and the practical

* "Germania," c. 19.
† "Hist. of Rome," vol. i., p. 184.
‡ *Ubi supra.*

limitation of that power. We cannot indeed suppose that the *jus vitæ necisque* was harshly or capriciously exercised, when we find that full-grown men, with full personal and political rights, were willing to abandon those rights and formally to consent to place themselves under this tremendous power. Yet this was done* in every case of adrogation, a proceeding which was of ordinary occurrence at Rome. Nor can we think otherwise of the power of sale, when we remember that even under the Republic this power was used merely as an instrument of conveyancing. Men rarely do all that they have the power to do, and it is not likely that the archaic House Father was in this respect exceptional.

The provisions in default of Sons.

§ 5. We have seen that the primary object of every Household was the maintenance of its succession. In other words, it was necessary that the House Father should have a legitimate son. For this purpose it was essential that he should marry; and if his wife failed, from any defect on her part, to give the Household a son, that failure was a sufficient ground for divorce. Sometimes, however, this remedy might be ineffectual or inconvenient. In these circumstances, various other expedients were adopted to secure the desired succession. It would seem that, originally, a brother or other near agnate was commissioned to raise up, even during the husband's lifetime, seed unto his brother. On this subject the laws of Menu † are curiously precise. The privileges, or I should rather say the duties, of the substituted husband are strictly defined in time, and circumstances, and duration. The utmost care is taken to describe such a commission as a solemn and sacred obligation, and to guard against the slightest laxity of the domestic tie. In

* See Mr. Poste's "Gaius," p. 89, and the authorities there collected.

† ix., 59-60.

like manner we find * at Athens, in the law of Solon, that when the heiress of a property (ἐπίκληρος) was claimed by a kinsman whose age or infirmities precluded the hope of offspring, the husband's place was supplied by his next of kin. We may notice the width of the moral gulf between the age of the biographer and that of the illustrious subject of his memoir. Plutarch calls this law "absurd and ridiculous," and mentions various ingenious explanations, upon utilitarian principles, that had been suggested to account for so strange a provision. But when we remember that Solon, like a true statesman, professed not to have made the best laws, but the best that his people would accept, we may understand both the motive for his legislation and the depth and persistency of the sentiment which it recognized. So, too, if an Athenian died intestate, leaving no son, but an unmarried daughter, the next of kin who claimed the inheritance was bound to marry the daughter.† So imperative was the rule that the lady had no choice in the matter, and that the man, if he had been previously married, was obliged to put away his former wife that he might enter upon this new marriage. The son of the heiress took the name of his maternal grandfather, and became his heir. Similar rules were in force among the Dorians, by whom the heiress was called not ἐπίκληρος but επιπαματίς. "Regulations concerning heiresses," says K. O. Müller,‡ "were an object of chief importance in the ancient legislations, on account of their anxiety for the maintenance of families, as in that of Androdamus, of Rhegium, for the Thracian Chalcidians, and in the code of Solon, with which the Chalcidian laws of Charondas appear to have agreed in all essential points."

* "Plutarch's Lives," Solon, c. 20. See also Müller's "Dorians," vol. ii., p. 211.

† Smith's "Dict. Ant.," *s. v.* ἐπίκληρος.

‡ "Dorians," vol. ii., p. 209.

There was another Indian expedient,* of a less questionable character, which also finds its direct parallel at Athens. A man who had a daughter, but no son, might give his daughter in marriage on the express condition that the son of that marriage, or one of its sons, should belong to him. Thus his grandson became, in contemplation of law, his son, without adoption or any other process. So common was this custom at Athens that a special name (*θυγατριδοῦς*) was used to express the relationship.

The most general method, however, of providing for the continuity of the Household in cases where nature had denied an heir was adoption. By this practice, the adopted son left his own Household and his own House Spirits, and became a member of the Household and a worshipper of the House Spirits of his adoptive father. When his initiation into the new worship had taken place, he became as much a member of the Household as if he had been born in it. Even though he had previously been *sui juris*, he and all those, if any, who had been under his Hand came under the Hand of the new House Father. Like the wife, the adopted son, when he passed out from his former Household, ceased to have any connection with his former relatives. He was no longer of kin to his natural father or to his brothers in the flesh. He could not inherit from them, nor they from him. He was no longer responsible for their actions, nor they for his actions. He could no longer offer the old prayers at the old tombs. He was a stranger in his father's house, his inheritance lay with another kin, and his kin were descended from a different blood.

Adoption was only an expedient, and its practice was consequently subject to several limitations. It was admis-

* Menu, ix., 177.

sible only when the necessity for it actually existed. The adoptor must have been married, must be without sons, and must be without any reasonable hope of having a son. If a man had, or was likely to have, a son of his own blood, it was not competent for him to disinherit that son by the adoption of a stranger. Nor, on the other hand, could a man pass by adoption into another Household, or if once adopted, return to his original Household, unless sufficient provision were made for the continuance of the *sacra* which he abandoned. Subject, however, to these conditions, the process was twofold. There was the relinquishment of the original Household, the *detestatio sacrorum*, as the Romans termed it; and there was the *transitio in sacra*, or the formal initiation into the new worship. By the former proceeding, the natural House Father released his son from his *manus*, and discharged him from his Household. By the latter proceeding, the adoptive House Father received the person so discharged, and admitted him to the new allegiance.

Another method of supplying the want of a natural heir was appointment. I use this word in preference to testation, because the latter term suggests irresistibly the idea of a modern will; and because a modern will is not only in its nature but in its history distinct from the method which I am about to describe. Failing all other heirs, whether by nature or adoption, a man was permitted, with the consent apparently of his kinsmen who had a reversionary interest in his property, to declare his wish that some person whom he mentioned should be his successor, and should continue both his duties and his rights. We are not told what was the precise legal effect of such a declaration. But we may infer that no immediate relation was created between the parties, and that the grant was, in fact, conditional upon the death of the grantor. Probably the transaction bore some resemblance to that famous conditional gift of Telemachus to Eumæus, on which Justinian * relies for his enactments respecting donations *mortis causa.* Such a form of appointment was known to the Hindus. We find among the Norsemen † a similar custom in the 'Brande Erbe,' or the inheritance for burning, when the kinless man left, for the performance of his funeral rites, his land to some friend who pledged himself to perform the duties of an heir. It is probable that the earliest form of this method occurs in Rome. The appointment was there made in the presence of the army when marching out to battle, ‡ and was called "*testamentum in procinctu.*" We may trace in this declaration in the presence of the embattled clan the characteristics that I have indicated. It was made in the presence of the clan because the consent of the kinsmen was required to bar their rights as remainder-men; and the proceeding was adopted when the declarant was about to go upon a dangerous service, and there was neither leisure nor opportunity for the negotiations that the method of adoption must have involved. The practice was extended to times of peace at the *comitia calata*—the *Bod Thing*, § or bidden meeting of. the Frisons—that is, the assembly of the Curies specially convened for the particular purpose. It may be doubted, however, if the proceeding at these *comitia* was ever a favourite method at Rome. Certainly it had become obsolete in the time of Cicero. Long before that time other modes of legal procedure had been introduced by which the ingenuity of lawyers contrived to make, in a more convenient manner, sufficient provision for the devolution of the property of the childless.

* Inst., ii., 7, 1.

† Robertson's "Scotland under her Early Kings," vol. ii., p. 323, *n*.

‡ Mr. Poste's "Gaius," p. 101.

§ "Edin. Review," vol. xxxii., p. 9.

I have described these several proceedings as expedients in default of a legitimate son. That this was their true character is readily apparent. They were all contrived for the benefit of the grantor, and not of the grantee. It was plainly for the sake of the son-less House Father, and not for that of his agent, that the commission to the Levir or other agnate was given, or that the daughter's son was reserved. It is true that adoption was, in time, regarded * as an important means of providing for younger sons. But its original character is distinctly shown by Isaios.† In a case where he was opposing an attempt to invalidate an adoption, the orator's contention was that, if the process were set aside, an injury would be done, not to the person adopted, but to the adoptive father. An adverse judgment would result in the adoptive father having died without a son; and, consequently, no person would offer sacrifices in the dead man's honour, no person would offer him the funeral repast, and he would be without worship. Nor can we suppose that a donee *in procinctu* was regarded in the same light as we now regard a legatee. He was, in truth, a trustee, who in an emergency undertook for his friend an onerous duty; and who, if he received any advantage, received it only because the estate of the donor was held to be indivisible, and the property was inseparable from its burthens.

§ 6. It is needless to describe the position of a slave. The Dependents.
In the golden days of Greece and of Rome, he had no rights, but was merely subject to duties. He was an *ἔμψυχον κτῆμα*, a *vocale instrumentum*, a human chattel, or a tool that speaks; and, in contemplation of law, he in no way differed from a bullock. Yet, in early days his lot

* Plato, Laws, xi., 923.
† ii., 10, 46.

was not so hard. He was, in his humble way, a member of the Household. He was under the protection of the House Spirit. His entrance upon his service was marked by a formal ceremony in the nature of an initiation. He joined in the same devotions. He shared the same sacrificial meal. He was laid in the common tomb. The place where a slave was buried was declared by the early doctors of the Roman law * to be "*religiosus.*" The religion of the Lares, as Cicero † assures us, was established alike for masters and for slaves. This religion, indeed, was the slave's true and only religion, and that which was his great safeguard against his master's tyranny. Cato, ‡ in describing his model *villicus* or steward, represents him as never troubling himself about any other worship than that of the gods of the hearth and of the field; and as leaving, like a true slave, all dealings with gods, as well as with men, to his master. It is true that the slave was in the Hand of the House Father. He could acquire no property. He might, without any redress, be beaten, or sold, or put to death. But in these respects he was not in a worse position than the son of the house. All members of the Household, without exception, were subject to the one sovereign; and in sovereignty, as I have already stated, there are no degrees. But under this outward resemblance there was necessarily a broad distinction between the son and the slave. The authority was alike in both cases, but the spirit in which it was exercised was widely different. How much broader the distinction grew when the limits of the Household were overpassed, and the son became the member of that State-community from which the slave was excluded, I shall have occasion in a subsequent chapter to consider.

* "Dig.," xi., 7, 2. † De Leg., ii., 11.

‡ Mommsen, "Hist. Rome," vol. ii., p. 369.

The Household contained another class of persons which requires our notice. It had not only its children, and its slaves, but also its dependents. From various causes free men came under the Hand of the House Father. In other words, persons who were not included in the classes already mentioned were admitted as a kind of inferior members of the Household. They were duly initiated. They shared in the common worship, and were buried in the common tomb. It followed that, even though they did not live under the same roof, they were subject to the House Father. In return for his protection they owed to him allegiance. This class was composed, in the first instance, of emancipated slaves. If a slave received his liberty, his connection with the Household did not thereby cease. If it ceased, liberty would, in archaic society, have been equivalent to a sentence of outlawry and starvation. The manumitted slave remained a member of the Household, although in a somewhat different character. He was free, but he was dependent. His servile status was removed, and, as against strangers, he was free; but he still had a right to the common tomb,* and he was still in the Hand of his former master. Custom, however, required that the master's power should be exercised in a different way, and upon different principles from those which had guided it before the liberation.

Another division of the same class consisted of refugees, especially of refugees for homicide. It seems to have been an ancient belief that the stain of human blood, however incurred, required purification. There was also the danger of the blood-feud from the kinsmen of the deceased. The homicide, therefore, generally fled from his home, and sought a person who could both purify him from his sin, and also

* Niebuhr's "History of Rome," vol. i., p. 320.

protect him from the avenger of blood. If such a suppliant applied to a House Father in the proper form, as recognized by that House Father's worship, and addressed him by the proper adjuration, such a request could not be refused. The stranger had brought himself under the protection of the House Spirits, and they would resent any wrong done to their suppliant. Away from his hearth, indeed, and without the appropriate ceremonial, the House Father might at his pleasure grant or refuse his mercy to any person who sued for it. But the suppliant in the technical sense of the term, the ἱκέτης or man who came to the holy hearth, was a different case. Him the House Father was bound to receive; and when he had received him the stranger was initiated, and became, at least for the time, a member of the Household.

There were other classes, too, of persons who must be ranked as members of the Household, although their presence was not essential to it, and was probably rare in earlier times. There were, first, those free men who voluntarily attached themselves to some wealthy man and followed his fortunes, sharing his wealth, aiding him in his troubles, and faithful to him to the death. Although the relation between the House Father and these his companions, or followers, was of the closest and most intimate kind, it was the necessary consequence of that relation that these persons were not less subject to their House Father than were his own sons. Secondly, there were the resident aliens, or outsiders—men who, in pursuit of gain or from motives of convenience, had settled in a community which was not their own; and who were obliged, for the purpose of obtaining legal recognition, to place themselves under the protection of some House Father. Thirdly, there were those persons of free birth but inferior condition, usually the remnant of a conquered population, who, under the protection of a conquering chief, cultivated, for in a great measure his benefit, the lands that were once their own. It may be doubted whether these classes, or any of them, were found—at least to any considerable extent—in the archaic Household. That at an early period of history they make their appearance, and that at a later period they largely modified the course of events, is certain. In any case their place in the Household was from the first distinctly marked. Over all of them the paternal authority existed in full vigour. But custom and a sense of justice, besides those other considerations to which I have already referred, modified its exercise; and relations of semi-freedom that extended over several generations necessarily tended to produce some fixed and not wholly intolerable rules. Thus there grew up in the Household, or by its side, a body of men—not servile, and yet not fully free, having among themselves important differences of condition, clearly distinguishable from the slaves, but distinguishable also from the immediate members of the Household.

CHAPTER V.

THE CLAN.

Description of the Clan.

§ 1. WHETHER our ancestors at any time actually lived in families which ended with the death of the parents or the maturity of the children, and without any further or other organization, is a question which I do not venture even to discuss. There may have been such a time, just as there may have been a time when they had a distinct consciousness of the meaning of each element in every composite word. Such a state of existence is certainly conceivable. But we have in our race no direct evidence of such a state. Among the Aryans the history of society, like the history of language, begins at a much more advanced stage of development. It is, indeed, to the evidence of language that we are indebted for much of our knowledge of pre-historic society. We cannot, therefore, trace that society beyond a period when an inflexional—that is, a comparatively well-developed—form of speech existed. Whatever may have been their condition in some remote past, our ancestors, at the time when our knowledge of them commences, both spoke a well-developed language and possessed a clear and well-marked social organization. The Household, not in its rudimentary stage, but in the advanced form that I have attempted to describe, existed in full force among them, but it was not the sole institution that they possessed. It was the unit of a larger and more complex body. That body was the Gens, or Kin, or Clan.

I proceed, then, to inquire into the structure of this larger organism.

In every Aryan country, and in every age, we find men living together in communities of considerable size. These communities are generally known as tribes, clans, peoples, or by some similar expression. They were distinct from that other association which is familiar to us as the State. Their members always assumed the fact of their consanguinity. They did not assert exclusive jurisdiction over any considerable territory, or over all persons within such territory as they possessed. They were simply the owners of, it might be, a few square miles on which dwelt men of a common lineage with their dependents and followers. Generally, but not necessarily, they were surrounded by neighbours whose blood was more or less kindred with their own, and with whom they recognized some slender community of worship. But as regarded their neighbours the several clans were strictly independent; no common authority controlled their actions. They might be friends, or they might be enemies; but their choice of these alternatives rested with their own free will. Between members of the same clan, indeed, very intimate relations existed. The clan had a common worship and a common tomb; it had common property; its members had mutual reversionary rights in their separate property; they took charge of the person and the property of any clansman that was under any incapacity; they exercised full powers of self-government, and maintained for the purpose a suitable organization; they acted together in avenging wrong done to any of their members; they rendered, in case of need, mutual help and support. Further, although upon these points I shall have occasion subsequently to treat, they obeyed and honoured a common head, the representative of their founder, and the nearest to him in blood; and in the course of time they branched out into numerous sub-clans, each of which was in its turn subdivided, and tended to become a separate and independent community.

In those societies with which we are best acquainted, the clan system has long since disappeared. No record of its peculiarities has come down to us. Save a few casual allusions, we know nothing of the constitution or the functions of the Hellenic γενῆ, of the Roman Gentes, or of the Kins of our own forefathers. Those who might have observed the Keltic clans in the British Islands suffered, for the most part, the opportunity to escape. It is but lately that the old writings of the Hindus and of the Persians became known to us, and their incidental notices of the clans were strange and unfamiliar. The living clan society, either among the Rajpúts or the Slavs, was, until lately, practically unintelligible to us. Yet it is even still possible to obtain some description of clan relations which, however incomplete, will assist us to realize their position.

A writer in the last century,* who had travelled in the Highlands of Scotland and observed the manners and customs of the Gael, thus describes them:—"The Highlanders are divided into tribes or clans under chiefs or chieftains, and each clan again divided into branches from the main stock, who have chieftains over them. These are subdivided into smaller branches of fifty or sixty men, who deduce their original from particular chieftains, and rely upon them as their more immediate protectors and defenders. Next to the love of their chief is that of the particular branch whence they sprung, and in a third degree to those of the whole clan or name, whom they will assist, right or wrong, against any other tribe with which they are at variance." This description accords with the old High-

* "Letters from an Officer of Engineers," cited and adopted by Mr. Skene, "Highlanders," vol. i., p. 156.

land genealogies. They represent the country as divided originally among five great divisions or tribes, each of them tracing descent to a common ancestor, and each containing a number of kindred but independent clans. Thus the MacDonalds, the MacDougalls, the MacNeils, the MacLaughlans, and some other clans, although they were severally independent, traced their descent to a common Eponymous hero, or, as we should perhaps rather call him, Genarch—Conn of the Hundred Battles. They were, consequently, distinct from the descendants* of another archaic hero—Ferchar MacFaradaig. Of this hero the descendants multiplied exceedingly. From him sprang the old Maormors of Moray, the MacIntoshes, the MacPhersons, and the MacNaughtens. What is still more to our purpose, they include the newer Houses of the Camerons,† the Nasicas of the North, the MacLeans, the MacMillans, and the Munroes. These Houses again were subdivided, as some leading Eponym arose, and as fortune favoured; but I need not repeat such well-known names as Glengarry, Keppoch, or Lochiel.

If from Scotland we turn to that distant eastern land where so many Scot names have acquired additional lustre, we shall find in the description of the Rajpúts ‡ a similiar state of society. There are thirty-six Raj-Kulas or royal races—that is, I presume, pure-blooded clans, of the Rajpúts. Most of these Kulas are divided into numerous branches called *Sachas*, and these sachas are subdivided into innumerable clans or *Gotras*. A few Kulas have never ramified, and these are termed *eka*, that is, single. From the gotra or gote comes the patronymic ending *ote*, equivalent to the ιδης of the Greeks, the Latin *ius*, and our own *ing*. Thus, of the Sooryavansas, or sun-race, the Rajpút

* Mr. Skene's "Highlanders," vol. ii., p. 211.

† *Ib.*, pp. 169, 193, 267. The name Cameron means "crooked nose."

‡ See Tod's "Rajasthan," vol. i., p. 82.

Herakleids, as we may term them, one *Kula* is called from a famous chief, the Grahilotes, or Gehlotes. This Kula comprises twenty-four sachas, two of which—the Aharya and the Sesodia—have at different times given their name to the entire clan. When a kingdom was formed, the founder of the kingdom seems usually to have become a new Eponym. Thus, in the district of Murwar,* which was separated from Melvar, Rao Rimmell had twenty-four sons, each of whom obtained a separate grant of land and became the founder of a clan. Twelve of these clans maintained their position, and the others became dependent upon some greater clanships.

Similar divisions may be traced at Rome. The *Nomen*, or Gentile name, marked the main stock, from which branched various *Cognomina* or *Familiæ*. In some cases these Familiæ grew into sub-clans, from which in turn *Agnomina* or secondary Familiæ were produced. Sometimes the word Agnomen is used in a different sense, and denotes merely a title, or personal dignity. Thus, Caius Julius Cæsar Augustus corresponds precisely with another celebrated name, Siddharta † Gautuma Sakya Buddha. In both cases there is the name first of the individual; next, of his clan; then, of the branch of that clan to which he belonged. Finally, the person thus described bears the complimentary designation of, in the one case, the August; in the other case, the Enlightened. It is, however, with the former meaning of the Agnomen that we are now more particularly concerned. The Virginian Gens, for example, was divided into two Familiæ, called respectively Ruffus and Tricostus. The Tricosti produced three secondary branches, Cælimontanus, Esquilinus, and Rutilus. So, too, the Servilian Gens comprised the two Familiæ, Priscus and Vatia, each of which gave

* Tod's "Rajasthan," vol. ii., p. 17.

† This name is equivalent to Desiderius.

rise to a secondary Familia, called respectively Fidenas and Isauricus. The original Agnomen of the Familia Priscus was Structus, but, as we have seen that the Rajpúts do, its members changed that title for that of Fidenas, in honour of the success, at the capture of Fidenæ, of a distinguished clansman. Thus, the Dictator P. Servilius Priscus Structus, the conqueror of Fidenæ, became, so to speak, a new tertiary Eponym. His name marks an era in the Familia of the Structi, who were a branch of the Prisci, who were a sub-clan of the great Servilian Gens, which Gens belonged to the tribe of the Ramnes, one of the three tribes of which the Roman State was originally composed. Such a description, though to us it conveys little significance, would be readily intelligible to a Rajpút. He would at once recognize his Gotra, and his Sacha, and his Kula; while the Ramnes and the Tities would remind him of the Sun division and the Moon division of his race. So, too, the Hymans, the Dymans, and the Pamphylans of Laconia correspond to the five great tribes of Scotland. The *πάτραι* were the analogues of the MacDonalds and the MacNaughtens. The *ὦβαι* were the branchlets that formed among themselves special and closer combinations. Even in modern Ithaca the old divisions that existed in the days of Odysseus still linger. The three principal clans* into which the Ithacans are divided are called Petalas, Karabias, and Dendrinos. The chief families of the island all either bear these names, or, wherever branches of them have taken other appellations, the new patronymics were generally derived from some *sobriquet* applied to one of their ancestors. For instance, the family of Zabos is a principal branch of the Petalades, and came to be designated by its present name because its immediate founder had that epithet given to him (*ζαβος*, in modern Greek, meaning awkward, gauche).

* Sir G. F. Bowen, *Ithaca* in 1850, p. 17.

The *Sacra* of the Clan.

§ 2. Of the Gentile *sacra* we know but little. There appears, indeed, to have existed throughout the ancient world a profound reserve and reticence as to all matters connected with their domestic life, a reticence which to this day is observable in India, and among races of low culture,* and which is probably a survival of the special and exclusive worship of the hearth. Unhappily, too, that part of Gaius's work in which he treated of the Roman Gentes, and which doubtless contained, if not a full account of them, yet much that would have been very precious to us, is illegible. Through this thick darkness we can, however, dimly discern that these Gentile *sacra*, like the corresponding festivals among the Chinese,† were held annually at stated periods; that their expenses were charged ‡ upon the property of the Kin, or were defrayed § by joint contributions; that attendance || at them was compulsory upon every member of the Kin; and that the objects ¶ of the worship were the founder of the Kin ** and his successors, and perhaps also some divinity or hero that had been adopted as a patron saint. With this worship and these festivals no external authority was competent to interfere. In the celebration no stranger was allowed to participate. The place of their celebration was probably at the common tomb. Such a tomb we know to have existed, and in it were exclusively laid the remains †† of those who in life

* See Sir H. S. Maine's "Village Communities," p. 114; and Professor Max Müller's "Science of Religion," p. 58.

† See Mr. Doolittle, "Social Life of the Chinese," vol. ii., pp. 45-7.

‡ Smith's "Dict. Ant.," *s. v.* Gens.

§ Grote, "Hist. Greece," vol. iii., p. 75.

|| Niebuhr, "Hist. Rome," vol. i., p. 315.

¶ Willems's "Le Droit Public Romain," p. 24.

** So of the public worship, Ovid says:

Mille Lares Geniumque ducis qui tradidit illos
Urbs habet et vici numina trina colunt.—*Fasti*, v., 146.

†† Jam tanta religio est sepulchrorum ut extra sacra et gentem inferri fas negent esse.—*Cicero*, *De Leg.*, ii., 22.

had taken part in the common worship. It seems as if this tomb were to the Kin what the hearth was to the Household. It was the abode of the Gentile Lares. It was—at least in early times—situated in the common land of the Kin, and from that resting-place the Lares watched over and protected their own fields. These tombs were inviolable and inalienable. They could not be applied to any other purpose. They were excepted from any conveyance of the land.* A right of way to them, if the land were sold, was reserved by necessary implication. No title to them could be acquired by any adverse possession. No stranger could be buried in them. Severe penalties were attached to any trespass upon them. "Where is the man," asks Demosthenes,† "who will allow persons having no connection with the family to be placed in the ancestral tomb?" So exclusively were they reserved for the Kin that the Attic orators ‡ constantly adduce as evidence in support of the claim for admission to a *Gens* the fact that the claimant's father was buried in the Gentile tomb.

We have some evidence of the strength and the persistence of the feeling which, on this matter, influenced the archaic world. Among the Romans it was told,§ with admiration indeed, but yet with a full belief in the fitness of the act, that when the Capitol was beleaguered by the Gauls, a Fabius, in his sacrificial costume, and bearing in his hands whatever was needed for his rites, crossed the enemies' lines to offer on the Quirinal the sacrifices of the Fabian clan. Whether the occurrence did, or did not, actually take place, is not material for our present purpose. The story is good evidence of the belief, if not of the fact; and it is with the

* "Dig.," xlvii., 12, 5; viii., 1, 14.

† Against Eubulides.

‡ See Becker's "Charicles," p. 394, and the authorities there cited.

§ Livy, v., 46.

belief that we are now concerned. At a time more within the sphere of recorded history,* but at a conjuncture hardly less critical, another Fabius, the great Cunctator, was watching the movements of the terrible Carthaginian, and was carrying out, in circumstances of the utmost difficulty and danger, his famous policy of delay. Yet even then, when the day approached for the annual sacrifice of the Fabian clan, the dictator left his army, and returned to celebrate the worship of his Kin upon the holy ground of the Quirinal. Long after the introduction of Christianity, we find † popes and councils vainly denouncing these offerings to the dead. The repression of them among our own immediate ancestors ‡ seems to have formed a leading part of ecclesiastical discipline. And even at the present day the feasts for the dead continue, as we have seen,§ in full force among the simple peasants of most countries on the continent of Europe. Not the least noticeable trace of a survival of what once were Gentile *sacra*, is found in Croatia, where it is said ‖ that, at the present day, after the division of a joint family, the newly formed families continue to recite their prayers in common.

That Gentile *sacra* existed, there is no room for doubt. But that these *sacra* implied the worship of the common ancestors of the Kin, I have yet to show. If indeed it be true that the Kin was merely the expansion of the Household, this further consequence would follow as of course. It is therefore satisfactory to find that the facts, so far as we can ascertain them, correspond with this expectation. Writing of early India, Professor Max

* Livy, xxii., 18.

† Canciani, "Leg. Bar.," iii., 78, 106.

‡ Kemble's "Saxons in England," vol. i., p. 525.

§ See *supra*, p. 60.

‖ "Law Magazine and Review," Feb., 1878, p. 205.

Müller* observes:—"It is probable that different families had their own heroes, perhaps their own deities, and that they kept up the memory of them by their own poetic traditions. It is true that such a view is merely conjectural. But when we see that in some parts of the Veda, which are represented as belonging to different illustrious and noble families, certain gods are more exclusively celebrated; that names, which in Vedic poetry are known as those of heroes and poets, are afterwards considered as names of infidels and heretics; we have a right to infer that we have here the traces of a widely extended practice." In India, at the present day, it is said † of the village communities in Orissa and Bengal, that "the common people have no idea of religion but to do right and to worship the village god." Among the members of a pure Rajpút clan, too, Mr. Lyall ‡ tells us that "the ultimate source of all ideas upon things political, social, and even religious, is their Eponymous ancestor." We have similar evidence in the case of the early Persians. The Avesta § honours its Gentile heroes. "The bold Fravashis of the pure fight in the battle at their place, at their spot, as each has a place and a spot to watch over, like as a strong man, a warrior, keeps guard for a well gathered kingdom, with weapons ready for war." So, too, in reference to Greece, Professor Curtius || says:—"Every noble clan comprehended a group of families which either actually descended from one common ancestor, or had in ancient times united in one body of gossips. They were united by the common worship of the divinity of the clan, and its heroic founder: all its members were united by the obligation of avenging the violent death

* "History of Ancient Sanscrit Literature," p. 55.

† Mr. Hunter's "Orissa," vol. i., p. 95.

‡ "Fort. Rev.," No. 121, N.S., p. 100.

§ Spiegel's "Avesta," by Bleeck, vol. iii., p. 88.

|| "History of Greece," vol. i., p. 306.

of any one of their number, by a common sepulchre and by mutual rights of inheritance; every clan had one common place of assembly, and one common sacrificial hearth, and constituted one great House, a strictly exclusive and sacred social community." To the same effect is a striking passage in a Delphic oracle, which Demosthenes,* in one of his orations on a case of disputed inheritance, cites as confirmatory of the laws of Solon. The Athenians had sent to consult the oracle as to a sign which had appeared in the heavens, and to know what they should do, or to what god they should pray, in order that the sign might turn to their advantage. After directing certain sacrifices to the deities of Olympos, the oracle thus proceeds:—"And it is meet that ye offer sacrifice and gifts, according to the custom of the country, to your hero-founder from whom ye derive your name; and that honours should be paid to the manes of the departed, on the proper day, by the relatives, according to received usage." Thus, too, in Rome, the clan worship had a specific name, *sacra Gentilitia.* The connection of these *sacra* with the heroes of the clan is expressly stated. Dionysius,† when writing of the Roman Gentes, notices their worship of "the dæmons of their forefathers:" and an inscription ‡ is extant which commemorates the "*Lares Volusiani,*" the House Spirits, as it were, of the Volusian Gens.

The Inheritance of the Clan.

§ 3. I have already said that the possession of the property and the performance of the *sacra* were convertible expressions; whoever had the one had also the other. The right to the property correlated the duty of the *sacra.* The duty of the *sacra* gave the right to the possession of the

* Against Makartatos.

† xi., 14.

‡ Gruter, Inscript., 319, 9.

property. No *sacra*, while there was any property to maintain them, could be allowed to fail for want of an heir. Consequently, when the children and the immediate relatives failed, the kinsman succeeded to the vacant property and to the duties with which it was charged. On this point we have the express testimony* of the Twelve Tables:—"Si intestato moritur cui suus heres nec escit, adgnatus proximus familiam habeto. Si agnatus nec escit, gentilis familiam nancitor." To the same effect Menu † enacts that, failing the Sapindas, the Samanodocas shall inherit. In Athens,‡ if a deceased person left neither children nor agnates, the inheritance went to his γένος or clan. Nor can we doubt that a similar custom prevailed among the Teutonic § tribes.

This right of inheritance in the clan has been supposed to be analogous to the modern escheat. In the absence of any known heirs, the property now goes to the State; but in earlier times the ultimate body was not the State, but the clan. The motive, however, of the arrangement was very different in each case. The original principle of the escheat was the return to the donor of his gift when its conditions could no longer be fulfilled. At the present day it is merely a method to avoid the inconvenience and possible confusion that would arise from the presence of vacant possessions. But the object of Gentile inheritance was the continuance of the *sacra* in, so far as it was possible, kindred hands. Accordingly we find in early history, first, that the utmost diligence was used to prevent any failure in the succession; and second, that in these arrangements

* Tab. v., fr. 4 and 5.

† ix., 187.

‡ See Grote, "Hist. of Greece," vol. iii., p. 186.

§ See Grimm, "Rechts Alt.," pp. 467, 478.

no notice is taken of the State. "Nothing," says K. O. Müller,* "was more dreaded by the early Greeks than the extinction of the family and the destruction of the house, by which the dead lost their religious honour, the household gods their sacrifices, the hearth its flame, and the ancestors their name among the living." Against this evil provision was made in Sparta by various regulations, but all these regulations related to heiresses, adoptions, and similar forms of succession. The Attic mind † seems to have abhorred the desolation, as it called it, of any House, and insisted upon some person being found who should succeed to the property and the duties of the deceased. But it never thought of vesting the ultimate remainder in the City. So, too, Menu ‡ directs that, upon failure of the Sapindas and the Samanodocas—that is, of the Agnati and the Gentiles—the property shall go to the religious teacher or to the Holy Brahman. "Thus the obsequies cannot fail." Herodotus § tells us that the ancient Persians considered the possession of many sons to be, next after military prowess, the greatest proof of manly excellence. Even at this day the greatest misfortune that can befal a man in Persia is to be childless. When a chief's "hearthstone is dark"—such is the usual expression—he loses all respect, and hence the custom of adoption in such circumstances is universal. A similar feeling prevailed at Rome. "A house of his own," says Mommsen,|| "and the blessing of children, appeared to the Roman citizen as the end and essence of life. The death of the individual was not an evil, for it was a matter of necessity; but the extinction of a household or of a clan was an evil, even for the com-

* "Dorians," vol. ii., p. 202.

† Smith's "Dict. of Antiq.," *s. v.* Heres.

‡ ix., 188.

§ Canon Rawlinson's "Herodotus," vol. i., p. 221.

|| "Hist. Rome," vol. i., p. 59.

munity." It seems, however, to have been thought sufficient to vest the ultimate remainder in the Kin, without attempting to prolong the existence of a clan by transferring its ritual to strangers. In India, indeed, the religious teacher and the Holy Brahman are introduced; but we cannot doubt that they made their first appearance in the revision of the laws which belonged to the Brahmanic period. In practice, if a family become extinct, its share returns to the common stock of the village—in other words, to its Gentiles. In the maturity of Roman law* we meet, as we shall hereafter see, with a true escheat, or political remainder; but it was not until the time of the Empire that this change was effected. Whether the Gentiles were interested in their collective capacity, or in some way acquired individual rights in the property, we cannot tell. It seems probable † that there was no general law upon the subject, and that each Gens dealt with the property that fell to its share, and its attendant burthens, according to its own rules and views of expediency.

The Organization of the Clan.

§ 4. As the clan was an expansion of the Household, the organization of the one may be expected to resemble the organization of the other. This organization, indeed, is common to the Household, to the Clan, and to the State. Each of these bodies ‡ had its chief, whether he was hereditary or elective. Each had its council of advice. Each had its § children, its slaves, its freedmen. Even in their external relations the same resemblance may be traced. The various relations of clients, of friends, and of guests, may be found in the State and in the Kin as well

* See Ulpian, "Reg.," 28, 7; "Gaius," ii., 150.

† See Smith, "Dict. Ant.," *s. v.* Gens; Niebuhr, "Hist. of Rome," vol. ii., p. 157, *n.*

‡ Dean Merivale's "Fall of the Roman Republic," p. 155.

§ See Niebuhr, "Roman Hist.," vol. iii., p. 529, *n.*

as in the Household. Of these inferior, or extraneous parts, I do not now speak. It is the organization of the Kin itself that we have in this place to consider. First and most prominent in the clan, as in the House, stands the chief. He was the person who was nearest in blood to its Eponym, or founder. In other words,* he was the eldest male, or the heir of the eldest male, of the eldest branch. He, like the House Father, was the religious head of his special worship. He was the person whose duty it was to offer the customary sacrifices to the θεὸι πατρῷοι, the gods of the Kin. He was the natural leader of his kinsmen in war, and the administrator of their customs in peace. In all external relations he was their spokesman and representative. In domestic affairs, rank, and, consequently, a share in the public property, was, at least in some nations, determined according to the nearness to his blood. He was usually more wealthy than his kinsmen; because, in addition to his household property, he enjoyed a special endowment, and also certain lucrative incidents, such as customary gifts, fees of office, and license fees from such strangers as resorted, for purposes of trade or otherwise, to his district. But the chief was essentially one of his people. He ruled according to the customs of his clan. His authority rested not upon any external force, but upon the willing obedience and reverence that he received. "Nothing," says Mr. Freeman,† "of the pomp and circumstance either of modern or of eastern kingship surrounds him. His house is accessible to all: his personal life is spent in the same way—at once simple and public, as the life of any other members of the commonwealth. Divine as he is, no barrier parts him off from the other chiefs of his people. He is perhaps only one among many bearers of the kingly

* See "Ed. Rev.," cxliv., 187.

† "Comparative Politics," p. 145.

title.* Even within the narrow bounds of Ithakê, there were many kings besides the divine Odysseus." It is not difficult to understand how accidental personal differences necessitated, in the interest of the general welfare, some modification in the functions of the chief; and how, from the primitive simplicity of general and of judge, and of ruler and of priest, special organs were with the growth of the community developed. One function, however, survived every change, and by its persistency proved its antiquity. None but its accustomed head could perform the religious rites of the clan. Consequently, the name and office of Basileus and of Rex, although shorn of their original glory, long lingered among the Gentes of Athens and of Rome.

We have seen in the Household some traces of the family council. The presence of a similar body is observable also in the clan. I do not speak of the *Boulê*, and of its later political developments. But in the *Gens*, as it co-existed with the State, we find plain marks of independent legislative authority. The laws of Romulus,† and the laws of Numa, probably indicate the clan laws of the Ramnes, and of the Tities; and subsequent so-called legislation probably points to the similar rules of the Luceres and of the Plebs. So, too, Menu‡ enjoins a king, "who knows the revealed law, to inquire into the particular laws or usages of districts, the customs of trades, and the rules of certain families, and to establish their particular laws." We read

* "Kings were formerly as plentiful in Scandinavia as dukes at the present day at Naples; the son of a king, though without territories, bearing the same title as his father. In the Drontheim district alone, Harald Harfagra defeated and slew no less than eight kings."—Mallet's "North. Antiq.," p. 279, *note*. For the number of kings in early England, see Kemble's "Saxons in England," vol. i., p. 148; and for a lively description of a Rajpút Chief, see Mr. Lyall, "Fort. Rev.," No. 121, N.S., p. 99.

† Niebuhr, "Roman History," vol. ii., p. 284.

‡ viii., 41.

in later times* of a decree of the Fabian Gens prohibiting celibacy and the exposure of infants. The Manlian Gens expressed its abhorrence of the political conduct of an eminent kinsman by forbidding the use of the pronomen Marcus. The Claudian Gens forbade the use of the pronomen Lucius, because two kinsmen bearing that name had been convicted—the one of highway robbery, the other of murder. The familia of the Serani, a sub-clan of the Atilii, had a rule that their women should abstain from the use of linen garments.† At Athens,‡ the Eumolpidæ and the Butadæ are mentioned as having unwritten maxims of great antiquity. In cases of impiety, particularly in offences against the Mysteries, the Eumolpidæ had a peculiar tribunal of their own number, and exercised a special jurisdiction. We may, perhaps, compare with this council the Russian § senate of Village Starostas, who, under the presidency of their Starshina, make laws for the good government of their *Volost*, or township. We find traces also of councils apparently of this kind among the Hindus, the Kelts, and the early English. It is remarkable that in nearly all the Aryan communities both a council of this kind is found, and that the number of its members is almost always the same. So far as I know, in Wales alone, probably from some accidental circumstance, the number of the council is seven. In all other cases it is five. Why that particular number should have been chosen I cannot tell, unless it be due to that primitive numeration upon the hand which has left its mark all over the world. In India, the custom appears with a persistency that affords strong proof of its high antiquity. "The

* See Willems's "Le Droit Public Romain," p. 25, and the authorities there cited.

† Plin., xix., 1, 2, 8.

‡ Grote's "History of Greece," vol. iii., p. 90, *note*.

§ M. de Laveleye, "De la Propriété," p. 11.

Village Council," says Sir Henry Maine,* "is always viewed as a representative body, and not as a body possessing inherent authority; and whatever be its real number, it always bears a name which recalls its ancient constitution of Five persons." In Ireland, we read of the *Cuicer na Fine*, the five pledges of the *Fine* or Familia. Dr. Sullivan † describes these persons "as a kind of Family Council composed of five men, who regulated everything connected with the rights and responsibilities of the family." To this body, as the same writer ‡ suggests, the Reeve and Four Men of the old English township corresponded. That is, the Council of the Mæg became, when the cantonal element predominated, the representatives of the township. We may, I think, detect traces of a similar number in the Gentile institutions at Rome. It is said § that, while a father could order the exposure of his other daughters, he could not expose his eldest daughter or any son, unless the child were condemned, as monstrous weak or exceedingly deformed, by the judgment of five neighbours. Again, in the ceremony of mancipation, the number of witnesses, exclusive of official persons, was five. But mancipation was the solemn customary form by which the property of the Household was sold. It seems, then, not an unreasonable guess, although it is only a guess, that the sale may have originally taken place before the Council of the Agnates, whose presence both attested the fact and expressed their consent, at a time when that consent was essential to the transfer. Perhaps, too, a trace of this custom may be found in those five good House Fathers who were wont to go from Horace's Sabine Farm ‖ to Varia. The

* "Vill. Comm.," p. 123.

† "Introduction to O'Curry's Lectures," i., cciii.

‡ *Ib.*, ccv.

§ Dion. Hal., "Ant. Rom.," ii., 15.

‖ "Quinque bonos solitum Variam dimittere patres."—Ep., i., 14, 3.

passage has occasioned among the critics some controversy; and in the absence of definite information on Italian local self-government, I am not disposed to give way to fancies. But some future Horatian commentator may possibly think it worth his while to compare the *Punchayets* and the *Cuicer na Fine*, and to extend his inquiries to the Four Men and the Reeve, those five good House Fathers who used to go to their folkmote to represent their township.

In Greece, too, the Court of Five seems not to have been unknown. In the inscriptions still extant of some Hellenic cities, the number five frequently recurs in their legal business. Thus in Petelia,* an Hellenic city of Southern Italy, a deed of conveyance is attested by the signatures of the chief magistrates and of five *proxeni*, or citizens who represented foreign communities. Again, when much litigation prevailed in Calymna,† the people of that city, according to a practice very usual among Greek cities, sought judicial assistance from without. They obtained from the people of Iasus the desired help; and an inscription records that the people of Calymna honoured with a crown the five judges whom the people of Iasus had sent them.

We find also, in the archaic community, vestiges of an elaborate organization of inferior offices. Every Indian village contains a number of hereditary trades, which seem to be the relics of such a system. It is noteworthy that there are some trades in these villages which are not hereditary. The exceptions include those which belong to commerce rather than to trade—that is, which involve a supply of goods from distant markets. These employments, although lucrative and respectable, do not appear ‡ to be regarded as customary offices, or to confer any status in the community. Such, for example, is the business of the

* "Contemp. Rev.," vol. xxix., p. 76. † *Ib.*, p. 85.

‡ Sir H. S. Maine, "Village Communities," pp. 124-126.

grain-dealer. In early Greece the δημιόεργοι seem to be the analogues of these Hindu officials. Homer mentions the herald the prophet and the bard, the carpenter the fisherman and the leech, all of whom, although we cannot trace their exact position, appear to have exercised some kind of public function. Among the Keltic clans similar classes are known to have existed. It is probable that the Teutonic settlements were similarly supplied. We can, on this supposition, account for the abundance and the persistence of surnames taken from the names of certain trades, and for such expressions as the "Smith's Acre" and other local names. These names indicate at once the public function and the remuneration, in the form of a τέμενος or *sundergut*, by which its exercise was rewarded.

Admission to and Departure from the Clan.

§ 5. I have already said that, even in cases of children, and much more so in the case of strangers, a special initiation was required before any person could be admitted as a member of a Household. The same rule applied with respect to the admission to a clan, and to the withdrawal from it. No person could enter a clan or leave it at his own will merely, and without the consent of its members. If he sought to enter it, he must be accepted as a worshipper of his new gods. If he desired to leave it, care must be taken that he did not thereby imperil the worship of his former gods. Further, the person who entered a community acquired thereby a share in certain substantial benefits. On the other hand, by his withdrawal he weakened *pro tanto* the power and the repute of his clan. We find, accordingly, that this power of admission on the one side, and on the other side of expatriation, or, perhaps, I should rather say of exfamiliation, even when the change was absolute, and not merely a transfer from one Household to another, were always solemn public acts requiring the consent of the community. We read of the ceremonies with which the Greek and the Roman and the Teutonic youth were respectively presented to their kinsmen, and received from them a recognition of their claims. We know that at Rome adoption took place with the consent of the Gentile Parliament; and that at Athens, even in late times, every admission to a Clan was jealously scrutinized by its members. The process of abandonment was similarly guarded. Among the Greeks a man could make himself in their expressive language ἐκποίητος, but formal proceedings were necessary to effect this object. The old German law * tells us that when a man wished to leave his *parentilla,* or mæg, he was to go into the *mallus* or place of public assembly, with four alder sticks, and to break them into four pieces and to throw them into the *mallus,* and make his renunciation in a prescribed form of words; and thereupon his power of transmitting an inheritance to his former Kin, or of receiving it from them, ceased; and they were no longer liable for, or entitled to, his wer-geld. In our own early law,† traces of a similar custom exist in the process known as foris-familiation. A son was said to be foris-familiated if his father assigned him part of his land, and gave him seisin thereof, and did this at the request, or with the free consent of the son himself, who expressed himself satisfied with such portion. The heirs of the son could not afterwards claim any greater portion of their grandfather's estate. So, too, we read of the ceremonies that attended the expulsion of an offending Gesith. He was escorted by a guard to the verge of the forest, and there they watched in silence his departure so long as he could be distinguished. But when he had at

* "Lex Salica," s. 63. Canc., "Leg. Barb.," ii., 107.

† Reeves, "Hist. Eng. Law," vol. i., p. 110 (first ed.).

length disappeared, the whole body raised three times a loud shout, partly perhaps as the final *vale* to their former comrade, who was now dead to them, and partly, as it is said, lest the fugitive might wander back to the point from which he had set forth. "Some such process," says a learned writer,* "must have been absolutely necessary in every archaic community. Some circumstances must have been held to justify the expulsion, and probably some ceremony may have indicated that the member of the community who rebelled against the custom was cast out, and had become 'friendless,' 'flyma,' or 'exlex.'"

We may, perhaps, obtain a somewhat clearer notion of the exclusive character of these old Kins by observing the accounts given of the Swiss cantons at the present day. A Switzer cannot move from one canton of the Confederacy to another, as an Englishman moves from one shire or one colony to another shire or another colony. Each canton has its own property, to which various lucrative incidents are attached. A tariff of admission † to these advantages is in each case established, and thus each canton becomes a sort of joint-stock company. In the case of married couples the rate of admission is considerably higher than it is for single persons, because the danger of their increasing the divisor of the communal property is more imminent. The celibates must obtain permission to marry, and this permission it is often difficult to procure.

The Help to Clansmen and their Redress.

§ 6. The mutual obligations that prevailed between clansmen were of the closest kind. Every clansman was bound ‡ to assist and support, in all his difficulties, every other clansman. It is mainly from later times, when the

* "Anc. Laws of Ireland," vol. iii., p. 107.
† Mr. Dixon's "Switzers," pp. 74-80.
‡ Niebuhr, "Rom. Hist.," vol. i., p. 315.

clan was comprised within the State, that we derive our knowledge of these kindred duties. It appears* that, if a man were condemned to pay a fine, or if he incurred expense in any public office, or if he were taken in war, his kinsmen ought to contribute to his needs. If he were accused, they attended in court to maintain his cause. If he were wronged, they helped him to procure redress. No clansman was competent to give evidence against another. If a clansman were advanced to honour, his whole clan, or at least that portion of it which was more directly connected with him, shared in his advancement. If he were punished, the penalty extended to all that belonged to him. Thus, in the old English poem, "Beowulf,"† certain warriors are described as having deserted their prince in the time of trouble. The punishment which his successor awards to them is not that they, individually, but that the whole mægsceaft, or near kindred, of each of them should be deprived of their folk-right. It is probable that, in our day, it was the application of this principle of root and branch punishment that furnishes the true explanation of those massacres, in the form of public executions, which the Chinese Government perpetrated under the superintendence of Commissioner Yeh.

Even still, where the Clan society survives, this essential incident survives with it. "I have," writes Dr. Faucher,‡ "been witness (in the Government of Moscow, in the summer of 1867) to the fact that a whole village, which had been destroyed by one of the numerous conflagrations of that year, and which had lost everything—whose inhabitants, besides not feeling at ease where they were, resolved to return to the mother village of their village, situated

* See "La Cité Antique," p. 118.

† Kemble, "Saxons in Eng.," vol. i., p. 235.

‡ Cobden Club Essays, "Systems of Land Tenures," p. 355. (The passage is quoted without grammatical alteration.)

two hundred and fifty miles off, and which they or their ancestors had left nearly fifty years ago. They collected money for this purpose from the neighbouring gentry; and even the neighbouring villages, which fully appreciated the resolution, contributed their share." It is probable that these poor Russian peasants would have felt less difficulty than some learned critics have felt in the narrative of Herodotus* respecting the immigration of the Minyæ from Lesbos to Lacedæmon. The Lacedæmonians, seeing that strangers had occupied Mount Taygetum, sent to ask who they were and why they came. The reply was that, "driven from their own land by the Pelasgi, they had come, as was most reasonable, to their fathers; and their wish was to dwell with them in their country, partake their privileges, and obtain allotments of land." The Lacedæmonians acknowledged the claims, and received the Minyæ into full citizenship. The tale may, or may not be true; but the sentiment on which it depends must have appeared worthy of respect.

If one kinsman wronged another, the remedy must be sought in the *forum domesticum*. If, however, the wrong were inflicted or sustained by a stranger, the case was different. The clan was collectively liable for the wrong done by any of its members; and was, on the other hand, bound to redress any wrongs that any of its members might have endured. If a bone were broken or a limb were lost, the wrong-doer was liable to the like infliction; and it was the duty of the next agnate to inflict the retaliation.† If a clansman were killed by a stranger, it was the duty of the clan to take vengeance upon the homicide or upon some of his Kin. When the action of the

* iv., 145.

† "Si quis membrum rupit aut os fregit, talione proximus agnatus ulciscitur."—*Cato*, Orig. apud Priscianum, vi., p. 710.

State had withdrawn from private hands the execution of the vengeance, it was the duty of the clan* to put the law in motion against the offender. When compensation was made for homicide, it was to the Kin of the slaughtered man that the money was paid; and it was upon the Kin of the wrong-doer that, either wholly or in part, the burthen of making that compensation fell. Nor was it among men of the Aryan race exclusively that this rule as to homicide prevailed. No rule in the ancient world was more rigorous, or more widely spread. None occupies a larger space in legal history. But the question of the blood feud—important and interesting though it be—is only incidental to my present undertaking.

Theories respecting the Origin of the Clan.

§ 7. Much has been written concerning the origin of the clan, and various theories on the subject have been proposed. Two only of these require our present notice. Some writers have thought that the gens, at least as it existed at Athens and at Rome, was a merely artificial association, the work of some forgotten legislator, united by the tie of a fictitious consanguinity. Others have regarded it as the aggregation, whether spontaneous or artificial, of several originally independent Households. I do not propose to enter at any length into these controversies. As to the former theory, it is needless to resort to a mere unsupported hypothesis, which hardly, if at all, accounts for the phenomenon, when we have a *vera causa* that affords a simple and complete explanation. That institution cannot have been the work of any particular legislator, which was as general among the Aryans as is the verbal root by which its meaning was expressed. The kin was not a fictitious but a real relationship. Its members thought so themselves,

* Canon Rawlinson's "Herodotus," vol. iii., p. 308; Müller's "Dorians," vol. ii., p. 234.

and acted upon that opinion. The word itself, or its equivalent, implies community of blood. The kinsmen, as we have already seen, bore a common name, and that name was a patronymic. They had a common worship of a common Eponym, they held their land in common, they had reciprocal rights of tutelage and of inheritance. For the proposition that their relationship was merely imaginary, there is absolutely no proof. It seems to rest partly upon a misconception of early relationship, and partly upon a consequent misconstruction of certain passages in Greek and Roman authors. Archaic men did not, as we do, understand descent in the light of a purely physical fact. There is no doubt that with them the kin both included persons whom we should regard as strangers, and excluded persons whom we should regard as our nearest relatives. This result, which is equally and even more conspicuously true of the Household, was produced by the two well-known principles, agnation and adoption. The inference is, not that the kin was an artificial combination, but that it was founded on a principle different from that with which we are familiar. Ancient kinship, in short, consisted not in community of blood, but, as Plato * expressly tells us, in community of worship.

The other theory to which I have alluded, relates not to the motives which led to the association of kinsmen, but to the actual structure of the institution. This theory holds that the clan or kin was an aggregation of independent Households. It supposes that so many separate Households combined to form a kin; that so many kins combined to form a tribe; that so many tribes combined to form a State. There is a regularity in this theory that renders it at first sight agreeable, and it is not without some amount

* "Laws," v., 729.

of plausibility. But it is essentially misleading. It resembles the famous doctrine of the social compact, and it is open to similar objections. It was probably suggested by the supposed relation of the gentes and the familiæ at Rome, although it is readily refuted by the ordinary facts of Roman history. The Roman gentes were older than the familiæ: the latter were merely branches of their respective parent stocks. There were many familiæ of the Claudii and of the Cornelii; but there were Claudii and Cornelii before any of those familiæ came into existence. On the other hand, there were gentes—such as the Manlii and the Marii, who never seem to have branched into any familiæ. Thus, there were gentes before there were familiæ, and even after familiæ were known there were gentes without familiæ. The clan separated into Households, but the separate households did not, by any voluntary association, form a clan.

That, also, is an erroneous representation of the true theory of the gens, which describes* the gens as "merely the patriarchal family in a state of decay." Except so far as decay is incidental to growth, there is no decay in this case. The gens is the patriarchal family, in a state not of decay, but of development. It arises from the natural growth of such a family. It reproduces many such families. There is, indeed, change; but the change is not that of death and decay, but of life and expansion. From the simple homogeneous Household are evolved numerous distinct and related Households, which, in the aggregate, form a whole, and that whole is the gens.

Most of the controversies relating to the gens have assumed that the gens was of one kind only. As usually happens where such an assumption is erroneously made, there is much truth on both sides of the question. These

* Mr. Hunter's "Roman Law," p. 658.

conflicting arguments are reconciled when it is understood that there are two classes of gentes—similar, but distinct. One is the gens in the strict sense of the term, the pure genealogic clan which *bonâ fide* springs, or believes that it springs, from some common ancestor, and in which the rules of descent are—at least in its perfect condition—scrupulously observed. The other is the non-genealogic clan or tribe, where men of different origins voluntarily unite for some definite purpose in a brotherhood which simulates the gens, and yet preserves, in the several branches of that brotherhood, traces of their descent. It is easy to see that much that Niebuhr and Grote have said as to the artificial origin of the gens may apply to these non-genealogic tribes, while it does not apply to the pure clans. So, too, Mr. Lyall has shown how that large intermixture of foreign elements, which embarrasses Sir Henry Maine and Mr. McLennan from the point of view of the genealogic clan, can be explained when the process of formation of a non-genealogic tribe has been recognized.

The Household, as I have attempted to describe it, has a natural limit, which is soon reached. That limit, indeed, is not in nature marked by any definite line. It is not determined by the life of the House Father, or by any term of years, or by any particular number of the members of the Household. On all these points we must, as we shall presently see, admit that the archaic Household differed widely from those modern families of which alone the nations of Western Europe and their descendants have experience. Yet, sooner or later, a time must come when the original Household can no longer hold together. Its bulk becomes unmanageable. Like the primary cell in organic nature, it divides into a number of distinct cells. Each new cell goes through a similar process, and all these cells are related both to the parent cell and to one another.

Thus, whatever may be the rate of this development, a homogeneous body, after attaining a certain bulk, spontaneously divides, as we might expect, into several similar bodies, and among these cognate bodies a relation exists. The aggregate of these related bodies is called the kin, or clan. That such a body, distinct from the Household, and yet including it, and similarly organized, did actually exist, is not a matter of dispute. The difficulty is to account for its existence, not to prove it. I hope to be able, in a subsequent chapter, to show the point at which archaic custom drew the line, and the reason, as founded in the old religion, why it should be so drawn. But, given a body like the Household, held together by its domestic religion, the production of a larger body similarly united follows from the known laws of evolution. The anticipated operation of these laws is verified by the existence, in all the Aryan nations, of such a body as that which we were prepared to expect. Or if we accept the clan as a fact, we can account for its existence by showing that it proceeds naturally from an institution which—at least in our present state of knowledge—we must accept as an ultimate fact in the history of those nations. In either aspect of the question, it follows that the clan must be regarded as the natural development of the Household.

Many circumstances tend to support this proposition. The clan was an original institution common to all the Aryan races. Its rights and duties, as they survived in those later times when we are best acquainted with it, were a development of the rights and duties of agnation—that is, of the Household related in the male line. We may, therefore, reasonably infer that agnation was the principle upon which the clan was founded. Its structure and its functions, too, pre-suppose and depend upon that Lares-worship which, as we have seen, was the corner-stone of the

Household. Again, a familia, as such,* had no special *sacra.* Its worship was included in that of the gens. There was, indeed, a difference in the form of the offering to the nearer and to the remoter ancestors; but this difference was a part of a common ritual, and did not amount to a distinct operation. There was nothing between the worship of the Household and the worship of the gens. Further, when we examine the definitions of the gens which the early Roman lawyers have left to us, they furnish strong confirmation of these views. According to Cicero,† the Pontiff Scævola, in discussing the learning of inheritance, defined in effect 'Gentiles' to mean those free-born persons who bore a common name, who had not in their pedigree any servile taint, and who had not themselves incurred any legal change affecting their personal condition. The force of these limitations will become more apparent as we proceed. It is now sufficient to observe that they were meant to cut down a too general proposition. All kinsmen bore the same name; but all who bore the same name were not necessarily kinsmen—or, at least, had not the *jura Gentilitia,* with which the Pontiff was then concerned. It was necessary to except—first, the clients or other dependents, all of whom bore the name of the clan; second, those members of the clan who were not "perfect in their generations;" thirdly, those who had left the clan, or otherwise undergone those changes of status that the Roman law grouped together under the title "*Deminutio Capitis.*" But the common name, as other Roman writers ‡ expressly admit, implied and recognized a common descent, that is, according to the rules which in those days regulated descent.

* See Smith's "Dict. Ant.," *s. v. sacra.*

† Top., vi., 29. See Niebuhr, vol. i., p. 321.

‡ "Gentilis dicitur et ex eodem genere ortus, et is qui simili nomine appellatur, ut ait Cincius."—*Paulus Diaconus,* p. 94. See also Varro, "De Ling. Lat.," viii., 2.

That name was always a patronymic. It never was suggestive of local origin or of political contrivance. But it in plain and unambiguous terms declared that those who bore it were the children, or if he were then alive would be in the *manus*, of the *pater familias*, whether actual or adoptive, whom the clan adored as its founder.

This resemblance of the Household to the clan suggests itself even to the contemporary observer of Slavonic life. "The peasant family of the old type," says Mr. Wallace,* "is a kind of primitive association in which the members have nearly all things in common. The village may be roughly described as a primitive association on a large scale." Mr. Wallace proceeds to show the points of resemblance and of difference between the two institutions. In both there is a principal personage, who is the ruler within and the representative without. In both the authority of this ruler is limited; in the one case by the adult members of the Household, in the other by the heads of Households: in both there is community of property: in both there is common responsibility. In both protection is given, in case of insolvency, by a rule corresponding to the wainage of our old law, by which the house and implements, in the one case, and the land in the other, are exempted from seizure. On the other hand, the commune is much larger and the relation is less close. The partnership, too, in the Household extends to every kind of gain, while in the commune the Households farm separately, and pay into the common treasury a certain fixed sum.

* "Russia," vol. i., p. 183.

CHAPTER VI.

THE SYSTEM OF ARCHAIC KINSHIP.

Kinship traced from the Eponym.

§ 1. KINSHIP implies a reference to some standard. Two men are related to each other because they are severally related to a third. As we determine the likeness or the unlikeness of two terms, or of two propositions, by comparing them with a third term, or a third proposition, so we affirm or deny kinship by a reference to a common ancestor. Lawyers still look with respectful admiration upon the first purchaser. But among archaic men the position of the ἄρχηγος, or Præpositus, awakened, for reasons that I shall presently endeavour to explain, a far deeper feeling. With them kinship comprised every social relation, every tie that binds man to life; and with them kinship implied a constant and vivid reference to the founder of their kin, the Eponymous hero of their clan, or of their race.

There is ample evidence as to the existence of the belief in these Eponyms. They were indeed the crown of the system of House-worship. The Eponym was the original House Spirit, and was often regarded as the representative of the spirits that were descended from him. His name—that by which he is now generally known—proves the prevalence of the belief among the Greeks. There is, however, more direct evidence in the case of that people. "In the retrospective faith of a Greek," says Mr. Grote,* "the ideas of worship and ancestry coalesced. Every association

* "History of Greece," vol. i., p. 110.

of men, large or small, in whom there existed a feeling of present union, traced back that union to some common initial progenitor, that progenitor being either the common god whom they worshipped, or some semi-divine person closely allied to him."

The same remarks are equally applicable to the Romans. Among them the senior House Spirit appears very conspicuously as "Lar Familiaris." It is noteworthy, too, that the Roman writers rarely use, in reference to an individual Household, the plural Lares, but usually speak of the Lar as if he were a single person. In India, at this day, the members of the genealogic clans are always careful to refer their position to their Eponym, and speak of him with a certitude that, as Mr. Lyall observes, "would impress Niebuhr."* "It does not follow," says the same acute observer,† "because a tribe claims its descent from a god, that the divine founder is a personage entirely mythical, as certain comparative mythologers do vainly imagine. He is quite as likely to be a real hero deified, for the founder of at least one Rajpút State, who is as authentic as any historic personage can be in India, is freely worshipped by his clan to this day." It is still a fundamental article of belief ‡ with every Russian peasant that every family must have a House Spirit, and that that spirit is the founder of the family. The Persians § derived their three orders of priests, and warriors, and husbandmen from the three sons of Zarathrustra, just as the Norsemen || derived their three classes of society from Thrall, Karl, and Jarl, the three sons of Heimdall. It may, indeed, be said ¶ generally that the

* "Fort. Rev.," No. 121, N.S., p. 100.

† "Ed. Rev.," cxliv., p. 183.

‡ Mr. Ralston, "Songs of Russia," p. 126.

§ Spiegel's "Avesta," by Bleeck, vol. iii., p. 92.

|| Mallet's "North. Ant.," p. 366.

¶ Niebuhr's "Hist. Rome," vol. i., p. 13.

names of countries and of settled districts are derived from those of their inhabitants, and that the names* of these inhabitants are always patronymics. Mr. Kemble† enumerates 1,329 names of places in England that are either patronymics or directly formed from patronymics, and every patronymic implies an Eponym. So we are told that the Picts called themselves Cruithneach, and that their Eponym was Cruithne. Of the Gaelic clans and their Eponyms I have already spoken. In short, wherever there was a clan there was an Eponym, or founder, whether real or legendary, of that clan.

To this original chief or genarch, the nearest in blood was the natural successor. This nearest person was generally the eldest son of the eldest branch. Disputes, indeed, long prevailed as to the course which should be pursued when the eldest son pre-deceased his father, but left a son surviving him. In such circumstances, it was doubtful whether the son of the deceased elder brother or the living younger brother was nearer to the Eponym. In Germany this perplexing question was, in the 10th century, in the reign of Otho I., determined,‡ "*inter gladiatores*," that is, by the conclusive method of trial by battle. In political affairs, however, such a decision is not often accepted as final. Even in our own history, the Wars of the Roses attest the fierceness of the quarrels between the representatives of the elder and of the younger generation. Yet, in that struggle, and even two centuries afterwards, at the time of the Revolution, no person wished to go out of the royal line. For, in a large community, the dispute was not, as in matters of private right, between individuals, but between corporate Households, or even between clans. Little regard was paid in

* Kemble, "Saxons in England," vol. i., p. 61.

† *Ib.*, Appendix A.

‡ Grimm's "Deutsche Rechts Alt.," p. 471.

times of difficulty to the rights of the elder or the rights of the younger. It was not the interest of the individual for which men were solicitous; they sought the assurance that a man of the founder's blood sat in that founder's seat. If only the founder's kin was represented, it was little matter what particular member of that kin was the representative. Thus all the difficulties about succession are easily explained when it is understood that the standard was proximity to the Eponym; and that proximity was usually satisfied by a reference to the corporate House or kin, and not to the individual heir.

In the same line, however, there may be many Eponyms. When, from any cause, a man breaks away from his own clan, and makes a fresh start elsewhere, if he distinguish himself in any conspicuous way, he forms, as it were, a new point of departure, and founds a new clan of his own. Like Napoleon, he is his own ancestor. Thus, Battos, of Kyrenê, belonged to the Minyan family of the Euphemidæ.* That is, he was descended from the Eponym, Euphemus, one of the Argonauts who belonged to the great clan of the Minyæ. Here we find two new Eponyms. The original Eponym was Minyas, or, perhaps, Menu—the Adam, if I may so speak, of the Aryans. Euphemus founded a clan among his kinsmen; and, many generations after him, Battos succeeded in repeating the process. But the kings of Kyrenê were always known as Battiadæ, and, except on special occasions, would not be called Euphemids, much less Minyæ. So, too, Alexander the Great traced his descent to Perdikkas, who claimed † to be a Temenid from Argos; and the Temenidæ were a branch of the Herakleidæ. Had Alexander founded a dynasty, he would probably have become in his turn a great Eponym; and the Herakleids,

* Herodotus, iv., 150.

† *Ib.*, viii., 137.

the Temenids, and the Perdikkids would all have been merged in his absorbing renown.

Kinship among the Aryan nations Agnatic.

§ 2. There are three possible ways in which consanguinity may be traced. One is, through the father alone; the second is, through the mother alone; the third is, through both the father and the mother. Again, the line so traced may, in each of these cases, be the male line or the female line, or both the male and female. Of these forms, the last is that with which, under the name of cognation, in modern times, and among races of European descent, we are familiar. The second form, that of uterine succession, still prevails among many of the less advanced races. With these two forms I am not now concerned. The former belongs to the history of law; the latter is, at least at the present time, peculiar to races different from our own. It is to the first form—or, rather, to a branch of it—that I desire to call attention. This form at one time prevailed among all the Aryan nations, and, from its name in Roman law, is usually called agnation. Agnation, as distinguished from cognation, means relationship through the male line only. It traces through the father alone; and it traces through his sons, not through his daughters. A man's brother's son, for example, is his agnate; his sister's son, or his mother's brother, is his cognate. In an agnatic system, therefore, the descendants—male or female—of a sister were not related to the brother or his descendants. In like manner, two half-brothers by the same father were as fully agnates to each other as if they were of the whole blood; but two half-brothers by the same mother were not related to each other at all. Thus the agnates were properly a part of the cognates, although, when the words are contrasted, the one denotes kinship through males, the other kinship through females. But while agnation had much narrower limits than those which our modern notions assign to kinship, it, in one respect, exceeded those limits. An adopted son was, for all purposes, deemed to have been naturally born in the Household that he entered. Consequently, an adopted son, although we should not regard him even as a cognate, was always considered as an agnate of his new family.

It is easy to accumulate evidence to show the prevalence of agnation among the nations of the Aryan race. Although, at a later period of the history of each of these nations, the more liberal principle of cognation has been established, yet, in the earlier stages of their development, agnation was universal. Everywhere we find the descent from a common male ancestor, the succession of males, the exclusion—sometimes absolute, sometimes relative—of females from the inheritance. It is remarkable that, in the folk-lore * of all the Aryan nations, the House Spirit is always masculine. In the immense assemblage of spirits that, in the imagination of archaic men, peopled earth and sea and sky, the division of the sexes is usually observed. But it was not so with the House and its precinct. We read of Oreads, and Dryads, and Naiads, besides the gods and the goddesses of Olympos; but we never hear of an Oikad. It was to his father's spirit, and not to his mother's, that the Aryan man offered sacrifice. It was his father's spirit, not his mother's, that ruled over the Household; just as, in life, it was his father, and not his mother, that was that Household's acknowledged head. We read, too, of disputes as to succession between the sons of deceased elder brothers and their paternal uncles; but we never hear of such disputes where the paternal aunt or the maternal uncle is a party. Even where daughters are admitted to the succession, there is a tone of apology for what is clearly an innovation, or the

* Grimm, "Deutsche Mythol.," vol. ii., p. 467.

compromise of a marriage with the next agnate is required. "In Hindu law," says Sir Henry Maine,* "which is saturated with the primitive notion of family dependency, kinship is entirely agnatic; and I am informed that, in Hindu genealogies, the names of women are generally omitted altogether." At Athens, Demosthenes † cites the law, which provides that, in case of intestacy and failure of issue, the property shall go—first, to the father's next of kin, as far as the children of cousins, "and males, and the children of males shall have preference if they are from the same ancestors, even though in degree farther removed." Second, failing the paternal relatives, the mother's next of kin to the same limit succeeds. Finally, failing both these, the succession goes to the clansmen of the father.

For the Roman law, it is enough to cite the words of the Twelve Tables, "Si intestato moritur cui suus heres nec escit adgnatus proximus familiam habeto." So, too, among the Teutons,‡ the words of the Salic law may be taken as representing that of all the other nations, "De terra Salica nulla portio hereditatis mulieri veniat." It is noteworthy that, in Germany proper, this restriction applied only to the "alod," or hereditary property. In all other kinds of property, the daughters inherited with the sons, share and share alike. Among the Norsemen, however, even this relaxation from the rigour of the old rule found no favour. In Scandinavia and, as it seems, in old Friesland, the universal maxim was, without any qualification—"The man goes to the inheritance; the woman from it." In the Slavonic house communities of the present day, § the woman is always under ward, and is entitled, not to the

* "Ancient Law" p. 150. † Against Makartatos.

‡ See Canciani, "Leg. Barb.," iii., 50. Grimm, "Deutsche Rechts Alt.," pp. 407, 472.

§ M. de Laveleye, "De la Propriété," p. 24.

inheritance, but to receive a dower. So it was also with the Keltic nations. The Welsh laws * declare that "a woman is not to have patrimony." We meet with similar provisions in the Brehon † laws. It is not yet fifty years since the last trace of this venerable principle, that rule of inheritance which excluded the half-blood, was removed from the law of England. Originally ‡ this rule, as it was known in Normandy, was limited to the case of uterine brothers. But by a subsequent mistaken extension, at a time when the reason on which it rested had been forgotten, it was applied to all half-brothers, without distinction; and philosophic lawyers racked their brains for reasons to vindicate the wisdom of a rule of which history alone furnished the true explanation.

Alleged traces of opposite system.

§ 3. The universality of agnation among the Aryan nations has not been undisputed. Certain facts have been supposed to contradict this rule, or at least to indicate an earlier and a different state of society. Of these facts, the most noteworthy is the case of the Picts. Cæsar § describes a system of polyandry, generally among brothers, as existing among the inland tribes of Britain. A later historian, Dio, attributes a similar custom to the Caledonians and Mæatæ, that is, the Picts of Scotland. Bede ‖ tells us that the Picts of his day were accustomed, in cases of doubt, to elect their king from the female line of the royal house, and not from the male line. Other ancient authors also notice this Pictish right of succession on the female side. In the list, too, of the Pictish kings, brothers, sons of the same father, often

* "Anc. Laws of Wales," vol. i., p. 175.

† "Anc. Laws of Ireland," vol. iii., p. cxiv. "O'Curry's Lectures," vol. i., p. clxx.; vol. iii., p. 183.

‡ See Sir H. S. Maine, "Ancient Law," p. 151.

§ "De Bel. Gal.," v., 14.

‖ "Hist. Eccl.," b. i., c. 1.

succeed each other; but there is no instance throughout the whole period of the Pictish kingdom of a son succeeding his father. It is alleged that this form of succession is the natural result of such a system as that which Cæsar describes, and that it is always found where polyandry exists. There is also a statement of Polybios * that three or four Spartan brothers had often one and the same wife, "the paternal land being just sufficient to furnish contributions for all to the public mess, and thus to keep alive the citizen-rights of all the sons." Several passages, too, have been collected from the old Hindu writings that allude, or appear to allude, to a similar practice. But polyandry is inconsistent with agnation, and is the foundation of that widely different system of relationship which traces descent through the mother and not through the father. There is, therefore, evidence that among some Aryan tribes agnation did not exist, or, at all events, during one period of their history did not exist.

Uterine succession—that is, succession through the mother alone—is contrasted not only with agnation, but with cognation. It differs both from the earlier and more rigid form of agnation, and from that later form of it under which daughters were, in default of male heirs, allowed to succeed to their father's inheritance. It differs also from cognation, that is, from the modern mode of including as relations all the kin, whether male or female, of both the parents alike. It ignores kinship through the father, just as agnation ignores kinship through the mother. For the proof, therefore, of this principle, it is not enough to show succession through the mother, for such succession is consistent with cognation. The further negative must be proved, that succession did not take place through the

* See Grote's "Hist. Greece," vol. iii., p. 536.

father, or, at all events, that in matters of succession the maternal line was preferred to the paternal line. If, then, Mr. McLennan's contention * be true—which, however, I by no means admit—that the kinship of the "Eumenides" is later than the kinship of the Iliad, this fact does not even tend to prove the existence in early Greece of uterine succession. It would be, indeed, a very remarkable fact, if Mr. McLennan could prove that the blood feud in the time of Homer † extended to relatives on the female side. But even if it did so extend, we know that it also included the agnates. If the universality of such an extension could be established, it might affect our views as to the relative priority of agnation and of cognation, but it would not prove that cognation was a development of a polyandrous system. Although, in theory at least, uterine succession does not necessarily depend upon polyandry, it is certain that neither agnation nor cognation can exist without marriage. Marriage, indeed, is of itself insufficient to account for agnation, and the explanation of that phenomenon must be sought in the worship of the House Spirit. According to the principles of that religion, kinship was established, not necessarily between the descendants of the same couple, but between one sex of such descendants, actual or constructive, traced through persons of that same

* "Fort. Rev.," iv., 580.

† Tlepolemos, a Herakleid, killed his mother's brother, Likymnios, and was, consequently, obliged (*Il.*, ii., 665) to fly, "for the other sons and grandsons of the mighty Herakles threatened him." It is not easy at first to see what concern the Herakleidæ had with a mere connection by marriage. But as the Herakleidæ were a separate people, they would have married among themselves, but in different clans. Likymnios, therefore, would have been a Herakleid, and his avengers of blood would, of course, have been υἱέες υἱωνοί τε βίης Ἡρακληείης. Mr. McLennan describes Likymnios as the brother (rather, the illegitimate brother) of Alkmene, the mother of Herakles. But this statement rests on the authority of later writers. Homer does not make it.

sex. But this religion, in which marriage formed one of its most important rites, was, as we have seen, of the very essence of archaic Aryan society. It is, therefore, difficult to admit, unless in some exceptional circumstances, the existence among any Aryan population of a contradictory system.

So far as my present inquiry is concerned, it is of little moment whether at some remote time the progenitors of the Aryans were, or were not, polyandrous. It is with the Aryans themselves, as they are actually known to us, that I have to deal. Within the time of which any record of them exists, they have been monogamous. Marriage was an institution of the race before its dispersion. It is at that point, at the clan life on the banks of the Oxus, as comparative philology reveals it to us, that I pause. What may have been the previous history of the race I cannot tell. Some history doubtless there was, but we have at present no certain means of tracing it. For my purpose, therefore, I may accept marriage, and recognized paternity, and descent through fathers, as ultimate facts. All that I have here written might well stand, although at some distant time our institutions were in a much lower state of development than that which I have assumed. We are not absolved from the necessity of the study of both the body and the mind of the Aryan man because his ultimate progenitor may have been an Ascidian; and we must trace the history of Aryan institutions, even though they may have originated in Ascidian habits. I do not desire to enter into any controversy on the subject of primitive marriage. Yet, I will say that we ought not, without very conclusive proof, to accept a hypothesis that agnation is merely a development of polyandry. I venture to think that, beyond some ingenious conjectures, no evidence has on this subject been hitherto adduced; and that the difference between the two systems, the one arising from monogamy, and the other from polyandry, is fundamental. I may add that this hypothesis merely assumes that kinship through the mother gave rise to, or at least preceded, kinship through the father; but it does not explain why kinship through the father was limited to males, or why this limited form preceded instead of following the more general form under which daughters were first admitted in the absence of sons, and ultimately admitted upon an equal footing. But these questions are, as we shall presently see, answered by the theory of House-worship.

When we examine the proofs upon which we are required to believe in Aryan polyandry, there appears little reason to alter the conclusion to which general reasoning has led us. Small reliance can be placed upon the practice of a country so exceptional as Sparta, even if the evidence for that practice were wholly free from doubt. The passages from the Indian writings, in some instances at least, censure the acts in question as a scandalous breach of public morality. Those passages in Menu that relate to the duty of the childless husband's brother, depend, as we shall presently see, upon a wholly different principle. There remains, then, only the case of the Picts. So doubtful a case will scarcely be supposed to be sufficient to contradict the unanimous testimony of ancient writers, and the still stronger, though silent, witness of national customs and institutions. It may have been that, as Mr. Skene supposes, Cæsar and Dio were mistaken or misinformed. It may have been that Cæsar's information applied to some aboriginal tribes, and not to Kelts. Certainly Tacitus knew nothing of the custom which Cæsar described, and the evidence as to the succession does not go beyond the case of the royal family. Even if we admit the facts, it is reasonable to suppose that, in all the cases, whether in Sparta, or in India, or in Britain, local circumstances such as the pressure of population, and perhaps the example in some cases of Turanian neighbours, may have induced certain tribes to deviate from their ancestral customs. In such circumstances,* acts are often alleged to have been done in pursuance of immemorial custom, when, in truth, the origin of the practice can be proved to be of very recent date.

As to the peculiarity of the royal succession, we know how readily, especially in the case of great men, accident is converted into a custom, and a theory is supplied to explain that custom. Thus the Moghul Emperors,† although they were Mohammedans, were not circumcised; and the belief was generally accepted that there was a law of the House of Timour that no person with any mutilation should sit upon his throne. No such law ever existed, and it is known that the custom originated in a mere accident. When, however, it was once established, it prevailed even against the general rule of their religion. But this exceptional case does not prove either that the Moghuls were not Mohammedans, or that circumcision was not an ordinance of the Mohammedan creed. So, too, the peculiarity of the Pictish succession, whatever its origin may have been, does not disprove the general prevalence in that people of agnation.

The principle of Exogamy.

§ 4. Assuming the principles of Eponymy and of agnation—that is, assuming descent from a common male ancestor, and the limitation to males through the male line of the resulting relation—we have yet to take into account another influence. The lines of descent are marked out as I have described them, but further provision is necessary to keep them distinct. That provision is found in the

* See Sir H. S. Maine's "Vill. Comm.," p. 17.

† See Sir J. W. Kaye's "Sepoy War," vol. ii., p. 685.

principle of exogamy. It cannot be supposed that, in any Aryan Household, so important a duty as the selection of the mother of the future House Father would be left to chance. Two fundamental rules—one positive, the other negative—regulated the bridegroom's choice. He must marry a daughter of his own people: he must not marry a woman of his own kin. The race on the one side, and his own name on the other side, marked the limits of his selection. In other words, the law of marriage was that every man should take his wife from some cognate clan. This law involves two propositions. All marriages must take place within the people. No marriage must take place within the kin. As to the larger division, endogamy was the rule; as to the smaller division, exogamy prevailed. To the rule of endogamy an exception was made in favour of those communities between which an alliance was established, and the right of intermarriage was, by special favour, conceded. But, as regards exogamy, the rule, at least in the pure clans, was imperative. No man could lawfully marry a woman who bore his name.

The first portion of these rules can be readily proved. In India,* it is a universal law that no legitimate marriage can take place between members of two entirely different castes or tribes. Menu, in a passage I have already cited,† indicates the reason of this rule. It is the duty of the wife to prepare the proper sacrifices and oblations, but neither gods nor Manes will eat offerings that have been defiled by a stranger's hand. At Athens, the law, at least in its later history, was equally imperative. Those only were Athenians ‡ who were born from two Athenians. If an alien lived as a husband with an Athenian woman, he was

* Mr. Lyall, "Fort. Rev.," No. 121, N.S., p. 101.

† *Supra*, p. 87.

‡ Plutarch, "Perikles." Becker's "Charicles," p. 477.

liable to be sold as a slave, and to have his property confiscated.* If an Athenian lived with a foreign woman, she was liable to the like proceedings, and he to a penalty of a thousand drachmæ. The person, too, who gives a foreign woman in marriage to an Athenian, representing her as belonging to himself, was liable to disfranchisement and the confiscation of his property. At Rome the capacity for civil marriage† was restricted to either a Roman citizen or a Latin or foreign woman who had received the *jus connubii.* Tacitus ‡ observes that the Germans abstained from marriages with foreign nations. Other authorities § have incidentally noticed the same practice among the Goths and the Saxons. Nor is the prejudice, amongst ourselves, against a foreign marriage so long extinct that we can have much difficulty in comprehending this restriction.|| The proof of the rule as to exogamy is more difficult. The words of Menu,¶ indeed, are precise. "She who is not descended from his paternal (or maternal) ancestors within the sixth degree, and who is not known by his family name to be of the same primitive stock ** with his father (or mother), is eligible by a twice-born man for nuptials and holy union." The present practice of the pure Indian tribes accords with this rule. "We begin to appreciate," says Mr. Lyall,†† "the immense influence of the idea of kinship upon

* See the text of the law in the Oration against Neæra.

† "Gaius," i., 56.

‡ "Germania," c. 4.

§ See Canciani, "Leg. Barb.," iv., 88.

|| Writing of the Chinese, Sir John Davis observes :—"Marriage between all persons of the same surname being unlawful, this rule must, of course, include all descendants of the male branch for ever ; and, as in so vast a population there are not a great many more than one hundred surnames throughout the empire, the embarrassments that arise from so strict a law must be considerable."—*China,* vol. i., p. 326.

¶ iii., 5.

** The Hindu word is "gotram," literally a cow-stall.

†† "Fort. Rev.," *ubi supra,* p. 102.

primitive minds, when we perceive that widespread and numerous clans in Central India are nothing else but great circles of affinity, including, perhaps, a hundred thousand persons who cannot lawfully intermarry." But although this evidence is, so far as it goes, conclusive, it is the only direct evidence that we possess. It is by this one example that we must reconstruct the custom as it probably once existed throughout the Aryan world. For such a reconstruction something more than the Indian precedent is required. Some explanation should be given of the disappearance of the rule in other countries. Some vestiges, too, however faint, of its former existence in some at least of those other countries should be traced. Both of these conditions can, I think, be fulfilled. The disappearance of exogamy is probably due to the action partly of the State and partly of the Church. When a State is formed, the rule of exogamy is not likely to find favour. It tends to create and to maintain internal divisions, which it is the policy of the State to efface. As the Gentile lines gradually disappear, so the importance of the rule diminishes, until it at length vanishes because nothing is left for its operation. The State absorbs the clans, and the decay of the clans involves the decay of the rule. In Christian times, too, and in countries where the action of the political solvent was not felt, the whole question of marriage fell into the hands of the Church. There the canons effaced the rules of kin. Christians, indeed, must intermarry with Christians; but within the Church there were no clans, and there was no sympathy with clans. The whole system of the Church, like that of the State, rested upon the recognition of individual action, and was inconsistent with corporate morality.

Several traces of the law of exogamy may, I think, be observed, although I must acknowledge that they are not very distinct. Mr. McLennan, in his "Primitive Marriage," with much ingenuity urges in its favour the marriage ceremonies indicative of capture, and the legends which point in the same direction. I cannot persuade myself to accept his evidence, or his conclusions, with the same unwavering faith that animates Mr. McLennan; and I should much like to have some proof of the operation of the rule at a later period than that to which he seems to refer. I will add, therefore, a few examples which may, perhaps, be thought to have some relevancy. Herodotus * tells us that the Minyæ, who had been settled in Lemnos, were driven from that island, and came to Sparta, and sought admission there on the ground of a common descent. The claim was recognized, and the newcomers were admitted to citizenship. Thereupon "the Minyæ forthwith married Spartan wives, and gave the wives whom they had married in Lemnos to Spartan husbands." Of course the truth of the story is, for our present purpose, not material. The evidence as to the custom is good, even if there had been neither Minyæ nor Spartans. But it is difficult to account for the supposed exchange, and I have not met with any explanation of it. To me it seems a case of exogamy. The Minyæ were bound to marry within their people, that is, after their adoption among the Lacedæmonians. Their former marriages were therefore void, or, as we should rather say, were voidable. But their former wives were in their *manus*, and were assumed to be, whether by adoption, as in the case of the Indian Meenas,† or otherwise, members of their kin. It was thus the duty of the Minyæ to marry, and to marry Lacedæmonian wives; while the women of their kin were in their turn available for marriage by their Spartan cousins. In Rome, under the

* iv., 145.

‡ See Mr. Lyall, "Fort. Rev.," No. 121, N.S., p. 106.

later republic, the line of forbidden degrees was drawn * at the seventh degree, that is, marriage was prohibited within the limits of the *agnatio*, or, as it was then called, under the more extended sense given to it in the Prætorian jurisdiction, the *cognatio.* It is not improbable that by this time the *cognatio* may have practically superseded the *gens,* although the latter institution lingered for many years afterwards. It may also be observed that, in recalling the names of those Roman matrons of whom we have knowledge, we do not find any that bore her husband's Gentile name. Cornelia marries a Sempronius, Fulvia an Antonius, Calpurnia a Julius. But such an induction, *per enumerationem simplicem,* is not very strong, and is always exposed to its characteristic danger of the contradictory instance. It would be very difficult to establish conclusively this negative proposition, yet in the absence of better evidence it ought, until it is rebutted, to have some weight. Happily there is direct evidence in support of these probabilities. Plutarch,† writing of the Romans, says that in former days men did not marry women of their own blood, or as he in the preceding sentence calls them, kinswomen (συγγενίδας), as in his own day they did not marry their aunts or their sisters; and he adds that it was long before they consented to wed with cousins. Tacitus ‡ tells us that the Germans were usually contented each with a single wife, except in the case of a few who, on account of their nobility, were courted for many nuptials. This result is one of the usual consequences of stringent marriage rules. The very poor clansmen § cannot procure marriages for their daughters; and the rich

* See Willems's "Le Droit Public Romain," p. 67, *note.*

† "Quæstiones Romanæ," c. 6.

‡ "Germania," c. 18.

§ See Mr. Lyall, "Fort. Rev.," *ubi supra,* p. 111.

clansman is incessantly importuned to take a portionless girl, if only nominally, off the hands of a poor and proud neighbour. That which produces this result among the Rajpúts of this day may, in a similar state of society, be regarded as the cause of the like effect among the Germans in the days of Tacitus.

There is, however, in this matter a distinction which it is material to note. The rule of exogamy applied only to the formation of a new Household. When a Household was already established, a different principle came into operation. In that case the object was to maintain the existing House, and the heir succeeded to the wife as a part of the "Familia." It was a case of inheritance, and not of marriage, in the proper sense of the term. The Household must be carried on; and the heir stood, in all respects, both as regards his duties and his rights, in the place of his predecessor. One of these duties was to raise up male issue for the House by the woman who had been specially appointed for that purpose. The marriage of the heir with the widow did not, in principle, differ from the Levir's commission. Both cases were consequences of the corporate character of the Household, and of the disregard for the individual in the desire to promote the welfare of the general body. A wife must be chosen from a different clan; but the rule, when properly construed, was not inconsistent with the other rule which prescribed the universal succession of the heir. The same principle applied also to the succession of the heiress. This also was a rule of inheritance; but as the former case suggests the Levirate, so this case suggests the reservation of the daughter's son, the *θυγατριδοῦς*. The heir took the inheritance as it stood, with all its advantages and all its encumbrances. His duty was to provide the House with a son, who should have the right to perform the *sacra* and the means of performing them. Whether the woman were maid or widow was not material. In the one case by right of selection, in the other case by right of birth, she was the proper mother of the desired son. In her case, therefore, it was not the law of exogamy, but the law of inheritance that prevailed.

The theory of Agnation.

§ 5. It is not difficult, when we have realized the nature of an archaic Household, to account for the prevalence of the system of agnation. Kinship was based, as we have seen, upon a community of worship, and not necessarily upon a community of blood. But the community of worship could be perpetuated by males only. The *sacra* were offerings made to deceased House Fathers; and they could be performed by sons, whether actual or constructive, and by no other persons. If a woman remained in the Household, she could not have a legitimate child. If she had a legitimate child, she must have passed into another Household, and another worship. No female was counted in the series of descents, because no offering was made to a female ancestor. "No sacrifice," says Menu,* "is allowed to women apart from their husbands—no religious rite, no fasting: as far only as a woman honours her lord, so far she is exalted in heaven." The Hindu,† at stated times, makes his offerings to his father, his father's father, and his father's grandfather; but he has no offering for his mother, or his mother's father, or for any person in the maternal line. It was the House Father, too, that made these offerings, and not his wife or his daughters. None but males could present the funeral repast to the Manes. None but males, therefore, could, as regards each other, be fellow partakers of the cake, or fellow givers of the water.

* v., 155.

† Menu, ix., 186.

Agnation was a consequence of the doctrine of House-worship in the male line. But what was the cause of that particular form of House-worship? Admitting the worship of the House Spirit, why was that spirit always a male, and never a female? Why, too, was the celebration of his worship always limited to males? Until an answer can be given to these questions, our explanation of the subject, although it may be true so far as it goes, is obviously incomplete. We must connect our theory with some principle of human nature, or at least with some ultimate form of Aryan belief. I do not entertain any such ambitious design as that of establishing a natural law of religious development. All that I shall endeavour to do, is to carry our inquiries a step further, and to connect this worship of males with a certain theory of archaic physiology.

The theory to which I refer is that of generation. It was, and in some countries still is, a common belief, that a child proceeds from his father alone; and that the mother supplies to it nutriment and gives it birth, but nothing more. Many of the lower races * hold that there is an intimate physical connection between father and child. They hold that what is done to the body of the one directly affects the body of the other. Hence, they infer that the food, or the exercise taken by the father, materially affects the health of the unborn, or newly-born child. When a child is born among these people, the father is always subject to numerous and severe restrictions, both as to his food and his conduct. Some tribes of cannibals have been known † to procure from their own women children by their prisoners, and to bring up these children for the shambles, like bullocks, as being the flesh and blood of their enemies. Among many tribes,

* Mr. Tylor's "Early History of Mankind," p. 298.
† Southey's "History of Brazil," vol. i., p. 218.

in various parts of the world,* in both Americas, in the West Indies, in West Africa, in the Eastern Archipelago, among the Dravidian tribes of South India, in parts of Eastern Asia, among the Basque population of Europe, the doctrine culminates in a less horrible but sufficiently grotesque form —that of the *couvade*. Of this custom, it is in this place enough to say, in the words of the widow to Sir Hudibras, that, under it—

> "Chineses go to bed,
> And lie-in in their ladies' stead."

No traces of any such custom are found, so far as I know, among any Aryan people. But although the Aryans early abandoned, if ever they entertained, any notion of a direct physical connection between father and child, they, for some purposes, held the theory of paternal generation in its full extent. "The son of a man," says Menu,† "is even as himself;" and his daughter "is closely united with his own soul." The same authority ‡ tells us that "the woman is considered, in law, as the field, and the man as the grain." Euripides uses the same metaphor when he makes Orestes defend his preference of his father's claims upon his duty to those of his mother. In the "Eumenides," in reference to the same famous case, Æschylos discusses the question at large. Klytemnestra, having murdered her husband, Agamemnon, is herself slain by her son, Orestes, as the avenger of blood. This conflict of natural and of legal duty is the subject of the drama. Orestes is pursued by the Furies, and is ultimately tried before the gods at the Areopagus. His defence is, that his mother was not of his blood; and, on this ground, judgment is given in his favour. Perhaps Justinian alludes to this theory when, in describing certain changes § made by

* See Mr. Tylor, *ubi supra*, p. 300.

† ix., 130.

‡ ix., 32.

§ Inst., ii., 13, 5.

him in the law of disherison, which placed both sexes on the same footing, he somewhat ostentatiously assigns as the reason of his reform, that each parent is equally concerned in the procreation of the race. This theory, therefore, is one upon which large bodies of men have for ages acted, and still habitually act. It was recognized in India, in Greece, and probably in Rome. If we do not find it among other Aryan nations, its absence is readily explained by the scantiness of our evidence. It is, in these circumstances, no unreasonable inference to conclude that this theory was part of the Aryan stock of beliefs. Assuming, then, the existence of this premise, we may trace the course of thought in some such direction as the following:—A male was the first founder of the House. His descendants have "the nature of the same blood" as he. They, in common, possess the same mysterious principle of life. The life-spark, so to speak, has been once kindled, and its identity, in all its transmissions, must be preserved. But the father is the life-giver. He alone transmits the life-spark which, from his father, he received. The daughter receives, indeed, the principle of life, but she cannot transmit it. She can, at most, be the medium for transmitting another, and quite different, life-spark. None but males possessed this capacity of transmission. None but males, therefore, could maintain the identity* of the

* "It appears to me, however, at least open to question, whether the continuation of existence in the person of the heir, which we now call a fiction, was not, in earlier times, stated as a solemn physical truth. It is difficult otherwise to account for the broad and general terms in which this continuation is appealed to as a fact, not only by Roman lawyers, but by lawyers of other countries. The Hindu lawyers, when discussing the rights of succession, seem to assert the physical identity of father and son, and also of father and daughter, quite as strongly; and, whenever they have to deal with a disputed question of succession, treat this identity as a self-evident truth."—*Mr. Justice Markby's Elements of Law, sect.* 552. So also, an Afghan poet, complaining of his traitorous sons, writes:—"My hand could reach them even now: But I will not destroy my own soul."—*Elphinstone's Caubul*, vol. i., p. 285.

original life-principle, or could perform the worship of which that principle was the centre. Thus, males were exclusively the lineal representatives of the founder of the kin; and as collateral kinship means only the fact that certain persons are alike lineal representatives of a common ancestor, it follows that all relationship, whether lineal or collateral, so far at least as it implied the possibility of celebrating the House-worship and the consequences of that worship, was confined exclusively to males.

CHAPTER VII.

THE NEAR KIN.

The Agnati and the Gentiles.

§ 1. Between the equal members of the same kin, Nature placed an obvious distinction. The descendants of common ancestors are usually brought more closely together in proportion to their nearness to the common stock. In ordinary circumstances the descendants of a common father have stronger associations, and acknowledge a closer tie, than the descendants of a common grandfather; and the descendants of a common grandfather than the descendants of that grandfather's grandfather. This feeling of propinquity may be indefinitely strengthened by that kind of partnership, with unlimited liability, which appears in certain forms of archaic society. But although community of property acts as a powerful cement to hold together a relation that has been already established, it is not the cause of the union. The sentiment of consanguinity exists prior to it, and independently of it. Whether the family partnership be prolonged, or whether it terminated in the death of the first House Father, or even before that event, the custom of the Aryan race has always recognized the mutual obligations of those who were nearest of kin. The associations thus formed were, however, mere subdivisions of the larger body, and were not substantive institutions. They had, as I have already said, no exclusive worship. The gens, indeed, had its special *sacra*, but a familia, as such, had none. There was, as we shall see, a difference in the character of the offerings made to the nearer and to the more remote ancestors; but the kindred Penates seem to have been comprised in the general worship of the clan. The offerings to the common ancestor probably were taken to include all his descendants who were themselves House Fathers. In this way the various sections of the kin reciprocally adored, although with the more distant form of veneration, their respective House Spirits.

The typical example of this division of the clan, as of so many others of our early institutions, is found in India. In that country the degrees of kindred, as I have already observed, were determined by the nature of the sacred rites in which the kinsmen shared. The nearer relations offered to their deceased ancestors the *pinda* or sacrificial cake. The more distant relatives made an offering of water. The former are called "Sapindas," or persons connected by the cake. The latter are called "Samanodocas," or persons connected by equal oblations of water. The relation * of the Sapindas ceases with the seventh person, that is, with the sixth degree of kindred. The relation of the Samanodocas ends only when their birth and their family name are no longer known. The Sapindas have the primary right † of inheritance to a deceased person; and failing the Sapindas, the Samanodocas succeed. In other words, all those persons are Sapindas who have a common great-grandfather or other nearer ascendant, that is, second cousins and all nearer relatives. All those persons are Samanodocas who have a common great-great-grandfather, or other more remote ascendant, that is, third cousins and all more distant relatives. In the former case, the common ancestor who marks the limit is the father's grandfather. In the latter case, it is the grandfather's grand-

* Menu, v., 60. † *Ib.*, ix., 187.

father. Thus, the Prince of Wales and the Ex-Crown Prince of Hanover are Sapindas, because they trace descent from the same great-grandfather King George III.; but their children fall into the wider circle of Samanodocas or more remote kinsmen.

A like distinction, although we are not fully acquainted with its details, existed among the Persians. The Zend Avesta incidentally notices, in an ascending scale, four classes of society, houses, kins, villages, and provinces. Taking as the social unit the house, and omitting (partly in the absence of further information, and partly as dependent probably upon local conditions) the provinces, we have the two forms, the less and the greater, the *zantu*, or kin, and the *wik*, or village. The account that Herodotus* gives of the Persian social system confirms this view. He tells us that there are many γένεα of the Persians, and he enumerates ten. "Of these, the Pasargadæ (or more correctly the Parsagadæ) are the best; and amongst them there is a φρήτρη, the Achæmenidæ, whence the kings of the Persians are born." It thus appears that the Persians consisted of a number of clans; that these larger clans contained sub-clans; that the Greek names for these divisions were respectively, γένη and φράτραι; and that the arrangement seemed to Herodotus to be in no way unusual, or to call for any special observation.

This distinction also prevailed in Greece and in Rome. The Iliad † tells us that the warriors of old time fought marshalled in their φῦλα and their φρήτραι. These terms, at a later period of Athenian political history, acquired special meanings; but when used of the primitive order of battle, they are generally acknowledged to imply combinations similar to those known to have in the like circumstances existed elsewhere. In the Odyssee ‡ we meet with what

* i., 25. † ii., 362. ‡ xv., 273.

appears to be a similar distinction expressed by the words ἔμφυλοι on the one side, and κασίγνηται τε ἔται τε on the other. In Sparta we read of the πάτραι and the ὦβαι. In the Attic orators the nearer relatives are usually called ἀγχιστεῖς, as opposed to ἐγγενεῖς. Sometimes* the contrasted terms are συγγενεῖς and γεννῆται. At Rome the Familia, or Cognatio, as in later times it was called, was long distinguished from the gens. In the Twelve Tables,† as we have already seen, the distinction between the agnates and the Gentiles appears as sharply as it does in Menu. Ulpian, too, in discussing‡ the various senses in which at different periods the word "Familia" was used, expressly notices this division. He says that Familia in one sense included all the agnates, and in another sense included all those who "*quasi a fonte quodam memoriæ*" were descended from the blood of the same remote ancestor, such as the Julian gens.

Among the northern nations a similar division may be observed. We know from Cæsar§ that the Germans occupied their lands "*secundum cognationes gentesque.*" We know from Tacitus|| that they were arranged in battle according to "*familiæ propinquitatesque.*" The difference which the great Roman writers thus described was expressed by the Germans themselves in the words, Mæg, or Sib, and Kin. The Norsemen, while they retained the word kin, appear to have called the smaller divisions frændr,¶ and to have specialized the word sib, or sif, and confined it to relatives by marriage. Among the Slavs the name for the "*Familia*" is "Bractwo," a form, apparently, of φρατρα, while the kin or clan was, at least

* See Grote's "Hist. Greece," vol. iii., p. 88, *n.*

† Tab., v., fr. 4 and 5.

‡ Dig. L. xvi., 195.

§ "De Bel. Gal.," vi., 22.

|| "Germania," c. 7.

¶ See "Cleasby-Vigfusson Icelandic Dict.," *s.vv.*

in the old language,* called Rod.† Among the Keltic nations the division was familiar. I have already cited the passage from Captain Burt, which notices this division among the Highlanders of Scotland. Among the Welsh ‡ the Aelodeu appears to have been equivalent to the Mæg, while the Kin, or Gentiles, were called Boneddigion. Among the Irish, the "Fine" was the smaller division, and those who passed its limits were included in the "clan," or "cinel."

The boundary between the Agnatio and the Gens.

§ 2. Between these distinctions thus existing throughout the Aryan nations there are, besides the mere coincidence in the division itself, other points of resemblance. Even the very names of the Indian classes find their analogues in Rome and in Greece. The Sapindas remind us of the Confarrei—the *companions*, or those who shared the holy bread—and of the original form of marriage *per confarreationem*. The Samanodocas suggest the true meaning of the ὁμογάλακτες of the Greeks. A Greek writer § of high authority tells us that the members of a γένος were called γεννῆται and ὁμογάλακτες, not that they were related by birth, but they were so called from their festal assembly. I think that the true meaning of ὁμογάλακτες in this passage is those who offer the same milk, and not those who are nourished by the same milk. The latter meaning is inadmissible—first, because it would then apply only to brothers, and there is no reason to assume any such limitation; on the contrary, the term γεννῆται implies much more distant kinsmen.

* Mr. Ralston, "Songs of Russia," p. 83.

† Thus, in a recent novel, we read that "The House (Bractwo) of Malinofski belongs to the Rody or clan of Zadora."—*Blue Roses*, p. 31.

‡ Robertson's "Scotland under her Early Kings," vol. ii., p. 322.

§ 'Οι *μετέχοντες τοῦ γένους ἐκαλοῦντο γενῆται καὶ ὁμογάλακτες, γένει μὲν ὀυ προσήκοντες, ἐκ δὲ τῆς συνόδου ὄυτω προσαγορευόμενοι.*—*Pollux* viii., 9, 111.

Second, because the degrees of kindred were counted through the male and not through the female line. Third, because the idea of relationship is expressly excluded, and the name is said to have been given ἐκ τῆς συνόδου. Further, milk was a common offering both with the Greeks and the Italians. Thus the ὁμογάλακτες correspond to the Samanodocas, just as the Sapindas find their equivalent in the Roman "Confarrei." In each case a like relation was expressed by a name denoting community of oblation, although in one country the oblation was of water, and in the other it was of milk.

There is, however, a resemblance between the practice of the various Aryan nations in this respect far more important than any of these fainter analogies. In all cases, so far as we know the facts, the smaller division merges into the larger at the same point. That point is the sixth degree of kindred. The sixth degree represents second cousins, that is, those persons who are descended from a common great-grandfather. This rule is a consequence of that other rule under which the Hindu makes his offerings, not only to his father, but to his father's father, and to his father's grandfather. As to both these rules, the Indian evidence * is precise. One kind of offering is made to the three immediate paternal ancestors; another kind of offering to their three predecessors. To this distinction, as we have seen, the rules of inheritance correspond. It is also noteworthy that the Hindu had special names for his ancestors up to his great-grandfather, but not beyond him. Thus the offering to the great-grandfather, and the priority of the second cousin in inheritance, went together. The rule at Rome was similar. I have already noticed the distinction as to the right of inheritance between the agnati and

* See Menu, iii., 216, 284; ix., 186, 187.

the Gentiles; but in Roman law * the agnates were counted up to the sixth degree—that is, they included all the male descendants of a common great-grandfather. In later times, when the principle of cognation superseded that of agnation, the Prætor, acting apparently on the principle that equity follows the law, counted the degrees of cognation in the same manner. In Athens † the right of collateral descendonts ended with second cousins, that is, the children of παῖδες ανεψιῶν were ἔξω τῆς αγχιστέιας, outside the Mæg. Among the Teutonic nations ‡ this "Sipzal," or system of relationship, had specific names up to six degrees. These names were taken from the head and the joints of the arm and hand. Head, shoulder, elbow, wrist, first finger-joint, second finger-joint, were all specific; but the seventh degree, and all subsequent thereto, are described under the general name of Nagel Kyn, or nail-kin. In the laws of the Langobards,§ to take but a single instance, it is provided that, "omnis parentela in septimum genuculum numeretur," the Mæg shall be counted up to the seventh person. So it is said in the Welsh laws, "The ancestors of a person are his father, and his grandfather, and his great-grandfather: the co-inheritors are brothers, and cousins, and second cousins." ‖ We may observe, I think, a similar rule in the difficult case of the Irish ¶ *Fine.* The ingenuity of the Brehon professors multiplied distinctions which are not found in the laws of other countries, and it is not easy distinctly to understand their writings on this subject. I venture, however, to suggest that "Fine," like Familia, was used in various

* "Inst.," iii., 6, 8.

† Hermann, "Grec. Ant.," p. 235.

‡ See Robertson's "Scotland under her Early Kings," vol. ii., p. 309.

§ Canciani, "Leg. Barb.," i., 73.

‖ "Anc. Laws of Wales," vol. ii., p. 427.

¶ See Dr. Sullivan, "Introduction to O'Curry's Lectures," i., clxiii.

senses, and included both the more limited and the wider bodies; that, of the six kinds of Fine enumerated in the Brehon laws, the first three include the *Sui heredes* and *Agnati*, and that the remaining three are subdivisions, how far practically important we cannot tell, of the Gentiles. The Geil-Fine included the fifth descent, which, if the *Ego* were not counted, brings us to the sixth degree, as in other cases. The other three Fines, taken together, extend to the seventeenth degree, at which point all traces of kinship are assumed to be lost.

I must point out, however, that there is some diversity, or apparent diversity, in the practice of the Teutonic nations. Thus the Salic law extends the parentela, or Mæg, "*usque ad sextum genuculum.*" The law of Rothar and that of the Bavarians prescribe "*usque ad* or *in septimum genuculum.*" This difference may be easily explained by supposing that the former excludes, and the latter includes, the seventh degree, or nail-kin. But the Ripuarian law and the Anglican law fix the limit, "*usque ad quintum genuculum,*" and the old Saxon Mæg ended at the fourth degree. Probably this case resembled the former one, and the "fifth knee" marked, according to this computation, the nail-kin; and the Mæg would, therefore, have terminated "*ad quartum gradum.*" If this were so, the old Mæg would have ended with first cousins, and would subsequently have been extended to include second cousins. This is the view taken by Mr. Robertson, who compares the "near kin" of the Hebrews. There is also some, although not conclusive, philological evidence, as we shall see in a subsequent chapter, in favour of this contention. But the difficulty admits, I think, of a simpler explanation. The Saxons may have commenced to count, as Grimm * hints, with first cousins—that is, the father

* "Deutsche Rechts Alt.," p. 469.

and the son were not included in the Mæg. To use the language of a different, and perhaps more familiar system, the *Sui heredes* were distinguished from the agnates, and the agnates only were reckoned in the Mæg. The whole Teutonic system would, on this supposition, be consistent in itself, and would coincide with the practice of the other Aryans.

There is thus some apparent diversity as to the precise point at which the Gentiles begin. There is a similar discrepancy as to the precise point at which they end. Generally, six degrees of lineal ascent were counted, that is, the last recognized collateral relation was the fifth cousin. Thus Menu* says "to three ancestors must water be given at their obsequies; for three is the funeral cake ordained." With this statement agrees the assertion of one of the commentators on Menu, that the Samanodocas end with the fourteenth degree. That degree means that the relatives were fifth cousins, and descended from a common third grandfather. In the Roman law the six generations, both upwards and downwards, are clearly marked, and have their appropriate names. It is sufficient here to describe the ascending members—as the grandfather, or "Avus"; the second grandfather, or "Abavus"; and the third grandfather, or "Tritavus." Beyond the Tritavus the Roman lawyers declined to proceed. All the ancestors beyond him were included† under the general term "Majores"; and all the descendants beyond the Trinepos, or third grandson, were classed as "Posteriores." To this rule some exceptions are found. The Welsh counted seven degrees—that is, they went one generation higher than the Tritavus, and thus extended their kinship as far as sixth cousins. The Irish Fine extends collaterally to the

* ix., 186.

† Dig., xxxviii., 10.

seventeenth degree, and this system, computed lineally, gives, exclusive of the seventeenth person, the same number of ascents as that which the Cymry used. We have an unexpected parallel in Greece, where Plato * described the pride that the Athenian aristocrat felt in the enumeration of his seven wealthy ancestors. It is probable that these rules were of less practical importance, and, consequently, were more liable to variation, than those which marked the boundary of the agnates. The superior limit of kinship was not, at all events, connected with the religion of the clan. There was no such distinction as regards sacrifices between any of the Samanodocas as there was between them and the Sapindas. It is not, therefore, surprising that some variations should have arisen in the practice of the various nations. Perhaps a more reasonable cause of surprise is their uniformity.

The Joint Undivided Family.

§ 3. I have now to describe another institution, which, although it may seem to have required an earlier place in these pages, I have, for reasons that will presently appear, reserved for consideration in this place. I mean that continuation of the archaic Household which is known to Indian lawyers of our day as the Joint Undivided Family. The notices of it in ancient writings are few and obscure, but modern instances are not uncommon. In some of the more remote parts of France, † far into the eighteenth century, and even within the last forty years, survivals, so to speak, of the corporate Household have been observed. There is a Swedish ‡ proverb—"it is good for brethren to dwell together"—which seems to indicate a conflict between custom and law, and a desire to retain undivided the common

* Theæt., p. 174 E. See also Hesychius, in "Wachsmuth," vol. i., p. 247.
† See M. de Laveleye's "De la Propriété," 238, *et seq.*
‡ Geijer, "Hist. of the Swedes," vol. i., p. 83.

property. But the principal living examples of the system are found among the Hindus and the Slavs. The Joint Undivided Family of modern Indian law is described by the Judicial Committee of the Privy Council * as "Joint in food, worship, and estate." Its members have a common worship, a common meal, and a common purse. On the death of the House Father, the eldest son, as a rule, succeeds to the management; and the family keeps together, generally, till the third generation. The facilities for separation are now so great, that its duration seldom exceeds, seldom indeed attains, that period. Its existence, however, shows that in the earlier law the chiefship—subject, doubtless, to some not clearly defined power of election—continued in the eldest male heir. It is rather the fact of such chiefship, than the mode of determining it, with which I am now concerned. By whatever method the new *pater familias* was ascertained, his authority, and the consequent subordination of his younger brothers, followed as of course upon his recognition. And so we can appreciate the force of Menu's † injunction, "A man shall regard his elder brother as equal to his father." In Russia,‡ the family is a kind of corporation with perpetual succession, and governed with an authority that is almost absolute by its chief, who is styled "Elder." All its property is in common. There is, as a rule, neither inheritance nor partition. The house, the garden, the implements of husbandry, the cattle, the crops, the chattels of all kinds, remain the collective property of all the members of the family. No one thinks of claiming an individual share. On the death of the House Father, the authority and the administration pass to the eldest of the Household, in some districts to the eldest son, in others

* See Moore's "Indian Appeals," vol. ii., p. 75.

† iv., 184.

‡ M. de Laveleye, "De la Propriété," p. 23.

to the eldest brother of the deceased, provided that he occupies the same house. Sometimes the members of the Household elect a new chief. If the surviving members of the Household are all under age, some relation comes to live with them, and becomes a co-proprietor.

A similar custom,* with, in some cases, the succession to the youngest, not to the eldest son, prevails among those Southern Slavic tribes that spread from the Danube to the Balkan. In an old national poem † entitled "The Judgment of Libusa," the ancient constitution of the Household is clearly laid down. Two brothers, Staglav and Hrudos, dispute over their inheritance—a contest which is described as something unnatural and monstrous. The matter was referred to Queen Libusa, whose judgment was delivered in the following terms:—"Brothers, sons of Klen, descendants of an ancient family which has arrived in this blessed country under the leadership of Tchek, after having set free three rivers: You must agree, like brothers, on the subject of your inheritance, and possess it in common, according to the holy traditions of our ancient law. The House Father governs his House, the men cultivate the land, the women make the garments. If the chief of the House dies, all his children keep the property in common, and choose a new chief, who, on the great days, presides in the council with the other House Fathers." So well have the national customs been maintained, that a learned Slavonian author ‡ observes, that, at this day, Queen Libusa might set up her throne of justice anywhere in Southern Slavonia, and pronounce, amid the applause of the village chiefs, the same judgment that, in days of old, upon the hill of Visegrad, determined the contest of the mythical brothers, Staglav and Hrudos. In these southern countries, indeed,

* Sir H. S. Maine, "The Nineteenth Century," vol. ii., p. 809.

† M. de Laveleye, *ubi supra*, p. 202. ‡ *Ib.*, 204.

the Household sovereignty is less strict, and the rule of election appears to be more common, than it is in the north. Still, whether the House Father be the eldest son as of right, or the eldest son subject to confirmation, or some agnate whose title rests upon election only, he is the House Father; and the other members of the family are subject to his authority, and are concluded by his acts. He is the administrator and the speaker of the Household. In their private affairs he governs according to the usages of the House. In public affairs, and their dealings with other Houses, he is the organ by which his Household expresses its opinion.

I pass over the notices in Greek writers of the *συσσίτιαι* or common meals, which were found in many Hellenic States. They are more likely to receive, than to afford, light, in the course of modern inquiries. But it is possible to trace in that country vestiges of such an association, and even of its struggles with a stronger system. From some observations of Aristotle, scanty indeed and obscure, but still precious, we learn that in Massalia, Ister, Heraklea, Knidos, and other cities, disturbances arose because one person only of each Household had any share in the government. "Those," he says,* "who had no share in the government ceased not to raise disputes till they were admitted to it—first the elder brothers, and then the younger also; for in some places the father and son are never in office at the same time, in others the elder and younger brother." This passage seems to point to a time when the head of the House alone took part in public business, and when all those who were in his Hand, whether they were his sons or his brothers, were bound by his acts. But it implies the continuance of the headship in the elder brother as against

* "Politics," v., 6.

the younger. We read, too, of the large increase in the number of citizens that in some places occurred, and it is not unreasonable to suppose that this change was effected by the emancipation of the younger sons. In opposition to these movements, Philolaos * is said to have made laws for the Thebans, in order that the number of the lots, that is, of the original properties, might be preserved. A similar enactment is ascribed † to Pheidon the Corinthian, "one of the oldest of legislators," as Aristotle observes. The restoration of the original lots was also a favourite object with the conservatives of Sparta. But this restoration of the lots implies, or rather means, the restoration of the system of the Joint Undivided Family. At Rome, when our knowledge of its history commences, the law of division was firmly established, and only a few hints suggest the former existence of the corporate system. We know that land was held in common, that the persons holding ‡ it were called *consortes*, or joint-lot owners, and that this tenure was different from the *condominium*, or joint ownership of later times. Further, the *actio herciscundæ familiæ*, that is, the legal mode of dividing a Household and making partition of its goods, seems to have been in early times an important part of legal business. This verb, "*herciscere*" or "*erciscere*," for both forms seem to have been used, is a later compound; and its component parts, although obsolete in the times of the classical writers, help us in the present inquiry. "*Erctum*" appears to mean § an inheritance taken as a whole, and "*ciere*" means to divide. Hence it is probable that the expression Joint Undivided Family is a sufficiently accurate translation of the old Roman "Familia ercta non cita." But when we look at the Roman doctrine

* "Politics," ii., 12. † *Ib.*, ii., 6.

‡ See the authorities cited in Smith's "Latin Dictionary," *s. v.* Consors.

§ Heineccius, "Ant. Rom.," p. 581.

of inheritance, at the "successio in universum jus quod defunctus habuit," there is no room for doubt that there are before us the remains of the law of a corporation; and if a corporation, the principle of the Joint Undivided Family must have once applied. The original corporation might at an earlier or a later period have been made to reproduce other corporations like itself, but there must have been a time in which it was undivided.

Identity of the Joint Family and the near Kin.

§ 4. We are now in a position to estimate the relation between the Household and the Clan. The household tends to expand into the clan. The clan tends to reproduce new households. Further, the point at which the household passes into the clan is fixed. It occurs in the fourth generation. The Household includes the descendants of a common great-grandfather, but goes no further. The reason for the selection of this particular point is connected with religion. Up to this point there was only one form of ancestral worship. Beyond this point a second form appeared. What was the cause of this religious difference, I cannot tell. I can only conjecture that the line of separation marks the extreme limit at which men can have any personal knowledge of their forefathers. Archaic men may have thus expressed the distinction between those whom they knew and loved, and those more shadowy ancestral forms of whom—like the poet * uninspired by the Muse—they heard merely a report, and did not know at all. But the clan, when it was once formed, was maintained by the constant reproduction, not of individuals, but of households. These households repeated the same process until they produced new or secondary clans. Thus there were two, and only two, archaic institutions. There was the

* Ἡμεῖς δὲ κλέος οἶον ἀκούεμεν οὐδέ τι ἴδμεν.—Il., ii., 486.

Household, and there was the clan. These two shaded into each other. There was an enlarged Household, and there was a smaller clan. For each of these minor forms, special names have been invented. But, in fact, neither of them was an independent institution. There was nothing but the Household and the clan, and the transition between them. The process of transition might, indeed, be viewed from different aspects. It might be regarded as the upward passage of the Household. It might be regarded as the downward passage of the clan. Still, under any aspect, it remained one and the same, its structure uniform, and its functions unchanged.

There has been some speculation as to the supposed sequences of these bodies, and it has been thought that the Patriarchal or Natural Family, the Joint Family, and the Village Community, mark separate stages of social development. To me these social forms appear, at least among the Aryans, to be not successive, but simultaneous. When outside of a community a new Household is formed, it is Natural Family, Joint Family, and Clan all at once. I mean that it is the only social tie which its members are supposed to recognize; and that it expands until, in its natural course, it, so to speak, bursts and forms several similar households. These related households are thenceforth called a clan. The households of which the clan consists are, or become, some larger, some smaller. To the larger households, which are on the way to become separate sub-clans, the name of Joint Family is given. The newly-formed and, therefore, smaller households are sometimes called Natural Families, by which expression is meant the presence of a living House Father and his descendants. But the latter households are corporate as well as the former; and will, in due time, become, unless they are interrupted, Joint Undivided Families. Interruption, however, may occur; and, in such cases, the Joint Family is not permitted to complete its course. This interruption generally takes place when the Household is drained of its members—that is, when the sons are emancipated and leave the Household, one only remaining to carry on the old stock. The result is, the increase of the number of smaller households in the community. In a clan, on the other hand, every clansman has not only his distant but his near kin, because he is the member both of a clan and of a Household. In due course that Household, which may at first be merely a small or so-called natural Household, grows into a large household—that is, into a Joint Undivided Family; or, as it is called in relation to the clans, a Mæg. This body, in its turn, is developed into a Kin or secondary clan. In this new clan a similar process may take place, and thus concentric circles of kinship are established.

Sir H. S. Maine * observes that "there can be no reasonable doubt that the House Community of the Slavonians is the Roman gens, the Hellenic γένος, the Celtic sept, the Teutonic kin. It is also the Joint Family of the Hindus." With this idea, as thus expressed, I cannot agree. I think that the Joint Undivided Family corresponds to the Familia, not to the Gens. I trust, however, that the difference between Sir Henry Maine and me on this subject is only verbal, and that I may claim the weight of his authority in support of my contention. He seems to use the term gens and its equivalents in a less definite sense than I do. He did not think it necessary in this case to distinguish between the near kin and the remote kin of Greece and of Rome. But that he contemplates the former and not the latter body appears from his identification of the House Community with the Joint Family of the Hindus—a body which, as I

* "The Nineteenth Century," vol. ii., p. 799.

may observe, he elsewhere rightly compares with the Agnates or Familia, and from the distinction which he draws between the Slavonic institutions and the Village Community. If we compare the Slavonic and the Indian Family with the Mæg of Western Europe by the same tests which Sir Henry Maine uses in comparing the two families with each other, we shall find that they agree in having a thoroughly ascertained common ancestor, a genuine consanguinity, a common property, and, if not a common dwelling, at least adjacent dwellings. I may add that they had a common worship, a corporate character, reciprocal rights of inheritance, of tutelage, of aid and defence. In both cases, too, there were the agnatic system, the authority of the chief, and the semi-hereditary, semi-elective, mode of appointing a new chief. It is true that the men in Western Europe ceased to inhabit a common dwelling, but this circumstance did not affect the closeness of their relation in other respects. In one point, indeed, the proof is defective. There is no direct evidence as to the time at which the Joint Undivided Family ends. Sir Henry Maine speaks of several generations. M. de Laveleye thinks there are usually three generations. But the members * in the Slavonic communities rarely exceed sixty persons. And it is elsewhere said that they vary from ten to about that number. The Highland sub-clans contained forty or fifty. These numbers are about those which, in the fourth generation, a man, his wife, and all their descendants might in favourable circumstances attain. An incidental observation of Sir Henry Maine supplies better evidence. He says † that "the Joint Family of the Hindus is that assemblage of persons who would have joined in the sacrifices at the funeral of some common ancestor, if he had died in their

* "The Nineteenth Century," vol. ii., p. 810.
† "Early History Inst.," p. 107.

life time." In other words, as I understand him, the Joint Family consists of the Sapindas. If this be so, the argument stands thus. The Slavonic House Community coincides with the Joint Family of the Hindus. That Joint Family is the Sapindas. The Sapindas, as we have seen, are the Agnates or Familia or Mæg. Therefore the Mæg and the Joint Undivided Family are one and the same institution.

The development of the Joint Family.

§ 5. I have assumed that a clan society exists, and that corporate Households are formed within the clan. In such circumstances, and apart from any question as to the beginning of society, the difference between the Joint Family and the so-called Natural Family is, that the one runs a certain definite course, and the other arises from an interruption of that course at an early period. Thus the Joint Family is the older form of the two. In the natural order of events the change is from the homogeneous to the heterogeneous, from the simple undivided family to the complex group of related Households. We consequently understand and expect the change from the Indian household to the Roman, but in ordinary circumstances a change from the Roman to the Indian would be inexplicable. There is, too, the notable fact that the differentiation proceeded only so far as the males were concerned, and did not originally affect the females. The daughters, unless they had left the Household, remained under Power; and, so far as they were concerned, the Household always continued undivided. Further, in those countries where it has been superseded, traces of the archaic system may be observed. In those countries where that system yet lingers, the process of disintegration may be seen in actual operation. There is historical evidence that, where the two systems were known to exist, the system of separation was regarded as an innovation. Nor can we feel surprise that the archaic system is little known amongst us, or that our scanty information respecting it has as yet been scarcely digested. It is from Rome and Germany that we derive our domestic law. It is from these countries, and from Athens, where the State at an early period asserted its supremacy, that our knowledge of antiquity has been mainly obtained. Partly from these causes, and partly because the older variety now vanishes when it is brought into contact with modern ideas, and still more with modern law, we have become accustomed to regard the family, in its modern form, as an institution of Nature, and coeval with it. The existence of any different form is thus almost inconceivable to us. Yet it is certain that the family, as we now know it, is not the only form of domestic relation; that it is not the earliest form; and that it is a development from a much earlier state.

It is a question of some interest to ascertain the circumstances which led to this modification in the archaic system. In the normal state of that system, the Joint Family or Mæg remained undivided until it formed a clan. Then, within the clan, the same process was continued until sub-clans were produced; and this process, so long as external circumstances were favourable, might be repeated indefinitely. Two modifications of this system, as regards its duration, are possible. One relates to the continuance of the Household, the other to its close. Either a separation of the Joint Family may take place at some period, whether it be on the death of the House Father or during his life, earlier than its natural termination. Or the Joint Family may continue for its full term; but upon its dissolution no further relation between the separating parts is recognized.

When a Joint Family, outside of a clan, coheres until a clan is formed, its function has been fulfilled. It then enters the conditions of clan life. But when, within a clan, a Household is established, there are reasons why its cohesive tendencies should be reduced. The imperative need for mutual support no longer exists. The larger body affords sufficient protection and assistance. Nor is there any religious motive to remain in the same dwelling. Menu recognizes * not only the innocence but even the advantage of separation. "Since religious duties are multiplied in separate houses, separation is legal and even laudable." The continuance of the Joint Family thus became a question of convenience, and this was in a great measure determined by the form which the clan had happened to assume. If that form were a community, the clan, as we have seen, undertook to provide for each of its members; and the son of a Household, on attaining the proper age for admission to the clan, received his allotment of public land, and was henceforth in a position to take care of himself. If the form of the clan were that of a chieftaincy, the practice was, as in a subsequent chapter I shall more fully show, to grant to each House Father a certain portion of land, out of which he was bound to maintain his relatives up to the sixth degree. In other words, the principle of the Joint Family continued to operate, and no disturbing force intervened. But, whether the separation took place sooner or later, the custom of the Household was in other respects unchanged. The Household was still a corporation, and its government was still the rule of the House Father. Many small households took, in certain circumstances, the place of a few large households, and that was all. If, however, from any cause, the relation of the several households, after their separation, were interrupted, and the formation of the clan were thus checked, the results would be different. Each Household would then be compelled to perform for itself those functions

* ix., 106.

which otherwise would have belonged to the clan. In these circumstances, all tendency to early separation would be checked, and the cohesion would continue to the end. Each Household would thus be a clan in a state of arrested development.

Thus the Joint Family and the Clan may co-exist on equal terms, or the family may be weakened while the clan is increased, or the clan may be repressed while the family continues to flourish. The two forms are rarely at their best together. There is a tendency that one should increase at the expense of the other. With these views the facts appear to coincide. "In India," says Sir H. S. Maine,* "the Joint Family and the village community are often found side by side; sometimes, indeed, bound together by complex common relations. Even there, however, it has been observed that when joint families are abundant, the village organization is weak and village communities are rare; and this is notably the case in Lower Bengal." But the most conspicuous example of the natural development of an archaic society is Russia. In that country the process has gone on for a long time, under favourable conditions and with little external interruption. There, with land in excess of the demand of its population, the village or clan continues to reproduce itself indefinitely. In these circumstances society has undergone no structural alterations. When the pressure of population in any village is felt, a swarm is thrown off, and a new village is formed, which maintains relations of filial affection with its metropolis or *mutter-dorf*. When combined action against the Eastern nomads became necessary, Russia assumed the sole form in which, with her experience, co-operation seemed possible. She appeared as a great village, governed by its chieftain

* "The Nineteenth Century," vol. ii., p. 820.

or clan father, occupying land which was common property, self-sufficing in all respects, and dealing with strangers in its corporate form. "This," says Dr. Faucher,* "is still the conception which the Russian people entertain of their State." Such a society is substantially the archaic form carried out upon a large scale. Probably a similar and not less instructive example will be found in the history of China. Probably, too, the socialistic and nihilistic agitation of which we hear in Russia is only an attempt to resist the external tendency to convert an archaic into a political society. It seems incredible that reasonable men should desire the destruction of all government; but it is not at all incredible that many persons should prefer the old system of clan society to the Imperial government of the Tsar. However this may be, the history of the Southern Slavs † is very different. With them the Joint Family has taken the place of the village. They had been subject to Mohammedan rule. The effect of this influence is easily traced. It has repressed all tendency towards independence, and consequently all Gentile development. It has not afforded, at least to its Christian subjects, that protection for person and property under which, in well-governed countries, the free action of the individual is rendered possible. It has at the same time, for its own convenience in fiscal and other matters, encouraged the formation of smaller associations, just as in the middle ages associations of villeins were encouraged on the feudal estates. The Mohammedan government seems to have been well contrived for purposes of repression. It was good enough to maintain a fair amount of peace. It was bad enough to check all economic advancement. Thus the Southern Slav—prevented from expanding, secured from

* "Cobden Club Essays," vol. i., p. 358.

† See Sir H. S. Maine, *ubi supra*, p. 798.

the dangers, both of war and of peace, that usually beset archaic societies, excluded from the benefits of a political organization, yet required to maintain some collective character—retained the form of the Joint Family, because, by external disturbing forces, the natural course of its development was interrupted.

The proprietary rights of its members.

§ 6. It is difficult to give an adequate description of the Joint Family or Mæg without some reference to its proprietary relations. This subject, however, requires full and separate treatment. While, therefore, I must reserve to another chapter the consideration of the evidence, I may in this place venture, by way of anticipation, to present a summary of the conclusions at which, upon this subject, I have arrived. The settlement of Europe was made by clans. Each clan occupied a certain territory—much, I suppose, as an Australian squatter takes up new country. The land thus occupied was allotted by metes and bounds to each branch of the clan; the remainder, if any, continuing the property of the clan. Each branch thus set up, as it were, for itself, and dealt with its own members as if it were an independent community. It distributed to each Household, according to the number of adult males therein, an allotment of arable land. To this allotment certain grazing and other rights on the other parts of the property of the branch clan were appurtenant. The Household cultivated this land in common, and for their common advantage. If an adult member died, the allotment was reduced by his share. If an adult male member were added, either by adoption or by a boy being admitted as of full age to the clan, he, or the Household for him, became entitled to a further proportionate share from the public estate. When a division of the property of the Household took place, each member received an equal share, but the shares were calculated *per stirpes* and not *per capita.* That is, each person in respect of whom a portion of land had been received was, for the purpose of distribution, reckoned a member. But the young man who had not been admitted into the clan and still remained in his father's Hand—the *knecht,* or *knabe,* or *sven,* for by these among other names he was called—succeeded to his father's share, or if he was one of several such sons, to a share of that share. His elder brothers, however, for whom provision had already been made, and who had left their father's hearth, had no portion of the inheritance. While the Household held together, the property was, in effect, vested in the House Father in trust for the joint benefit of himself and his companions. Each person, as he married, received a separate house and *lararium:* but the land was cultivated by their common labour, and its proceeds went into the common purse. The general management rested with the House Father. He, according to the customs of the family, could assign the separate severalties, if any, and from time to time alter their distribution. He was bound to provide maintenance for each member, if he needed it, from the common fund. When the limits of the *Mæg* were reached, the retiring members of the family, if I may so call them, were entitled to receive for their separate use a final share of the Household estate, and to commence each for himself the foundation of a separate family. If such a man died childless, his lot reverted to the Household from which he had received it. If a Household became extinct, that is, if a man died without either children or near kin, its territory went back to the clan.

CHAPTER VIII.

THE DISTINCTION OF RANKS IN THE CLAN.

The division of the Free Population.

§ 1. THE clan was, as we have seen, built up of separate though related Households, in each of which were various degrees of rank. The whole must exhibit the character of its component parts, and, consequently, traces of these differences may be expected in the composite body. As the Household had its House Father, his sons, and his dependents, so these several classes find their place in that aggregation of Households which is called the clan. There is the Clan Father or chief; there are his relatives, according to their respective degrees of nearness; and there are the outsiders, or the inferior population. Thus, a sort of double aristocracy presents itself. The House Fathers formed a privileged class as against the unenfranchised members of their respective Households; and the whole body of the race, the Patricians as distinguished from the Patres, formed an aristocracy as compared with their freedmen or other dependents, or with the metics or strangers that sojourned among them, or with the alien population that were permitted, on terms more or less hard, to cultivate their lands.

The Irish language has special terms to denote these various relations. "Cinél," or, as the Welsh called it, "Ceneal," comprised * "the several Houses deriving from

* Dr. Sullivan's "Introduction to O'Curry's Lectures," vol. i., p. lxxviii.

a common ancestor or head," that is, the men of pure descent. "Cland or clann," that is, "the children," included both the "cinél" and also their clients and retainers. A similar distinction is expressed in the Roman phrases,* *habere gentem* and *in gente esse*, expressions somewhat similar to the more familiar distinctions between *servire servitutem* and *in servitute esse*, and between *possidere* and *in possessione esse*.†

These distinctions are sufficiently clear; but there is another distinction, which, though not less important, is less readily intelligible. Among the members of the clan itself, within the "cinél," in the strict sense of the term, and apart from the exceptional privileges of the royal house, there was a well-marked difference. That difference was between the noble and the free, or, as it may otherwise be expressed, between gentle and simple. Both classes were equally members of the clan, and, to a certain extent, had equal rights. But both by public opinion, and by the custom which supplied the place of law, certain sections of the community possessed, in comparison with other sections thereof, an acknowledged superiority. Their descent was purer; their wealth was greater; their wer-geld was higher; their share in the public lands, or in the distribution of booty, was larger; they were the natural leaders of the community in war, and its natural councillors in peace. Accordingly, we observe in the early history of all the Aryan nations the presence of what may be called a natural aristocracy as the leaders and the kinsmen of a natural democracy.

It is in Greece and in Germany that this division is most conspicuous. Every reader of the "Iliad" is familiar with the broad line which separates the kings and heroes of kin to Zeus from their followers. In the "Odyssee," too,

* See Heineccius, "Ant. Rom.," Muhlenberg's note, p. 480.

† Mr. Poste's "Gaius," p. 641.

the princes and the sceptred kings are carefully distinguished from the ordinary freemen. Among the continental Teutons there are the Adeling and the Friling: among our own ancestors, the Eorl and the Ceorl. To these correspond the Primus Mediocris and Minor of the Burgundians and of the Alemanni, and the Holdr and the Odel Bondr of the Norsemen. But the other nations also exhibit similar phenomena. I do not speak of the Populus and the Plebs, for that great division may be placed in a class different from that we are now considering. But the Roman analogues appear in the *Ingenuus*, in the old sense of the word, and the *Liber;* or, in a different aspect, in the *Adsiduus* and the *Proletarius* of the Twelve Tables. In India, setting apart the Brahmans as a literary or professional class, and taking the Sudras as an inferior and conquered population, there are * the Kshatriyas or nobility, and beneath them the Veisyas or free cultivators. The Zend Avesta speaks of the *Qaetas* or owners of the land, with their attendant friends, and the *Verizenas* or actual workers of the soil. In other passages of the same work, the Atharvas appear to occupy † a position similar to that of the Brahmans; while the "Rathaestras" and the "Vastrya-fshuyans" correspond to the Kshatriyas and the Veisyas respectively. Perhaps the Avesta ‡ indicates a similar distinction in the different consequences of giving bad food to the owner of a noble house, and to the owner of a middling house. Among the Kelts a like division prevailed. The Irish had their *Flaths* and their *Bo-aires.* The Welsh had their *Brcyr* and their *Boneddigion.* The Highland distinction § between the Duine Uasals and the

* See Dr. Muir's "Sanscrit Texts," vol. i., p. 292.

† *Ib.*, vol. i., p. 293; vol. ii., p. 454.

‡ Spiegel's "Avesta," by Bleeck, vol. i., p. 105.

§ Robertson's "Scotland Under her Early Kings," vol. ii., p. 303; vol. i., p. 237.

ordinary clansman is well known. Even in the case of the Slavs,* who now show this difference the least among all the Aryan nations, there seems reason to suppose that, before the levelling force of the Tatar invasion, they resembled in this respect their brethren in Western Europe.

§ 2. I have next to inquire into the cause of this wide-spread distinction. It is not difficult to understand that some Households should be more prosperous, more numerous, and more wealthy than others. Yet these advantages are rather the effects than the causes of such a difference as that which we are considering. Even if there were no evidence that, in at least certain societies, land was distributed according to the rank of its holders, they are inadequate to explain all the facts of the case. They may account for the differences in modern society, where individuals rise and fall with a rapidity foreign to archaic nations. But they do not explain the strongly marked lines, so difficult, if not impossible, to cross, which intersected the society of the ancient world. The preceding inquiries into the structure of archaic society point, for the cause of this difference, to some sentiment connected with the peculiar religion of our forefathers, and consequently affecting their descent. The facts correspond to this expectation. A certain series of pure descents was sufficient to establish freedom and a share in the government of the community, and in the distribution of its lands; but another and a larger series was necessary for the full enjoyment of all the honours and all the consideration that the community could give. A minimum of four degrees of kinship, traced collaterally, secured to a man the protection and support

The causes of Nobility.

* Robertson's "Essays," p. xliii.

which a *Mæg* or *Sipsceaft* was able to afford. This meant two generations in lineal succession, or, including the person himself, three descents. But even the Mægman—much less the man who, from whatever cause, failed to attain his *Mægthum*—was not the foremost in his community. That place was reserved for those who could trace their Mæg three times: who not only themselves had their free grandfather, but whose grandfather and whose grandfather's grandfather had severally their Mæg. Thus freedom, and the practical rules as to the succession to property, and as to the wardship of women and of minors, were determined by collateral kinship; but lineal descent was the test of nobility. The man who could trace his six uninterrupted degrees of unsullied lineage was not merely free-born, but full-born. His birth entitled him to land and office; but neither land nor office, even if they could be otherwise acquired, could compensate for any deficiency in his birth.

This rule of nobility seems to be the result of two other rules. One is that fundamental principle which I have already noticed, of taking the common great-grandfather as the stock, or founder, of the Joint Family or Mæg. The other is a rule which, in the present chapter, I shall more particularly consider, known as the custom of the Three Descents. The effect of this latter rule was that, for the purpose of acquiring full rank in any particular status, the claimant must show that his father and both his grandfathers had held that status. Consequently, a man who claimed to belong to the nobility of his clan must show that his grandfather was noble—that is, that his grandfather had a kin, or in other words, had a great-great-grandfather who was a freeman. Therefore, a nobleman must trace, at least, five ancestors—that is, must be the sixth in lineal succession of freedom. I have already mentioned the double set of three ancestors in India and in

Rome, and the still more extended pedigrees of the Greeks and of the Kelts. But, however strong the probability may be, direct evidence has hitherto been wanting to establish that the completion of such a pedigree was essential to nobility. I think that the uniting link is supplied by the Athenian practice. An old writer * states that "the Thesmothetæ are Eupatrids, διὰ τεττάρων." That is, it was not sufficient that a candidate for the office of Thesmothete should be himself a Eupatrid, but his father and his mother, and both his grandfathers must also have been Eupatrids. But the position of a Eupatrid implies, as we have seen, the presence not only of a near kin, but of a full or remote kin; and as the near kin terminated at second cousins, the full kin implies an additional step—that is, it requires a minimum of four lineal descents. If, therefore, the grandfather of the candidate was a Eupatrid, and if a Eupatrid was a man who could show his grandfather's grandfather, it follows that the candidate himself must have been required to prove his third grandfather—that is, to name his Tritavus. At Rome, again, all the elements of the case exist. The Tritavus was known to the law: every Patrician had a gens. The rule of the Three Descents was, as I shall presently show, recognized. It is not, then, an unreasonable inference that the test of nobility was the same in Rome as it was in Athens. In modern times † the system of heraldic quarterings, once a matter of great practical importance, indicates the existence in Western Europe of a similar practice. The latest actual example of the rule seems to be that of the Norsemen. Among these people, the sixth inheritor of an Odel property was an Odel Bondr; but it was only the sixth inheritor of such a property, who could trace his descent

* See Hermann, "Grec. Ant.," p. 297.

† Robertson's "Scotland Under her Early Kings," vol. ii., pp. 321, 323.

through the maternal as well as the paternal side, that was perfect in his generations and so entitled to rank as an Holdr.

The Chieftaincy.

§ 3. In this nobility there were degrees. There was one branch nobler than the noble, and in the nobler branch there was one person noblest of all. Amongst all his clan the chief stood proudly eminent. Their nobility, indeed, was not due either to his favour or to any popular grant. It was the result of birth alone. The clansmen were their chief's brothers * and kindred. He was their chief, their acknowledged senior and first man, but in no sense their master, or the source of their honours or of their wealth. He was their natural leader in war, he was the natural arbitrator of their disputes in peace. Above all, he was charged with the care of the Gentile worship. This last function, indeed, was that which was specially characteristic of archaic royalty. Generals might be chosen for special services, if occasion so required. Judicial business, if archaic proceedings deserve that name, might be transacted before officers appointed for the purpose. But the worship of the *Gens*, like the worship of the Household, required the services of a particular celebrant. That celebrant should be the heir of the Eponym—that is, he ought in strictness to be the eldest male, or the representative of the eldest male, of the eldest branch. Thus, Mr. Lyall † assures us that, in "Rajpútána, the chief is supposed to be the nearest legitimate descendant, in direct line, from the founder of the State, according to the genealogy of the tribe; and the heads of the branches from this main stock are the leading Rajpút nobles, the pillars of the State." Such were those hereditary kings with definite prerogatives,

* Tod's "Rajasthan," vol. i., p. 198.

† "Edin. Review," cxliv., p. 183.

of whom Thucydides and Aristotle speak. Such were the Highland and the Irish chiefs. Such were the kings whom the Teutons chose by reason of their nobility, while they chose their generals, or herzogs, for their valour. Such are, at this day, the Rajas of Jodhpoor and Jeypoor. "In the actual condition," says Mr. Lyall,* "of the Rajpút clan society, with its tribal chief at the head of a cluster of families and sub-families, each having a separate representative, we find . . . . the conception of an aristocracy deriving from blood alone, the families being noble according to the degree of the nearness of their consanguinity with the pure blood of their chief, and nobility depending entirely upon a man's position in his own clan; while, outside of all the clans, there is no nobility at all."

In all large genealogical communities amongst the Aryan nations there was a clan to which the royal dignity was exclusively attached, although, within the limits of that clan, the right of election was more or less freely exercised. Such, among the Persians,† was the great clan of the Achæmenidæ, to which King Darius, in the Behistun inscription, boasts that he belonged. Such, in the view of Homer, were the Pelopidæ in Greece and the Dardanidæ in Troy; and such, in post-Homeric times, was the illustrious race of the Herakleidæ. We read in Herodotus,‡ to take but a few of the less familiar examples, of the royal tribe of the Kimmerians, and of the Herakleid kings of the Scyths; of the Herakleids and of the Mermnadæ in Lydia, of the Battiadæ of Kyrenê, and of the Aleuadæ of Larissa. Multitudes of other examples have been collected§ by writers on Grecian antiquities. Of Ireland, Dr. Sullivan ||

* "Edin. Review," p. 191. † Herodotus, i., 125

‡ i., 7; iv., 10, 11, 150.

§ See Wachsmuth, "Hist. Ant. of Greece," vol. i., p. 225.

|| "Introduction to O'Curry's Lectures," vol. i., p. ccxxxii.

thus writes:—"The descendants and relations of a king formed an exclusively royal class, analogous to the Anglo-Saxon Athelings or Clitones, the descendants of Woden, and the Bavarian Agilofings. The story told by Tacitus of the Cherusci sending to Italy for a Romanized Cheruscan, after the extinction of all the members of the royal family at home, may be paralleled by similar instances of a strict adhesion to the royal line in Ireland." Among Teutonic nations this practice * seems to be universal. All the reigning families in Northern Europe—Anglican, Saxon, Dane, and Norwegian—traced their descent from Odin. Among the Ostrogoths the clan of the Amali was pre-eminent; among the Visigoths, the Balthæ; among the Bavarians, the Agilofings; among the Franks, the Merwings; among the Vandals, the Asdings; among the Lombards, the Gungings and the Lithings. Among the Indian clans of the present day, the royal houses, as we might expect, are carefully defined. Thus, to take but a single instance, the Rana of the Rajpúts † must belong to the Sesodia *Sacha* of the Gehlote *Kula* of the Sooryavansas.

I have said that the Genius of the Founder became the Lar of the Household. The same principle continued to operate when the Household had expanded into the clan. This spirit was in some way supposed to dwell in the House Father or the Clan Father for the time being. That chief continued upon earth the existence of the sainted Genarch. How long this belief actually continued, or whether it ever were practically driven out by beliefs that logically were inconsistent with it, it is hard to tell. At all events, the sentiment which it had generated remained unchanged. We may thus, to some extent, comprehend the deep feeling of devotion with which the son regarded his father and the

* Prof. Stubbs's "Const. Hist. of England," vol. i., p. 142.
† See Tod's "Rajasthan," vol. i., p. 82, *et seq.*

clansman his chief. "A father," says an old Slavonic maxim,* "is like an earthly god to his son." "The ordinary Highlanders," says Captain Burt † in 1730, "esteem it the most sublime degree of virtue to love their chief, and pay him a blind obedience, although it be in opposition to the Government." I need not cite authorities in support of so well known a fact as the absolute self-abnegation of the Keltic clansman. But as a proof of its persistency I may observe that, so lately as three and a half centuries ago, this sentiment was in full force, not only among the Keltic Irish, but among the English settlers, in favour of a fugitive child who was sprung from a great Anglo-Irish line. An English officer ‡ in Ireland thus writes, in the year 1538, to his superior officer in London:—"I assure your Lordship that this English Pale, except the towns and some few of the possessioners, be so affectionate to the Geraldines, that for kindred, marriage, fostering, and adhering as followers, they covet more to see a Geraldine to reign and triumph than to see God come among them; and if they might see this young Girot's banner displayed—if they should lose half their substance, they would rejoice more at the same, than otherwise to gain great good."

A strange case of the same kind, from Rajpút history, is narrated by Colonel Tod.§ When we remember the intense superstition of the parties, and the terror which such superstition excites even in the boldest among uncultured people, the devotion of the Rajpút chief will probably be thought to deserve no mean rank among the recorded deeds of self-sacrificing heroism. Jeswunt Sing, the Raja of Marwur, a celebrated Rajpút prince, lost his senses in consequence of

* Sir H. S. Maine, "The Nineteenth Century," vol. ii., p. 801.

† Mr. Skene's "Highlanders," vol. i., p. 156.

‡ Professor Richey's "Lectures on Irish History" (2nd series), p. 115.

§ "Rajasthan," vol. ii., p. 36.

the alarming apparition of a Brahman to whom, when in life, he had given just cause of offence. "He was generally believed to be possessed with a wicked spirit, which, when exorcised, was made to say he would only depart on the self-sacrifice of a chief equal in dignity to Jeswunt. Nahur Khan, 'the tiger lord,' chief of the Koompawut clan, who led the van in all his battles, immediately offered his head in expiation for his prince; and he had no sooner expressed this loyal determination than the holy men who exorcised the spirit caused it to descend into a vessel of water, and, having waved it thrice round his head, they presented it to Nahur Khan, who drank it off, and Jeswunt's senses were instantly restored. This miraculous transfer of the ghost is implicitly believed by every chief of Rajasthan, by whom Nahur was called the 'faithful of the faithful.' Previous to dying, he called his son, and imposed on him, by the solemnity of an oath, the abjuration of the office of *Purdhan*, or hereditary Premier of Marwur, whose dignity involved such a sacrifice; and from that day the Champawuts of Ahwa succeeded the Koompawuts of Asope, who renounced the first seat on the right for that on the left of their prince."

The Custom of the Three Descents.

§ 4. Between the two extremes, the noble and the slave, there were some intermediate conditions. There was the freeman, who was below the noble. There was the freedman, who was but little above the slave. The freeman, too, was either full-born or merely free-born, as he was, or was not, a member of a Mæg. The question, to which of these classes any man belonged, was determined by his pedigree. The general rule seems to have been that a man was held to possess the full rights belonging to any condition, if his father and his grandfather, with their respective wives, had occupied the same position, although with imperfect rights. Thus, although the freedman had ceased to be a slave, and was for certain purposes free, it was not until the third generation that his grandson acquired the full rights of a free-born man. So, too, three generations of freedom were required for a full-born man—that is, a man whose Mæg, or family association, was complete. In like manner, three generations of full-born men must be completed before a gentleman was made—a man perfect in his generations, the member of a gens, or kin, or cinél, and one of the Eupatridæ of his community. Thus the minimum space between a noble and a slave was, counting inclusively, ten generations. The noble himself marked one generation, his ancestors up to and including his "Tritavus" counted six, and this "Tritavus" was the fourth in descent from the Libertus, or emancipated slave. In other words, there were before the "Tritavus" three generations of semi-freedom. Questions of descent are so perplexing to those who are not familiar with their intricacies, that I make no excuse for treating this subject in some detail.

When a slave was emancipated, he did not thereby become at once independent. Independence, indeed, so far as individuals were concerned, was in early times unknown. A man must belong to some aggregation of men, or at least to some person who did so belong. The freedman, therefore, remained in his old Household. But he had obtained promotion in it. His person was now safe. His proprietary rights were acknowledged. He was, indeed, still under the authority of the House Father; but however absolute this sovereignty might in theory be, in practice it was exercised in a very different spirit over the freedman and over the slave. But still the former slave was far below the free born. Not only was his social estimation less, but his share of the corporate property and the estimated value of his life and limb were also less. He might even, in case of misbehaviour, be reduced once more to the servile ranks. On his death, if he had no children, his property escheated to his Patronus, because, as having been a slave, he could have no agnate either near or remote by whom he might be represented. The like conditions attached to his children. The sons of the freedmen, the Libertini, lingered, to use the expressive phrase of the Roman law, in the same state of imperfect freedom as their father. It was not until the third generation that the first free-born man of the race made his appearance. He, although he did not himself possess all the rights of freedom, was capable of transmitting them. Accordingly his son, that is the fourth in descent from the freedman or emancipated slave, was both free by inheritance, and was the stock to which his free-born posterity traced their descent. Still, the free-born man was far from attaining to all the rights and privileges of perfect birth. He was free-born, but not full-born. A full-born man must have an independent family association; and for such an organization the presence of two living generations of free-born men was essential. Thus a full-born man must have at least two pure descents. His grandfather and his grandmother on each side, as well as his father and his mother, must have been free-born. As the Liber was the third in descent from the Libertus, so the Ingenuus was the third in descent from the Liber. The full Mæg or "Cognatio," as the later Roman writers call it, was thus formed, a body capable of protecting its members, and answerable jointly and severally for their misdeeds. It was upon this Mæg that the duty of waging the blood feud for a slain kinsman devolved. It was to the Mæg that the wer-geld of such a kinsman was paid. It was the Mæg of the homicide that had to make or to guarantee the proper compensation, and against every member of which, in the absence of such compensation, the avenger of blood might lawfully extend his hand.

There was, however, a further distinction. The Mægman or Ingenuus possessed, indeed, full heritable blood, and formed one of a distinct self-governing association. But he did not thereby acquire in the fullest degree all the advantages that resulted from such a position. It was not reasonable that a newly-formed Mæg should have the same power or the same importance as one which had been established for many generations. We thus arrive at a difference between full-born freemen. Mægs were older and younger. The younger Mæg stood by itself, and had within the community to which it belonged no further or other special connection. It was only an inchoate kin. But the older Mæg, that which had continued for three descents of Mægthum, expanded not only into a kin, but into a kin of a very high rank. That is to say, the full-born member of a Mæg, whose two grandfathers had been themselves Mægmen, was thereby the member of a kin, the most advanced and highest form of blood relationship with which the ancient world was acquainted. But the clansman who could reckon his six ancestors upon both sides of unblemished descent, was not only free-born, but full-born; and not only full-born, but well-born.

Historical evidence of the Three Descents.

§ 5. I now proceed to state the evidence in support of the existence of this custom of the Three Descents. The Romans had specific names for each step in the first part of the progression, Libertus, Libertinus, and Liber. It is expressly stated* that the class Libertini formerly included both the Liberti and the sons of Liberti. There is also the custom of the Fasti,† in which the names both of the father

* Suet., "Claud.," 24.

† Niebuhr, "History of Rome," vol. iii., p. 295.

and of the grandfather are recorded. Further, in a speech in Livy,* the speaker, Appius Claudius Crassus, contrasts with the men of Patrician descent the ordinary Quirite, the descendant of two free men. The Greeks had the remarkable word *τριγόνια,* which implies, in its secondary sense, fulness of the condition described; and the force of this evidence is not weakened by the fact that, in the great orators and poets, the use of the word is generally figurative. Thus Demosthenes describes an opponent as evil from the third generation; that is, he alleges that this opponent was a free citizen of Evil, and could show his "Vier ahnen" in crime. So, too, the unhappy Œdipos,† when, in his misapprehension at the cause of her alarm, he strives to encourage Iocastê to proceed with the terrible inquiry, assures her that her nobility will remain unstained, even though he should be proved thrice a slave from the third mother; that is, even though his servile state were established by lawful inheritance, and he were a slave not merely of the third, but of the fourth generation—not merely capable of transmitting slavery, but actually inheriting it as a right. In like manner, Euripides‡ speaks of a man as thrice a bastard; that is, as one in whom base descent had become hereditary. It is noteworthy, too, that Homer usually gives the names, not only of the father, but of the grandfather, of his heroes. At Athens§ it was necessary that the Archons and the Priests should prove their descent as citizens for three generations. So, too, Strabo‖ states that among the Massiliots three generations were necessary to qualify

* An hoc, si Claudiæ familiæ non sim nec ex patricio sanguine ortus sed unus Quiritium quilibet, qui modo me duobus ingenuis ortum et vivere in libera civitate sciam, reticere possim?—vi., 40.

† Œd. Tyr., 742, 1063.

‡ Androm., 637.

§ Hermann, "Grec. Ant.," p. 296, and note (5).

‖ iv., 179 c.

a man of alien origin for admission among those who were capable of municipal honours.

Among the Gothic nations the custom of the Three Descents appears to have been universal. Among the Scandinavians,* the three gradations of the Frigiven man, his son, and the Bondr, were marked as clearly as the corresponding ranks were marked by the terms Libertus, Libertinus, and Liber, in early Rome. In the Sachsen Spiegel, the rule is laid down in precise terms:—"Si qui in quatuor suis generationibus, hoc est ex duobus avis et duobus aviis, ac patre et matre indiffamati juris est, illum in jure suo nemo infamare potest." So among the Franks, if a man was claimed as a *colonus*, and alleged in defence that he was an *ingenuus,* he had to prove that his father and his grandfather were *ingenui* on both sides. The whole system of succession to property † among these northern nations seems to have been based on this principle. Three descents of freedom were necessary to give the right of inheritance in allodial property. Three descents of military service were necessary to give the right of succession in benefices. Three descents were, in like manner, necessary to establish "native right" in the inferior classes that were attached to the soil. Among ourselves, some curious cases of survival in this matter may be noticed. In the first place, there is the old proverb, that "it takes three generations to make a gentleman." In the second place, when the order of baronets was established, it was, among other things, required that each candidate should prove that he was descended in the male line from a grandfather at least who had borne coat armour. Again, under an Act of Parliament ‡ which long regulated the subject, the test of British nationality was that a man's

* Robertson's "Scotland under her Early Kings," vol. ii., p. 322.

† *Ib.*, vol. ii., p. 313.

† 13 Geo. III., c. 21.

father and grandfather had been natural-born subjects of the Crown. I do not mean that the framers of that Act, or even the law officers of King James the First thought of, or perhaps knew anything of, the old rule of the Three Descents. But to stand on the old ways is very dear to the legal mind; and it is not unreasonable to believe that these lawyers followed in both cases the traditionary rule.

The Keltic nations also exhibit traces of a similar custom. In Cymric law, the descendant of the original *Alltud*, or stranger to the district, was, after the lapse of three generations, ranked as a "Briodwr;" and thenceforth became irremovable, and was entitled to his share in the land of the "vicinity." In Scotland, a similar rule applied to serfs, although it is possible that in this case the rule may have been introduced from England. In Ireland,* the descendants of a Bo-aire, or Ceorl, might, when they possessed land for three generations, aspire to become Flaths. So, too, a "*Fuidir* Family,† in the fourth generation—indeed, in the third, for the Daer Bothach had also right of settlement—could not be ejected from the land." That is, the third descendant was capable of transmitting heritable right, and the fourth of acquisition by virtue of such right. There is a curious application of this rule in early Irish church affairs. If a churchman left his original church and went to another, where he died, his "clan-naighe" goods were divided in certain fixed proportions between his old church and the new. "The rights of the original church," observes the learned editor‡ of the Ancient Laws of Ireland, "did not cease with the division of the clan-naighe property of its former member, but, although in a decreasing ratio, affected the similar property of the two first generations of the descendants of

* Dr. Sullivan's "Introduction to O'Curry's Lectures," vol. i., p. cix.

† *Ib.*, p. cxxi.

‡ vol. iii., p. lxix.

the deceased. It may be conjectured that the next generation would be wholly discharged from the claims of the church of their ancestors of the third generation, and that the church in whose district they resided would then be considered as their original or native church."

The importance of genealogies.

§ 6. These considerations indicate the triple distinction of the ancient free population. It consisted of freedmen, of freemen, and of nobles. The distinction rested exclusively upon blood, and could not, therefore, be removed by grant either of people or of king. By the operation of time, if there were no disturbing influence, each lower class naturally passed into the one next above it. Each step of promotion brought with it increased consideration, additional strength and influence by reason of a more numerous kindred and more extended alliances, and no small material advantage, both direct and indirect. At a later period, when the dependent portion of the Household became developed, and the Gasindschaft was established, other varieties of rank arose. Nobility was then derived, not from birth, but from official position and attendance upon the throne. But, even in these circumstances, native right—the right of a beneficial interest in the public land that the chief held and distributed—was determined by the rule of the Three Descents. The same principle, too, established the right of the lord to the personal services of his dependent. Hence the preservation of pedigrees and their accuracy—matters which now seem merely solemn trifling—were duties of urgent practical importance. They were the evidences of a man's social position at a time when social position implied much more than it now implies. Whether they were long, or whether they were short, they were alike essential, according to the nature of the case, for the establishment of rights. Writing of the Rajpúts, Colonel

Tod * tells us that "each race (*sacha*) has its *Gotra Acharya*, a genealogical creed describing the essential peculiarities, religious tenets, and pristine *locale* of the clan. Every Rajpút should be able to repeat this, though it is now confined to the family priest or genealogist." "India," says another writer,† "singularly barren of authentic historical records, has preserved, by oral tradition and with scrupulous care, the genealogy of even obscure families. In every village the *mirasi*, or bard, can repeat the names of every proprietor who has held land in the village since its founding hundreds of years before; and the proof of the correctness of the genealogy is the fact that the village lands are to-day held in the very shares which the descendants of the original founders represent." So it is said ‡ that, in Ireland, the genealogies of the royal houses "appear to have been critically examined and discussed at the general conventions of the states and provinces of Erin. When revised and approved of, they were recited at the fairs, so that they should be preserved in the memory of all, and be subject to the control of public opinion." The same care, and for a like reason, was taken as to the pedigrees of low as was taken of the pedigrees of high. In the old English and Scoto-Norman charters, the pedigrees of serfs, traced with much care, frequently occur.§ It is probable that it was in the interest of the lord, and not of the serf, that this care was taken. But whatever may have been the motive, the rule of law at that time was, that the mutual rights and duties of the parties were determined by the fact of the descent.

* "Rajasthan," vol. i., p. 82.

† Griffin's "Rajas of the Punjab," p. 451.

‡ Dr. Sullivan's "Introduction to O'Curry's Lectures," vol. i., p. ccxxxii.; see also, Sir John Davies's "Historical Tracts" (Ed. 1787), p. 258.

§ Robertson's "Scotland under her Early Kings," vol. ii., p. 314; Kemble's "Saxons in England," vol. i., p. 225.

But if pedigrees were in former days muniments of title, it was necessary that the proper chain of title should be complete and unbroken. This necessity suggests the explanation of another phenomenon of early society. We can thus appreciate, not only the importance that our forefathers attached to pedigrees, and their anxiety for their preservation, but also the extreme rigour shown towards mesalliances and to any lapse from female virtue, and the indifference with which masculine aberrations were regarded. It was not the immorality of the act that shocked our ancestors, but the blot that it might cause in the family pedigree. The restriction, therefore, did not extend beyond its cause. The apprehended danger to the House * was sternly forbidden and mercilessly punished. But the wandering loves of the men were of no interest to their archaic companions. It was upon considerations of expediency, and not upon considerations of morality, that the rules relating to the intercourse between the sexes were originally founded. Of this state of things there are two curious survivals. One is the difference in the legal consequences between adultery on the part of the husband and adultery on the part of the wife; the other is the history of the word libertine, a word which originally denoted the son of a freedman, and, afterwards, a freedman himself, but which—because the conduct of the freedman was unrestrained either by public opinion or by law—subsequently acquired its present meaning.

* Grote's "Hist. Greece," vol. ii., p. 115.

CHAPTER IX.

COMMUNITY.

The territorial relations of Clansmen.

§ 1. THE kin, or gens, or clan, was thus a body of men of common descent, so far, at least, as its principal members were concerned, and united by a common religion which was essentially commemorative of that descent. But it was something more. These kinsmen or fellow-churchmen —although the latter term now describes all too feebly the closeness of the old religious tie—were also settled on the same land, and were joint-owners of it. The primary bond of kindred union was, indeed, the community of their worship. But in addition to this tie, and dependent upon it, was the further tie to which the community of their land gave rise. The land belonged to the clan, and the clan was settled upon the land. A man was thus not a member of the clan, because he lived upon, or even owned, the land; but he lived upon the land, and had interests in it, because he was a member of the clan. This secondary tie, which survived, and even superseded, the earlier relation, was originally threefold. The clansmen lived together: they held joint interests in landed property: they managed, for certain purposes, that property in common. Thus they were at once kinsmen, neighbours, co-owners, and partners. But intimate as their connection thus was, their individuality was not lost. In the next degree of kinship after brothers the House Spirits began to differ. Uncle and nephew, much more first cousins, had no longer the same Lares.

Even brothers, when they were separated, may have had some difference of ritual. Thus, each Household had its separate worship, and, consequently, its separate hearth, its separate property, and its separate administration of that property. There were, therefore, in an archaic township two distinct classes of conditions. These conditions may, in the expressive language of the middle ages, be described the one as immunity, the other as community. In the former case, the House Father was absolutely free from all external control. So long as his Household remained, he could do what he liked with his own. Neither the community as a whole, nor any member of it, had any concern with his domestic affairs. These affairs belonged to his particular House Spirits, whose will it was his duty to ascertain and to express. No other person, therefore, ought, or wished, to intermeddle in them. Such an interference would have seemed to the archaic mind something much more serious than a mere unauthorized intrusion. It would have been an offence to the House Spirit who was thus approached by stranger hands, and would have challenged his just resentment. But outside the authority of the special House Spirit, matters were changed. There the authority of the common spirits of the clan began. The House Father was no longer independent, but was, on the contrary, bound in every act and in every forbearance by stringent rules framed in the interest of other persons. The tie between him and them, at least in secular matters, was the community of their land. But this community varied according to circumstances. There were always the community of neighbourhood and the community of joint-ownership. In other words, the clansmen always lived in the same village, and owned collectively the same territory. But the management of that land by the kinsmen, and, consequently, the conditions of their partnership, varied according to the nature of the property. Sometimes some portion of the land was required for the cultivation of cereals, or for meadow lands, or for plantations. Sometimes all these purposes were in demand; sometimes none of them. The conditions of production differed in different soils, and climate, and circumstances; and the conditions of the partnership varied accordingly. But whatever the difference in the details might be, some kind of partnership always existed; to this extent, at least, that interests in the common property were not enjoyed without reference to other proprietors, but could be used only under precise and rigorous rules.

The Land of the Clan as regards strangers.

§ 2. It was in this manner, by independent groups of men united by some personal tie, whether of blood or of religion or of both, and also occupying collectively each its own portion of land, that entire countries* were originally inhabited. The names by which we now know the great European monarchies were once mere geographical expressions, and did not denote political societies. These countries were inhabited throughout their whole extent by a multitude of small independent organized bodies, of which the boundaries of one ceased when the boundaries of another began. There was no land, whether it was cultivated or was in its natural state, that was not included within the boundaries of some community. Of course, each larger community had its sub-divisions; and the right to its own portion of land was guarded by each branch against other branches of the same clan, as carefully as the whole territory was protected from the intrusion of strangers. But the fact that a certain portion of public

* See "Einleitung zur Geschicte der Mark-Hof-Dorf-und Stadt-Verfassung und der offentlichen Gewalt."—Von Georg Ludwig Von Maurer. Sect. 3.

land had not been granted to any such sub-division, raised no presumption of its abandonment. It remained, as before, a part of the original patrimony of the whole community.

Thus a question was lately raised in India as to the extent of waste land in that country. The answer* in effect was, that there was no waste land in India, none at least in the sense with which we are familiar when we speak of the waste lands of the Crown. Of uncultivated land there is abundance; but, with some trifling exceptions, the entire country is appropriated and is divided among the different village communities. These local bodies, as we should call them, whether they be communities or clans under chieftains, are entirely independent. None of them admits any right cf any other to control its conduct. "Every State," Colonel Tod † writes of the Rajpúts, "presents the picture of so many hundred or thousand minute republics without any connection with each other, giving allegiance and rent to a prince who neither legislates for them nor even forms a police for them." What is still true of India, was once true of the most famous communities of Europe. To take but a single instance, Mr. Kemble, ‡ in describing early England, observes that "the country was covered with a net-work of communities, the principle of whose being was separation as regarded each other, the most intimate union as respected the individual members of each."

As to the size of these primary cells of the political organism, there was nothing even like uniformity. Some of the old German marks were very large. Others, again, contain only some hundred, or perhaps some thousand acres. Mommsen calculates that the original *Ager Romanus* comprised, at the utmost, 115 square miles, that is 73,600 acres;

* Sir H. S. Maine, "Vill. Com.," p. 121.
† "Rajasthan," vol. i., p. 495.
‡ "Saxons in England," vol. i., p. 70.

but this area included the territories of several cantons. Mr. Hunter * describes the remote district of Parikud, in Orissa, as "exhibiting an almost perfect picture of the primitive Aryan commonwealth. A Raja is at the head, and exercises unquestioned hereditary control. His domains extend over 70 square miles, divided into 54 communities of agriculturists, whose homesteads, 900 in number, cluster together into villages; each village having a perfectly defined extent of land attached to it. In these rural communes the distinctions of caste are rigidly preserved, and the gods are worshipped according to the ancient rites." This statement gives a territory of 44,800 acres which forms the original mark, containing 54 separate and kindred marks. The average size of each of these smaller marks is about 830 acres, and the average number of houses in each village is about 17. Such was the Patria of the Romans, the Ethel of our ancestors, the true Fatherland that held all that was dear to its sons. How deeply rooted in the popular mind was this form of society, we may judge from its persistency. Thucydides describes the grief of the Attic peasants, long after the political integration of Athens, when they were forced to abandon their villages, and to take refuge from the invading Spartans within the walls of the city. The Gás, or political divisions of England before the consolidation of the Monarchy, have long ago disappeared, and left not a trace behind them. But the marks, which were a natural † and not an artificial division, retained their individuality under every change that has befallen our race. To this day traces of the old marks may be found in most of the countries of continental Europe. For India I will repeat an often cited extract from the writings ‡ of

* "Orissa," vol. i., p. 32.

† Kemble's "Saxons in England," vol. i., p. 81.

‡ Elphinstone's "History of India," p. 64, citing Sir C. Metcalfe.

a great Indian statesman, approved and confirmed by the experience of another not less eminent authority:—"The village communities are little republics, having nearly everything they can want within themselves, and almost independent of any foreign relations. They seem to last where nothing else lasts. Dynasty after dynasty tumbles down: revolution succeeds to revolution. Hindu, Pathan, Mogul, Mahratta, Sik, English, are all masters in turn; but the village community remains the same. In times of trouble they arm and fortify themselves: a hostile army passes through the country; the village communities collect their cattle within their walls, and let the enemy pass unprovoked. If plunder and devastation be directed against themselves, and the force employed be irresistible, they flee to friendly villages at a distance; but when the storm has passed over, they return and resume their occupations. If a country remain for a series of years the scene of continued pillage and massacre, so that the villages cannot be inhabited, the scattered villagers, nevertheless, return whenever the power of peaceable possession revives. A generation may pass away, but the succeeding generation will return. The sons will take the places of the fathers; the same site for the village, the same positions for the houses, the same lands, will be re-occupied by the descendants of those who were driven out when the village was depopulated: and it is not a trifling matter which will drive them out, for they will often maintain their post through times of disturbance and convulsion, and acquire strength sufficient to resist pillage and oppression with success."

The Land of the Clan as between Clansmen.

§ 3. As between members of the same clan, land was held not as each man thought fit to occupy it, but according to certain definite rules. But, in the distribution of its land, the clan did not deal directly with the individual or even with the Household. If there were a people, that is, a combination of several clans, each clan received its grant. If there were merely a single clan, it made its grants to its several sub-clans. The latter bodies dealt with their respective households. Thus the land of the whole community was divided into portions of suitable size; and these portions were assigned to the several branches, sub-clans, or villages. This assignment was, according to the ancient practice, regarded as temporary; and a redistribution of lands took place at certain intervals, with the object of establishing equality in their respective shares. Each village, upon the assignment to it of its share, proceeded to distribute its proper share to every Household, according to its rank. The chief received the largest share; the clansman who was perfect in his generations received more than the ordinary freeman. Such was the mode in which, in Cæsar's * time, their lands were distributed, *gentibus cognationibusque*, to the Cyns and the Mægs of the Germans. Such was the mode † in which the first settlers in New England organized themselves. Such, at this day, is the mode in which the Afghan clans ‡ distribute and redistribute their lands.

A well known passage of Tacitus,§ which has given rise to much controversy, thus finds its explanation. Writing of the early Germans, the historian says—"Agri pro numero cultorum ab universis in vicos occupantur, quos mox inter se secundum dignationem partiuntur. Facilitatem partiendi camporum spatia præbent. Arva per annos mutant; et superest ager." For the words "*in vicos*"

* "De Bell. Gall.," vi. 22.

† Sir H. S. Maine, "Vill. Com.," p. 201. Merivale's "Colonization," p. 96.

‡ Elphinstone's "Caubul," vol. ii., p. 15.

§ "Germania," c. 26.

some editions read "*in vices.*" On critical grounds this lection is objectionable.* According to the text above given, the passage seems to suggest some important inferences. In the first place, the occupation of the land was collective, *ab universis*—that is, the whole land was the property of the entire community. Secondly, the land was occupied *in vicos*, so as to form villages—that is, as Cæsar tells us, by Cyns and Mægs. Thirdly, the quantity of land granted to each Mæg was proportioned to the number of households which that Mæg contained. Fourthly, after the grant had been made (*mox*), the Cyn or Mæg which had received it proceeded to distribute it among its households, according to their recognized Gentile rank. Fifthly, the great extent of available land gave facilities for distribution. Thus the Mægs are able to take up new ground for cultivation every year, and still the community has land to spare.

The actual use of the land by the householders of each Mæg was regulated by definite usages. These usages may be briefly stated. The whole land was divided into three parts—town lands, arable lands, and pasture lands. To these was, in some cases, added a fourth division—namely, meadow lands. Within the limits of the town or village all the kinsmen dwelt. Each habitation was separated, and was surrounded by its own enclosure. Each Household had, in absolute property, its own hearth, and the area that was requisite for its dwelling and its yard. It was further entitled to its due share of the arable land of the community, as the usages of the clan might from time to time determine. It was also entitled to its share of the grass and other natural products of the pasture lands. Thus, to use the language of our own legal system, every

* See Ritter's Note *ad locum*.

House Father held his house and garden in fee; was entitled, subject to certain reservations, to a lease renewable for ever—for one, three, or four years, as the case might be, of a shifting portion of the arable land; and was also entitled to certain rights of common appurtenant, and other similar rights in the waste land of the community.

These various rights, and the duties that they imply, were regarded as forming parts of a whole. Each right depended upon the other. It was not that one man had a right to a house and yard, another to a share in the cultivated land, and a third to a given amount of grazing. But the owner of the house, or, rather, the family of which he was for the time being the organ, was entitled to a definite share in each part of the common property. That share was called *κλῆρος*, or sors, or loos, or ethel, or alod—terms which always indicate an aggregate of rights and duties in regard to the patrimony. This aggregate the Northmen called *Tompt*, or, as we retain the word, Toft, and the Germans, among many other names, *Pflug*. Whatever variety of names may have been used, the fact itself is clear. There is an old maxim of Germanic law * which declares that "the tompt is the mother of the field." The house determines the share of the field; the field determines the share of the pasture; the pasture determines the share of the forest; the forest determines the share of the rushes to thatch the roof; and the rushes determine the share of the water for the nets. In old documents,† separate *mansi*, in different villages, each with its proper accessory rights, are expressly declared to be respectively an *integritas* or independent whole. It is certain that the two *jugera*, the customary allotment of the Romans, although somewhat larger than the courts of the Teutonic dwellings, were by

* Grimm, "Deutsche Rechts Alterthumer," p. 539.

† Von Maurer's "Einleitung," sect. 57.

themselves insufficient * to maintain a Household. It is only on the assumption that this allotment was the representative of other subsidiary rights that we can regard the statements of the Roman historians as coming within the limits of physical possibility. Our own law,† too, preserves, in the doctrines of common appurtenant and common *pur vicinage*, some curious relics of this mutual dependence of rights. In the former case, the right of the commoner to depasture his stock in the summer was limited by the number of stock that he could maintain during winter, a number which was necessarily regulated by the extent of his farm buildings and the produce of his cultivated land. The latter form is substantially the result of commonable rights over lands for certain purposes held as separate property. But the law carefully distinguished between rights of common of pasture which arise out of some other holding and are incident thereto, and rights of pasture in gross which result from an ordinary agreement between parties in respect to grazing.

§ 4. The town was simply a collection of houses, and not in any way a corporate body or independent existence. It was not the basis of the community, but merely that portion of the clan's land which was used for purposes of residence. In addition to the several houses and their respective gardens, it contained lines of streets giving access to the various dwellings. It contained also a public space in which meetings were held, and public business transacted. It was surrounded by a wall, or a hedge, or some similar enclosure. Within it, or near to it, was the stronghold, a place more or less fortified, in which the inhabitants might find shelter in time of need. Sometimes, though not as it

The Township and its Houses.

* Mommsen, "Hist. Rome," vol. i., p. 194, *note*.
† See Cruise's "Digest," Title xxiii.

seems necessarily, the sacred places of the clan were within this fortress. The houses stood each in its separate enclosure. No buildings were erected with party walls. No person was even allowed to build or to cultivate up to the very edge of his land, but a space * of at least two feet was left for eaves-drip, or, as the Twelve Tables call it, *Ambitus.* In later times, however, when towns, in the modern sense of the term, grew up, and space under the pressure of population became valuable, this rule seems to have been relaxed. Each enclosure had, like the village, its separate hedge or other fence. The Greek classical writers call this enclosure ἕρκος. The same word occurs in Roman authors, under the form *herctum,* and with the like meaning. Tacitus notes the existence of the custom among the Germans, who called the space surrounding the house *hof* or *curt.* Among the Northmen it was known as the *toft;* in the Brehon laws, where it is the subject of much minute legislation, it is styled *Maighin.* In Russia it still exists as *Isba.* In India the same phenomenon also survives, with an additional peculiarity. In that country not only the precinct, and its inviolability, continue, but also an extraordinary secrecy of domestic life, a secrecy which is said to be maintained even by people in very humble circumstances, and in conditions of the utmost difficulty. It is probable, as Sir Henry Maine † observes, that this custom of secrecy will explain much that seems strange to us in primitive society. But it receives its own explanation in that separate character of the Household worship to which I have already adverted. Everything done in the house or its precinct was private because it was holy: and it was holy because it was under the care of its own especial House Spirit.

There is little room for doubt that the sanctity which,

* See Kemble's "Saxons," vol. i., p. 45.

† "Village Communities," p. 115.

as I have shown, belonged to the hearth, extended to the enclosure within which that hearth was erected. The House Spirits that guarded the one guarded also the other. The Greek poets speak of the ἱερον ἕρκος, the same epithet qualifying the enclosure which is commonly used to qualify the hearth, whether domestic or public. So that when the authority of Zeus was adopted among the ordinary household gods, Ζεὺς ἑρκεῖος took his place alongside of Ζεὺς ἐφέστιος. The Greek writers translate the Latin term Penates by ἑρκεῖοι. I have already observed that Jupiter Herceus, of whom Ovid and Lucan write, was called by the Romans, Jupiter Penetralis. If, then, the enclosure were holy, that is, were under the protection of the Lares, it might be expected that the house and its precinct were descendible according to the rules which determine the succession of the House Father. This expectation is fully realized. "*In horto heredium*" was the Roman maxim. I have already noticed the strict rules of inheritance in nearly all the Aryan nations. I have also said that the inheritance included the collection of rights of whatever kind arising out of the land, that the clansman enjoyed. It was not merely that the *hortus* descended to the clan; but all the *jura in re*, or interests in and upon the common land, ran with the *hortus*, and were enjoyed by its owner.

§ 5. I have said that, so far as related to his house and its enclosure, the House Father was absolutely independent. His actions, even those which would now come under the cognizance of the State, were subject to no control. Like the Cyclopes of the poet, he there laid down the law to his wife and his children, and cared not for other men, as other men cared not for him. But outside the charmed circle his position was very different. In every single act The Arable Land.

he was bound to care, and to care very much, for other men. These others, in their turn, took a very lively interest in his proceedings. He was no longer at liberty to do what he liked with his own. On the contrary, it was his duty to do with it what the custom of the community required. He held certain rights in the arable mark—that is, in the agricultural reserve of the community; but both these rights, and the modes of his enjoyment of them, were strictly defined. Out of the public land a certain portion was set apart for purposes of cultivation. This portion was divided, somewhat like shares in a company, among all the households of the village. The size of these reserves, and of the allotments into which they were divided, varied in different places. The rules of cultivation in like manner varied according to local requirements, but in each community they were uniform.

The allotments were held subject to an elaborate code of minute regulations, of which the object * was to secure uniformity of cultivation among the several proprietors. Thus, among the Teutonic tribes, the arable mark was divided into three fields. Of these fields, one was left fallow, one was used for wheat, and one for some spring crop; but the whole of each field was, at the same time, either left fallow, or cultivated with the same kind of crop. In these circumstances, the lot of each household was divided into three parts—one for each field. Each of these parts was, from the nature of the case, at some distance from the other parts, and never formed one consolidated property. These allotments were granted for agricultural purposes, and for none other. Consequently, when the crop was removed, the rights of the commoners to the use of the soil revived. After a given day, the temporary fences were removed, and

* Sir H. S. Maine's "Vill. Com.," p. 109.

the cattle of all the clansmen* were allowed to depasture on the stubble. On the fallow field, on the baulks of land dividing the fields, and on the meadow lands after the hay harvest, the right of common pasture in like manner prevailed.

If it be asked how the original distribution of the arable mark was determined, the answer must be that it was settled at the first formation of the community. If the community were in the nature of a colony, or of the settlement of a branch or sub-clan, its portion was assigned to it by the formal act by which the colony was established or the branch was endowed. If it were an original settlement, the land was "roped out" by the elders or the chief, as the case might be, with reference, doubtless, to some custom which existed, or was assumed to exist, among the settlers, or was simply assigned by lot. Sir Henry Maine † describes the curious growth of what was practically new legislation in Indian villages, where the village authorities have been compelled to develop imaginary customs for the novel business of retailing water supplied to the community by the State, just as English judges were forced to apply the rules of the Common Law to the modern exigencies of railways or of insurance. In no circumstances, however,

* "The fields of arable land in this county (Norfolk) consist of the lands of many and divers several persons lying intermixed in many and several small parcels, so that it is not possible that any of them, without trespass to the others, can feed their cattle in their own land; and, therefore, every one doth put in their cattle to feed *promiscuè* in the open field. These words, 'to go shack,' are as much as to say, 'to go at liberty,' or 'to go at large,' in which the feeling of old times is to be observed, that the severance of fields in such small parcels to so many several persons was to avoid enclosure and to maintain tillage. . . . *Nota.*—A good resolution, which stands with reason . . . which I thought fit to be reported, because it is a general case in the said county; and, at first, the court was altogether ignorant of the nature of this common called 'shack.'"—*Sir Miles Corbet's Case*, 7 Reports, 5*a*.

† "Vill. Com.," p. 110.

do the duties and the rights of these joint purchasers of water depend, directly or indirectly, upon mutual agreement. "Authority, custom or chance," Sir Henry Maine well observes,* "are, in fact, the great sources of law in primitive communities, as we know them, and not contract." If we may rely upon the evidence of language, chance has been the prevailing power among the three great races of Western Europe. Certainly, such words as κλῆρος, sors, loos—all indicating primarily lot, and, secondarily, a portion of freehold land with its accompanying rights—point in that direction. But whatever may have been its title, the partition, when once it had been made, remained constant. The original number of lots continued unaltered, notwithstanding any changes that time may have made in their holders. Thus, in the Punjab, where the village is said † to exist in its strongest and most complete form, every villager has his share, which is generally expressed in plough lands. A plough land is not a uniform quantity of land, but a share in the particular village. There may be 64, or 128, or any other number of shares; one man has two ploughs, another a plough and a half, another half a plough, and each holds land representing his share.

Early in the present century, in Friesland, in the bailiwick of Norden and Bertum, land customs were still observed, which take us far back in the history of our race. I cite at length the following passage ‡ from the pen, it is said, of the late Sir Francis Palgrave, because it illustrates not only my present subject, but also other matters which are discussed in these pages. "The land is considered as being divided into portions or *Theels*, § each containing a stated

* "Vill. Com.," p. 110.

† Sir George Campbell, "Cobden Club Essays," vol. i., p. 156.

‡ "Ed. Rev.," vol. xxxii., p. 10.

§ "From the Frisick *Tellan*, Eng. *to till.*"

quantity: the owners are called Theel-men, or Theel-boors; but no Theel-boor can hold more than one theel in severalty. The undivided or common land, comprising the theels not held by individuals, belongs to all the inhabitants of the Theel-land, and is cultivated or farmed out on their joint account. The Theel-boor cannot sell his hereditary theel, or alienate it in any way, even to his nearest relations. On his death, it descends to his youngest son. If there are no sons, it descends to the youngest daughter under the restrictions after mentioned; and in default of issue, it reverts to the commonalty. But elder sons are not left destitute. When they are old enough to keep house, a theel is assigned to each of them, be they ever so many, out of the common lands, to be held to them and their issue, according to the customary tenure. If a woman who has inherited a theel becomes the wife of a Theel-boor, who is already in possession of a theel, then her land reverts to the commonalty, as in case of death without issue."

The Waste Land.

§ 6. I have said that the main bond of union among the clansmen, so far as their property was concerned, was neither mere neighbourhood nor the uniform system of tillage, but the joint ownership and occupation of their territory. Although of late years scholars have given to the history of the arable mark an almost exclusive attention, yet in many places where pasture and not tillage was required, no community of cultivation existed; and even among cultivating communities the waste land seems to have played no inconsiderable part in their development. From what I have already said, it follows, first, that none but members of the kin were entitled to derive any advantage from the use of the public territory; and, second, that the extent of any individual interest therein depended upon the grant of the whole community. The first proposition, indeed, may be somewhat modified. In those cases where the land had been acquired by conquest, there were generally some remains of the conquered population who retained more or less interest in the lands that were once their own. But as between the conquerors themselves, it was the clansmen, and the clansmen only, who were entitled to derive any advantage from the land that the clan had acquired. The outsiders, the men who lived with the clan but who were not of the clan, were no part of the folk, and had no share in the folcland. No services rendered, no participation in the common danger, no endurance of the burthen and heat of the day, could create in an outsider any colour of right. Nothing short of admission to the clan, and of initiation in its worship, could enable him to demand as of right the grass of a single cow, or the wood for a single fire. He was permitted to reside among the clan, and that was all. Whatever advantages he derived from that residence were matters of grace, and were neither rights nor the foundation of rights. We may perhaps derive some assistance in forming an idea of this system, which exercised so great an influence in the early world, from the curious survival of it which is at this day found * in Switzerland. In that country every commune has its separate property, and declines to admit any stranger to a share in its privileges without due consideration. Every commune, therefore, charges an entrance fee. Many communes have regular tariffs, adjusted according to market rates. Of late years, a party has arisen which seeks to remove these internal distinctions, and to allow a Switzer free right of settlement in any part of Switzerland. But this innovation is far from popular. "Vaud's communal revenues are vast, and

* Mr. Dixon's "Switzers," p. 74, *et seq.*

she imagines that revision will compel her to admit the Bernese settlers, who are very numerous in her hamlets, to a share in all these village gifts."

Among those persons who were entitled to the use of the public land, there seem to have been three principal modes of enjoyment. The land was occupied in common, subject, of course, to regulations for its reasonable use; or it was granted to some individual or some community in absolute property; or it was so granted during a term for purposes more or less restricted. The first mode was the general rule, to which special grants to individuals were the exception. Every householder* had, by virtue of his position, the right to depasture upon the public lands—subject, as I have said, to what may be called the close season of tillage or of meadows—a certain number of cattle, probably as many as he could otherwise maintain during the winter. These cattle fed together, according to their kind, each under the charge of a common herdsman. Every householder was entitled to use the common ways, and to cut wood in the public forest. He had, in like manner, the right of fishing in the public waters, and of hunting and of fowling over the public land. All these rights belonged as of course to every clansman, without any grant, and were, as I have said, appurtenant to his town lot.

It is probable that, in cases of conquest, allotments of arable land were assigned in absolute property to the conquerors and their heirs, and that the size of these grants was proportioned to the rank of the grantee. In time of peace, however, public services were sometimes rewarded by a special grant of public land. In Greece, such a grant was called τέμενος. The τέμενος occurs in Latin under the

* Von Maurer's "Einleitung," sections 67, 68.

form *templum*, a word, however, which was soon specialized. In Germany we meet with the significant terms *Sondergut* and *Sonder-eigen*, denoting arable land or forest or *hof* cut off from the public land, and carved into a separate and individual property. In England, where such lands were more frequent than on the Continent, they were called "Boc-land," or land conveyed by special grant, and not held under the ordinary custom. They seem to have originated in grants made to the Church; but the practice was afterwards extended to lay grantees, and especially, after the power of the Crown had become developed, to the Royal Thanes. Their devolution was determined either by the form of the grant or by the declaration of the original grantee; and, if he so desired, they might be subject to a kind of perpetual entail. The reason of admitting such a perpetuity was probably the desire to follow the analogy of the Ethel or primitive allotment. Boc-land was, from the nature of the case, a "conquest" or private acquisition, and so did not come within the rules which regulated the "*hereditas aviatica*," or family estate. But the analogy of that estate was readily applied to it, and the character once impressed could not by any subsequent process be effaced. When, however, the grant was made by the king alone, without the action of his great council, under whatever name that council was known, grave doubts seem to have been entertained for many centuries as to the legal effect of such a grant as regarded either the heirs of the grantee or the successor of the king. The opinion seems to have long lingered that the heir succeeded only by the assent of the grantor, and that a new king was not necessarily bound by the grants of his predecessor, and might consequently revoke them at his discretion.

A method, more usual than that of Boc-land, of creating separate interests in the waste lands was by way of tenancy.

The land still remained public property, but was occupied, with the consent of the community, by some kinsman, with or without some compensation in the form of service or rent. The tenure of such an occupier was, as regards the community, a mere tenancy at will; but as regards other persons, amounted to the full rights of ownership. Such was the *possessio* of the Roman law, a principle which had its origin in the *Publicus Ager*, first of Rome, then of Italy; and which, when the doctrine of the *Publicus Ager* was extended to the Provinces, became the basis of the law of Real Property in the greater part of Europe. The Teutonic tribes* seem to have followed a similar practice in their "gewere," a term which denoted the protection given by the community to the tenant of public land in respect of his tenancy. Such a tenancy was probably temporary in its origin; but, by a development that is almost inevitable, it grew in course of time into a hereditary right.

* Von Maurer's "Einleitung," sec. 44.

CHAPTER X.

IMMUNITY.

Indepen-dent House-holds co-existed with Com-munes.

§ 1. I HAVE hitherto described the association of freemen whose rank was equal, or but slightly different, and who lived together upon terms of equality. Outside this association there were two other forms of society. There was the Household, considered as a corporate body, without any relation to other Households. There were the relation of the Household to its inferiors, and the mutual relations of these inferiors arising from their common subordination. This independent position of the Household may be called Immunity, as opposed to the Community. It implies the possession of property, both real and personal, held by separate right, and without either the benefits or the burthens arising from association. In such circumstances, relations, unmodified by external control, necessarily arose between the House Father and his unfree dependents. These dependents might be relatives for whom, by the custom of his clan, he was bound to provide; or might be friends who lived in his house on terms of acknowledged intimacy; or might be settled as an inferior class in their own dwellings upon his land.

I do not think it can be successfully maintained, although at first sight the theory is very alluring, either that private property was evolved from communal rights, or that the modern king was a development of the Fürst or Alderman. That for the most part the immunity gradually superseded the community is certain. But I think that this result followed rather from the survival of the fittest, than from any natural process of evolution. The 'Gasindschaft,' in my opinion, arose spontaneously, side by side with the 'Gemeinde.' Its development was later; but gradually it absorbed the older and at one time more important form. The two organisms were closely connected. The one was the Household itself, under conditions favourable to its growth. The other was the development of the relations between several associated Households. It was by the advantages derived from this association, that, in many cases, the development of the independent Household became possible.

The clan, as I understand the matter, assumed one of two forms. Either the Household from which it sprung kept together, or it dispersed. In the latter case, the result was a community such as in the last chapter I described: in the former case, the result was a chieftaincy. The type of the chieftaincy was thus, of necessity, the Household; and its standard of rank was the nearness of kin to the chief. Like the House Father, the chief had the management of the corporate property. Like the House Father, he held the property, not for his exclusive use, but for the benefit of the entire body. Important practical consequences in the history of the society followed from this original difference in form. Sometimes the two systems, to some extent, co-exist even in the same society. There may be chieftaincies in the sub-clans, while the headship of the clan is in abeyance. The clans may assume the form of communities, and yet may combine in their devotion to a single chief. Of the former case, Mr. Lyall * mentions an example in Rajpútána. There the eldest branch of the

* "Edin. Review," vol. cxliv., p. 195.

great Rathore clan has sometimes assumed the form of a community—or, rather, of a number of households more or less loosely connected. It has thus failed to retain its natural headship, or even to grow into a separate power. The only use that these Rajpút Legitimists make of their birthright is to decline all obedience to a younger branch of the clan, the Raja of Jodhpoor, who is now the acknowledged political head of the Rathores. Of the opposite form, a form much more consistent with political advancement, the most remarkable example is Russia. In that country, as I have said, the type of society is the village community, or, as we might call it, the democratic clan. But every clan, and every member of every clan, whatever may be their equality among themselves, recognizes, without a limitation and without a murmur, the *Patria Potestas* of the Tsar.

Assuming the existence of an immunity—that is, of a Household, either wholly or in part, not included in any commune—it is not difficult, when it assumes any degree of importance, to predict either its character or its conditions. Its possessions must, in such a state of society as we are now supposing, consist in a rude plenty rather than wealth. In the absence of any disturbing influence, this state implies a number of persons who will consume that plenty, and sympathize with and assist the person who bestows it. Those persons will be in the hand of the House Father—that is, they will owe him allegiance and be subject to his authority. If they had previously been members of a commune, or of other households, they will abandon that position as involving rights and duties inconsistent with their present relation. But there is a second consideration. Whence does this plenty arise? Cattle must be tended, and fields must be cultivated. Abundance, at least in temperate climates, means labour; and labour is not usually agreeable to the class of men who live at other men's expense. There is no reason to suppose that the Gesiths in any Aryan people were an exception to this rule. There must, therefore, have been, under some form, a labouring population, who, upon whatever terms, supplied the wants of the House Father and his friends. I have, thus, after I have traced the rise of the immunity, to consider—but only so far as the immediate subject is concerned—first, the position of the free-born retainers; secondly, the sources of the inferior population; and, thirdly, the relation of that population to their respective superiors, especially with reference to the tenure of land.

Distinction between Inheritance and Acquisition.

§ 2. The structure of the commune affords little room for progress. The limits of its growth were soon attained; and its powers were expended, not in its own increase, but in the work of reproduction. When in a commune the pressure of population is felt, if there be vacant territory, the people form new communes *ad infinitum.* If there be any other available outlet, they seek their fortunes in that direction. If there be neither land nor outlet, population adapts itself to the exigencies of the case. The death rate increases, and the birth rate diminishes, until equilibrium is restored between the mouths and the means of feeding them. But, although the constitution of a commune is not favourable to any great increase of wealth, it generally provides means of escape from its restrictions. Under its shelter the infancy of industry is nurtured; but when the plant has taken root, it must be speedily planted out into some freer soil. It is not worth while to examine the causes which render one household in a community a little richer than another. The true point of interest is the method by which escape has become possible from the restrictions both of the Household and of the clan. This method consisted in the recognition of the difference between things * patrimonial and things not patrimonial—in other words, between inheritances and acquisitions.

At an early period of communal history, if not from its commencement, a distinction was drawn between property included in the partnership or directly derived from its funds, and property acquired by a partner in some separate operation. The property of the corporation, or the natural proceeds of that property, whatever may have been the purpose for which the association was formed, belonged, as I have said, to the corporation; but property otherwise acquired was at the disposition of the individual who owned it. If, indeed, the property were acquired by the exercise of the calling which was the ordinary business of the corporation, that property formed part of the inheritance; but if it were acquired in any other manner, the corporation had no claim upon it, except in the way of ultimate remainder. I shall now state the evidence as to the universality of this distinction—a distinction which, like several others that I have noticed, has an importance in the history of law far beyond that which in these pages I have attempted to trace.

Menu,† in reference to the Joint Undivided Family, says —"What a brother has acquired by labour or skill, without using the patrimony, he shall not give up without his assent; for it was gained by his own exertion. And if a son, by his own efforts, recover a debt which could not be recovered before by his father, he shall not, unless by his free will, put it into parcenary with his brethren, since in fact it was acquired by himself." In a case where a dispute had arisen respecting the gains of a dancing-girl,

* "Res vel in nostro patrimonio sunt vel extra nostrum patrimonium habentur."—*Gaius*, ii., 1.

† ix., 208.

the High Court of Madras * recently decided that "the ordinary gains of skill belong to the family, when this skill has been imparted at the family expense, and while receiving a family maintenance. But the case is otherwise where the skill has been imparted at the expense of others, not members of the learner's family."

In the Odyssee, we find Laertes in the possession of an estate which he had acquired by the produce of his own exertions, † and which seems to be distinct both from the ordinary share of a member of a community, and from the special estate attached to the Crown. In Sparta ‡ it was discreditable to sell any land, but the sale of the ancient lot was illegal—a distinction equivalent to that between the *Terra Alodis* and the *Terra Comparata* of the Franks. The most notable illustration of this subject in any Grecian city is found at Athens, under the legislation of Solon. Plutarch § tells us that the great Athenian lawgiver acquired reputation by reason of his law respecting wills. "For, formerly, it was not lawful to make a will, but the goods and the house must remain in the gens of the deceased person; but he (*i. e.*, Solon) permitted a man, if he had not children, to leave his property to whomsoever he wished, and thus honoured friendship more than kinship, and favour more than obligation; and made the goods ‖ to be the acquisitions of their holders." In other words, he enabled the heads of houses to deal with their hereditary property as they would have done if that property had been acquired by their own labour or their own capital. Thus alienation was facilitated, since the consents pre-

* See Sir H. S. Maine's "Early History of Institutions," p. 110.

† See Mr. Gladstone's "Homer and Homeric Age," vol. iii. p. 59.

‡ Grote's "Hist. of Greece," vol. ii., p. 556.

§ "Solon," c. 21.

‖ τὰ χρήματα κτήματα τῶν ἐχομένων ἐποίησε.

viously required were no longer necessary, and the power of testation in its modern sense became possible.

At Rome, the operation of this distinction was felt in the limitation, or rather the evasion, of the paternal power. The person *in manu*,* whether he were son or slave, could neither own nor possess anything in his own right. Whatever he acquired, he acquired for his House Father. If property were bequeathed to him, his acceptance of it depended upon the direction of his House Father. If he did accept, his possession was held to be for the use of his House Father. All the produce of his own labour in like manner went to the same ever present authority. Thus the acquisition of separate property by the son was, at least in ordinary circumstances, impossible. His House Father might allow him to use certain property, which was termed his *peculium*; but of this the son had merely the administration. The ownership, and even the possession,† were in the House Father. But there was one direction in which the authority of the House Father did not operate. That authority arose *jure privato;* but outside the House, and in the service of the State, the son was *publici juris*, and was then on an equality with his father. What the son acquired in war was not the result of any capital or skill that belonged to the Household. Besides, booty was the property not of the captor but of the State; and the son's share of it was given by the State to him, as one of its citizens, in consideration of services rendered by him in the performance of a public duty. Accordingly it was held that, so far as regarded his *peculium castrense*—that is the property he had acquired in war, a *Filius familias* was to be regarded as though he then were a *Pater familias*. By a well known fiction of law, this principle was gradually

* "Gaius," ii., 87.

† *Ib.*, iv., 148.

extended. In the case of certain civil offices and liberal professions, the *peculium* was said to be *quasi-castrense*—that is, it was dealt with as it would have been dealt with if it had been acquired by a soldier in war. Justinian * legislated directly in the case of property that came to the son by bequest or other similar means. This property was called *peculium adventitium,* and was distinguished from *peculium profectitium,* or property derived from the gift or consent of the House Father. In regard to the latter, the old law remained unaltered. In regard to the former, an estate for life was given to the House Father, but the son had a vested remainder.

With respect to the Teutonic races, it is sufficient to observe that Sir H. S. Maine † considers that it is among them that the most extensive use of this classification of property has been made. In England, the laws ‡ of Henry I. provide—"Let the eldest son succeed to his father's fee: his purchase, and all that he may have acquired, let the father bequeath to whom he will." In the assizes of Jerusalem, and in the old customary law of France, the same distinction prevails. The provisions of the Brehon law are strikingly similar. The oldest rule on the subject in that law appears to be expressed in the words—"The proper duties of one towards the tribe are, that when he has not bought he should not sell." Various modifications of this rule were at different times introduced, mainly in favour of the Church. It recognizes, however, the two principles, that the acquisitions might, and the inheritance might not, be sold. "As to acquired property," says the learned editor,§ "a distinction was drawn between the case in which the

* "Inst.," ii., 9, 1.
† "Ancient Law," p. 281.
‡ lxx., 21.
§ "Ancient Laws of Ireland," vol. iii., p. lxiv.

means of acquiring additional property arose from the industry of the owner, and the produce of the land in the ordinary course of husbandry, the power of alienation naturally being greater in the former than in the latter case. Property acquired by the exercise of an art or trade was placed in almost the same position as property the result of agriculture—two-thirds of it were alienable; but in a state of society in which the exercise of particular arts and professions were caste privileges, the profits of any such social monopoly were naturally distinguished from those acquired solely by individual ability; and, therefore, the emoluments accruing to any man by the exercise of 'the lawful profession of his tribe,' were subject to the same rights, for the benefit of the tribe to which he belonged, as ordinary tribe land."

The evidence which the Slavic nations give us on this subject is very instructive. With them the rule of the freedom of acquests has been less strictly observed than in other European countries, and with them, accordingly, the community continues in its fullest vigour. I do not mean that the rule is unknown to the Slavs. The contrary, indeed, is stated* on good authority. But the application, at least, of the rule has been strict, and the consequences of this strictness are very striking. The villagers argued, and not unreasonably, that a son of the village, who had left home with the consent of the village, and had been educated at its expense, ought not exclusively to profit by opportunities which, without the aid of the village, he could never have enjoyed, or could never have turned to account. It is, therefore, the established custom that, if any villager becomes prosperous abroad, the profits of his industry belong to the village. Further, where a particular form of

* See Mommsen, "History of Rome," vol. i., p. 75.

industry is established in a village, all orders obtained abroad by any villager are held to be orders not for himself but for his village, and the execution of them is distributed among the villagers by common consent. From this system two remarkable consequences have followed. One is, that a peasant who emigrates from his village to a city must account to the village for his earnings, or must pay to it a rent for his own labour and his own skill. The other is, that in Russia the ordinary process of the division of employments has adapted itself to the requirements of the form of society there existing, and has taken place, not individually, but by villages. Hence arises the explanation of that singular economic phenomenon—the existence of entire villages engaged exclusively in a single occupation. There are villages in Russia * in which the inhabitants make nothing but boots. There are others in which they are all smiths, or are all curriers. In others, again, they make exclusively tables and chairs, and in others earthenware. In one particular village all the inhabitants are employed in training birds, and in the bird trade. Some prosperous communities follow the lucrative occupation of begging. That is, where an Englishman follows, for his own advantage and at his own risk, a certain trade, that trade is in Russia carried on by an entire community. These trading villages are not assemblages of artisans that have become integrated, and simulate the form of a community. They are ordinary communities in which a particular industry is carried on in common. "The associations," says Baron von Haxthausen,† "are open to all, and the members are united only by the bonds of communal life." They are not artisans who are associates, but associates who have become

* Haxthausen's "Russian Empire," vol. i., pp. 16, 56, 141, 154, 190.

† *Ib.*, p. 154.

artisans. Their trade is not the foundation of their union, but merely one of its effects. Among the Southern Slavs, the same rule, although perhaps not to the same extent, appears to operate. "In Montenegro," writes Sir H. S. Maine,* "the dominant notion is that, as the community is liable for the delinquencies of its members, it is entitled to receive all the produce of their labour; and thus the fundamental rule of these communities, as of the Hindu joint families, is, that a member working or trading at a distance from the seat of the brotherhood ought to account to it for his profits. But, as in India, all sorts of exceptions to this rule tend to grow up; the most ancient, and most widely accepted, appearing to be, that property acquired by extremely dangerous adventure belongs independently to the adventurer. Thus, even in Montenegro, spoil of war is retained by the taker; and on the Adriatic coast, the profits of distant maritime trade have, from time immemorial, been reserved to sea-faring members of their brotherhoods."

The Extra-communal Household.

§ 3. When, from any cause, a family was established on its own property apart from a community, if it possessed sufficient coherence, its development might assume a non-communal form. It might prosper so as to become a considerable body; and yet the relations of its members among themselves would, for a long time, be different; and might, by proper means, be kept different from the relations which existed among members of separate but associated Households. The property of the single Household would, of course, be vested in its chief for the time being; subject, however, to certain trusts for the benefit of his relatives. These relatives were those who formed his

* "The Nineteenth Century," vol. ii., p. 805.

Agnatic, or *Mæg*. They were all entitled—not to an inheritance in the land, but to a maintenance from it, whether that maintenance was provided by the occupation of some portion of the land, or, if need were, at the personal expense of the chief. When a man's father and grandfather were so entitled, his hereditary claim was established; and, by the rule of the Three Descents, he acquired a right to a definite share in the land itself. When this right accrued, the kinsman was no longer in the *Mæg* of his chief, and fell into the position of an ordinary clansman. He was no longer an *agnatus*, but a *gentilis*. If, then, the affairs of such a society were reviewed upon the death of its chief, its continuance on the Household type might be indefinitely prolonged. The new branches that from time to time were formed recognized the primacy of the parent stock. Like adult and emancipated sons of the Household, they were freed from parental control; but they willingly accepted the paternal advice and direction. Thus, the chief of such a society was bound to maintain his kinsmen up to the degree of second cousin. His relatives beyond that degree were not entitled to maintenance. In lieu of it, they received, as it seems, in discharge of all claims, a definite allotment of land in absolute ownership; and thereupon they commenced to form, upon similar principles, a new branch of the clan. This allotment was not a mere township or building lot, but a portion of territory sufficient for the use of the entire Household, and capable of being organized in the same manner as the clan itself had been. Thus, the Mæg, or near kin of the chief, stood to him in a very close and intimate relation. They were, in a certain sense, the members of his own family; and the permanent establishment of their descendants depended upon the proof of their kinship with him. The two systems, that of a community and that of a chieftaincy, appear to have co-existed in most Aryan countries. In India, we have, on the one side, the village communities of Bengal, and, on the other side, the Rajas of the Rajpút clans. In Hellas, the Homeric kings seem to have closely resembled the Rajas and the Keltic chieftains. In Germany, Tacitus distinguishes the *gentes quæ regnantur* from the *civitates*, or communities. In England, the communities are found * in Kent and the eastern counties, while Wessex and Mercia were true kingdoms. Among the Keltic peoples the same distinction may be observed, only that the Cymry seem to have preferred the community, while the kingdom flourished among the Gael. Of the interest of the chief's kin in the public land, as I have above described it, I shall cite proofs from India at the present day, and from mediæval records of Western Europe.

Writing of certain princes in Oude, Sir William Sleeman observes—"His brothers do not pretend to have any right of inheritance in the share of the lands he holds; but they have a prescriptive right to support from him for themselves and their families when they require it." † And again, in another case, he observes—"He was succeeded by his brother Sookraj, whose grandson, Madhoo Persand, now reigns as Raja, and has the undivided possession of the lands belonging to this branch. All the descendants of his grandfather, and their widows and orphans, have a right to protection and support from him, and to nothing more." In Europe, there is a remarkable illustration of the same principle, in the Tenure by Parage—a mode of tenure noted, indeed, by Glanville, but which at an early date died out in England, although it was widely prevalent among the Continental noblesse. I translate its description from

* Robertson's "Scotland under her Early Kings," vol. ii., p. 264.

† "Journey through Oude," vol. i., pp. 169, 173.

the old* Norman French—"Tenure in parage is that in which the person who holds, and the person of whom he holds, ought, by reason of their lineage, to be peers and parties in an inheritance which descends from their ancestors. In this manner, the younger holds of the elder up to the sixth degree of descent; but, thenceforward, the younger are bound to do fealty to the elder. And in the seventh degree, and thenceforward, that will be held in homage which previously was held by parage." That is, the tenant who, up to the sixth degree, or the limit of the Mæg, was the peer or *ὁμοῖος* of the lord, ceases, when he passes that degree, to retain that position; and becomes his "man," under the obligation not of agnation, but of pledged fidelity. Mr. Robertson † remarks that this principle was widely prevalent, if not universal, amongst nearly every people of Celtic as well as of German origin. Its application gave no little trouble to the Anglo-Irish lawyers. An old record ‡ recites that The O'Callaghan is seized of several large territories, as lord and chief of Poble (*i. e.*, people) O'Callaghan, and that by custom there is a Tanist who is seized of certain lands, and then proceeds —"The custom is, further, that every kinsman of The O'Callaghan had a parcel of land to live upon, and yet no estate passed thereby, but that the lord and O'Callaghan for the time being may remove the said kinsman to other lands;" and that certain persons were seized of several plough lands according to the said custom, "subject, nevertheless, to certain seignories and duties payable to The O'Callaghan, and removable by him to other lands at his pleasure."

* "Grand Coutumier," c. 30.

† "Hist. Essays," p. lxii. And see "Scotland under her Early Kings," vol. ii., p. 258, *et seq.*

‡ "Inquisition taken at Mallow," Harris's Ware, vol. ii., p. 72.

I add another witness concerning Ireland, partly on account of the trustworthiness of his evidence, and partly because he incidentally illustrates some observations that, in other parts of these pages, I have made. Sir John Davies, then Attorney-General of Ireland, writes, in the year 1607, to the Earl of Salisbury a report of his inquiries "touching the state of Monaghan, Fermanagh, and Cavan." From that report * I extract the following passage—"We had present certain of the clerks or scholars of the country, who knew all the septs and families, and all their branches, and the dignity of one sept above another, and what families or persons were chief of every sept; and who were next, and who were of a third rank, and so forth, till they descended to the most inferior man of all the baronies: moreover, they took upon them to tell what quantity of land every man ought to have by the custom of their country, which is of the nature of gavel-kind, whereby, as their septs or families did multiply, their possessions have been from time to time divided and subdivided, and broken into so many small parcels as almost every acre of land hath a several owner which termeth himself a lord, and his portion of land his country. Notwithstanding, as M'Guyre himself had a chiefry over all the country, and some demesnes that did ever pass to himself only who carried that title, so was there a chief of every sept who had certain services, duties, or demesnes, that ever passed to the tanist of that sept, and never was subject to division."

Several points in this passage deserve notice. First, the scholars of the country, like the Indian bards, profess to know both the genealogies of every person in their clan, and the quantity of land to which each clansman is entitled. Secondly, the land-right of the country was in the nature

* Sir John Davies, "Historical Tracts," (ed. 1787), p. 258.

of gavel-kind—that is, the children inherited in equal shares. Thirdly, this system led to a great subdivision of property. Fourthly, each of these small estates was held by a 'lord,' and was regarded as his 'country'; that is, it was not an estate, in our sense of the term, but was an allotment for a Joint Family or Mæg. Fifthly, both the chief of the clan, and the head of each sub-clan, had certain lands and lucrative incidents pertaining to their respective offices, which were not subject to the ordinary rule of distribution, but, as the endowment of the office, passed to their successors, and not to their heirs.

The Comitatus.

§ 4. There is a difference, although there are many points of resemblance, between a chieftain and a lord, and consequently between the near kin of a chief and a comitatus. Any person who had sufficient reputation to attract followers, and sufficient means to provide for them, could form a body of retainers. The chieftaincy, although it was favourable to the existence of a comitatus, and generally gave rise to it, primarily depended, as I have shown, not upon its dependents, but upon its kinsmen. The latter form rested upon birth, the former upon personal qualities and wealth. It is obvious that the maintenance of a large number of non-producing able-bodied men involves not merely political but economic considerations. I proceed, therefore, to examine the circumstances which are favourable to the development of this remarkable institution.

The economic conditions of the comitatus, or gasindschaft, or thanehood, are not difficult to determine. A wealthy and unoccupied class; a class less wealthy, but equally accustomed to rely upon the labour of an inferior population, and, consequently, holding industry disgraceful; the natural increase of a proud and poor youth, ready to fight, but not ready to work; the absence of manufactures and of commerce, and of the liberal professions which successful industry maintains; the absence of a strong central government—such are the elements out of which retainers are made. The rich chief and the bold and needy youths gravitate to each other by a silent but irresistible attraction. The former cannot spend his means exclusively upon himself; and is, therefore, not averse to share them with others, on whose help, when he needs it, he can depend. These others are not unwilling, in effect, to transfer their services for pay. Yet it would be a false and imperfect explanation, to describe the conduct of either party as exclusively influenced by these or any similar motives. It would be nearer to the truth to say that the chief spends his money upon those objects which his education has taught him to admire, and which the public opinion of his own world approves. The retainer follows a gallant leader with an open hand, in a spirit of generous loyalty and self-sacrificing devotion. If the lord ought to be liberal to his poor gesith, the gesith must fight to the death for his lord. For his lord's honour and renown he must sacrifice all, even life itself. It was infamy to survive the fall of his lord: it was worse than infamy to abandon him in his peril. If the gesith's kinsmen fought on one side, and his lord on the other, it was to his lord* that he must cleave. All that the gesith won, he won for his lord; and the lord, in no churlish spirit, rewarded, of his own bounty, the bravery and the honour of his true gesith.

I have said that the gesiths were in the hand of their lord. They were, therefore, not *sui juris;* and they lived, not under the protection of the community, but at the personal will of the House Father. All their property, and all their possessions, were his; whatever they used they

* See Kemble's "Saxons in England," vol. i., p. 172.

derived from his bounty, and they had the administration of it—not the ownership. If they committed any offence, it was to his justice that they were amenable; and over them he had the power of life and death. In other words, their relation to him was the relation of the son to his House Father, as I have already described it. The war-gear * and the loaned land, the heriot and the benefice, were in the nature of the *peculium*. They belonged to the lord, and reverted to him when the relation, in view of which their use had been permitted, was dissolved. The gesith could make no will, because he had no property to bequeath. He could not marry, for he had nothing wherewith he could endow his wife. If he acquired property, or married a wife, or left his goods to his children, he could only do these things with the consent and assistance of his lord. But still the gesiths, although they were thus dependent, were of noble birth. They were free to come or to go at their pleasure. If they were ill-treated or dissatisfied, they could enter the service of another lord. In time, they might become lords in their turn; and even if their former position continued unchanged, they could hold a benefice, or grant, of a portion of their lord's land, out of which they could maintain their own dependents and establish a gasindschaft of their own.

I do not know to what extent the comitatus is noticed in early Indian writers. Its main features, however, may be traced in the Sepoy army. Writing of the Sepoy, Sir John Kaye † observes—"His predominant sentiment, indeed, was fidelity to his salt; or, in other words, to the hand that fed him. But if he thought that the hand was unrighteously closed, to withhold from him what he believed to be his due, he showed himself to

* See Kemble, *ubi supra*, p. 179.

† "Hist. of Sepoy War," vol. i., p. 206.

be most tenacious of his rights, and he resolutely asserted them." In the whole history of the Sepoy force that Sir John Kaye narrates, it is clear that the Sepoy is not merely trustworthy, but as devoted as any true gasind, when two conditions are fulfilled. His master must be successful, and must be liberal. In such circumstances, the Sepoy will give his whole heart. He will be faithful even to an abstraction, such as the Company was, if it realize his ideal. He will be true to his salt—a significant expression—even though the hand that gives it, so it be open, is invisible. The same writer* notices clear indications of the comitatus among the native princes. Scindiah, the Maharajah of Gwalior, had a body of Mahratta horsemen of his own kindred or caste. These men are described as Scindiah's companions by day and night, inseparable from his pleasures and his state. So too, the Talookhdars, of Oude, are described† as having large bodies of armed retainers, whose position and functions seem closely to have resembled those of the retinue of European barons.

As to Persia, the Avesta speaks of the "Airyanəm," the friends or companions of the landowners there described. The Slavic nations, among whom, with abundant land and no inferior population, the commune simply expanded itself indefinitely, had little inducement to adopt this practice. It is in Western and Southern Europe that we find its chief examples. It is sufficiently distinct in Homer, where kings and heroes are the *ἑταιροι*, and the *θεράποντες* of more distinguished princes. In the Macedonian period it again appears in the *ἑταιροι* and the *πεζέταιροι*, the Horse Guards and the Foot Guards of Philip and of Alexander. Even in the traditions of early Rome some glimpses ‡ of the custom

* "Hist. of Sepoy War," vol. iii., p. 313. † *Ib.*, p. 422.

‡ Mr. Freeman, "Comparative Politics," p. 478.

may possibly be discerned in the fierce band of youths that attended Romulus, and charged with the dictator at the Lake Regillus. But neither in Athens nor in Rome, during the ascendancy of these cities, does the comitatus present itself in any definite form. It is indeed, as Mr. Freeman has remarked, "an institution which is not well suited for the atmosphere of a city life." Accordingly it is among the Teutons and the Kelts that it appears in its most complete development. In both these nations, in the description of Cæsar and the description of Tacitus, the difference between the warrior friends and the humbler clients is conspicuous; and the word "soldier" still denotes something of that devotion to his chief that the Soldurii of Gaul, and the Gesiths of Germany, were wont to show to Dumnorix and to Segestes.

The Inferior Population.

§ 5. Distinct from the comitatus or military retainers, and yet essential to the existence of that body, was the despised and non-combatant class which performed the humble duty of cultivating the warrior's fields. It may be stated, generally, that this class was composed of men outside of the kin, although dependent upon it or upon some of its members, and that it was derived from a conquered and alien race. In most of the countries whither the Aryan nations wandered, they appear to have found hostile populations of a race different from their own. It may, perhaps, be gathered from the philological evidence that, even in their primitive seats, our forefathers had to contend with neighbours of this description. Similar troubles awaited them when they journeyed east and west. So far as their history is known, they always conquered, and either absorbed or enslaved, their opponents. In Russia, the process of absorption seems to have prevailed; and as the Slavic settlements were constantly pushed to the north, the

Finnish tribes either retired before them or seem to have amalgamated with them on equal terms. In Scandinavia,* in Northern Germany, and in Italy,† the aboriginal population, if any, does not appear to have affected settlement. But in India, and in Western Europe throughout Spain, France, the Low Countries, and the British Isles, the Aryans found and subjugated non-Aryan peoples. In Greece, also, many instances of subject populations occur, although most of these appear to have been of the same race, if not of the same division of that race, as their conquerors. In India, these unfortunate persons are known as the Sudras, the lowest class, or, rather, the people outside the classes, of Hindu society. In Greece, we read of the Helots of Lacedæmon, the Thetes of Attica, the Klarotæ of Krete, the Penestæ of Thessaly, the Maryandynians at Heraclea on the Pontus. Among the continental Saxons, and other Teutonic tribes, we meet with the Læts, that is, persons to whom a permissive occupancy of land was, on certain terms, conceded, and who were distinguished from the Alodists, the owners of the land in full right. In England, the laws of Ethelbert mention the Læts in Kent; and Bede ‡ notices, incidentally, "folclic and dearfende" men, who seem to have tilled the soil to which they were attached, and to have supplied the wants of the martial owners of the land. In Ireland,§ such people are known as "daer" classes, servile or base tenants, not of the blood of the privileged clan. It may have been that, in many cases, these subject persons were, as in Greece, the remains of Aryan tribes vanquished by invaders of their own race. We can trace, too, some, at

* Robertson's "Early Kings," vol. ii., p. 235, *note*.

† Mommsen's "Hist. Rome," vol. i., p. 8.

‡ "Hist. Ecc.," vol. iv., p. 22.

§ See Dr. Sullivan's "O'Curry," vol. i., p. cxiv. Robertson's "Essays," p. 154.

least, of what K. O. Müller * calls "the fundamental laws of ancient Greek bondage." The serfs could not be put to death without a trial. They could not be sold out of the country. The amount of their tribute, or gifts as it was called, was permanently fixed. Doubtless, also, there were degrees in the condition of the subjects, and their treatment differed in different countries, and at different times. But it is clear, that at least in Western Europe, the basis at least of this class was non-Aryan. Much attention has of late years been given to the presence of these non-Aryan Europeans.† The result seems to be that both archæology and history concur in declaring that, before the Aryan immigration, an Iberian or Basque population inhabited Spain, France, Belgium, Great Britain, and Ireland. This population was generally of a smaller size, had longer heads, darker complexions, and more delicate organizations than the Kelts and the Northmen who invaded them. To this race belonged the Silures, the Ligures, the Iberi, the "Fear Bolgæ" of the south of Ireland, and various other tribes; and their modern representatives as a separate people are the Basques.

The Land-rights of the Dependent Classes.

§ 6. I do not wish to discuss the rights of war, or the relations of the victors to their vanquished enemies. These relations varied more or less according to differences in time, place and circumstance. Nor is it necessary now to speak of tributary tribes, or even of those persons who were dependent upon the clan as a whole, or upon the State. That portion of the inferior population to which I now refer, and whose fortunes have had most influence in history,

* "Dorians," vol. ii., pp. 62, 66.

† See "British Quarterly Review," October, 1872; Mr. Dawkins, in "Fortnightly Review," September, 1874; Prof. Huxley, in "Nature," vol. i., p. 514.

is not that which lived under communes, but that which lived under separate lords. I shall not attempt to narrate the history of these people, for I should then have to write no small part of the legal and political history of Western Europe. It is enough to say that the demesne lands of every great proprietor, that is, the lands which he retained in his own possession, were cultivated by men of this class. According to the custom of the Three Descents, these cultivators were held to have acquired, in the third generation, a native right, as it was termed, in the soil: in other words, the occupier could not be removed from the land so long as he performed his customary obligations. These obligations could not be increased, and the tenant-right thus acquired was hereditary. Sometimes the lord settled upon his waste land freedmen, for whose maintenance after their emancipation he was bound to provide; sometimes he found there a place for some of the broken men who, homeless elsewhere, sought his protection. In due time the descendants of these persons acquired the customary right. When such persons came to a chief of a clan, and were settled by him upon the Folc land, they necessarily* strengthened his power, since they considered themselves as personally attached to him; and they, at the same time, weakened *pro tanto* the aristocracy of the clan, or at least checked its growth, by reducing the extent of its pastures. The influence of these dependents—first, in strengthening their lords against their own clans, or other public authorities; secondly, in forcing their way, in favourable circumstances, not indeed over the close barriers of the genealogic tribe, but into the new political association in which those tribes were absorbed; and thirdly, by securing their own rights in the land against

* See Mr. Hunter's "Orissa," vol. i., p. 57.

lords or communes—will some day, when the story is told, be recognized as no inconsiderable portion of political and legal history.

I have said that, after three generations, the native right, as it was called, became hereditary; and the tenant, if he performed his stipulated duties, could be neither rack-rented nor evicted. But whether he could himself leave the land was another question. It may safely be said, that the native, or *geneat*, or by whatever other name the hereditary *colonus* was known, had no such power. But freemen seem often to have accepted a base tenure, and the test of freedom was the power of unrestricted locomotion. Thus we find that the right of withdrawal was the leading distinction between the different classes of cultivators. "Domesday Book" constantly and carefully distinguishes between the man who can, and the man who cannot, go whither he will. The former class the Burgundian and Lombard laws * describe as "Faramanni"; the latter are styled, in the Northern and Danish law,† "Færbena"; that is, in the one case, men who might fare or travel; and, in the other case, men who were forbidden to fare. In Ireland there is a similar difference between the "Daor Ceile" and the "Saor Ceile," only that in that country ‡ a man was bound not to the land, but to the lord personally, from whom alone he could accept stock. In India § we find a similar distinction, although in that country the relative position of these classes is strangely inverted. There are resident cultivators and migratory cultivators. The former hold by tenant-right, and are regulated by custom. The latter are strangers induced by the lord to take up waste land, and their position is

* Canciani, "Leg. Barb.," iv., 29.

† Robertson, "Early Kings," vol. ii., p. 244.

‡ Robertson's "Essays," p. 157.

§ See Mr. Hunter's "Orissa," vol. i., p. 57.

determined by contract. But the customary tenants hold a much better social position than the lessees. The emigrant loses his place in his own village, and is regarded with little favour in his new settlement. What is a still greater misfortune, he is to some extent confused with the landless low-caste. Like them, he has no local connection, no Mæg, no hereditary rights. He has neither *Sedem* nor *Penates*, as other men have. In a word, he is not, in the estimation of those among whom he lives, a respectable man.

These rules respecting the dependents suggest several considerations. In the first place, it is apparent how easily a court of law might misunderstand their vague tenure, and what difficulty might be experienced in enforcing it. It was admitted that "no estate passed." The lord, therefore, must have appeared to be the absolute owner. In such circumstances the dependents could, in the eye of the law, have nothing more than, at the most, a moral claim upon his bounty. Thus, without any intentional injustice, a substantial wrong was done; and the ownership was held to be vested in the chief, free of all trusts and of all limitations. In the next place, the origin of the bulk of the peasantry may be discerned. The peasants, generally, are the lineal descendants not of the *cinél*, but of the gillies or dependent members of the clan. They probably comprised some families of pure descent, which, when the old organization was broken up, were unable, from whatever cause, to retain their old position. But the mass of these dependents were not connected by any tie of consanguinity with the clansmen of pure descent. If this be so, it helps to explain a very singular fact, the readiness with which the Keltic peasantry transferred their attachment to Norman settlers. When Fergus M'Ivor commended, before his death, his clan to Waverley, he said—"You cannot be to them Vich Ian Vohr." These words were true, so far as the cinél or pure-blooded clansmen were concerned; but they were not true as regards the inferior population that was connected with the clan. Both in Scotland and in Ireland, the "native men and kindly tenants" accepted, without any difficulty, a new lord, if only that lord did his duty towards them. The Frasers, and the Chisholms, and the Campbells were supported by their tenants as heartily as were the Macintoshes, the Mackenzies, or the Macdonalds. The Irish tenant saw no difference between Strongbow's Knights, and his native Flaiths. Both parties were alike strangers to his blood. No sentiment of nationality at that time existed. So long as his rights of occupancy were respected, it was of comparatively little interest to the tenant in whom the ownership was vested. Further, we can thus trace the origin of those proprietary claims which so long lingered among the Irish people. When the clan system was broken down, and the rights of occupancy were disallowed, a natural confusion arose among the tenantry as to their position. They knew that their ancestors had belonged to the clan, and had rights in the land. They had no standard by which they could ascertain the precise extent of either of these claims other than the inappropriate rules of English law. They alleged, therefore, that they represented the pure clan, and that they were entitled to the ownership of that clan's lands. Such pretensions were, in most cases, unfounded. I do not, however, mean now to revive a useless controversy. I only wish to point out that, in that and every similar controversy, the issues are strictly matters of history. They depend upon an examination of the structure and the usages of archaic society. It has been a favourite labour-saving contrivance of political writers to explain these and similar difficulties by a simple reference to some assumed qualities of the Keltic race. Perhaps these alternative explanations may appear to illustrate Mr. Mill's * remark that, "of all vulgar modes of escaping from the consideration of the effect of social and moral influences on the human mind, the most vulgar is that of attributing the diversities of conduct and character to inherent natural differences."

* "Political Economy," vol. i., p. 390.

CHAPTER XI.

THE COMBINATION OF CLANS.

The Natural Expansion of Clans.

§ 1. I HAVE shown the growth of the domestic and of the Gentile relations. I have now to notice a further development. As the Household expands into the clan, so the clan expands into a people. In course of time, and with the increase of its numbers, the simple homogeneous body becomes in the usual way a collection of heterogeneous related bodies. This wider relation is thus substantially an extension of an actual Gentile relation. It marks the fact that the clans of which it is composed acknowledge a common descent. A single clan might, in course of time, expand into many autonomous clans; but, although each of these new bodies would practically be independent of all the others, the old community of worship would, in favourable circumstances, still be maintained. Such worship had, indeed, little influence upon the daily life of the co-religionists. Each clan had acquired its own peculiar gods, who were nearer and dearer to it than those far-away gods, who were content with a smaller oblation, and who returned a less careful regard. Still, these shadowy gods must be treated with proper respect; and provision must be made for continuing the old worship and for commemorating the old descent. This union, then, was not made, but grew. It was the natural consequence of the increasing number of clans. It was a survival from the time when there was but one clan and one worship. To a certain extent it served to keep together communities that otherwise would have been hopelessly scattered. Thus the Hellenes found a bond of union in the worship of the old Zeus at Dodona. The Italian tribes preserved the worship of their hereditary Mavors. The European Scyths,* if, indeed, they were of Aryan descent, recognized as their only lords, Tabiti and Papæos, that is Vesta the Queen of the Scyths, and Zeus their ancestor. Nor can we doubt that the respective descendants of Ing, of Hermin, and of Isco, had their common worship, even if every Teuton did not offer, as he may have offered, sacrifice to the common progenitor, Mann.

In describing these larger divisions of society, language gives us little help. There are, in most of the Aryan languages, words that may be used to express considerable aggregations of men. But these words are vague, and vary in each language; and it may be doubted if in any instance this meaning is more than secondary. For the most part, proper names are used in preference to any of these general words. The Hellenes, for example, were said to be divided into the Ionians, the Dorians, and the Æolians; and no accurate distinction was drawn in the application to any of these bodies of the word *γένος* or *ἔθνος*, or of any similar terms. Still, the fact that there is some such wide-spreading connection remains, and some expression for it should be found. The advance of physiology has tended to bring into prominence the conception of race. Still more recently, the discoveries of comparative philology, acting upon troubled social and political conditions, have given practical importance to the theory of nationality. There is also the word nation, which is at present used almost as a synonym with State. It would be fortunate if

* Herodotus, iv., 59, 127.

this word could be rescued from this loose meaning, in which it is wasted, and applied strictly, as its etymology suggests, to the expanded kin. In general use, however, it denotes a political relation, while race seems to express community of physical descent.

For the description of the expanded gens, or people, I know nothing better than the description which Herodotus* gives of the Hellenes generally. They were of the same blood; they spoke the same language; they observed similar customs; they had a common worship and common rites. They thus, in many important respects, resembled each other; and they were, in those very respects, unlike other people. There was, consequently, a sympathy between them—a tendency, as it were, towards union; but the sympathy was weak, and the tendency was easily counteracted. This relation was merely personal. It was in no sense political. It was in no sense territorial. It did not arise from an occupation of the same country, and it was not limited by such occupation. The names of the great modern powers were once mere geographical expressions without the least political signification. So Hellas, as the Greeks understood the term, was not the country that we now call Greece. It included every land in which Hellenes were settled. In other words, the Hellenes were not the inhabitants of Hellas, but Hellas was the land occupied by the Hellenes. In Central India, at the present day, the first, and perhaps the hardest, lesson which a European statesman has to learn, is, that he is in a country where the idea of political citizenship is unknown, and where the idea of territorial sovereignty is only just beginning to arise. "Geographical boundaries," says Mr. Lyall,† "have no correspondence at all with distinctive institutions or grouping of the people, and have comparatively slight

* viii., 144. † "Fort. Rev.," No. 121, N. S., p. 98.

political significance. Little is gained toward knowing who and what a man is by ascertaining the State he obeys, or the territory he dwells in, these being things which, of themselves, denote no difference of race, institutions, or manners. Even from the point of view of political allegiance, the government under which a man may be living is an accidental arrangement, which the British Viceroy or some other distant irresistible power decided upon yesterday, and may alter to-morrow. Nor would such a change be grievous unless it divorced him from a rule of his own tribe or his own faith."

Difficulty of Co-operation in Clans.

§ 2. So far as it went, this sentiment of nationality, if I may so call it, was undoubtedly a social force. The Hellenes always drew a sharp line between themselves and the barbarians, a term by which they designated all non-Hellenic people. In times of great external danger, appeals might be made to this Panhellenic sentiment, not without success. The Highlanders, as Captain Burt* relates, "had an adherence one to another as Highlanders, in opposition to the people of the low country." Among both the Greeks and the Romans,† a still further advance may be observed; and public opinion, and afterwards positive law, forbad that any Hellên, or any Quirite, should be reduced to slavery. But the integrative tendency went no further. On the contrary, vicinity and similarity of habits increased the surface of contact, and, consequently, the occasions for dispute. Achilles had no quarrel with the Trojans, who had never made a foray in the fertile fields of populous Phthia, since between him and them lay the shadowing mountains and the resounding sea. Between Achilles and his Hellenic neighbours such amenities may have been not

* Mr. Skene's "Highlanders," vol. i., p. 156.

† Becker's "Gallus," p. 201.

infrequent. Hence the immediate and personal causes of quarrel soon overpowered the feeble tendencies to union. Even when their common interests most urgently pressed for co-operation, the old enmities were too strong. One chief would never accept the authority of another chief; and if both of them were to submit to a stranger, it was with the mental reservation that the submission was only to last so long and to extend so far as each subordinate thought fit. A memorable example of this state of feeling is found in the history of the Highland clans. The clans, each with its own desires and its own objects, sometimes united in some political enterprise, in which they professed a common interest. But this tie was too weak to bear any lengthened strain. They quarrelled with each other upon their private grudges; or, when their personal convenience seemed to require, they left the army and went home. "Hence it was," says Lord Macaulay,* "that, though the Highlanders achieved some great exploits in the civil wars of the seventeenth century, those exploits left no trace which could be discerned after the lapse of a few weeks. Victories, of strange and almost portentous splendour, produced all the consequences of defeat. Veteran soldiers and statesmen were bewildered by these sudden turns of fortune. It was incredible that undisciplined men should have performed such feats of arms. It was incredible that such feats of arms, having been performed, should be immediately followed by the triumph of the conquered and the submission of the conquerors. Montrose, having passed rapidly from victory to victory, was, in the full career of success, suddenly abandoned by his followers. Local jealousies and local interests had brought his army together. Local jealousies and local interests dissolved it. The Gordons left him because they fancied that he neglected them for the Macdonalds. The Macdonalds left him because they wanted

* "Hist. of England," vol. iii., p. 338.

to plunder the Campbells. The force which had once seemed sufficient to decide the fate of a kingdom melted away in a few days, and the victories of Tippermuir and Kilsyth were followed by the disaster of Philiphaugh." Mr. Lyall * notices a curious case of the same kind in India. Little more than sixty years ago, the Rajpút clans were in great danger and distress. Ameer Khan, a Pathán filibuster, was moving at large among them, at the head of a well appointed army of 30,000 men. They had been almost destroyed by the Marathas, and were only saved from entire destruction by British interference. Yet, at this very time, the two great chieftainships of Jodhpoor and Jeypoor waged an internecine war on account of a quarrel between their respective chiefs for the hand of the Princess Kishen Konwar, of Oodeypore. "The fact," says Mr. Lyall, "that these two states, surrounded by mortal enemies, and in the direst political peril, should have engaged in a furious blood-feud over a dubious point of honour, shows at once that the Rajpúts were a people quite apart from the rest of India, and strikes the primitive note in their political character. The plundering Marathas and Patháns, to whom such a *casus belli* must have appeared supremely absurd, encouraged, and strenuously aided, the two chiefs to destroy each other, until the dispute was compromised upon the basis of poisoning the princess—a termination which very fairly illustrates the real nature of barbaric chivalry."

Many comments have been made upon the want of concert among uncivilized people. Herodotus † says of the Thracians, that, if they had one head, or were agreed among themselves, they would far surpass all other nations. Thucydides ‡ expresses a similar opinion respecting the

* "Edin. Review," vol. cxliv., p. 177.
† v., 3. ‡ ii., 97.

Scythians. The folly of the different nations who allowed Rome to deal with them one by one, instead of combining against her, has been the subject of much sterile wonder. The explanation of the phenomenon is simple. These barbarous tribes could no more combine for any great operation than they could make a chemical analysis, or run forty miles in an hour. They were mentally and morally unequal to the task. Their state of society did not admit of the training necessary for concerted efforts. Thrace, for example, was not a country in the sense in which at the present day we use the term. It merely denoted the locality in which some fifty* independent tribes were settled. Every one of these tribes was, in its structure and in its social life, independent of all the others. Every one, so far from habitually acting with the others, regarded them as its rivals, and often as its enemies. All their habits tended not to confidence and co-operation, but to hostility and distrust. Each clan, in short, had its own individual existence; and as it was complete after its kind, it was not capable of further integration. Even among civilized men nothing is more difficult than co-operation. Many generations of failures are needed before even a little success can be obtained. In our own day the course of the disciplined armies of two great allied nations does not, as we know, always run smoothly. To expect permanent and efficient co-operation among uncultured clans is as unreasonable as it would be to look for grapes from brambles, or figs from thistles.

§ 3. There is another form of grouping, which, in archaic societies, is of only too frequent occurrence. It is that of conquest. One man, or one society, by force, or the fear of

Association of Clans by Conquest.

* See Canon Rawlinson's note on "Herodotus," *ubi supra.*

force, compels the submission of several societies. In such a state of things, the conquered society is usually bound to pay to the victor a certain tribute, or to yield a proportion, for the most part either a third * or two-thirds, of its land and stock; and also to obey, generally, any order that he thinks fit to issue. These orders, however, are always special, and do not prescribe such general rules of conduct as we understand by the term laws. Each society, notwithstanding its conquest, continues to live according to its own usages, and conducts its ordinary business in its own way. It is, in fact, impossible to form, in any other manner, any great empire of which the object is simply the collection of tribute. The more extended the empire, the more difficult is its administration, the greater are the demands upon the conquering force, and the more perilous is its position. That force may, in ordinary circumstances, be adequate to compel obedience to a few simple duties; but where locomotion is difficult and slow, the task of establishing new and odious customs among numerous and scattered peoples is hopeless. Further, archaic conquerors never felt any such wish. To them it seemed natural and right that every race of men should have its own religion, and observe its own usages. Without these essential supports society could not, in their view, be maintained. The victors had no desire to deprive their subjects of necessaries which they themselves could not have used, and they would have scorned the notion of extending to the vanquished their own privileges. They knew that their gods were stronger than the gods of other people; and they were content that the matter should so rest. They did not care what the customs of their subjects were: they had no desire to alter these customs. They

* See Niebuhr's "Hist. Rome," vol. i., p. 419; vol. ii., p. 45. Robertson's "Scotland under her Early Kings," vol. ii., pp. 210, 358.

probably did not even suppose that it was possible to alter them. All that concerned them was that their tribute should be regularly paid, and their orders promptly executed. In the emphatic words of the Behistun inscription, "Says Darius* the king: 'These are the provinces which have come to me: by the grace of Ormazd they have become subject to me: they have brought tribute to me: that which has been said to them by me, both by night and by day, it has been done.'" Tribute and obedience, such were the requirements of the great king. If he were secure of these, he cared little for the laws of his subjects.

So simple and so well known is this class of societies, that I shall only cite one illustration. "The empires of the East," says Professor Rawlinson,† "have uniformly arisen from the sudden triumph of conquering nomadic hordes over more settled and civilized communities. . . . In every case a conqueror rapidly overruns an enormous tract of territory, inhabited by many and diverse nations, overpowers their resistance, or receives their submission; and imposes on them a system of government, rude and artificial indeed, but sufficient ordinarily to maintain their subjection, till the time comes when a fresh irruption and a fresh conqueror repeats the process, which seems to be the only renovation whereof oriental realms are capable. The imposed system itself is, in its general features, for the most part one and the same. The rapid conquest causes no assimilation. The nations retain their languages, habits, manners, religion, laws, and sometimes even their native princes. The empire is thus of necessity broken into provinces. In each province a royal officer, representing the monarch—a Satrap, a Khan, or a Pasha—bears absolute sway, responsible to the Crown for the tranquillity of his

* Canon Rawlinson's "Herodotus," vol. ii., p. 491.
† *Ib.*, vol. ii., p. 460.

district, and bound to furnish periodically, or at call, the supplies of men and money which constitute the chief value of their conquests to the conquerors."

Such, generally, was the character of every empire, even the Athenian, prior to the great domination of Rome. They all were, as Sir Henry Maine * has well expressed it, tax-taking and not legislative. But such a form of empire is merely inorganic. Its forces act from without, and not from within. It is composed, indeed, of separate organisms, but these organisms are distinct from each other and from their common ruler. The case, in short, is that of one organism preying upon another, not that of new structures built up out of the changes of the old. The empires of Attila and Tamerlane were not more organic than a number of wool bales under a hydraulic press, or a mob of cattle under the charge of a drover.

Association of Clans by Agreement.

§ 4. There was yet another form of archaic association. It arose neither as the spontaneous memorial of a common though remote ancestry, nor as the forcible domination of one society over another. It was the result of specific agreement upon equal terms. Like the alliance of kinship, this consensual alliance rested upon a common worship. There was, however, a difference between them. In the former case, it may be said † that the association existed for the sake of the worship. In the latter case the worship was established to mark and consolidate the association. When the men of old desired to form any intimate and lasting alliance, they knew, as I have so often said, one way, and one way only, for the purpose. They united in a common worship. They retained, indeed, their old corporate personality. The several clans and sub-clans

* "Early Hist. of Inst.," p. 384.

† Mr. Freeman, "Hist. Fed. Govt.," p. 187.

remained unchanged, and the gods of their respective Fathers continued to receive their customary honours. But several clans might combine under a new and special worship. When they did so, they followed the familiar precedent. They were independent; they desired to unite; and they naturally imitated that powerful form of association of which alone they had experience. They formed what may perhaps be called an artificial and concurrent kin. They adopted, so to speak, certain new deities to form their common or public Penates; and they became brothers by sharing in the new worship and partaking of its common meal. This was the first step in all such combinations, and it was essential. No permanent association could, according to the beliefs of the archaic world, exist without the establishment of its special cult.

But when the intention of union was formed and its principle was accepted, it became necessary to determine the character and the objects of the association. On the one hand these objects might be temporary, or might be special. On the other hand the association might be designed to last for all time, and to include all purposes. It is needless to consider mere transitory alliances. Such agreements must have been familiar in every state of society, and probably were not supposed to require any community of worship, even though the presence and the sanction of the deities, whether common or separate, were invoked to guarantee the contract. But when a permanent union was formed, it might be either general, or intended for some special object. Of these special associations, the highest temporal aim was usually the establishment of friendly relations between its members, or, at all events, the mitigation of the usages of war. Such seems to have been the character of the great Amphictyonic Assembly at Delphi, whose venerable oath has been preserved to us, binding, among other things, the belligerent Amphictyon not utterly to destroy his hostile brother and not to cut off the water from that brother's stronghold. Multitudes of minor Amphictyonies,* each practising its own cult and associated for its own purposes, existed through every part of Hellas. Of a similar character were the Feriæ Latinæ,† which marked the unity of the Latin race. "The test of union," says Mr. Robertson,‡ "in an Italian confederacy of early times, seems to have consisted in participating in a solemn sacrifice, of which the supreme director would have been, in a certain sense, a *Rex Sacrorum* appointed by the members of the confederacy. The leading man of Veii, affronted by being passed over on the occasion of one of their solemn festivals at the Fanum Voltumnæ, when another priest (alius Sacerdos) was appointed to direct the sacrifice, procured his own election to the position of Rex of Veii; and, accordingly, in their subsequent contest against Rome, the Veientines were left by the Etrurian confederacy to their fate. Thus the choice of a *Rex* by the Veientines was equivalent to a dissolution of their connection with the Etrurian confederacy: and in the legend of the expulsion of the Tarquins may be seen, apparently, a similar, but more successful assertion of independence by the Romans, who henceforth 'chose their king' from among themselves, and ceased to receive him from Etruria." So, too, Tacitus§ describes what, by a somewhat hybrid phraseology, may be called the Amphictyony of the seven Volkerschafts that worshipped Hertha; and the Amphictyony of which the Lygii were the most prominent members, and which worshipped the Dioskuri under the

* Grote's "Hist. of Greece," vol. ii., p. 324.
† Mommsen, "Hist. Rome," vol. i., p. 43.
‡ "Essays," p. 218.
§ "Germania," cc. 40, 43.

name of Alcs. These associations, however, exercised little influence upon men's ordinary conduct. They were, in fact, mere confederations of independent communities for particular purposes. They might be, and they sometimes were, utilized to some extent for political objects; but they had no more tendency to build up a State than the Crusades had to establish a universal European monarchy.

The true character of these Amphictyonies is thus apparent. At first sight they present * the appearance of an organized political association, or, at the least, of the material out of which such an association could readily be constructed. Yet, in no case has this result followed. There is no instance of any Amphictyony having become a State. There are few instances where any Amphictyony has prevented—or, except within the terms of its alliance, softened—war between its members. The reason is either that, in some cases, the remains of the old homogeneous force were unable to restrain the natural tendency to differentiation; or that, in other cases, the integration was attempted between bodies whose organization, though not high, was complete of its kind, and whose independent life would not readily merge in a new form of existence. Nor need we feel surprised at the small success of the early reformers of war. For eighteen centuries the precepts of a far purer religion, in a far more advanced condition of society, have not been at all times able to secure the peace of Christendom.

§ 5. It must not, however, be assumed that these associations, although they have not materially affected the course of political history, failed to excercise any moral influence. Archaic society was, as I have said, composed of a number

Moral effects of such agreements.

* Mr. Freeman, "Hist. Fed. Govt.," p. 133.

of small, complete, and mutually repellent organisms. No social tie was recognized other than a personal relation, and that relation must be created in a particular way. "There is no sense of obligation then existing," writes Mr. Grote * of legendary Greece, "between man and man as such, and very little between each man and the community of which he is a member; such sentiments are neither operative in the real world nor present to the imaginations of the poets. Personal feelings, either towards the gods, the king, or some near and known individual, fill the whole of a man's bosom: out of them arise all the motives to beneficence, and all the internal restraints upon violence, antipathy, or rapacity; and special communion, as well as special solemnities, are essential to their existence." In these circumstances it was a great advance when men were brought together with new sympathies and common obligations. To some extent this result was obtained by the festivals that commemorated community of descent. A further and distinct advance was made when Amphictyonies of non-cognate kins were formed on terms of mere agreement. A step in the same direction was taken when, without any actual alliance, two or more tribes reciprocally sent legations to offer sacrifice at each other's festivals, and to partake in the consequent recreations. By these means they brought themselves, as Mr. Grote † observes, "into direct connection each with the god of the other, under his appropriate local surname." Another similar step followed when strangers were invited as guests to the festival of some particular community. So powerful, indeed, was the sentiment thence resulting that, in Greece at least, it amounted to something almost approaching a national union. Very practical consequences, too, followed sometimes from

* "Hist. of Greece," vol. ii., p. 108.

† *Ib.*, vol. ii., p. 324.

this interchange of friendly sentiment. During the holy period all hostilities were suspended, and these truces were, under the religious sanction, faithfully observed. Such were the truces at the Olympian and the Pythian games; such was the Samian truce,* which bound all Triphylians. Such, too, was the famous truce of God, by which the Christian Church succeeded in curbing, for three days out of seven, the ferocious habits of its northern converts. It was thus that the ideas of common duties and of common enjoyments were raised in those contracted minds; and sympathies, and a sense of mutual obligations, were generated in communities whose normal state was, if not actual war, at least invincible suspicion and distrust. "It may," I again quote the words of Mr. Grote,† "be affirmed with truth that the habit of forming Amphictyonic unions, and of frequenting each other's religious festivals, was the great means of creating and fostering the primitive feeling of brotherhood among the children of Hellên in those early times, when rudeness, insecurity, and pugnacity did so much to isolate them. A certain number of salutary habits and sentiments, such as that which the Amphictyonic oath embodies in regard to abstinence from injury, as well as to mutual protection, gradually found their way into men's minds; the obligations thus brought into play acquired a substantive efficacy of their own, and the religious feeling which always remained connected with them came afterwards to be only one out of many complex agencies by which the later historical Greek was moved."

Minor forms of association.

§ 6. Some minor forms of association may be briefly noticed. One kin is sometimes absorbed by another. The *sacra* of the one merges into the *sacra* of the other; and the

* "Hist. of Greece," *Ib.*, p. 326.
† *Ib.*, p. 332.

two bodies no longer maintain a separate existence, but form a united clan. Such a process is analogous to arrogation, or the adoption of a man *sui juris*. The adopted person lost his independent condition, and became merged in the household of his new Father. Thus, in the Odyssee,* Menelaus expresses his desire that Odysseus should settle in his country, and offers lands to him for himself and his people. So the Claudian gens emigrated to Rome, and was there admitted to full communion with the people of Quirinus. In like manner, Livy† describes the Samnites as admitted by the people of Capua to a partnership in their city and their lands. But this political adoption merely added to the bulk of an existing society, and did not alter its structure or change its relations.

There were other alliances of an intimate nature, but which stopped short of complete amalgamation. Some of these were meant to be permanent, some were in their nature temporary, some were limited to specific purposes. Of the first class, the arrangement which Xenophon‡ describes Cyrus as having made between the Chaldeans and the Armenians, whether the story be true or fictitious, affords an instructive example. It was stipulated that the parties should be mutually independent, and that they should have, reciprocally, four rights. These were—the right of intermarriage, the right of cultivating and the right of depasturing each other's lands, and the right to assistance in case of attack. Of temporary and special alliances, examples are found in those cases in which several independent clans placed themselves, in time of war, under the command of some Herzog, or Dux, or Tagos, and resumed their former

* iv., 174. † iv., 37.

‡ καὶ ἐλευθέρους μὲν ἀμφοτέρους ἐπ' ἀλλήλων ἐῖναι συνετίθεντο, επιγαμίας δ' ἐῖναι, καὶ ἐπεργασίας καὶ ἐπινομίας καὶ επιμαχίαν δὲ κοινὴν ἐι τις ἀδικοίη ὁποτέρους.—*Cyropædia*, iii., 2, 23.

independence when peace was restored. To this class belongs that immortal federation which sought redress for the Atreidæ before holy Ilion. Such, too, was the military system of the Teutonic tribes in the time of Tacitus.* Such, too, with only the difference of the choice of a leader by lot and not by merit, was the system of their descendants in England. "These same old Saxons," says Bede,† "have not a King, but a number of Satraps, set over their nation, who, when war is imminent, cast lots on equal terms; and whomsoever the lot points out, him during the war they all follow as their leader, him they obey; but when the war is over, all the Satraps again become of equal power." These transient combinations resemble the hunting expeditions of the Red Indians, or the journey of an Eastern caravan. On these occasions men place themselves under the control of a single chief, and observe, for the time, strict discipline. When the hunt is over, or the journey is at an end, they separate, and their union is dissolved.

Clans, also, sometimes established, whether by force or by better influences, an authority of varying extent over other clans. This authority might practically range between alliance on the one side, and domination on the other. From the term used by Thucydides in describing the Athenian supremacy, it is now generally known as Hegemony. "A powerful canton‡ induced a weaker to become subordinate, on such a footing that the leading canton acted for the other as well as for itself in its external relations, and stipulated for it in State treaties, while the dependent canton bound itself to render military service and also to pay a tribute. But this union was always loose; and its central authority, whether in peace or war,

* "Germania," c. 13.

† "Hist. Eccl.," b. v., c. 10.

‡ Mommsen, "Hist. of Rome," vol. iv., p. 226.

was feeble. Its existence, indeed, depended upon its weakness; for, so soon as its strength increased, its tendency was rapidly towards dominion. Examples of this class of cases are numerous, especially among the Hellenes and the Kelts. The Hellenic instances are too well known to require further notice. Among the Kelts, the Romans * found, in the North of Gaul, a Belgic league, extending into Britain, under the headship of the Suessiones; and in Central and Southern Gaul were formed the rival confederations of the Arverni and the Hædui. In the time of Cæsar, the Belgæ † still held their headship in North-Eastern Gaul, but without, as it appears, their British dependencies. By their side the league of the Armorican or maritime cantons had grown up in what now is Normandy and Brittany. In Central Gaul the Sequani had taken the place of the Arverni, and carried on the old struggle with the Hædui. And so, among the Highland clans, ‡ the Campbells and the Macdonalds, in the seventeenth century, collected their tributary clans, and fought as their forefathers had fought in the days of the great dictator.

* Mommsen, "Hist. of Rome," vol. iii., p. 168.

† *Ib.*, vol. iv., p. 226.

‡ Macaulay, "History of England," vol. iii., p. 315.

CHAPTER XII.

GENTIS CUNABULA NOSTRAE.

The Primitive Aryans.

§ 1. At some remote, but unascertained period, on the table-lands of Central Asia, where the Oxus and the Yaxartes begin to flow, and extending westward probably to the Caspian Sea, dwelt the forefathers of our race. The men who then occupied these regions were of one blood, spoke one language, had a common stock of beliefs, of manners, and of customs. They had a common form of social organization, although they did not form a nation as we understand the term; and they drew a clear line of distinction between themselves and the barbarians, or tribes of alien race and alien speech, by whom they were surrounded. How these men came there, what was their descent, or what their previous history, we know not. That such a history did exist, we may well believe. That, a century hence, some portion of that history may be discovered, no person, who remembers the absolute ignorance of our grandfathers upon this subject, will venture to deny. But in the existing state of knowledge, we must accept the Aryans as an ultimate fact. We must be content to take them as we find them. We know so much of them, and we know no more. From these original settlements, at some unknown periods, there streamed to the south on the one side, and to the north-west on the other side, many bands of emigrants. Under their various names of Indians and of Iranians, of Hellenes and of Latins, of Kelts and Slavs and Teutons, these emigrants have borne the Aryan speech, and the Aryan beliefs and customs, through all the lands that extend from the Ganges westward to the Pacific Ocean, and from Iceland to the Darling Downs. All these nations are descended from the original race as directly as the Italians or the Portuguese are descended from the children of Quirinus, or as the dwellers in America or Australia are descended from the realm of England. It is, then, an inquiry of no common interest, to ascertain something of the primal Aryan polity. If we can obtain a true notion, so far as it goes, of this early society, we shall at all events understand the problem which the historian of the future will have to solve. The roots of the present are deep down in the past; and modern civilization must be affiliated to the thoughts and the actions of the tribes that, under their elders, used to roam, thousands of years ago, over "*Airyanem Vaejo*," the cradle of our race.

The Comparative Method of Inquiry.

§ 2. A distinguished writer on Physical Science remarks that Shakespeare and Newton were the descendants of savages. Whether in fact they were so or not, I do not pretend either to assert or to deny. But I venture to allege that, so far as any trustworthy evidence on the subject is at present known to exist, savages were not the acknowledged progenitors of these great men. The ultimate fact, in the present state of knowledge upon this subject, is the condition of the Aryans. We cannot connect these Aryans with any other race, nor can we go behind the evidence which their language and their institutions afford. It may be positively asserted that the men who spoke that language, and possessed these institutions, were not in any reasonable sense of the term savages. It is by the aid of Comparative Philology that we are enabled to form some definite conception of the material condition of our archaic forefathers. There is nothing in the conclusions of that science to suggest the low moral state, the wandering and precarious existence, the berries and the acorns, of the noble savage. The Aryans knew the arts* of ploughing, of making roads, of weaving, and of sewing. They built substantial houses, they used cooked food and fermented drinks. They counted† as far at least as a thousand. They were familiar with many useful plants and their properties. They had domesticated the animals most useful to man—the cow, the horse, the sheep, and the dog. They had property,‡ and they knew the meaning of wealth. All these things, and others of the same kind, may be learned from the study of language. But as regards their social and moral conditions, the method of inquiry is somewhat different. It is, at first sight, a very alluring project to reconstruct from language archaic society, and thence to deduce the varied forms of modern civilization. Only a very slight practical attempt is needed to reveal the hopelessness of this method. In the first place, the linguistic evidences are too meagre to be of themselves practically useful. In the next place, many political and legal terms are used in a secondary meaning; and hence the existence of the word in the original language proves nothing as to its use at that time in this secondary sense. Thus there is no doubt that the Aryans had a word to express *hand;* but this fact does not prove either that they used or that they did not use this word in the technical sense of *manus* and of *mund.* By a combination, however, of the results of Comparative Jurisprudence and of Comparative Philology, by verifying the inferences that the one suggests by the conclusions of the other, by reading, as it were, the terms of

* Prof. Max Müller's "Science of Language," vol. i., p. 223.

† See "Vergleichendes Wörterbuch der Indogermanischen Sprachen," Von August Fick, p. 70.

‡ *Ib.*, pp. 11, 22.

the archaic language in the light derived from the study of archaic institutions, it is perhaps not impossible to attain some trustworthy conclusions. If for these several institutions, which from other evidence the Aryans might have been expected to possess, corresponding words can be shown to exist in the original language, the evidence is at all events as good as the nature of the case admits.

I have shown that, among all the Aryan nations, the early history of their institutions, so far as it can now be discerned, agrees in certain particulars. The Household, in the sense in which I have endeavoured to describe it, is the primary unit. This body is governed by a House Father with supreme authority, and comprises the House Mother, the children, the slaves, and the dependents. By the natural expansion of the Household kins are formed; and these kins in turn form within themselves smaller bodies of near kinsmen, intermediate, as it were, between the Household and the entire kin. The kins were known by their respective names, usually—probably, indeed, invariably—patronymics. A distinction of ranks prevailed among the freemen, according to their membership or non-membership of a kin; and probably, to some extent, between the kins themselves, according to the purity and the length of their descent. Each kin was settled upon a portion of land, which it owned in its collective capacity. Its members lived together in villages, in which each Household held in full property a house and garden. The arable land was cultivated in common; the produce, when the Household continued undivided, being shared among its members, and when separate Households were formed, becoming the separate property of each Household. The pasture lands were undivided, and the amount of cattle that each Household might depasture was settled by certain rules. Such, briefly, were the main features of archaic society at a period before anything resembling political institutions was formed. Such, then, or of a similar kind, are the features that we might expect to find among the primitive Aryans. I have now to consider what traces, if any, of these institutions may be discovered in our forefathers' language.

The Household.

§ 3. The Aryan House Father was certainly the husband of one wife; and the House Mother was the true and honourable wife of a single husband. The various members of their family had their specific names. We can still trace the terms that expressed the nearest degrees both of consanguinity and of affinity, and we can mark the friendly relations which these terms imply. But it is less easy to prove the peculiar corporate character of the Household itself, than to establish the existence of its component parts. The mere name of the House, or of the different members of the Household, proves nothing as to the technical sense of the former term, or as to the relations between those members. In express terms, the language tells us nothing of agnation, and nothing of paternal power. But the paternal power was the connecting bond and the external symbol of the Household's unity. If, therefore, any evidence of its existence can be obtained, its consequences may fairly be accepted. Three leading terms denoting paternity run through the Aryan languages. One of them, or rather one class of them, denotes the physical relation of parentage. Another of them may be described as a term of endearment. The third is a title of dignity. The first includes the words descended from the same root as that of the Latin *genitor,* or from other roots having a similar meaning. The second is found in the Greek *ἄττα* or *τάττα,* the Latin *Attus,* and *Tatius,* the Irish *Athail,* and our own familiar, though humble, "daddy." The third comes from a root which means to maintain and protect, and appears, among many other various but easily recognized forms, in the English father. I think that, from the use of this last-mentioned word by the Aryans, we may infer the existence among them of the paternal power. In other words, the term father, in its original sense, denoted a person who exercised a certain kind of authority; and this was the sense in which it was used by the Aryans at a time when its etymological meaning was more apparent than it has now become.

The root of father is PA, which means to support and protect. The term itself, as I have said, denotes not generation, but authority. It is applied by freemen to the gods, and by the slave or the dependent to the freeman. In Roman law,* it means not necessarily a married man, but, as we should say, the head of a house. The familiar expression *Pater Familias* correlates the *Familia* or Household, the body of dependents over which the *Pater* presides. It is nearly equivalent to our word lord, in its original sense of the Hlaford, or loaf-giver. With this word, indeed, it is sometimes in our old records expressly joined. When, for example,† the Saxon chronicle states that "in this year was Edward king chosen to father and to lord of the Scots' king and of the Scots, and of Regnold king and of all the Northumbrians, and eke of the Strathclyde Wealas' king and of all Strathclyde Wealas," the old record furnishes a full illustration of the surviving sense in which, a thousand years ago, our immediate ancestors used this word. In the Vedas, too, the words equivalent to father and *genitor* are used together, in reference to the same person, as mutually complementary, and severally expressing distinct ideas. Thus the form of the word, as it is found in all

* "Dig." L., 16, 195.

† See Mr. Freeman's "Norman Conquest," vol. i., p. 60.

the Aryan languages, proves its antiquity; while its history —the fact that in all these languages it has superseded the derivatives of other roots—proves the importance and the universality of the office.

It is notable that the Aryans had no special name for the relation of grandfather. The various languages express that relation each in its own particular way, for the most part by some periphrasis. The omission is the more striking because the Aryans had a special name, which is represented in the Latin *nepos* and our nephew, to express the relation of grandson. I think this singular omission may be explained by holding that the grandfather, or other highest living ascendent was the *Pater*. He was not the *genitor*, but he was the House Father. Special names were necessary to distinguish between the different members of the Household, but for all these members there could be only one head.

The contention may be thus stated. The word father was in use among the Aryans. Its etymology implies the exercise of some authority. In the earlier forms of all the derivative languages, the word is used in its etymological sense. It was, therefore, in this sense that it was used by the Aryans. The authority which, in the derivative language, it implies, is that generally known as the paternal power. Hence the inference is, that there existed among the undivided people a power similar in degree and kind to that which prevailed in each of the separate nations. To these considerations it may be added that there is no trace of any external authority among the Aryans, such as the modern State, which was likely to have interfered with the domestic rule of the House Father. It is not easy to prove, by the use of single words, the existence among the Aryans of such a relation as that of agnation. Still, by the aid both of that which is present, and of that which is not present, something may be done. The Aryans had * specific names, *patarva* and *bhratarva,* to express the father's brother and the son of the father's brother—that is, the paternal uncle and the first cousin on the father's side. But they had no such names on the mother's side; nor, on the father's side, did the list of special names advance beyond this point. There were, indeed, names for the immediate relations by marriage †—for the wife's father and the wife's mother, for the wife's brother and the wife's sister, and for the husband's brothers and sisters, and even for the husband's brothers' wives. But there is nothing to indicate any further relationship on the part of the wife. There is no special name to denote the wife's uncle, or aunt, or cousin, or any other of her kin. In this state of facts there are two matters for consideration. In the first place, there are special names for the persons who formed the Mæg, or near kin; and, in accordance with the principle of agnation, they all, excepting the wife's immediate family, are spear-kin and not spindle-kin; they are relatives on the father's side and not on the mother's side. There is thus some evidence in the language to confirm the presumption in favour of agnation to which the uniform custom of the derivative nations gives rise. In the second place, the specific names stop at the first cousin. But the Mæg, in the derivative nations, usually extended to the second cousin—that is, to the sixth degree. This difference suggests the possibility that, in primitive times, the line of the Mæg was drawn at the fourth degree—that is, at uncle's sons—and was subsequently extended. Such an opinion, however, is merely conjectural, and there is little, if any, external evidence in its support. In the present state of philological knowledge, the negative argument on such a point must not be pressed

* Fick's "Wörterbuch," pp. 1063, 1064.

† See Prof. Max Müller's "Chips," vol. ii., p. 31.

too far. There is nothing to explain either the original limitation or the subsequent abandonment of it. In these circumstances, a suspension of judgment is probably the wisest course, and it is enough to say that on this subject the philological evidence is not conclusive.

The House Spirit and the Hearth.

§ 4. The paternal authority, as it appears in historic times, was no arbitrary power. It was not the mere control of superior might. It was, as to a Roman ear its very name implied, a duly constituted authority. Its basis was the religion of the House, and the religion of the House consisted in the worship of the deceased ancestors that still dwelt at and protected the holy hearth. That hearth, and its ever-burning fire, at once the emblem of the comfortable element, and the organ of communication between the spirit-world and the earth, formed in the old days the centre of the spiritual life. There is as little doubt that this religion prevailed over the Highlands of Central Asia, as there is doubt of the presence there of the paternal power. But it is important to ascertain whether language affords any warrant for this belief. Its intimations are few, but suggestive. In the first place, there is philological evidence that the Aryans were a religious race. Their language contains an abundance of terms expressive of religious sentiment, of adoration, of piety, of faith, of prayer, and of sacrifice.* In the second place, that language contains nothing that is suggestive of public worship. It knows nothing of priests or of idols, of temples or of altars. In the third place, among the divided nations the names of their gods are simply the names of the various objects of nature, and were originally used with a full appreciation of their physical signification. All these objects had thus

* Pictet, "Les Origines Indo-Européennes," vol. ii., p. 690

received their names before they became objects of adoration. There was, therefore, a time when the language was spoken, but Polytheism did not exist. I do not thence infer, with M. Pictet, the original belief of the Aryans in the one true God. My inference is, that the Polytheistic Pantheon was not religious, but only scientific; and that it was designed merely to explain, in the rude fashion of an early time, the ordinary phenomena of Nature. Where, then, did the Aryans find the means for the satisfaction of those strong religious feelings which they certainly possessed? Language alone will not answer the question. It tells us that the Aryans had fire, and we know from other sources that fire, or at least a particular form of fire, was an object of worship among all the Aryan nations; but linguistic data alone do not warrant the assertion that the Aryans worshipped fire. So, too, the Aryan language contained the word that corresponds to ἑστίη or Vesta; but although this fact proves that the Aryans recognized the hearth, it does not indicate how far in their eyes that hearth was holy. The Aryans had several words for *man*, and the Hindus, the Greeks, the Kelts, the Scandinavians, and perhaps the Latins, spoke of their House Spirits as the men in the sky, or the men in the House, or the old men, or the men; but a missing link must be supplied * before we can allege that

* The Hindu expression is Naras. Nara is a recognized Aryan word, meaning man, and appears as well in other cognates as in the Greek ἀνηρ, and in the Latin names, Nero and Nerius. The temptation to identify Lares or Lases with this word is very great; and the more so as no reasonable explanation of Lares has yet been proposed. But the change of an initial *n* into *l* is a formidable difficulty. It is true that Priscian alleges that "solebant vetustissimi Græcorum n pro l dicere;" and that, in certain circumstances, the change in the middle of a word is regular. But I do not know any established case of such a change in the beginning of a word except that of νίτρον and λίτρον, and in our own language of noon-cheon and luncheon, which, after all, are but dialectic varieties. It is noteworthy that the Hindus are said ("Life in the Mofussil," vol. i., p. 115) to habitually interchange *l* and *n* at the beginning of English words.

the Aryans appropriated any such term to their deceased ancestors. Perhaps the most suggestive word on the subject is the name of the Hellenic fire god, Hephaistos. The attributes and the functions of the Olympic armourer were indeed very different from those of the gentle gods of the Household; but his name has been identified * with the Sanscrit *Subhyishtha*, a superlative form equivalent to the "sibest," if I may coin such a word, or the "kindliest" in its original sense, the guardian and the chief of the sib, the persons who shared in the same religious rites, and enjoyed the same divine protection.

The Clan and its Divisions.

§ 5. I have said that the Aryan nations, when they in their separate condition become known to us, lived in groups of clans connected by a descent, real or assumed, from a common ancestor; that each of these clans presented a structural division which may be called, in the terms of the Roman law, that of the Agnati and of the Gentiles; and that there was, further, a well-marked distinction among freemen into a superior and an inferior class, according as they were members of a kin and of a Household, or of a Household only. If we assume that similar arrangements prevailed among the undivided Aryans, the old language confirms our expectation upon each of these points. The Eponym of our race was Manu—the Menu of the Hindus, the Minuas of Orchemenos, the Manes of the Phrygians, the Minos son of Zeus of Crete, the Mannus son of Tuisco, whom, in the time of Tacitus, the German Sagas described

What we want is an instance of a Sanscrit word commencing with *n* that is represented by a Latin word commencing with *l*. The derivations of words, like the use of words, must be strictly judged; and the student must learn the painful, but wholesome, lesson, to abandon, upon cause shown, the most favourite effort of his ingenuity—"Quamvis invita recedant Et versentur adhuc intra penetralia Vestæ."

* See Pictet, vol. ii., p. 679.

as their founder. Just as the several nations were divided into cognate clans, as the Ionians, the Dorians, and the Æolians were descended from the three sons of Hellen; as Ing, Hermin, and Isco continued the race of Mann, so the Aryans had their several clans, each of which was known by its proper appellation. Individual names are of course necessary, at all times and in all circumstances, to distinguish individuals. But the pride of race which has always distinguished the Aryans appears to have given no small importance to the name of the clan. The word "name" has, accordingly, been preserved under a variety of but slightly differing forms all through the Aryan nations. It comes from the root *gna*, and means that by which one is known, the initial guttural being, by a strange coincidence, lost in every one of the separate languages.*

For the division of the clan there are appropriate words in the old language. These words are Sib or Kin for the one part, and for the other part the Wic. I cannot say that the language of itself proves any connection between these terms, much less such a connection as that which, in a former chapter, I have attempted to describe. The proof of that connection depends upon the resemblance in the customs of each of the separate nations. But when the existence of such resemblances is known, that knowledge may reasonably be applied to the interpretation of these Aryan words, which evidently denote different ideas. It is not clear whether the lower division ought to be called the kin or the sib. Both words exist in the Aryan language; but the latter, while it became obsolete among the Iranians, is used in the Vedas, and the former takes its place in the Avesta. Both these languages agree in the use of the wider term, the *wic*. Further, there are titles which show

* Pictet, "Les Origines," vol. ii., p. 380.

that each of these bodies was regularly organized, and was under the control of its special chief. The Avesta * notices four degrees in the social scale of the old Iranians. It speaks, and in this order, of the House-master, the kin-master, the wic-master, and the province-master; and it prescribes a tariff of purification for these, according to their rank. With the last-mentioned personage, who appears to have been merely local, I am not now concerned. But this passage gives the three ascending steps of the House, the kin, and the wic, with a master of each. In Sanscrit there are corresponding titles, except that for the "zantu pati," or kin-master, the "sabha pati," or sib-master, occurs. The House-master and the wic-master are recognized as original Aryan terms, but not so, apparently, the intermediate term. Yet, whatever difficulty may arise as to the use of a particular word, it may be confidently alleged that the Aryan House-master was the member of an organized clan under the presidency of a chief, and that he was also a member of a body of near kinsmen within that clan, by whatever name that body was called, and whether it had, or had not, a special president.

The word "wic" occurs, with but slight variations of either form or meaning, in all the Aryan languages. Its original meaning seems to have been simply a dwelling, and in this sense it appears in the Greek ὃικος, a digammated word, and in the Icelandic † Vic. But it also included a collection of houses or a village, and in this sense it occurs in the Latin *vicus*, our own wick, and under other forms in the Gothic, Keltic, and Slavonic tongues. The word kin, or gens, or zantu needs no comment. Its descent is unmistakable from that root with which, both in Greek and in Latin, we are familiar in the sense of generation. But the "sabha"

* See Spiegel's "Avesta," by Bleeck, vol. i., 57; ii., 2.

† Cleasby-Vigfusson, Icel. Dict., p. 687.

or sib deserves some further consideration. The Sanscrit word "sabha" is compounded of the preposition *sa*, which is the Latin *cum*, the Greek *συν*, and of the root *bha*, which occurs in the Latin *fui* and its cognates.* It means an assembly, and, secondarily, a place of worship. Hence are derived various adjective forms, meaning, generally, worthy of the assembly, and then faithful and distinguished in society. In the Rig Veda the word "sabheya" is used as an epithet of a son who is distinguished in the "sabha," and is the glory of his father, or of a priest who is learned in the customs of the family. Sometimes "sabha" is used in the sense of a tribunal; and the words "asabhya," meaning worthless—that is, out of the sabha, and "pasabha," meaning violence, or conduct in opposition to the sabha, also occur. Corresponding to these terms is the Gothic "unsibis," illegal; all which words suggest the idea of an assembly having jurisdiction. In Irish, the word "sabh," or "sibhe," a chief, belongs to the same source. The word occurs in the Slavonic languages, with the significant sense of a person who has a share in a common field-mark. In the Norse language it is said † to mean relationship by marriage as opposed to that by blood; but from the use of the technical term afsifja, ‡ to forisfamiliate, I suspect that this was a later meaning. From the old German sippe, it has come to ourselves, and survives in our language. Sib, in the sense of related, is still used in the Lowlands of Scotland, and appears in the writings of Sir Walter Scott. It is also found in the humble but deeply interesting word, gossip. This word, degraded as it now is, takes us back, with a twofold interest, at once to the

* Pictet, "Les Origines," vol. ii., p. 382, *et seq.* Fick, "Wörterbuch," p. 195.

† Cleasby-Vigfusson, p. 526.

‡ *Ib.*, p. 9.

cradle of our race and to the cradle of our faith. It was originally applied to persons who were sib, or related to each other in God; and especially meant those persons who, by taking part in the same baptismal rite, were regarded as forming between each other a new relation, of which God was the bond. As the Hindu belonged to a "sabha," of which the bond was the offering to Agni, so the Christian entered, through baptism, into a spiritual kinship, of which the members were in a special sense brethren in Christ. How intimate this tie was once held to be we may gather from a curious passage of an old Irish * annalist. When he desires to express the climax of misery and disorder in his unhappy country, he declares that "there was no protection for church or fortress, gossipred, or mutual oath." Hence gossips came to mean intimate friends; next, gossip meant the light, familiar talk of such friends; and, finally, with a dyslogistic connotation, any frivolous conversation. To such base uses may the noblest words, like the noblest men, come at last.

The Aryan vocabulary contains † the word "vasupatar," and its feminine, "vasupataryâ," meaning one who has a noble father. The words immediately recall the Homeric epithet of Helenê, *εὐπατερέια*, and the Athenian noblesse, the *εὐπάτριδες*. But a noble father is a relative expression, and connotes a state of things where inferior parentage is not unknown. We are thus reminded of that remarkable division of freemen which, as I have shown, is found among almost all the Aryan nations, and which, in our own early history, is familiar to us under the names of Eorl and Ceorl. How far a similar distinction originally prevailed, I can only surmise. But clans, and divisions of clans, existed among the Aryans. The words that I have

* "Annals of the Four Masters," 1050.

† Fick's "Wörterbuch," p. 186.

cited are evidence that, before the dispersion of the nations, ranks were distinguished, and that the basis of that distinction was birth. Among the separate nations distinctions of rank prevailed, and I have stated my reasons for believing that the line was drawn at membership of a kin. In these circumstances, it is not an unreasonable inference that, in this respect also, the practice of the Aryans resembled the practice of their descendants.

The Mark System.

§ 6. It remains briefly to notice the traces among the Aryans of the mark syetem, such as I have already described it. In the first place, the word *Masg* is found * in the sense of the mark itself. There are, as I have said, a variety of names for the house; and âra,† which reappears in the Latin *area* and various Sanscrit and Slavonic cognates, occurs in the sense of what our old law called the "precinct." The village was known as "vaika or vik." But it had also other names, amongst which is our word "tribe." This word ‡ is the Sanscrit trapa, the Keltic treabh, the Lithuanian troba, the Latin tribus, the Umbrian trefu. In the Gothic languages, it appears under some variety of the well-known "dorf," or, as in England it is called "thorpe." The Russian word is "derewnia," and the Scandinavian is "trup." It is probable § that these words are connected with troop, troupeau, and the like, and that the primary idea is aggregation for the purpose of protection. But it may be observed that these words do not support the meaning of the word "tribe" as an extension of the community; in other words, of an aggregation of clans. I suspect that such a meaning came from the Latin tribus, and that this word was of

* Fick's "Wörterbuch," p. 151. † *Ib.*, p. 20.
‡ Pictet, "Les Origines," vol. ii., p. 291.
§ See "Cobden Club Essays," vol. i., p. 351.

entirely different origin from those we have been considering. It denoted * merely a political division, and is analogous to our "riding." Both in Greek and in Latin, it was τριπτυς or τριττυς, the third of some primitive whole. In this aspect it would be a comparatively modern word, and has little interest. In the other sense it claims, of course, a high antiquity; and it denotes the community itself, and not any extension of it. I do not know that there is any express evidence of either the arable mark or the pasture mark. There seems, however, to be one word which points to a system of collective occupation. This is † the Sanscrit samanya, the Oscan comonom, the Latin comoinis, or, as it was in classic times written, communis, the Gothic gamainths, the modern German gemeinde. All these forms imply an undivided property, and probably have especial reference to pasture lands. To them may perhaps be added the Greek κοῖνος and the Irish cumme. There is another word, "vara or varata," ‡ which seems to imply a fenced place, and of which traces still remain in the final syllable in such words as Kenilworth, Lutterworth, Tamworth. It is possible that this word may relate to the house and its precinct only; but it may also, and a kindred word among the Germans did, denote a *sundergut* or immunity.

At the same time I must add, that neither in the case of tribe, nor of common, nor of worth, does Fick include in his Aryan vocabulary any corresponding primitive term. The evidence of the experts is, therefore, not so decisive as it was in those other cases, where they were all agreed.

§ 7. Philology affords also some negative evidence. The Aryans had no word for law. They had no word for king. The Negative Evidence.

* See Mommsen's "Hist. Rome," vol. i., pp. 45, 74.

† Pictet, vol. ii., p. 406.

‡ *Ib.*, p. 80.

There is no trace among them of any organized priesthood, or of any system of public worship.* There is no trace among them of anything that approaches to what we call a State. These omissions, however, are less formidable than they might at first sight appear. The experience of India shows that, even at the present day, men can live without the aid of any political organization. If we bear this fact in mind, these negations, taken along with some positive hints, will help us to understand the social condition of these distant forefathers. If there be no Aryan State, there are plainly enough the clan and its organization. If there be no Aryan word for law, there is an Aryan word † for custom. If the king be wanting, we find chiefs in their several degrees—the chief of the House, and the chief of the wick, and the chief of the kin. If they had no established religion, our forefathers had strong religious sentiments, even if we can but dimly discern the objects of their worship. The names of some of their divinities, the Devas, the Amukas,‡ Varana, seem to suggest an incipient Nature-worship. In "Bhaga" § again—a name that means a brother, the Zeus Bagaios of the Phrygians, the Boga of the Slavs, the degraded bogy of Christendom—there is probably a trace of the House Spirit. At all events, the vestiges of the agnatic Household may be seen; and where that is found, the House Spirit is not far away.

I do not, therefore, picture to myself the dwelling of an Aryan House Father as "a den ‖ which its savage owner shares indeed with his mate and his offspring, but which no other living being may enter except at the risk of his life."

* Pictet, "Les Origines," vol. ii., p. 690.

† See Fick's "Wörterbuch," p. 101.

‡ *Ib.*, p. 12. § *Ib.*, p. 133.

‖ Mr. Cox's "General History of Greece," p. 11.

The rule of the precinct was not altogether so alarming. To me the evidence seems to point to a number of clans connected, like the Hellenes, in a general way, and worshipping a common genarch. These clans had each its peculiar *sacra*, and bore each its special "nama" or Gentile designation. Each of them was independent, and lived upon its own land, or wandered perhaps over its own beat, under the direction of its hereditary chief. They knew nothing of State affairs; but clan life, with its rules of marriage and of pure blood, of kindred help and kindred vengeance, was in full activity. Custom supplied the place of law; and their disputes were settled by their elders, or, at worst, were compounded under some system of wer-geld. They had property, both common and separate, and a distinct system of inheritance. To speak of such men as savages, in the same sense in which we so describe the lower grades of the Turanian peoples, is a mere abuse of words. They may have been in some respects far from the standard of modern civilization; but there never was any risk of an Aryan having been mistaken for an Anthropoid.

CHAPTER XIII.

NON-GENEALOGIC CLANS.

The Household the type of archaic Association.

§ 1. I HAVE hitherto described the normal growth of the primitive association. Starting from a single Household, it expands into a Joint Undivided Household, which separates into several related Households, which become a kin or clan. Such seems to be the regular course of events when it is not interrupted by the action of external forces. Disturbing forces do, of course, intervene; and there must have been, and must still be, countless instances of kins that have been cut short at every stage of their existence. Superorganisms have their perils not less than the organisms of which they are composed; and the apparent waste of vegetal and animal life finds its parallel in the fate of societies. War, pestilence, famine, all the ills to which flesh is heir, scatter the elements of which the rising societies are formed. Even prosperity brings with it its own dangers. The stronger and more luxuriant the growth, the less necessity exists for those expedients by which, in less fortunate circumstances, the ranks of the society are recruited. The rules of descent become rigid, and are strictly enforced. Any lapse from the strict standard, any imperfection in the pedigree, brings with it expulsion. Not unfrequently this strictness is fatal even to the body that it means to protect. In the absence of new blood, the old genealogic clan dwindles, and at last its place knows it no more.

The genealogic clan, however, is not the only, although it is probably the earliest, form of Aryan association. There are other similar bodies, for all of which the old clan forms the model, and for some of which it supplies the materials. I have said that from various causes, either from some defect in the pedigree, or from some misconduct, or from the pressure of debt or of a blood feud, or from some similar misfortune, men are expelled from, or are obliged to leave, their kin. In archaic society, such a relinquishment, whether compulsory or not, means something very different from what it means when the State is supreme. It implies that the person so cast out has no longer, unless he be sold into slavery, a place in the world. He must begin life anew. He belongs * to no brotherhood, is subject to no custom, has no hearth. His hand is against every man, and every man's hand is against him. But man is a social animal, and the scattered elements of society, by an unfailing attraction, gravitate together. Forthwith they commence to organize themselves according to the law of their being. Of that law, the Household is the type. Nor is misfortune the sole cause of such new combinations. Sometimes there is a natural reproduction of the parent stock. Sometimes there is a separation, whether in friendship or in anger, of the old body. Sometimes men desire to associate for the accomplishment of some common purpose, for the advancement of some religious belief, for the prosecution of some special form of industry, for the cultivation of some special art. In all these cases they have recourse to the one prevailing type. Human association presents itself to archaic man in the form of a Household, and that Household is arranged on certain definite principles. There is no reasoning upon the matter, no balancing of

* Ἀφρήτωρ ἀθέμιστος ἀνέστιος ἐστιν ἐκεῖνος.—Il., ix., 63.

powers, no calculation of the greatest happiness of the greatest number. They accept the one familiar form as an ordinance of nature; and they no more desire to innovate upon it than they think of altering their stature or changing the colour of their skin.

The formation of artificial Associations.

§ 2. The principles on which the Household was based, and which, in the formation of artificial households or analogous groups, men had to apply, were the existence of an Eponym, Agnation, and Exogamy. Of each of these subjects I have already treated, and nothing more is now necessary than to notice the method of their application to the new circumstances. The first step is to find an Eponym. Ordinarily, some man of ability and note supplies the want with a degree of efficiency proportioned to his reputation. Some successful soldier, some person of high, although perhaps blemished descent, some person of peculiar sanctity, in short a person possessed of any qualities calculated to excite public attention, attracts a following. Nothing succeeds like success; and the association, if it once secure a foothold, soon augments its numbers. The leader of one generation becomes the Eponym of the next. After his death, his spirit is acknowledged as the *Lar Familiaris* of the new society, and his followers are regarded as his adopted sons. So far, there is no difficulty. The train of thought is sufficiently intelligible, and I shall presently show that this was the actual course of events. What was the position of the leader during his life, is not so clear. It appears as if, in ancient times at least, it was usual to accept as the patron some hero or some god; or, in Christian times, some saint; and this patron, separately during the life of the Eponym, and conjointly with the Eponym after his decease, formed the Penates of the association. Yet even the worship of a living man, or rather of his genius or spirit, is not inconceivable. The Romans blended the divinity of Augustus with their Lares, as grateful Greece did that of Castor and the mighty Hercules. Asiatic provinces could not be restrained from erecting altars to the emperors. Even in our own time we are at once shocked and amused at the accounts of the determined efforts of the Hindus to worship, during his life-time, the brave General Nicholson; and of that much-aggrieved officer's escape from apotheosis by the unsparing application to his votaries of the cat-of-nine-tails. In all circumstances, however, the name and the repute of the Eponym form the cement of the association. Its members derive from him a common name, a common worship, and a common pride of descent. They have lost or forsaken all other ties, human or divine; and they form under their new organization, for good or for evil, an independent and self-sufficient community.

Yet, although these men are thus connected by their allegiance to a common head, each of them within that limit becomes himself the founder of a line of his own. Those who once had a lineage and Gentile customs, introduce in some fashion their old ties into the new place. As the Englishman in Australia and America revives old memories by giving to his homestead and his township the long-familiar names; as the surviving son of Priam founded, in his exile,* his little Troy, and Pergamos modelled upon its great original; as the Roman colonist,† wherever he went, always established a miniature and semblance of the Roman people; so the Rajpút, driven into the jungle, strives to perpetuate the memory of his kin. Thus the process which I have hitherto endeavoured to describe is inverted.

* Procedo, et parvam Trojam, simulataque magnis
Pergama, et arentem Xanthi cognomine rivum
Agnosco, Scææque amplector limina portæ.—*Æn.*, iii., 349.

† Effigies parvæ simulachraque Populi Romani.—*Aul. Gellius*, xvi., 13.

Instead of a Household expanding through kins into a people, the tale commences with a people in miniature, ready formed, and with its component clans marked out from the first. That which practically keeps together the larger connection, and keeps asunder the smaller groups, is the law of Exogamy. Men must marry within the people, and must not marry within the clan. It is noteworthy how men are found to obey the letter of these laws, while they adopt various contrivances to avoid the inconvenience to which, in an early state of society, their pressure gives rise. When the domestic supply of wives fails, recourse is had to abduction: but the women so taken are formally adopted—* although the adoption of females seems, as I have elsewhere said, to have been irregular—into one clan, in order that they may be married into another. When there are enough women in the tribe, but their distribution among the clans is unequal, a re-examination of pedigrees takes place. Some plausible case of distinct ancestry is always made out, and one clan is divided into several clans, each of which has, of course, both as between themselves and the other clans within the tribe, reciprocal rights of *connubium*. These and the like expedients would not be tolerated in the older and more successful clans; and they will probably cease among those who now use them, as time strengthens and confirms their hereditary tendency.

Such seems to be the process by which clans were formed otherwise than by descent. So little is known of the history of any clans, or of their formation, that it is difficult to illustrate, by any well-authenticated case, any part of their development. As to these impure clans, an example is given by Mr. Lyall from his personal observation in India. In that country there exists a great tribe of robbers and

* Mr. Lyall, "Fort. Rev.," No. 121, N.S., p. 107.

caterans named Meenas. "This name," Mr. Lyall says,* "represents four great sections of one tribe, which inhabit four different and distant tracts, and are evidently fast separating off into alien clans by reason of distant habitations. Each section is, of course, distributed off into manifold circles of affinity; and these circles, being in various phases of growth and consistency, can mostly be traced back, by the clue of their names or other characteristics, to their real distinction of origin. Some of them preserve the name of the higher clan or caste from which the founder of the circle emigrated and joined the Meenas: some names denote only the founder's original habitation, while other circles bear the names of notorious ancestors. We can perceive plainly that the whole tribe is nothing else but a Cave of Adullam, which has stood open for centuries, and has sheltered generation after generation of adventurers, outlaws, outcasts, and refugees generally. It is well-known from history, and, on a small scale, from experience of the present day, how famines, wide-desolating invasions, pestilences, and all great social catastrophes, shatter to pieces the framework of oriental societies, and disperse the fragments abroad like seeds, to take root elsewhere. Not only have these robber tribes received bands of recruits during such periods of confusion, so common in Indian history, but there goes on a steady enlistment of individuals or families whom a variety of accidents or offences, public opinion or private feuds, drives out of the pale of settled life and beyond their orthodox circles. Upon this dissolute collection of masterless men, the idea of kinship begins immediately to operate afresh, and to re-arrange them systematically into groups. Each new immigrant becomes one of the Meena tribe; but he, nevertheless, adheres so far to his

* *Ubi supra*, p. 105.

origin and his custom as to insist upon setting up a separate circle, under the name of his lost clan, caste, family, or lands."

This description suggests the commencement of a far more famous society, and the old Asylum on Capitolinus between the Two Groves. It is clear that the legendary origin of Rome, whether those legends be in fact true or false, did not appear to the men among whom the tale was told as in any way absurd. It is equally clear that, to a native of Central India, at the present day, the stories of the Asylum and of the Rape of the Sabines would seem mere ordinary occurrences. A prince in distress, but miraculously preserved; a band of brave but broken men collecting under his banner; the contemptuous rejection of *connubium* by the neighbouring genealogic clans; the successful abduction; the foundation of a great power—to the story of all these events a modern Rajpút would seriously incline, without any misgivings as to antecedent improbabilities. In times that, in our view, are more within the region of actual history, the Roman annals record some cases that seem to be parallel. One of these was that of the Cilician Pirates, whom Pompeius Magnus extirpated. At one time it seemed as if a great robber-State was about to establish itself in the Levant. "The pirates," says Mommsen,* "called themselves Cilicians; in fact, their vessels were the rendezvous of desperadoes and adventurers from all countries, discharged mercenaries from the recruiting-grounds of Crete, burgesses from the destroyed townships of Italy, Spain, and Asia, soldiers and officers from the armies of Fimbria and Sertorius; in a word, the ruined men of all nations, the hunted refugees of all vanquished parties, every one that was wretched and

* "Hist. of Rome," vol. iv., p. 40.

daring." The organization of these men was complete. They afforded mutual help; they acknowledged any agreement made by any of their members; they collectively avenged any wrong that any such member had sustained. They showed,* in an eminent degree, "the inviolable determination to stand side by side, the sense of fellowship, respect for the pledged word and the self-chosen chiefs." "We cannot tell," adds the historian, "how far the internal political development of this floating State had already advanced; but its arrangements undeniably contained the germs of a sea-kingdom which was already beginning to establish itself, and out of which, under favourable circumstances, a permanent State might have been developed." Perhaps the history of Sertorius points in the same direction. If that distinguished general had been content with his Iberian position, he might have founded a Spanish kingdom. The Spaniards, just as the Teutons and the Kelts would have done, insisted † upon becoming his 'men.' But his object was to re-conquer the headship of his native country. He fell in the attempt, and his clan, that might have been, fell with him.

The Religious Association.

§ 3. A union which, like the Household, rests upon a religious sentiment, was obviously suited for the extension of religious communities. Accordingly it is found that in India such communities spring up with wonderful rapidity, and all with similar features. Some person, sometimes a devout man, sometimes an impostor, starts some new tenet or professes some new revelation. He organizes a new society, of which he becomes the Eponym. Sometimes he fails, and no more is heard of him or his society. Sometimes his memory lingers in some obscure tomb or

* "Hist. of Rome," vol. iv., p. 42.

† *Ib.*, p. 20.

shrine. Sometimes his success is assured, and the religious community may attain even to national proportions. Such was the case of the Sikhs, who were originally a religious fraternity; and such, on a still greater scale, were the faiths of Bouddha and Mohammed. Of the practical operation of these principles on a small scale, Mr. Lyall gives some interesting illustrations.* He says:—"A boy may be noticed sitting by the roadside, who can be known at once to belong to a religious order by the large trident painted in a special fashion on his forehead, having for vestments only a light martingale of yellow cloth around the loins. Being questioned as to his circumstances, he explains that he has forgotten his people and his father's house; that his parents both died of cholera, a year or so back, whereupon his uncle sold his sister into a respectable family, and presented the boy to a mystic who had a new revelation, and was developing a religious fraternity thereupon. To that fraternity he now belongs, and all other ties of blood or caste have dropped away from him. Or if one question, in like manner, any strange pilgrim that comes wandering across central India from the shrines upon the Indian Ocean towards the head-waters of the Ganges in the Himalayas, he may describe himself simply as the disciple of some earlier saint or sage who showed the Way. The point to be remarked is, that he undertakes no other definition of himself whatever, and declines all other connections or responsibilities." I need do no more than indicate the analogies in Christian countries. If any person, in a country where the Roman Catholic creed prevails, enter 'religion,' that is, become a member of some religious order, he is deemed to be civilly dead; and has, in contemplation of law, no other interests save only such

* "Fort. Rev.," No. 121, N.S., p. 100.

as belong to his monastery. In regard to secular things, such a person has practically ceased to exist. There are in this connection some matters, otherwise difficult of explanation, which now become intelligible. Sir H. S. Maine * justly explains certain difficulties in Irish ecclesiastical history, by showing that each monastic house constituted a family, or tribe; and he observes that the founder of the house "afterwards nearly invariably reappears as a saint." He offers no explanation of this phenomenon, but it does not seem difficult to find one. The canonization merely represented the apotheosis. The founder became the Eponym, the *Lar Familiaris*, of his community. If Herodotus were to describe such a personage, he would probably say of him, as he does say † of Miltiades, "And to him, when he had made his end, they offer sacrifices, as is the custom to a founder." In such circumstances, the monks and their successors became the saint's kin. Each monk may have had his secular kinsmen, and for certain purposes notice was taken of them. But the spiritual relationship was fully established; and each new religious community became, as it were, an additional clan of the great all-embracing community, the great spiritual nation, whose Eponym is Christ.

Religion, moreover, not only forms a bond of union, but also acts as a disintegrating force. If it brings peace on earth, it also brings a sword. The first great schism of which any information exists was that which arose among the Eastern Aryans, when those who worshipped the Devas emigrated into Hindostan, and their brethren, who clung to the old faith, remained in Iran. Unhappily, the disruptive power of religious belief, in modern times, needs no illustration. But in its milder form, as it appears in India, it

* "Early Hist. of Inst.," p. 236.

† vi., 38.

seems to furnish a method by which, in the absence of any legislative organ, the pressure of customs that have become unsuitable may be avoided. Religious societies break up and form new groups. Those who desire any change secede, and form a new religion of their own. Thus, the marriage with a deceased brother's wife is with some tribes an absolute duty, and is with others prohibited. The custom* has crept into one of the clans where it was previously forbidden. The result is that a sept has been detached from the rest of its brotherhood. "It appears," says Mr. Lyall,† "that a religious body with some distinctive object of worship, or singular rule of devotion, has usually, though not invariably, come to split off into a separate group, which, though based upon a common religion, constructs itself upon the plan of a tribe. The common faith, or worship, forms the outer circle, which has gradually shut off a sect not only from intermarriage, but even from eating with outsiders: while, inside their circumference, the regular circles of affinity have established themselves independently, just as families settle and expand within the pale of a half-grown tribe. Each body of proselytes from different tribes and castes has preserved its identity as a distinct stock, keeping up the fundamental prohibition against marriage within the particular group of common descent. But with some other groups of the sect it is essential to marry; and thus in the course of time has been reproduced, upon a basis of common belief or worship, the original circle of a tribe, beyond which it is impossible to contract a legitimate marriage."

I have taken the preceding illustrations chiefly from the present time and from Indian sources. There is nothing unusual in religious association, and we need not go far

* Mr. Lyall, "Fort. Rev.," No. 121, N.S., p. 103.

† *Ib.*, p. 113.

from our own doors to observe the power and the persistency of the force from which it springs. But that which I desire to show is the nature of such an association as an exclusive tie. The State has now become sufficiently strong to insist upon the allegiance of all its subjects, whether they are members of a religious body or not. But in archaic society, all the various combinations of men crossed each other, and yet remained distinct. In India, this condition of things still survives, although its end is probably not far distant. The information, therefore, which that country affords is inestimable. It is, indeed, fortunate that we have the evidence of so intelligent and trustworthy a witness as Mr. Lyall with respect to the events that are now actually taking place; and all students of social phenomena must earnestly desire that this very acute and judicious observer may, while there is still time, place upon record a detailed account of Rajpút customs and modes of thought. The weakness of the State, or, rather, the absence of any true State, in the remoter parts of India, has hitherto permitted these various societies to develop themselves by the side of the clans, or even in opposition to them—a result which, under a powerful central government, is hardly possible. We cannot, therefore, expect to find, either in modern States, or in the more advanced of the governments of antiquity, examples equally striking. But it must not be supposed that religious organizations, such as I have described, were unknown in Greece and Rome. In the latter city, indeed, the strong hand of the law was prompt to keep within bounds every kind of extravagance; and the senate, however tolerant to individual eccentricity in matters of worship, sternly repressed any organization that threatened the welfare of the State. In Greece, however, the case was otherwise. Of early Attica, Mr. Grote * observes that it

* "Hist. of Greece," vol. i., p. 264.

"was originally distributed into many independent demes or cantons, and included, besides, various religious clans or hereditary sects, if the expression may be permitted; that is, a multitude of persons not necessarily living in the same locality, but bound together by an hereditary communion of sacred rites, and claiming privileges, as well as performing obligations, founded upon the traditional authority of divine persons, for whom they had a common veneration." Such, on a larger scale, were the Orphic, and especially the Pythagorean, brotherhoods.* The latter famous association consisted of the disciples of a great religious and moral teacher. They adopted, as a symbol of their allegiance to him and of their union among themselves, a peculiar diet, ritual, and system of observances. Among themselves, they were bound by the most devoted attachment. Towards all persons outside of their brotherhood they made no secret of their contempt. Their social views are concisely stated in two verses of a descriptive poem that have been preserved.† "His companions he deemed equal to the blessed gods: all others he held of no account, either in value or in number." To this comprehensive rule they allowed no exception. It extended even to their nearest relatives, and the offence thus given is said to have been one leading cause of the misfortunes of the sect. With the history of the brotherhood I am not now concerned. I only desire to call attention to their characteristics as illustrating this form of association, to their intimate union, their exclusiveness, their devotion to their Eponym, their substitution of the new ties for the old domestic relations, and to the resemblance which their association seems to have borne to the Household.

"Hist. of Greece," vol. i., p. 31; vol. iv., p. 529, *et seq.*

† Τοὺς μὲν ἑταίρους ἦγεν ἴσους μακάρεσσι θεοῖσι.
Τοὺς δ' ἄλλους ἡγεῖτ' οὔτ' ἐν λόγῳ οὔτ' ἐν ἀριθμῷ.

§ 4. Other associations, formed for various other purposes, have been organized on principles similar to those that I have described. Such, especially, are those which have for their object professional purposes, and those which are purely industrial. The former class was conspicuous in early Greece. "As there were in every gens or family," says Mr. Grote,* "special Gentile deities and foregone ancestors who watched over its members, forming in each the characteristic symbol and recognized guarantee of their union, so there seems to have been in each guild or trade peculiar beings whose vocation it was to co-operate or to impede in various stages of the business." Such a class was the famous School of the Homeridæ—the bards who, with the great epic poet as their Eponym, formed what we should call the literary class of the time. Such were the Asklepidæ, or sons of the physicians, who, under the headship of Asklepios, formed the fraternity of medicine. Such were the Cheironidæ,† who inherited from the wise Centaur the knowledge of the virtues of medicinal herbs, a knowledge which they were bound to use without remuneration. Such, too,‡ were the Klytiadæ and the Iamidæ, the great augural clans of Elis, and the Talthybiadæ, the heraldic house of Lacedæmon. Thus, when Diomedes§ boasts that the children of the ill-fortuned were they that encountered his might, he does not intend to say, and in fact does not say, that those persons are unfortunate whose children meet him in battle; but he describes his opponents as being in very truth the children or descendants of misfortune. Misfortune was their Eponym, and they were so predestined to defeat that they could only be regarded as the clansmen of disaster. At Rome, the original history of

The Professional or Industrial Association.

* "Hist. of Greece," vol. i., p. 465. † *Ib.*, p. 249.

‡ Herodotus, vii., 134 ; ix., 33. Cicero, "De Div.," i., 41.

§ "Iliad," vi., 127.

such associations is remarkable. They were composed exclusively of ærarians and freedmen. No Quirite, much less a patrician, could belong to a guild. We may accordingly infer that these guilds were meant to provide an organization for persons who otherwise would have had no social ties. The State was not then sufficiently strong to dispense with the inferior social agencies. On the contrary, it eagerly courted their assistance. Thus, from the earliest times, or, in popular language, from the reign of King Numa, the artisans,* or, as we should say, the working classes, were arranged in nine guilds. These were the pipers, goldsmiths, carpenters, dyers, curriers, tanners, coppersmiths, potters, and all other workmen. To these must be added other guilds of great antiquity—bankers, merchants, watermen of the river, butchers, and scribes. "That each," says Niebuhr,† "as a true corporation, had its presidents, property, and special religious rites, may be asserted with perfect certainty, from the examples of later times." Of all these guilds, the greatest and the most powerful was that of the scribes or notaries. All the business now performed by clerks, book-keepers, and conveyancers, the preparation of all the public documents, and of all private written instruments, was in their hands. They formed the permanent civil service of the time; they were the solicitors, the scriveners, the accountants, of Rome. Under the Empire the old guild developed into two bodies—the *possessores* or public functionaries, and the notaries, who practised their profession independently. It is to the latter class that we owe, as Savigny has conjectured, the preservation, through centuries of peril, of the Roman law; and so, as Niebuhr ‡ has remarked, "The Manes of the heroes and

* Plutarch, "Numa."
† "Hist. of Rome," vol. iii., p. 298.
‡ *Ib.*, p. 300.

lawgivers of Rome owe it for the most part to a guild, in which they saw, not unjustly, a germ which might produce the destruction of the old noble institutions, and the pretensions of which rendered them indignant, that a late posterity is enabled to know and admire these institutions and their development."

From the Brehon laws it appears that organizations for professional purposes existed in Ireland, and were conducted on the principle of the family. There were similar associations for industrial purposes, of which the most important were grazing partnerships. It is, indeed, as Sir Henry Maine * observes, "most instructive to find the same words used to describe bodies of co-partners formed by contract, and bodies of co-heirs or co-parceners formed by common descent." In France, families of cutlers and of other trades were found in Auvergne and other rural districts, up to the time of the great Revolution.†

Closely resembling these industrial associations are the guilds of the Middle Ages.‡ These guilds had their origin in direct imitation of the family. The three earliest of which any record exists are English, and date from the beginning of the tenth century. They all agree in some significant particulars. Each has a patron saint; each makes provision for divine worship; each makes provision for a common meal. Between the members, strict rules for mutual help and support prevail. At an earlier period, indications, though less distinct, of similar associations may be found. It may be said, generally, that their character was similar. There was always a confraternity; and the basis of their union was a religious rite, symbolized by a common meal. In Christian times, to which alone our knowledge

* "Early Hist. of Inst.," p. 232.

† M. de Laveleye, "De la Propriété," p. 231, *et seq.*

‡ Brentano "On Guilds and Trade Unions," p. 16.

extends, these forms were applied to Christian purposes, and the saint superseded the Eponym. How wide-spread was this transformation we may infer from the multitude of industrial saints that still linger on the Continent of Europe. "The local gods," says Mr. Tylor,* "the patron gods of particular ranks and crafts, the gods from whom men sought special help in special needs, were too near and dear to the inmost heart of præ-Christian Europe to be done away with without substitutes. It proved easier to replace them by saints, who could undertake their particular profession, and even succeed them in their sacred dwellings. The system of spiritual division of labour was, in time, worked out with wonderful minuteness in the vast array of professional saints, among whom the most familiar to modern English ears are—St. Cecilia, patroness of musicians; St. Luke, patron of painters; St. Peter, of fishmongers; St. Valentine, of lovers; St. Sebastian, of archers; St. Crispin, of cobblers; St. Hubert, who cures the bite of mad dogs; St. Vitus, who delivers madmen and sufferers from the disease that bears his name; St. Fiacre, whose name is now less known by his shrine than by the hackney coaches called after him in the seventeenth century."

Some examples of Professional Associations.

§ 5. We can perhaps now appreciate some celebrated institutions of early history. We can understand the formation of associations—partly religious, partly professional—their structure, and their growth. The most conspicuous of these cases, because our attention has been of necessity directed to it, and because it still exists on a great scale, is that of the Indian castes. This subject, once so mysterious, is now tolerably well understood. "Caste," says Sir Henry Maine,† "is only the name for a number of

* "Primitive Culture," vol. ii., p. 110.

† "Village Communities," p. 219.

practices which are followed by each one of a multitude of groups of men, whether such a group be ancient and natural, or modern and artificial. As a rule, every trade, every profession, every guild, every tribe, every clan, is also a caste; and the members of a caste not only have their own special objects of worship, selected from the Hindu pantheon or adopted into it, but they exclusively eat together, and exclusively intermarry." There is even reason to believe that the great caste of Brahmans was, orginally, not a distinctive religion, but a professional or literary clan. "The office of Brahman," says Dr. Muir,* "was not one to which mere birth gave a claim, but had to be attained by ability and study." "Though the Brahman caste," says Mr. Lyall,† "is now a vast circle inclosing a number of separate Levitic tribes, which again are subdivided into numberless family groups, yet several of these tribes appear to have developed out of literary and sacerdotal guilds. Indeed, one distinctive tenet of the Hindu Broad Church, which rests (I am told) upon passages quoted from the Vedas, affirms that Brahmanism does not properly come by caste or descent, but by learning and devotional exercises. This is now laid down as an ethical truth: it was, probably, at first a simple fact. There is fair evidence that several of these Brahmanic tribes have at different periods been promoted into the caste circle by virtue of having acquired, in some outlying province or kingdom (where Brahmans proper could not be had), a monopoly of the study and interpretation of the sacred books; and, having devoted themselves for generations to this profession, at last graduated as full Brahmans, though of a different tribe from the earlier schools. Some glimpse of the very lowest rudimentary stage of a Levitic caste (that is, a caste

* "Sanscrit Texts," vol. i., p. 294.

† "Fort. Rev.," No. 121, N.S., p. 115.

with a speciality for ritual and interpretation of the sacred books) may still be obtained in the most backward parts of India." The case of the Magi seems to have resembled that of the Brahmans. Herodotus,* indeed, alleges that they were one of the six tribes into which the Medes were divided; but although they doubtless had an organization that simulated that of the tribe, it may be well doubted if they formed a true genealogic clan. Herodotus elsewhere † compares them with the Egyptian priests; and the manner in which he speaks of them seems to indicate that he regarded them more as a caste than as a nation. The better ‡ opinion seems to be that they were what is now generally understood as a caste. Little, indeed, is really known of the Magi. The name does not occur in the Avesta, where the priests are called Atharvas. It appears that the Magi were not merely a religious order, but were the learned men of the country; that they, or rather a particular class of them, interpreted dreams; § that they were experts in the use of the divining rod,|| and generally in a sort of magic which we probably should now term elementary natural philosophy. It is said,¶ also, that they were not only an order, but a family descended from one and the same stock. We may, therefore, conclude that they had an Eponym; that, as Herodotus seems to intimate, they contained various septs or divisions; and that, on the whole, they resembled, although perhaps on a larger scale, some of the Hellenic *γένη* which I have already mentioned.

In the same class ought, probably, to be ranked the Druids. These persons formed the literary order of the

* i., 101. † i., 140.

‡ See Canon Rawlinson's "Herodotus," vol. ii., p. 454, *et seq.*

§ Herodotus, i., 107.

|| Canon Rawlinson's "Herodotus," vol. i., p. 350.

¶ Ammianus Marcellinus, xxiii., 6.

early Kelts. In the old Irish records * they are habitually described as "men of science." The Druids of King Laeghaire, whom St. Patrick overcame by the great signs and miracles wrought in the presence of the men of Erin,† appear to be elsewhere spoken of as the "professors of science in Erin," and as "the Brehons and just poets of the men of Erin." It was their duty ‡ to interpret dreams, to use the divining-rod, to offer incantations, and generally to practise magic rites, in their case apparently very harmless,§ with the intention of securing benefit to their own friends, and of discomfiting their enemies. They also exercised jurisdiction, especially in cases of homicide, boundaries, and inheritances; the latter subjects, I may remark, depending upon the old customs founded upon the ancestral worship of the tribe, and requiring for their determination a knowledge of the genealogies and of the family rights of the tribesmen. Further, we hear ‖ of "a Druidical chief, or demigod, the great Daghda, as he was called, who was also their (*i.e.*, the Dadanann tribes) military leader." In other words, they had the usual organization under their Eponym. It is also said that the Druids were divided into several classes or branches.¶ Strabo mentions three; other writers enumerate five. The inference therefore is, that, like the Brahmans, or the Magi, they contained a number of separate clans, or, as Mr. Lyall calls them, smaller circles of affinity. It is not difficult to understand how, in their religious functions, they were superseded by the clerics of the Christian Church. But the old customs were less easily changed than the external modes of worship; and St.

* "O'Curry's Lectures," vol. ii., p. 189.
† "Ancient Laws of Ireland," vol. i., p. 15.
‡ O'Curry, *ubi supra*, p. 194.
§ See "The Incantation of Amergin," O'Curry, vol. ii., p. 190.
‖ "O'Curry's Lectures," vol. ii., p. 187.
¶ *Ib.*, p. 181.

Patrick * could not carry, against the Brehons, death as the punishment of homicide, in place of the Eric fine. That branch, at least, of the Druids which exercised judicial functions, maintained its ground; and there is little doubt † that the Brehons were the legitimate representatives of the Druids of Cæsar.

* "Ancient Laws of Ireland," vol. iii., p. 24.

† See Sir H. S. Maine, "Early Hist. of Inst.," p. 32.

CHAPTER XIV.

THE STATE.

§ 1. APART from mere alliance, or from external influence, or from domination, there are three principal cases, all resting upon a common principle, of combined action between separate clans. The first case is the community of worship between clans of common descent. This community is in no sense political, and is merely the expression of a natural sentiment and the recognition of a historical fact. It affords a sort of *primâ facie* case for alliance, as against strangers; but it does not afford any security for habitual friendly relations between the parties themselves. The second case is that community of worship which is established for the purpose of forming and securing a brotherhood of independent clans. These associations are, for the most part, limited in their object; and are always formed not between individuals, but between communities. Such a relation is mechanical, and not vital. It means juxtaposition—not integration. A confederacy of clans is thus formed, for objects more or less general in their nature. But federation, though apparently the simplest, is, in reality, the most difficult form of human association. Nothing is so hard to obtain as voluntary co-operation; and the difficulty, in itself sufficiently great as among individuals, is, as amongst separate masses of men, multiplied indefinitely. Neither the older, therefore, nor the later form of what I have termed Amphictyonic association, ever has been, or, as it seems, ever can be, sufficient to produce a State.

Comparison of social combinations.

All these cases of concerted action agree in certain respects. The co-operation is limited in time, or is restricted to some particular object; and the executive organ acts not upon individuals, but upon the clans in their corporate character. But there is a third result of community of worship, and this result is the State. There are cases in which two or more kins, while they severally preserved their identity, have formed a new combination, for an indefinite period and for general purposes. There are cases, too, where a society is formed merely of scattered individuals, and where, after its formation, that society at once proceeds to organize itself upon Gentile principles. In these cases, although the Gentile tie remains, the individual members of the clan enter into a wholly new alliance. Whatever may be their position within the clans, the members of the new association meet on equal terms. Between the same persons, two distinct relations of equality and inequality may exist; but these relations are not repugnant—they are only distinct. Admission to the one class does not necessarily imply admission to the other. There were members of the clan who were not members of the State: there might be members of the State who were not members of any clan. Thus the State is not composed of other social organisms. Its members may be members of other social organisms, and the activities of these other organisms may or may not clash, or tend to clash, with the activities of the State. But the organization of the State is complete within itself; and its power, within its own sphere and over its own members, is supreme. It has its own worship, its own property, its own functions, its own claims upon its members, its own duties towards them. It respects the rights and the duties of the other associations which it includes, and does not—at least in its earlier stage—seek to interfere with the relations of its members to any of those other associations. Of this union, community of worship, while the old beliefs continue, is at once the symbol and the cement. Without such a community, the State could not have come into being, or, if it had, could not have continued to exist. In the course of its evolution it has gradually developed new organs; and the former organs, which were adapted to its original condition, have served their purpose, and given place to their natural successors.

§ 2. It is no easy matter to give a complete definition of the State, just as it is no easy matter to give a complete definition of a man. Not only is the subject itself difficult, but verbal embarrassments are added. The word State means * sometimes an independent political society, sometimes the governing body of such a society. In its former sense, modern writers have not been very happy in their explanations of it. Mr. Austin,† whose power of analysis is unequalled, declares that the expression is not capable of precise definition. His description is in the following words:—"In order that a given society may form a society political and independent . . . the generality or bulk of its members must be in a habit of obedience to a certain and common superior: whilst that certain person, or certain body of persons, must not be habitually obedient to a certain person or body." For Mr. Austin's purposes, this description was sufficient. Analytical jurisprudence accepts government and law as they exist, and makes no inquiries as to their origin. It deals with a single function of national life. But for all ulterior questions as to the structure and the history of society, Mr. Austin's description has no value. Two observations respecting it suggest themselves. The first is, that Mr. Austin seems to have

The character of the State union.

* See Austin's "Lectures on Jurisprudence," vol. i., p. 249.

† *Ib.*, p. 233.

been misled, partly by the use of the correlated word sovereignty, and partly by an exclusive regard to European societies. He constantly speaks of the sovereign of a people as something external to that people, and superior to it. Such a view was, doubtless, not held by Mr. Austin. He knew that Government is usually the result, not of conquest or of usurpation, but of a genuine national evolution. But words react upon thoughts. It is, therefore, prudent to speak of the Government as the political organ of the State, that is, as the organ which, in the course of its evolution, is set apart to perform the principal functions of national life. The second observation is, that if the expression "political organ" be substituted for Mr. Austin's "sovereign," or its equivalents, the insufficiency of Mr. Austin's description, which I have cited above, becomes apparent. He attempts to define an organism by a reference to its external organs. The immediate result is a circle. To the question, "What is a political society?" he in effect answers, "A society that has political organs." To the further question, "What are political organs?" the answer at once describes them as "Those organs that are found in a political society." It is evident that the governing body of a political society is not the cause of that society, but one of its effects.

If we turn to the classical authors, our inquiries are, at least at first sight, equally unsatisfactory. Aristotle * says:—"A State, in one word, is the collective body of such persons (*i.e.*, citizens), sufficient in themselves for all the purposes of life." Cicero † says:—"Respublica . . . est cœtus multitudinis juris consensu et utilitatis communione sociatus." Neither of these statements appear to add much to our knowledge. On a closer view, however, a hint may

* "Politics," iii., 1.

† "De Repub.," i., 25.

be obtained from them. The word "*cœtus*," as Niebuhr * points out, is a technical term, and is equivalent to κοινωνία. The State is thus a species of κοινωνία, or community; and the force of this term the preceding pages have endeavoured to illustrate. From this starting point it may be possible to discover the qualities which distinguished this community from other communities; in other words, to ascertain the essential characteristics of political society.

The State, then, seems to me to have originally been a form of the non-genealogic clan or tribe. It was a true κοινωνία, that is, it was formed on the model of the Household; it established similar relations among its members, and it was kept together by a similar bond of union. But it was not a spontaneous growth, like a natural Household. It commenced in a voluntary association. In one of its forms the association was between clans fully organized. In another form, it seems hardly to have differed from those Indian forms of association which were described in the preceding chapter. From some of these forms it was distinguished, since it was not limited to the promotion of any special object, but was meant to secure the general well-being of its members. In this view, the characteristics of the original State may be thus enumerated:—First, it was constructed upon the model of the Household. Secondly, it was held together as natural households were held together, by the worship of its Eponym, whether that Eponym were a god, or a hero, or a deified founder. Thirdly, it was formed out of the members of two or more clans, whether those clans were antecedent or subsequent to the State; and it exercised over them, within its own sphere and by its own officers, its own jurisdiction. Fourthly, while it dealt with these members individually,

* "Hist. Rome," vol. ii., p. 44, *note*.

it preserved and recognized the clans of which they severally formed a part. Fifthly, the lands and public property of these clans were brought into a common stock, and formed the public land of the new corporation, and there were reciprocal rights of intermarriage. Sixthly, the union was intended to be permanent. Seventhly, the object of the union included all purposes of common interest, subject, however, to the duties and the rights of the clans in their several spheres of private life. Thus, the State was distinct from the clan, was wider than the clan, was, at least in the case of the pure clans, posterior to the clan. But the State was analogous to the clan, was formed upon the same pattern, was held together by a like principle, and was not substitutive for it, but accumulative upon it.

The evidence in support of each of these propositions may be briefly indicated. The analogy of the State to a Household is seen in the necessity, for each of them, of a common hearth. Aristotle says that rulers derive their honour from the common hearth, whether their title be Archons, or Kings, or Prytaneis. The Prytaneum was essential to the political life of every Grecian city; * and the Prytaneum contained the common hearth. The very names *πρυτανεῖον* and *κοίνη ἑστία* appear to have been used as equivalents. So, too, of Rome, Mommsen † says :—"As the clans resting upon a family basis were the constituent elements of the State, so the form of the body politic was modelled after the family, both generally and in detail." That the king was, in fact, the House-master of this political Household is evident, "for at a later period there were to be found, in or beside his residence, the always-blazing hearth and the well-closed store-chamber of the

* Wachsmuth, "Hist. Ant. of Greece," vol. i., p. 290.

† "Hist. of Rome," vol. i., p. 66.

community, the Roman Vesta and the Roman Penates, as indications of the visible unity of that supreme Household which included all Rome."

I need not speak further of the public worship, and the honours paid to the founder of the city and its guardian gods. Everywhere were the θεοὶ πολίαδες; everywhere the *auspicia publica*, or the knowledge of the signs by which these gods expressed their will. There was no city which had not its special public worship; and this worship was analogous to the worship of the clan, and to the worship of the Household. Nor is it necessary that I should labour to prove what no person disputes—the presence of clans within the archaic States. I shall merely advert to the well-known distinction between the political clans and the true clans, the 'φύλαι τόπικαι' and 'φύλαι γένικαι' of old writers. The former were merely statutory arrangements, specially created on the model of the older clans for purposes of political convenience—mere creatures of the State, and parts of it, without any independent existence. The latter are the true spontaneously-formed clans with which these pages are concerned. As to the dealings of the State with its individual members, and not with their clans, there is ample evidence. At Athens, the State sometimes thought fit to reward the distinguished services of some foreigner by the gift of citizenship. It had,* however, no power to order his admission into any clan. It could not make him the clansman of Apollo Patröos or of Zeus Herkeios. But the worship of these deities was an essential condition to the holding any public office. Consequently, these δημοποίητοι or State-made citizens were incapable of election to any magistracy. On the other hand, when a member of a clan became a member of the State, the State

* See Hermann, "Grec. Ant.," p. 195.

declined to recognize any disabilities to which, by clan-custom, he might be subject. Thus, a *Filius Familias* was, *publico jure*, on equal terms with his *Pater Familias*, was equally eligible for public office, and was equally capable of exercising public functions. He might even, as I shall subsequently show, be his father's political superior, although at the same time he was subject to that father's unrestrained power, within his precinct, of life and death.

Such an alliance involved community of public property, and reciprocal capacities for all the ordinary transactions of life. "The community of the Roman people," says Mommsen,* "arose out of the junction (in whatever way brought about) of such ancient clanships as the Romilii, Voltinii, Fabii, &c.: the Roman domain comprehended the united lands of these clans. Whoever belonged to one of these clans was a burgess of Rome." Every burgess—that is, every full member of the society—was entitled, as of course, to all the material rights and advantages of such an association, to the ἐπιγαμία ἐπεργασία and επινομία of which Xenophon speaks. But the principal right is that of intermarriage. It is this right † which practically forms the test of equality. A citizen must marry within his State, that is, he must marry with his peers. Those clans, then, with whom he may intermarry, are those whom he acknowledges, and who acknowledge him, as equal.

The assertion that the State union was originally meant to be for an indefinite time, and for indefinite purposes, does not admit of historical proof. I can only say that, from the days of the siege of Naxos to the days of the siege of Richmond, men have always acted upon this principle. Secession has never been recognized as a political right. It will perhaps suffice if, in these circumstances, I cite the

* "Hist. of Rome," vol. i., p. 65.

† See "Edin. Rev.," vol. cxliv., p. 192.

opinions of three great authorities. I do so, not because I think that they give any help towards the solution of the problem concerning the true functions of the State, but because they show the opinions of the best minds as to the indefinite character of the association. Aristotle says * that civil society was founded not merely that its members might live, but that they might live well. Bacon † insists that the "*Jus Publicum*" extends "*ad omnia circa bene esse civitatis.*" And Mr. Austin ‡ declares that "the proper purpose or end of a sovereign government is the greatest possible advancement of human happiness."

Historical evidence of this view of the State.

§ 3. There is an antecedent presumption in favour of this connection of the Household and the State. Early society was based on community of worship, and the form which the superstructure assumed was that of the Household expanding into the Kin. It might, therefore, be reasonably expected that the first attempts at any higher organization would proceed upon the same principle, that they would be founded on a community of worship, and that they would be modelled according to the prevailing type. Further, from the strong individuality and the inaggressive nature of the early cults, it might also be expected that the new combination would, at least in its early stage, not be intentionally antagonistic to its predecessor; but that the two systems would, at all events for some time, exist side by side. If this presumption coincides with the known facts of history—if the *à priori* argument be confirmed by actual experience, the consilience will furnish the strongest proof of the theory that the nature of the case admits. I proceed, therefore, to

* "Politics," iii., 9.
† "De Aug. Sci.," viii., 3. "Aph.," iv.
‡ "Lectures on Jurisprudence," vol. i., p. 298.

state the historical evidence which I have to offer upon this question.

There were two ways in which the known relations between clans and the State that comprised them might be established. I mean, of course, true clans, and not those local divisions to which I have already referred. Either the clans might be integrated into a State, or a State might be differentiated into clans. An association might be formed by separate clans, and these bodies might gradually become so co-ordinated that the life of the whole should predominate over the lives of its parts; or an association might be formed in the nature of a non-genealogic clan, within which new clans, or new branches of old clans, would, according to the Hindu model, naturally arise. Of these two methods there are, I think, examples in the two great States of antiquity. On the former principle, Athens was formed; on the latter, Rome.

Thucydides* alleges that, in early times, Attica was inhabited by separate communities, possessing each its own Prytaneum and its own rulers; that these bodies were not only mutually independent, but in some cases mutually hostile; that Theseus succeeded in uniting them into one city; and that, in the historian's own time, a commemorative festival was celebrated at the public expense in honour of the Goddess. He further alleges that, in his day, the various townships still continued to exist, and to celebrate their ancestral worship. But, although this latter worship was evidently that which was most familiar to them, all these people were also the votaries of the great Goddess of the Athenians, Pallas Athene, and were the citizens of one city. The historian vividly describes the reluctance and the grief of the people

* ii., 15.

when, at the commencement of the Peloponnesian War, they were forced to remove from the country into the city—feelings far more intense than those which the French peasants lately experienced when they were compelled to seek, beneath the walls of Paris, a temporary shelter from their German invaders. But, notwithstanding the strength of this local attachment, no person among them doubted that his political allegiance was due to Athens. The geographical name 'Atticans' was merged in the political name 'Athenians.' There was undoubtedly a time when Marathon and Dekeleia, Aphidnæ and Eleusis, were autonomous. For political purposes, as we should describe the proceeding, these communities merged that autonomy in the "*politeia*" of Athens. For religious purposes, and for the other objects of clan-life, they retained their original individuality. This union—lax, indeed, according to our modern notions, but far stronger than any similar association that had previously existed—rested, as I have said, upon the common worship of Athenê Polias. This worship did not interfere with the worship of Apollo Patrôos, or of Zeus Herkeios. The Goddess presided over the city as such; but Apollo was the god of the Ionian clans, and Zeus Herkeios was the common name by which the ancestral worship of each household was indicated. The gods of the city, of the clan, and of the household, were distinct, and their worship must not be confounded. But the public interest required that the domestic worship, according to its several rites, should be duly maintained. Thus, a common religion, and consequently common interests, were established for the whole of Attica; and yet that religion did not displace, but protected, the various forms of Gentile worship. At what time, and in what circumstances, this remarkable association was formed, there are no means of certain knowledge. But it is hardly an exaggeration of its importance to describe the event as "the beginning* of the political history of mankind."

Grecian history† presents many other, although perhaps less conspicuous, instances of this process. Tegea, in Arcadia, and Dyme, in Achæa, were formed each out of eight village communities. Mantinea was composed of four. Megara and Tanagra are also mentioned as having been similarly formed. Even after the Persian War, the city of Elis was the result of a like coalition. A hundred years after the foundation of Elis,‡ forty village communities coalesced to form Megalopolis, the Great City—Micklegarth, as our ancestors would have called it—by which Epaminondas thought to secure the unity of Arcadia. But without seeking other examples, it is enough to cite the authority of Aristotle§ that "the community formed out of several villages is a perfect city, having the limit of all self-sufficingness."

There are, substantially, two leading opinions as to the origin of Rome. One is that of the early traditions; the other is that of some modern historians. The former represents the city as springing from what I have called a non-genealogic tribe. The other regards it as the result of a *synoikismus*, or integration, among three pure-blooded clans. It is not necessary that I should undertake to determine this controversy. Whichever opinion be correct, there is little doubt that the city was united by a common worship; that it was organized on the model of a Household; and that the special cults of the clans, whether they were formed within the State or were prior to it, were carefully preserved, concurrently with the worship of the public Penates. Yet I may

* See Freeman's "Hist. Essays," vol. ii., p. 120

† Grote, "Hist. of Greece," vol. ii., p. 346.

‡ *Ib.*, p. 307.

§ "Politics," i., 1, 8.

be permitted to state a few of the reasons which have led me to the conclusion that the older idea is correct. The first reason is that the Romans thought so themselves. Little weight can be given to this argument in the presence of good evidence to the contrary. But in the present case I do not think that such evidence exists. Lord Strangford observes * that in Eastern countries, "wherever a rude and uncultivated people have been brought within the pale of Islam, they have never failed to connect themselves with the traditionary quasi-biblical ethnology of their conquerors or spiritual instructors, through some patriarch or hero of Scripture." No such general cause of error appears to exist in Rome. The Trojan legend is easily separable from the genuine tradition. The course of national development seems to have been fairly regular. The details of the story have, of course, been overlaid with the usual crust of fable, and it is idle to attempt to distinguish the true from the false. But where descent was of vital practical importance, and where all matters relating to it were carefully preserved, and where care was taken, by festivals and similar means, to perpetuate the memory of great leading events, the refusal even to admit the national traditions seems to be a misapplication of the rules of evidence. Again, both in its constitutional history and in its law, Rome, when it first appears in history, presents a remarkable advance as compared with most other peoples. Probably the determining point in the history of Rome is the start that it obtained in social evolution. To what causes this start was due, no evidence now remains to tell us. But the fact seems to suggest some fundamental difference between Rome and the ordinary run of pure clans. "A long succession," says Mommsen,† "of phases of political development must have

* "Letters and Papers," p. 58.

† "Hist. of Rome," vol. i., p. 55.

intervened between such constitutions as the poems of Homer and the Germania of Tacitus delineate, and the oldest organizations of the Roman communists." In place of these hypothetical changes, for which no proof exists, and no parallel is known, it is, I think, simpler to assume that the city of Rome was never like either the Hellenic or the Teutonic clans, but arose under dissimilar conditions. Again, there is no trace in Roman history of any royal *gens.* Such a body, the representatives in the eldest line of the divine Eponym, is essential in every pure clan. Even where several such clans have coalesced, some provision for the headship is made. Thus, at Athens, there were the Kodrids, in whom, even after the abolition of the kingdom, the royal dignity long lingered. But although the royal title survived for religious purposes at Rome, there is not a vestige, even in the legends of the regal period, of any clan with any hereditary claim to royalty.

Further, Niebuhr * has remarked that the proper names among the Oscan nations were usually Gentile names among the Romans. Such was the royal name of Tullius. Such were the famous literary names of Pacuvius, of Statius, and of Gellius. Niebuhr merely notices the fact, but the explanation of it seems to be possible in the light of the passages which I have cited from the Eastern experiences of Mr. Lyall. This explanation tends to confirm the old legend. A chief of pure blood, in consequence probably of some imperfection in his generations, makes a new settlement, at the head of a few followers and friends. The new community becomes successful. Its success attracts from other societies other adventurers. When any of these adventurers prospers, he becomes, in the new community, the founder of a clan. Of this clan, the principle of Exogamy

* "Hist. of Rome," vol. ii., p. 104, *note.*

serves to define and to preserve the limits. The clan takes its name from that of its genarch or founder. If the Eponym were a man of pure blood, he would introduce his hereditary *sacra*, and establish a new branch of his original gens. If he were not of pure blood, he would be known merely by his proper name. Not unfrequently, too, in the roughness of a new settlement, an old name, especially if it be unfamiliar to the new associates, is lost, and some accidental designation is acquired. In such circumstances the new appellation generally prevails; and men do not care, or perhaps are not without much trouble able, to resume their proper patronymic. If, then, the fact be as Niebuhr has alleged, the inferences from it are—first, that Rome was not the result of a pure clan or of a union of pure clans, but was a non-genealogic society; and next, that many members of this non-genealogic clan were broken men, who either had not in their own country attained the dignity of a kin, or who, in the course of their adventures, had abandoned their old associations.

The evidence with respect to the ancient Germans is less complete than it is in the cases of Athens and of Rome. It consists mainly of the sketch of Tacitus, which, masterly though it be, is sometimes highly tantalizing. From this source alone it would not be possible to reconstruct the old polity; but when that polity has been described from other evidence, traces of it quickly reveal themselves in the pages of the great Roman historian. With such aid, his distinction between the 'civitates' and the kins that compose them is apparent. It may be inferred that these 'civitates' were founded on a religious basis, both from his account of those Teutonic Amphictyonies that I have already mentioned, and from his statement* that, at the

* "Germania," c. 11.

meetings of the civitates, the priests were charged with the maintenance of order, and in the execution of this duty exercised plenary powers. Concurrently with the general power of the State, the operation of the "*Jus Privatum*," or the custom of the kin, may be discerned. The kin makes its appearance * in the order of battle, in the maintenance of the blood-feud, and in matters of inheritance. Foreign marriages,† too, are avoided; and in the ceremony of arming the young warrior,‡ the distinction between the "*domus*" and the "*respublica*" is broadly marked. In later times, mention is frequently made of communities associated under a common name. Such, for example, were the Picts, who were composed of the Caledones and the Mæatæ.§ Such were the Alemanni, and the great names of the Saxons and the Franks. But the nature and the circumstances of these unions are not sufficiently known to warrant any confident opinion on the subject. One instance is at least suggestive. The Angli and the Weringi, tribes mentioned by Tacitus, coalesced ‖ under the expressive name of Thuringi, or "Sons of Thor." Thus, the modern name, Thuringia, attests the principle upon which, fourteen centuries ago, the coalition of clans proceeded. The Scandinavians present a still stronger illustration. The Norsemen ¶ who settled in Iceland, "when they desired to form a community, built a temple, and called themselves by the name of Gothi or hof-Gothi, 'temple-priests;' and thus the temple became the nucleus of the new community." Many independent communities of this character sprang up all through the country, until, about the year 930, an integration took place. Ulf-lyot ** was the Theseus of

* "Germania," cc. 7, 21, 20. † c. 4. ‡ c. 13.

§ Mr. Skene's "Celtic Scotland," vol. i., p. 125.

‖ Canciani, "Leg. Barb.," iii., 31.

¶ Cleasby-Vigfusson, "Icelandic Dict.," p. 208.

** *Ib.*, p. 18.

Iceland. Under his influence the various Gothi formed an "Althing," or general legislative assembly, and Iceland became a State.

The relation of the Curia to the State.

§ 4. For the purpose of denoting social relations, all the Aryan languages contain a series of terms—not, indeed, etymologically connected, but expressive in each case of similar relations. To select the three most convenient examples, the first series contains the Gens, the φύλη, and the Kin. In the second series there are the Agnatio, the φρατρία, in its Homeric sense, and the Sibsceaft or Mæg. There is a third series, which consists of the Civitas, the πόλις, and the Volkerschaft. These last-mentioned terms imply, as I have attempted to show, a new union, based, indeed, on the idea of the Household, but including several Kins, and so having in certain respects a Gentile structure. If this view be correct, a fourth series of terms might be expected. There is still wanted a set of words which bear to the third series the same relation that the second series bears to the first. In other words, if the State imitate the Kin, what is the political analogue of the Sib? What, in the "*Jus Publicum*," corresponds to the Agnatio in the "*Jus Privatum*"? I think that the missing series may be found in the words Curia, φρατρία in its later sense (or, as the Spartans* called it, ὦβη), and, perhaps, Hundertschaft. These terms denote a political, not a Gentile division. They are not independent arrangements, but denote respectively the Civitas, the πόλις, and the Volkerschaft. They formed, as between their fellow-members, a closer connection than that to which their general political relations gave rise. Of four Quirites, two who were members of the same Curia were much more intimately related than two who were members of different

* Müller's "Dorians," vol. ii., p. 19.

Curiæ. The bond of union was a special worship; and Zeus Phratrios performs a function similar to that of Zeus Herkeios.

It is clear that the Curia was a political and not a Gentile arrangement. The Roman tradition * connects it, and it alone of Roman institutions, with the origin of the city. It is also noteworthy that the genealogical legends of the Teutons give genealogies of the clans, but not of either Volkerschafts or Hundertschafts. For the special relation of the Curia to the Civitas, a hint is found in the statement that Romulus gave each Curia one allotment. This statement suggests the grants to the Mægs, or villages, by the entire clan. In the case of the Curia, however, if reliance can be placed upon our authorities, this grant must be understood with reference to the township only. The extent of the grant is said to have been two hundred *jugera*, which was meant for one hundred householders, apart from their use of the common land. This measure was called *centuria*, and thus a sort of connection is established between the Curia and the Hundertschaft. It is not worth while, however, to inquire, even if there were any means of certain information, whether the estate of each Curia did or did not include more than building allotments. The rights incident to these allotments must have existed, whether they were exercised over the land of the Curia or the land of the city. It is sufficient for my purpose that the Curia was an intermediate body between the State and the Household; and that it received for its members, and distributed among them, grants of land, in the same way that the Mæg acted in the Gentile economy. The word "curia" itself appears to point to the Mæg, or Joint Household. Its etymology has long been a subject of as great difficulty as

* Mommsen, "Hist. of Rome," vol. i., p. 73.

its structure and functions. Recently, however, Corssen * has pointed out that 'curia,' or, in its older form, 'covisia,' transliterates with 'house.' If this view be accepted, 'curiales' will mean political Agnati, just as 'cives' were in effect political Gentiles.

§ 5. According to the view that I have thus endeavoured to present, the State, in its earlier form, was an independent association of men according to clans. In other words, its constituent elements, although they were individuals, were individuals in groups. There was thus a divided allegiance, and, consequently, a continual struggle, between the claims of the clan and the claims of the State. It was only by the complete subordination of the clan, and the direct communication of the State with each individual citizen, that true political society was established. These principles and this process may be observed, not on the civil side only of the State, but also on its military side. The community in peace and the community in war are, in fact, the same community under different aspects. It is not unreasonable, therefore, to expect that the development of the army should correspond with and illustrate the development of the State. As the history of law records the evolution of the individual from the corporation, in all matters relating to property, to succession, to personal rights; so military history narrates the evolution of the militant clansman into the professed soldier. The original army was simply the clan, or the people assembled in its clans. Each clan met according to its respective Mægs. The development of the army consisted in breaking down these divisions, and in the formation of a union independent of the clan. In this union the individual soldier found his place, not

The State and the Army.

* Fick's "Wörterbuch," p. 47.

according to his own convenience or his personal status, but according to his commander's view of the exigencies of the service.

Examples are scarcely needed of the rule that archaic men fought by clans. If the structure of their society be such as I have attempted to describe it, such a method is evidently that which, from the nature of the case, should have been expected. It is, however, prudent to verify inferences, however clear they may be, by a comparison with actual facts. Our earliest authority is Nestor's rule in the "Iliad,"* when he advises Agamemnon to marshal his men by Phyla and by Phratræ, so that Phratra might support Phratra, and Phylon support Phylon. The Teutons† acted upon the same principles; and their host was not a random crowd, but was composed of kins and Mægs. Of the early Roman system no information exists; but under the Servian reforms the army was organized with reference to its civic, if not its Gentile divisions. Nor is Mr. Robertson's suggestion impossible,‡ although I do not attach much weight to the fact, that the rule of the Imperial law, by which the property of the intestate soldier went to his comrades and not to the Fisc, may have been a far-off echo of the days when the Roman soldier stood in line—not with his Vexillatio and his Legio, but with his Cognatio and his Gens. In the Keltic people, however, the evidence is clear. There is no more interesting part of Lord Macaulay's great work than that in which he describes the Highland clans. He there§ shows that a clan was a regiment almost ready made. "All that was necessary was, that the military organization should be conformed to the patriarchal organization. The chief must be colonel; his uncle or brother must

* ii., 362. † Tacitus, "Germania," c. 7.

‡ See "Scotland under her Early Kings," vol. ii., p. 312.

§ "Hist. of England," vol. iii., p. 335.

be major; the tacksmen, who formed what may be called the peerage of the little community, must be the captains; the company of each captain must consist of those peasants who lived on his lands, and whose names, faces, connections, and characters were perfectly known to him; the subaltern officers must be selected among the Duinhe Wassels, proud of the eagle's feather; the henchman was an excellent orderly; the hereditary piper and his sons formed the band; and the clan became at once a regiment." A regiment so constituted possessed no small advantages. In it there were exact order and prompt obedience, and mutiny and desertion were unknown. Every man knew and trusted his comrade. Every man was devoted to his officers. No man thought of deserting his colours, because his colours represented to him his world. But although nothing was easier than to turn the clans into efficient regiments, nothing was more difficult than to combine these regiments into an efficient army. All within the clan was friendly. All without the clan was usually hostile. Between clan and clan there was always jealousy, and there was frequently hate. That general could have little confidence in the result of his most skilful combinations, who, in the words of Lord Macaulay,* "at any moment might hear that his right wing had fired upon his centre, in pursuance of some quarrel two hundred years old; or that a whole battalion had marched back to its native glen, because another battalion had been put in the post of honour." It is easy to perceive how unfitted for any large undertaking, for any enterprise that required time and patience and self-denial, such an army must have been. It was not until the clan system had been thoroughly broken up that the Highlanders became adapted for the purposes of modern warfare. A

* "Hist. of England," vol. iii., p. 338.

similar change is recorded in Roman history. Down to the time of Caius Marius, the Roman military system rested, as I have said, upon the Servian organization of the civic militia. The cavalry, which was composed of the wealthy classes, was difficult to recruit, and its temper had become absolutely intolerable. The infantry was less unmanageable, but still urgently needed reform. "The Roman method," says Mommsen,* "of aristocratic classification had hitherto prevailed also within the legion. Each of the four divisions of the *velites*, the *hastati*, the *principes*, and the *triarii*, or, as we may say, of the advanced guard, of the first, second, and third line, had hitherto possessed its special qualification as respected property or age for service, and in great part, also, its own style of equipment; each had its definite place once for all, assigned in the order of battle; each had its definite military rank and its own standard. All these distinctions were now superseded. Anyone admitted as a legionary at all, needed no further qualification in order to serve in any division: the discretion of the officers alone decided as to his place. All distinctions of armour were set aside; and, consequently, all recruits were uniformly trained."

Two points connected with these examples deserve consideration. One is, that the Gaelic clans, although they never formed among themselves any lasting confederation, sometimes accepted the command of a stranger. To a renowned foreign leader, like Montrose or Dundee, obedience might be rendered; but it was an obedience limited in its extent, and brief in its duration. The clans remained with the army until they fought with each other, or quarrelled with their general, or chose to go home. For any of these reasons they, without hesitation, abandoned the enterprise.

* "Hist. of Rome," vol. iii., p. 201.

That is, they formed a union, incomplete, indeed, and incoherent, but still, in some sense, a union, apart from their clan system, and distinct from a mere alliance or confederation of clans. What, in time, such a union might, in able hands and favouring circumstances, have become, we can only conjecture. But, at least, it was a union which was founded on a principle different from that of their ordinary clan association. Thus a political union was effected, not as a result of the clan system, but in spite of it. The second point to which I referred is, that the change to the army system involved a recourse to something like household discipline. The change in the structure of the Roman legion, which I have memtioned above, was accompanied by a change in its drill. "It is a significant fact," says Mommsen,* "that that method considerably increased the military culture of the individual soldier, and was essentially based upon the training of the future gladiators, which was usual in the fighting schools of the time." Thus, the principle of the Comitatus asserted itself at the expense of the principle of the clan. The necessity of an independent association, of a political, and not of a Gentile organization, was apparent. It is not from the alodial militia that the modern army is descended. Its roots are found in the Comitatus, in the discipline of the Household, and the undisputed commands of the House Father.

The disintegration of the State.

§ 6. Another indication of the practical distinction between the State and the clan, of the religious character of the former and of the tenacity of existence of the latter, is found in the opposite process to that which I have been considering. If the State could be made, so also it

* "Hist. of Rome," vol. iii., p. 201.

could be unmade. As the Roman Empire has been described,* not indeed with perfect accuracy, as a mere band which held together a bundle of separate communities, and as, when the Empire was dissolved, the communities still remained, so the communities themselves were capable of further reduction to their primary elements. The Greek language has special words for both processes. The integration of the State it calls *συνοίκισις*: the disintegration of the State it calls *διοίκισις*. Of the latter process, there are several examples. Xenophon † relates that, after the peace of Antalkidas, the Spartans resolved to inflict an exemplary punishment upon the Mantineans. The wall of Mantinea was accordingly razed; and the city was disintegrated into four parts, as in days of old they used to dwell. This reference to the past is especially remarkable, because Mantinea is described in the "Catalogue of the Ships" ‡ as if it were a single community. So, too, the Phokians, after their defeat in the Sacred War, were compelled to resume their village life. The effect of this desecration was the destruction of the State religion. The worship ceased, and the gods were forgotten. With the religion,§ everything which depended upon it—law, civic rights, property—fell also. The very gods became the property of the enemy; and if the Thebans erected a temple to Herê || on the ruins of Platæa, it was a Theban, and not a Platæan, Herê that was thereafter worshipped. By some such process as this, after its treachery in the Hannibalic War, the Romans reduced Capua ¶ to the rank

* Guizot, "Hist. Civilization," vol. i., p. 33.

† "Hellenica," v., 2.

‡ "Iliad," ii., 607.

§ See "La Cité Antique," p. 247.

|| Thucydides, iii., 68.

¶ "Ceterum habitari tantum tanquam urbem Capuam frequentarique placuit, corpus nullum civitatis nec senatus nec plebis concilium nec magistratus esse: sine consilio publico sine imperio multitudinem nullius rei inter se sociam, ad consensum inhabilem fore: præfectum ad jura reddenda ab Roma quotannis missuros."—*Livy*, xxvi., 16.

of a village. It was also the usual policy of Rome to break up all confederations among its vanquished subjects. The Classics contain many allusions to the use of the plough in the destruction of cities. The reason of this practice seems to have been that the foundation of the city was a religious ceremony, and its boundaries were marked by a furrow, in pursuance of an order of the gods given through the augurs. On the well known principle that every obligation which is formed in a particular manner should be dissolved in the like manner, it was felt that a city which had been duly consecrated, could not be desecrated, save by a similar ceremony. When we bear in mind the character of these ceremonies, we can appreciate the inclusion of the chapter* "*De Sulcis Circa Villas*," in the "*Indiculus Superstitionum et Paganiarum*," against which the Fathers of the Church thought fit solemnly to warn their Teutonic proselytes. There may, perhaps, be an allusion to some kindred practice in the abjuration of the Sax-note, or *Saxonicum consortium*, which we find in the "Laws† of the Barbarians." In a remarkable catechism, containing an "*Abrenundiatio Diaboli*," and also a profession of faith, and prefixed to the "*Indiculus*" that I have just mentioned, the catechumen pledges himself to forsake the devil and all the devil's guilds, and all the devil's works and words; Thor, Woden, and the Sax-note, and all those evil ones who are their associates. The words "Sax note" are explained to mean the tutelary gods, the θεοὶ πολίαδες, of the Saxons. It is known that Charlemagne dissolved the Saxon League; and it may have been that the method which he adopted for that purpose included that renunciation of which the form has been thus preserved.

* Canciani, "Leg. Barb.," iii., 102.

† *Ib.*, iii., 72.

CHAPTER XV.

THE MEMBERS OF THE STATE.

Jus Publicum and Jus Privatum.

§ 1. Mr. Austin criticizes with considerable severity the Roman division of law into '*Jus Publicum*' and '*Jus Privatum*.' He contends that the distinction is needless and perplexing, and that, in place of being contrasted divisions of a body of law, these two sections are merely chapters of the second part of the code, namely, of the law relating to persons. Yet, the old jurists had better grounds for this division than their distinguished critic supposed. The case is, indeed, one of the many which illustrate the difference between the analytical and the historical method in jurisprudence. No jurist at the present day would attempt to construct a code of existing law upon any such division. No Roman jurist—none, at least, of the older jurists—would have even thought of proceeding upon any other principle. The reason of the difference is found in the history of law. In the course of time the two expressions, '*Jus Publicum*' and '*Jus Privatum*,' have undergone a notable change. With us, they denote divisions of the same system of law. In their original meaning they denoted two perfectly distinct systems. In its earliest sense '*Jus Privatum*' meant clan-custom, including under that expression the customs of the Household. '*Jus Publicum*' at the same period meant State-law. When the State prevailed over the clan, the '*Jus Privatum*,' or, at least, so much of it as survived, became a portion of the commands of the State—that is, the State recognized and enforced the customs that had grown up under the old system. Gradually, as its legislative organs became developed, the State claimed and exercised the power of modifying these customs. Thus, '*Jus Privatum*' became, in fact, a part of '*Jus Publicum*' in its original sense. But with the development of the State, there grew up a body of law relating to the powers, privileges, and immunities of the State itself—that is, of the political organ of the community. To this new branch of law the phrase '*Jus Publicum*' was naturally specialized. Thus, in place of clan-custom and State commands, there was established "the law," properly so called. Of that portion of this general law which relates to persons, two branches separated. One of these branches contained the special provisions that relate to private conditions; the other contained the special provisions that relate to political conditions. Thus, '*Jus Publicum*' and '*Jus Privatum*,' originally separated and then united again, became contrasted.

In the infancy, then, of legal history, '*Jus Privatum*' denoted a body of rules which were not law, but, on the contrary, dealt with subjects that were expected from the control of the State. In order, therefore, to ascertain what law was, it was, in the first instance, necessary to determine what it was not. A description of the relations denoted by the familia and the gens ought, consequently, to have preceded, by way of limitation, a description of law in its strict sense. Even when the importance of this distinction had been reduced, its traces and the force of habit deeply influenced the form of law. Even in the maturity of Roman law, the '*Jus Personarum*,' the legitimate descendant of the old '*Jus Privatum*,' occupied the foremost place. Undoubtedly, in the order of logic, the '*Jus Rerum*' takes precedence of the '*Jus Personarum*.' But the position of the latter branch at the commencement of the Institutes proves the necessity which Gaius and his predecessors felt of distinguishing between the classes which were and those which were not the immediate objects of legislation. I propose, in this chapter, to follow in their footsteps, and to consider the large exceptions which, even as regards its apparent members, were made to the universality of the authority of the State.

Infant Sons and Members of the State.

§ 2. There is a wide difference between modern and archaic notions as to the legal position of a new-born child. With us he at once becomes a subject of the Queen, and is, in contemplation of law, entitled to the full protection and benefit of the State. The authority which the father possesses is, as regards the child, not a property, but a trust. It is understood to be given not for the advantage of the father, but for the advantage of the child; and it is subject to the controlling authority of the sovereign as *parens patriæ*. Very different views prevailed in the archaic world. The old definition of a man, as a naked biped, was not without significance. A new-born child was literally only that and nothing more. He was merely an animal; and the fact of his birth gave him no admission, as of right, into any social relation. He was not a member of any Household or of any clan, much less of any State. The reason was, that these societies were formed upon a community of worship; and that birth of itself could not, and did not, create any such community. I have already described the proceedings that were necessary to render the new-born infant the member of a Household. With these proceedings, or with the consequences of their omission, the State had no concern. It had nothing to do with an infant, either for its interest or against its interest, because the infant was not included in the State brotherhood. Initiation into the State worship was not less necessary than initiation into the clan worship; and in the one case as in the other, a peculiar ceremony was essential. At Athens the son of a citizen was, up to the age of sixteen, under the exclusive control of his father. At that age he was required to commence a course of training in the Gymnasia. After two years thus spent, he was enrolled in some deme. On this occasion* he was duly presented to the Assembly: he received, at its command, a shield and spear; and he took at the altar, on which a sacrifice was offered, the oath of a citizen, in which, among other things, he pledged his faith to the religion of the city. From that time he was regarded as a member of the State, and was admitted to many of the rights of citizenship. But he was required to attain two years' standing, and to perform certain military duties, before he was allowed to exercise the right of taking part in the Assembly of the People.

Not merely was a member of a clan not necessarily a member of the State; the converse was also true, and a member of the State was not necessarily a member of a clan. When the State† desired to confer upon foreigners the rights of citizenship, in recognition of special services rendered by them, such admission was within its acknowledged competence; but it could not, at the same time, admit them to any Phratria. Over these bodies the State claimed no control. Consequently, these naturalized citizens could not hold the office of Archon, or any priestly office, because they could not share in the worship of either the god of the clan, or of the god of the House—of Apollo Patröos, or of Zeus Herkeios. The State might admit

* Hermann's "Grec. Ant.," p. 239.

† *Ib.*, p. 195.

them to its own community,* or to any local phyle or deme, which were sub-divisions of the State. But no order of the State could make a man the member of a clan, into which he had not, either in consequence of his birth or by adoption, been admitted by the kinsmen. At Rome the practice was similar. On the 17th of March, at the festival of the Liberalia, the youth—at what precise age is a matter of dispute—dedicated to the Lares the badges of childhood, and changed his boyish dress for the garb of a man. He was then brought by his father and his friends to the Forum, and was there inscribed on the roll of some tribe as a citizen. From that time he assumed all the honours and all the burthens of citizenship, served in the field, and voted in the Comitia.

So, too, Tacitus † describes the ceremonies by which the attainment of the youthful Teuton's majority was celebrated. In the presence of the Assembly, the young warrior received from the hands, either of some man of rank, or of his father, or of his kinsmen, a shield and spear. "This," the historian adds, "is their toga, this the first honour of man's estate: before this they were regarded as a part of the Household, after this as a part of the State." It is probable that the practice, in the days of chivalry, of conferring knighthood was a survival of this ancient Teutonic custom. In its origin, however, the custom was a method of terminating the *Patria Potestas*, with a result varying in each case according to the nature of the transaction. The son was transferred by his father to another person for a specific purpose. The gifts of the arms indicated the acceptance of the transfer. When the arms were given by a kinsman, the youth became the son of that kinsman; but without, it is said, the revival of the paternal power.

* Hermann's "Grec. Ant.," p. 230.

† "Germania," c. 13.

If the arms were given by a chief, the youth was at once admitted into his following. If the father himself gave the arms, his act amounted to a complete surrender and formal abandonment of his power. The gift of the arms, in the presence of the Assembly, and with its concurrence, was an admission of the young man as a new member of the army of the State. In the two former cases, his newly-acquired rights were subject to the rights of his adopted father, or of his lord. But where the father was the donor, the acquisition of the new rights was absolute; and the youth, who was formerly *pars domus*—a member of his father's household—became at once *pars reipublicæ*. In this capacity he became at once entitled to all the advantages, and was bound by all the responsibilities, of a share in the commonwealth.

Political Rights of a Son under Power.

§ 3. It thus appears that boys, before they attained the age of early manhood, were not members of the State, although they were members of the Household and of the clan. It follows that they were, during their boyhood, under the exclusive authority of the custom of their kin. The State interfered neither for them nor against them. It simply ignored their existence. But boys had the capacity of becoming members of the State; and by usage, at least, if not by positive law, were entitled, upon attaining the proper age, to demand admission. If they were thus admitted, the question arises—What was the effect of their new allegiance upon their old allegiance? Did the new citizen live under State-law alone, and was kin-law confined to boys, to women, and to slaves? In all cases where there was no collision, as in matters of inheritances, and other instances, the two laws remained unaffected. But a difficulty arises at the point at which the two systems clashed—namely, the authority of the House Father. In

Athens the State seems to have been sufficiently powerful to override all conflicting claims; and consequently to extinguish the authority of the father over the citizen, who was bound to obey another and a higher law. But in Rome the Gentile tie much longer retained its power. It has often been observed that the Roman system of nomenclature, comprising, in addition to the personal name, the name of the kin and of the sib, while the latter name added merely the name of the father and of the clan to which he belonged, proves the greater duration and influence of the Gens above the γένος. But the mode in which the *Patria Potestas* was preserved at Rome is a still more striking proof of that difference. In Rome the rights of the *Pater familias* over his son, and the rights of the State over its citizen, were treated as conflicting rights; and no special provision for their adjustment appears to have been made. The father's power was strictly limited to matters within the jurisdiction of the clan. In matters of State-law, father and son met as equals. Inside the house, the father possessed over his son the power of life and death. Outside the house, the son, if he were Dictator, possessed the power of life and death over his father. Inside the house, the son could not possess any property, except by the consent of his father, and during his pleasure. Outside the house, the father might be subject, in purse and in reputation, to the decision of his son when acting as Prætor or as Judex. If an assault* were committed on a father who was a private citizen, and on his son who held or had held high public office, the father brought the action and recovered the damages; but the damages which he recovered for the injury done to his honourable son were much heavier than the damages which he recovered for the injury done to himself.

* "Dig.," xlvii., 10, 30.

These strange consequences, and others like them, were not accidental, or mere survivals of an extinct social state. In the maturity of Roman law, the rule remained in express terms. "Quod * ad jus publicum attinet, non sequitur jus potestatis." And, again: "Filius † familias in publicis causis loco patris familias habetur." The line between the two conditions was sharply drawn. Hence, notwithstanding his personal disabilities, *Filius familias* might hold any magistracy; or might act as a *tutor*, because that function was regarded as a public duty. He might bring actions ‡ in his own name where the wrong done affected his rights as a citizen. He might even, in his capacity of magistrate, preside at the proceedings § for his own adoption or his own emancipation.

So, too, if a *tutor* who had previously been *sui juris* was adopted, and so passed under the *Potestas* of his new father, the tutelage—except when the office was not personal, but incident to a position which the tutor, by his adoption, ceased to fill—was not affected. The reason was, that the change in the tutor's position was a matter of private concern only, and with which none but his kinsmen had an interest; while the 'tutela' was a public function, and was altogether apart from any Gentile arrangements.||

There is one case in which the political condition of the son seems to have materially affected his private condition. It was a fundamental rule ¶ of Roman law that a citizen could not lose either his liberty—that is, his independence—or his rights of citizenship, without his consent. Thus, in cases of arrogation, the person to be arrogated was pointedly asked whether he wished to become the son of the intending adopter, and to allow to that person the *jus*

* "Dig.," xxxvi., 1, 14.

† *Ib.*, i., 6, 9.

‡ See Mr. Poste's "Gaius," p. 67.

§ "Dig.,' L., 7, 3.

|| "Inst.," I. xxii. 4.

¶ Cicero "Pro Domo," c. 29.

vitæ necisque over him. When, therefore, a son became a citizen, and his *Pater familias* afterwards died, it followed that no other person could acquire over him, without his consent, a father's power. The son was therefore independent, and the family was practically broken up. I think that this is the reason why the *Patria Potestas* lasted, at Rome, during the father's life, and why it terminated at his death. The father's right existed when his son became a member of the State; and the two rights—the right of the Household and the right of citizenship—are not necessarily inconsistent. But when the father's right was extinguished, the right of citizenship prevented the creation of any new derogatory right without the citizen's consent. Thus the old Household was, *ipso facto*, brought to an end. If it were continued, it must be in the nature of a partnership, where one partner conducted the business for his own benefit and that of his co-partners, and not where a House Father governed his dependents with absolute sway.

After the power of the clan had passed away, the State did not hesitate to regulate the exercise of the parental authority. But, in the older times, both clan and State pursued each its own course. It is probable that no act of the son, in his public capacity, would have been regarded as a proper cause for the exercise of the paternal power. At least, the occurrence of such a case is specially noticed* as though it were unusual; and, yet, even there the State does not appear to have taken any notice, either in approval or in disapproval, of the proceeding. A recent historian† regarded this silence as a proof of the "languid voluptuousness" that is supposed to have prevailed in the Senate: a state of mind, however, which did not prevent

* Sallust, "Bel. Cat.," 39.

† Dean Merivale's "Hist. Rom.," vol. i., p. 148, *n.*

very prompt and vigorous measures being taken with other offenders on the same occasion. A simpler explanation is, that, according to the laws and usages which then prevailed, the Senate had no jurisdiction in the matter.

§ 4. The position of women in archaic law is a subject which many persons have found it difficult to comprehend. The solution of the problem, however, is simple. They had no position. Women were not only not members of the State, but were incapable of becoming members. Hence a woman was in perpetual tutelage. She could neither sue nor be sued in the courts of the State, because she had there no *locus standi*. It was, therefore, necessary that some citizen, some person who was capable of appearing in these courts, should act in her behalf. This disability is usually described by saying that women were, throughout their life, in a state of nonage. It would be more correct to say that women throughout their life, and infants during their minority, were alike subject exclusively to the custom of the clan. They were *pars domus*, and not *pars reipublicæ*. The State, therefore, neither recognized them nor interfered with them. "Women," says Ulpian,* "are removed from all civil and public functions, and consequently cannot act as Judices, nor hold offices of State, nor sue, nor intervene on behalf of another; nor be Procurators. Likewise, a person under age ought to abstain from all public functions."

Women not Members of the State.

The reason of this permanent disability has been sometimes sought in the presumed weakness of the sex, or, as Cicero rudely says, "Propter infirmitatem consilii." The Roman law, however, did not proceed upon any

* "Dig.," L., 17, 2.

such fanciful supposition. In the case of infants, the *auctoritas* of their guardians was not merely formal, but substantial. It controlled both the technical acts of the infant, and also the administration of his property. In the case of women it was otherwise. Ulpian,* in express terms, marks the difference. "Pupillorum pupillarumve tutores et negotia gerunt et auctoritatem interponunt; mulierum autem tutores auctoritatem dumtaxat interponunt." Gaius,† too, declares that he cannot see any reason for the tutelage of adult women; for the ordinary pretext of their liability to be deceived "levitate animi," is refuted by the facts, that such women administer their property, and that the tutor can be compelled, on application to the Prætor, to give his assent to their proceedings. Mr. Poste,‡ in his excellent commentary on Gaius, observes that "it is transparent that the wardship of women, after the years of puberty, was not designed to protect their own interests, but those of their heirs apparent, their agnates." I do not think that this explanation removes the difficulty—namely, why this restriction applied exclusively to women. The rights of the agnates were equally in danger from the conduct of a *Pater familias;* and a woman had the same powers in administering her property as her husband, or her father, would have had. The reason why a woman could not act in her own name, while a man could, was not that a woman was naturally more extravagant than a man, or naturally more inclined to defraud her agnates; but because the man had a *locus standi* in the courts of the State, of which he was a member, while a woman had no such membership and therefore no such position. This view is supported by the similar case of a stranger. The rule of the Twelve

* "Reg.," xi., 25. † i., 192. ‡ p. 140.

Tables was "adversus hostem (*i. e.*, peregrinum) æterna auctoritas;" that is, as an Athenian would have said, "a Metic must always have a Prostatês." Yet the stranger did not suffer from weakness of mind or any similar defect. He was simply incapable of any right under Quiritarian law.

A remarkable consequence of this exclusion of women from the State was their exemption from the operation of the ordinary criminal law. If a woman committed any crime, she was handed over to the person in whose *manus* she was, for trial, and, if need were, for punishment. A little after the war with Antiochus, in the year 186 B.C., the discovery was made at Rome * that the worship of Bacchus had for some time past been conducted, and was still conducted, in a manner which caused not only just and excessive scandal, but which directly led to the perpetration of the grossest crimes. The most vigorous steps for its suppression were adopted, and, for a time, terror reigned in Rome. It is said that not less than seven thousand persons, male and female, were implicated. The men were tried, condemned, and punished in various ways, according to their deserts; but it was found that no jurisdiction existed in the case of the women. They were ultimately surrendered to their husbands and parents, to receive their punishment in private. Long afterwards, Tacitus † relates how a lady of rank, the wife of a gallant officer just returned from a successful foreign command, was accused, *exteræ superstitionis*, probably of being a convert to Christianity, and was left to the judgment of her husband. He, according to the ancient custom, in presence of his near relations, tried his wife for a capital offence, and found her not guilty.

* Livy, xxxix., 8.
† "Annals" xiii., 32.

Slaves not Members of the State.

§ 5. All that I have said as to the exclusion from the State of infants and of women applies, *a multo fortiori*, to slaves. With the slave, the State had no concern; whether he lived or died was a matter of no public interest. "*Servile caput nullum habet jus.*" It is not correct to say that slavery imposed duties, but gave no rights. Slavery knew, so far as the law was concerned, neither duties nor rights. The law, of course, recognized the fact that such a state existed; but it did not attempt to interfere with it. It was not to the law that the authority of the House Father was due; nor did the law, for many ages, claim any right to regulate his power. It is probably this absence of State interference that is meant by the Roman jurists, when they said that slavery is not *jure civili*, but *jure gentium*. It certainly existed from the foundation of the city. It certainly was never a subject of the Prætor's peculiar jurisdiction. The allegation, therefore, appears to mean that slavery was a recognized fact, but that it did not depend upon, and was not regulated by, the old common law of Rome. It was within the sphere of domestic custom, and found no place in early law. I need not produce evidence of the uncontrolled power of a master over his slaves. In Greece and in Rome, their violent death was a matter of ordinary occurrence, and was justified both by law and by public opinion. In Germany, Tacitus * states that slaves were seldom cruelly punished, but were often killed in bursts of passion; and he adds, that no punishment attended such cases of manslaughter. Earlier writers would probably not have noticed this circumstance; but, for a century before the time of Tacitus, the law had interfered to check the cruelty of the slave-owners.

It is more to my purpose to consider the position of

* "Germania," c. 25.

a slave after the termination of his master's power. In modern communities, when a slave is liberated, he becomes —happily, I ought now to speak for most countries in the past tense—a citizen. He may not have all the political rights that the most favoured citizens enjoy; but, for general purposes, he is at once under the protection of the law as fully as is the noblest in the land. Such was not the case in the ancient world. At Rome, where, as usual, we see more distinctly than elsewhere the form and the working of legal principles, a man might, if he pleased, give freedom to his slave by any sufficient expression of his intention; and if he did so, he could not use any legal process to recover the right which he had disclaimed. But this manumission, although it gave freedom, did not give citizenship. For that purpose, the consent of the State was necessary; and that consent was given either directly or by some officer appointed for that duty. When wills were made at the Comitia Calata, the State itself concurred in the manumission by will; and, consequently, the slave so liberated became a citizen. Manumission *per censum* and *per vindictam*, which were attended with the same results, implied —the former, a deliberate recognition of the new citizen by the proper officer, the Censor; the latter, a judicial decision in his favour by the Prætor. In all these cases, the recognition by the State through its proper officers was essential. In Athens, the freedman was not admitted to citizenship, although, in that city, the State interfered for his protection much earlier than in Rome. He was ranked amongst the Metics, or resident aliens. At Sparta,* it appears that freedmen could never attain civil rights; and manumission, without the consent of the State, was probably not permitted. In Germany, a similar conclusion

* Hermann's "Grec. Ant.," p. 51.

may be drawn from the words of Tacitus,* that freedmen are only a little above slaves, and have no rights, "*raro in domo nunquam in civitate.*" In those clans only which were organized on the principle of a gasindschaft, not of a gemeinde—that is, in the *hird* of some wealthy House Father, their services were appreciated.

When the exclusive supremacy of the State was established, much was done to protect the slave against the caprices and cruelty of his master; but so long as the old '*Jus Privatum*' existed, it, and it alone, took notice of the slave. The '*Jus Publicum*' stood aloof, and did not seek to interfere in matters with which it had no concern.

Exemption of the House and its Precinct from Jus Publicum.

§ 6. The cases I have mentioned may be regarded as merely examples of a general principle. The especial seat of '*Jus Privatum*,' the condition under which it appears in the sharpest antagonism to '*Jus Publicum*,' is the House and its precinct. The house, and the enclosure of the house, were wholly exempted from the operation of State-law. Whatever was done or forborne therein was judged by its own tribunal according to its own standard of justice, and not otherwise. The utmost stretch of authority on which the State could venture was to require the House Father himself to execute right. So far as the State and its officers were concerned, every house was inviolable. Within the house and its enclosure the authority of the Household and of its representative, the House Father, was supreme. The House Father was as truly sovereign in that small precinct as any king is within his dominions. He administered, as I have said, his own justice. He kept his own peace. He was responsible for the conduct of all persons who were within his gates. No other person,

* "Germania," p. 25.

whether official or non-official, could exercise any form of process within his jurisdiction. He might, at his discretion, treat with the officers of the community for the extradition of offenders; but no officer could, in the execution of his duty, cross the holy boundary any more than the Queen of England could send a police constable to execute a warrant in Russia or in France. The House Father's relations with his neighbours were, if I may so speak, rather international than political. "What," asks Cicero,* "is more sacred than the house of every citizen? What is more guarded by every sentiment of religion? Here are his altars, here his hearth, here the gods of his Household; here are contained his sacred things, his worship, his ritual; this is so holy a refuge to all that no person may thence be dragged away." The same rule of law was continued six centuries afterwards in the legislation of Justinian. In the Digest,† Paulus thus states the rule:—"Nemo de domo suâ extrahi debet." Gaius, in the same work, goes still further, and declares that the general opinion of the profession was, that a summons could not be served upon a man in his own house: "Quia domus tutissimum cuique refugium et receptaculum sit,"‡ and every process of law implies a kind of compulsion. It was a maxim of the Spartans§ that "the door of his court or precinct was the boundary of every man's freedom: without, all owned the authority of the State; within, the master of the house ruled as lord on his own ground." These rights of domestic life, notwithstanding their frequent conflict with the public institutions, and notwithstanding the general tendency at Sparta to sacrifice everything to the supposed interest of the State, seem to have been respected. Our Teutonic forefathers

* Pro Domo, c. 41.
† L., 17, 103. ‡ *Ib.*, ii., 4, 18.
§ Müller's "Dorians," vol. ii., p. 296.

fully recognized the like inviolability. "Suam quisque sedem," says Tacitus, "suos Penates regit." Neither communal nor public officer was allowed to cross, in the execution of his duty, the freeman's door. Late in the eleventh century, a document, which is still extant, affords a notable illustration of the living efficacy of this rule. "Every house, every garden, shall have peace within its enclosure. No person shall enter upon it, no person shall burst it open, no person shall presume to inquire rashly after those that are set within, or to oppress them by violence. If any fugitive shall have entered the enclosure, he shall abide therein in security." * So too, in all the old English laws, from the earliest time to the reign of Henry I., the like principles are reiterated. A similar custom prevailed in Ireland. Around each residence, says the learned editor † of the "Ancient Laws of Ireland," "there was a space (maighim or precinct) of varying extent, within which the owner of the house had a right to insist that the peace should be kept." And he observes that the rules on the subject of the precinct that were laid down in the Brehon laws, are almost identical with those contained in the early English laws to which I have referred.

There are still extant, both in the form of survival and even of living institutions, traces of those times when '*Jus Privatum*' reigned supreme. To this day Englishmen like to be told that every man's house is his castle; and English lawyers still repeat their long-descended maxim, "domus sua cuique tutissimum refugium," although before the all-pervading energy of the State the castle is no longer a refuge, and the maxim only serves as a weapon for harassing the sheriff and his officers. In Russia, however, the old rule retains much of its pristine force. "A patriarch," says

* See Von Maurer, "Einleitung," p. 241.

† vol. iii., p. 102.

a recent writer, "is lord over his own house and family, and no man has a right to interfere with him, not even the village elder or the Imperial judge. He stands above oral and written law. His cabin is not only a castle, but a church, and every act of his done within that cabin is supposed to be private and divine." In India,* too, may still be seen the separate households, each despotically governed by its family chief, and never trespassed upon by the footstep of any person of different blood. There, too, may be seen, so far at least as native usages extend, the absolute immunity from all external interference. "From the remotest times," says Colonel Tod,† "*Sirwa* has been the most valued privilege of the Rajpúts, the lowest of whom deems his house a refuge against the most powerful." To the horror and consternation of the Eastern mind, this immemorial and prized immunity has, under British rule, been made to yield to the knock of the policeman, and the supreme control of the Queen over all her subjects. "To the extent," says Sir Henry Maine,‡ "to which existing Indian society is a type of a primitive society, there is no doubt that any attempt of the public lawgiver to intrude on the domain reserved to the legislative and judicial power of the *Pater familias* causes the extremest scandal and disgust. Of all branches of law, criminal law is that which one would suppose to excite least resentment by trespassing on the forbidden limits. Yet, while many ignorant statements are constantly made about the rash disturbance of native Indian ideas by British law and administration, there is really reason to believe that a grievance most genuinely felt is the impartiality of that admirable penal code. . . . I have had described to

* Sir H. S. Maine's "Village Communities," p. 113.

† "Rajasthan," vol. i., p. 526.

‡ *Ubi supra*, p. 115.

me a collection of street songs, sung in the streets of a city which is commonly supposed to be most impatient of British rule, by persons who never so much as dreamed of having their words repeated to an Englishman. They were not altogether friendly to the foreign rulers of the country, but it may be broadly laid down that they complained of nothing which might naturally have been expected to be the theme of complaint. And, without exception, they declared that life in India had become intolerable since the English criminal laws had begun to treat women and children as if they were men."

CHAPTER XVI.

THE TERRITORY OF THE STATE.

The principle of Vicinity.

§ 1. I HAVE shown, in the case of the genealogic clan, the close relation between the clan and the land. So close is this relation that some writers have included it within the definition of that body which in these pages is called a clan. They describe such a community as, among other things, consisting of a number of kinsmen settled upon the same land. This description applies only to genealogic clans. To the non-genealogic clans or tribes, so far at least as they are religious or professional and are not formed for the express purpose of land-occupation, the possession of common land is immaterial. For the most part, indeed, such tribes are landless. But even with the genealogic clans, the land, although its presence is usual and forms a highly important part of their organization, is not essential. A clan may be broken and spoiled of its territory, but it is a clan still. Several distinct clans, or even races, may occupy the same territory or the same town, either independently or in subjection to a common superior; and yet no integration may take place. Even a race that has become a nation may lose its political character, and yet retain for centuries its primitive Gentile structure. The tie which unites the kin is personal and not territorial; and, consequently, it may survive even so great a shock as that of its local displacement.

A memorable example of these propositions is the history of the Jews. I do not, however, press the illustration, both because they are not an Aryan people, and because it may be contended that their case is altogether exceptional. Another example, almost as striking, and not open to the same objection, is found in the case of the Armenians. "At present," says Professor Bryce,* "Armenia is a mere geographical expression, a name which has come down to us from the ancient world, and has been used at different times with different territorial extensions. The country, if we can call it a country, has no political limits, for it lies mainly in the dominions of Turkey, but partly also in those of Russia and Persia. It has no ethnographical limits, for it is inhabited by Tartars, Persians, Kurds, and the mixed race whom we call Turks or Ottomans, as well as by the Armenians proper. It has no natural boundaries in rivers or mountain chains, lying, as it does, in the upper valleys of the Euphrates, Tigris, Aras, and Kur. Of the numbers of the Armenian nation, or rather of Armenian Christians, for the nation and the church are practically synonymous, no special estimate can be formed. They are supposed to be about five or six millions. Others are scattered abroad in all sorts of places, India, Southern Russia, Kabul, Hungary, Abyssinia, Manchester. Wherever they go they retain their faith, their peculiar physiognomy, their wonderful aptitude for trade."

I have said that the State is one form of the non-genealogic clan. Yet it approaches very closely in some respects to the structure of the pure clan. Its object is not the promotion of a specific purpose, the advancement of some belief, the cultivation of some science, or the practice of some art. It has, indeed, its common form of worship; but this worship is

* "Trans-Caucasia and Ararat," p. 317.

merely its symbol, the outward visible sign of its unity. Its main object, the object to which the common worship is merely auxiliary, is the general material well-being of the community. Hence, like the pure clan, it tends to become localized. This tendency generally predominates; and neighbourhood, not kinship, becomes the basis of the national union. There is no need to offer proof of this territorial character, for the difficulty now is not to establish its presence, but to conceive its absence. At the present day, in all civilized countries, the territorial law is enforced upon all persons, whether strangers or natives, who are within its limits. Yet a State can certainly exist * apart from territory. The supreme court of the United States, † while it refused to recognize their right of property in the soil, acknowledged the Cherokee Indians to be a State capable of forming treaties, and of observing the duties and the rights of civilized men. This territorial principle, too, is a recent development. In India, ‡ territorial political titles are extremely rare, and are generally due, when they exist, to the English. In Rajpútána, the State takes its name from its capital, the residence and citadel of its chief, which, itself, almost always takes its name from the ancient chief who founded it. All the European States were originally personal, not territorial associations. Kings, § so late as the thirteenth century, were kings of peoples, not of countries. The various races that were settled in the same territory insisted, during many generations, on retaining each its separate law. The Frank lived according to Frank law; the Gallic Provincial lived according to Roman law; the Burgundian lived according to the law of the Burgun-

* See Austin's "Lectures on Jurisprudence," vol. i., p. 345.

† Wheaton's "International Law," p. 69.

‡ "Edin. Rev.," vol. cxliv., p. 179, *note*.

§ See Kemble's "Saxons in England," vol. i., p. 152. Mr. Freeman's "Norman Conquest," vol. i., p. 82.

dians; and the Lombard according to the law of the Lombards. So, too, the Englishman, and the Dane, and the Norman lived according to English, or Danish, or Norman law. It was long before there was a king of England; it was longer still before there was a king of France. It was a slow process by which the king's law extended, whether as a benefit or a burthen, to every individual in the kingdom. Yet although this was so, every important community, when it advanced to the condition of a political union, had a territory; and that territory became, if it had not originally been, the recognized basis of the association.

There are thus several points which require attention. The order of events is from kinship to neighbourhood, and not the reverse. The neighbourhood ultimately grows into a territory, and is absorbed by it. The principle of territoriality is comparatively recent; nor is it even yet regarded as essential to national life, although it may be essential to the highest forms with which we are acquainted of that life. Further, the two principles of personal allegiance and territoriality still co-exist, and have in recent times obtained a considerable development. I propose, therefore, to consider—first, the circumstances which led to the change from kinship to neighbourhood; next, the circumstances which led to the growth of the neighbourhood into the territory; and lastly, the two cognate doctrines of allegiance and territoriality, on which the modern nation is founded.

Vicinity as a source of Right.

§ 2. Of the methods by which the State modified the clan, one was direct and intentional; the other was the unforeseen and unexpected result of their mutual reactions. The direct method consisted, not in the alteration of the old clans, but in the substitution for them of artificial bodies, constructed on a similar principle. The original clans were prior to the State, and were the elements out of which it was composed. The reformed State, if I may so call it, was prior to the local clans, which were formed, not for their own sake, but as a means for securing the better working of the political association.

The basis of archaic society was community of worship; and common worship implied, at least in the higher classes, common descent, whether actual or constructive. The relations of members of the society were consequences of this primary principle. One of these relations was that of neighbourhood. Kinsmen were originally neighbours, and neighbours were kinsmen. But when the community prospered, it attracted an outside population, which in its turn became, in course of time, prosperous. Thus there were neighbours who were not kinsmen. These persons the State not unreasonably made liable to political duties; and they, with not less reason, claimed a share in political rights. On the assumption that such a claim was reasonable, the problem arose, how a community of worship between the old citizens and these petitioning outsiders could be established. Each party had its ancestral religion, and neither of them desired to abandon its own worship or to accept that of the other. But their religion was not exclusive; and another worship might be accepted which should be not destructive of the old worship, but cumulative upon it. The expedient was therefore adopted of forming a third religion, in which both parties, while they retained their respective *sacra*, might share. Of this new religion the foundation was not descent, but locality. The country was regarded as forming districts; all free-born men in each district formed a tribe; all tribesmen had a common worship; the aggregate of tribes, united in the common worship of the public Penates, was the State. The old clans continued for their own purposes, but their political functions were gone.

An example of this process is found in the reconstruction by Kleisthenes of the Athenian polity. Aristotle,* in describing the means by which an aristocratical government may be changed into a democracy, says:—"It is, moreover, very useful in such a State to adopt the means which Kleisthenes used at Athens when he was desirous of increasing the power of the people, and as those did who established the democracy in Kyrênê,† that is, to institute many tribes and fraternities, and to reduce the religious rites of private persons to a few, and those common; and every means is to be contrived to associate and blend the people together as much as possible, and that all former customs be broken through." Three distinct steps may here be traced. One was to form within the State new subsidiary associations. The second was to include in these new associations all persons whom it was desired to receive as members of the State, whether they were members of the old clans or outsiders. The third was to substitute, so far as was possible, these new associations for the former associations. The Kleisthenean tribes were carefully assimilated to the form of a pure clan. Each of them was called by the name of some Attic hero, and the statues of the Eponyms were placed in the Agora. Yet it was feared that these tribes might in time harden into exclusive bodies, not less formidable than those which had been with such difficulty broken down. To prevent this evil,‡ the territorial tribe no longer, like the

* "Politics," vi., 4.

† See for similar cases in Kos and Rhodes, Grote's "Hist. of Greece," vol. iii., p. 86, *note*.

‡ See Grote's "Hist. of Greece," vol. iv., p. 178.

genealogical tribe, occupied a contiguous territory. The several tribes were formed, irrespective of contiguity, or rather with a studied disregard for it, out of cantons in all parts of Attica. Thus a union upon the basis of territory was effected, and, at the same time, the strong centripetal force of neighbourhood was retained.

Some features in this great reform well merit attention. A great reform it surely was, although our knowledge of its details is meagre, for it not only laid the foundation of Athenian glory, but it established in human society a new and most fruitful principle. It is the first recognition of the principle that territory forms a basis for political rights and duties. Yet that principle was applied not without hesitation. It was not said that all men, or even all free-born men, in Attica should have full political rights. But it was provided that all such persons should be members of some newly organized society. Citizenship, pure and simple, was still too wide a generalization. It was necessary that every man should have his brotherhood and his kin; and then these kins might be farther combined into a city. Since the days of Theseus, that is, from time immemorial, the State had been formed of the old clans, into which, without special initiation, no stranger could be admitted. The change of Kleisthenes, and it was a great one, consisted in the formation of additional artificial clans for political purposes, and the extensive recognition of their new association by the State. "It was, indeed," says Mr. Grote,* "a striking revolution, impressed upon the citizen, not less by the sentiments to which it appealed, than by the visible change which it made in political and social life. He saw himself marshalled in the ranks of Hoplites alongside

* "Hist. of Greece," vol. iv., p. 219.

of new companions in arms—he was enrolled in a new register, and his property in a new schedule, in his deme and by his demarch, an officer before unknown—he found the year distributed afresh, for all legal purposes, into the parts bearing the name of Prytanies, each marked by a solemn and free-spoken ekklesia, at which he had a right to be present—that ekklesia was convoked and presided by senators called Prytanes, members of a senate novel both as to number and distribution—his political duties were now performed as member of a tribe, designated by a name not before pronounced in common Attic life, connected with one of ten heroes whose statues he saw for the first time in the Agora, and associating him with fellow-tribesmen from all parts of Attica. All these, and many others, were sensible novelties felt in the daily proceedings of the citizen. But the great novelty of all was the authentic recognition of the ten new tribes as a sovereign *demos* or people, apart from all specialties of phratric or Gentile origin, with free speech and equal law."

Vicinity as a source of Duty.

§ 3. Another cause which at least tended to the substitution of the local for the personal relations, was the need for military service. When the enemy is at the gates, there is no time to discuss questions of political equality. The recognition by the State came sometimes in the form, not of the bestowal of a right, but of the imposition of a burthen. Athens* required her Metics to fight side by side with her citizens. They were regimented, according to their ability to provide their arms, or, in other words, according to their wealth, with the Hoplites, or with some other division of the army. Such, too, appears to have

* Hermann's "Grecian Antiquities," p. 226.

been the design * of that famous organization which is attributed to King Servius Tullius. The whole object of that system was military, not political. It was meant to cast the duty of service upon all residents in Rome according to their means, not to give to strangers any political advantage. At a later time, a further step was taken, and political rights were conferred with the intention of thereby imposing political duties. That remarkable edict which, by the stroke of a pen, gave the freedom of the city to every subject of Cæsar, did not proceed from any high philanthropy or enlightened statesmanship. Its object was to include the greatest possible number of persons within the terms of an Act that imposed a convenient and productive tax. There is a curious parallel in our own history, although on a much smaller scale. The elective franchise was forced † upon the tenants of the lords with the avowed purpose of rendering them contributory to a rate for the wages of members of the House of Commons. But these events occurred when such rights were only slightly valued. The point to which I now invite attention is, that, when the privileges of citizenship were highly esteemed, and there was no inclination to share them, the State claimed the power to legislate for strangers within its territory. Such persons were assumed to owe, at least, a temporary allegiance, which might fairly be enforced. Undoubtedly, such a feeling must have led to unexpected consequences. Those who share the burthen have a strong moral claim to share the benefit. The tendency of such legislation must have been to prepare the way for an extension of citizenship. In the meantime, it taught men to believe that a reasonable ground for admission to citizenship was a residence within its

* Mommsen's "Hist. of Rome," vol. i., pp. 94, 100.

† "The Government of England," p. 496.

limits, and a share in common dangers and common burthens.

The failure of the City State.

§ 4. There are two difficulties to which City-States, such as those I have described, are exposed. One is the pressure of outsiders. The other is the inability to assimilate any considerable increase to their numbers. In other words, the City-State soon reaches the limit of its growth; and if any further addition be forced upon it, constitutional disturbances must ensue. The pressure from without is best known in those contests of Patricians and Plebeians with which, under various names, history is full. Neither as to the fact of these contests, nor as to their tendency, is there any doubt, or any occasion for illustration. But it is needful to consider the effect upon such States of the indefinite admission of strangers.

The organization of the City-State is of the simplest kind. It consists of an assembly of all its citizens. It implies the personal presence, at all its meetings, of all its members. That presence must be given on a certain day, and at a certain place. The furthest concession that can be made is that of a quorum. The vote of those who are present may be accepted as the vote of the whole body, and consequently binds those who are absent. The organ for administrative business was equally simple. It consisted in the election, for a certain term, of an officer or of officers by the whole body of the citizens, whose powers the person so chosen exercised. For the preparation of legislation, and for general supervision, a council of State was formed, on the analogy of the council of the clan. Such an organization was suited to the requirements of a small town; and accordingly, Aristotle, when he says that the πόλις or city must be of a certain though indefinite size, observes, by way of illustration, that a city could not consist of ten myriads.

Just as it might be said that a man must be of a certain size, but that a being a hundred feet high could not be a man, so the great philosopher urged that a collection of a hundred thousand human beings could not be a State. He did not allege that no such number of persons could live together. His proposition was, that no political institution, that is, no City-State, could contain such a number. When, therefore, from any cause the bulk of the State exceeded its power of assimilation, its end had come.

The City-State which aspired to empire—that is, to what we should call a national development—had thus but a choice of ruin. If it adhered to its original constitution, it was destroyed by the pressure of its discontented subjects. If it freely admitted these subjects to its citizenship, it fell by its own weight. The history of the great City-States of antiquity furnishes an illustration of each of these tendencies. "What else," said the Emperor Claudius,* "was the cause of the destruction of the Lacedæmonians and of the Athenians, powerful though they were in arms, but that they used to repel their subjects as aliens?" On the other side, the policy of Rome was, as the same emperor contends, a freedom of admission which, to the descendants of a pure clan, would have seemed impossible. Yet, "the civic community † of Rome had broken down from its unnatural enlargement." As compared with the Hellenic City-States, the course which Rome pursued was the nobler and the manlier one. Still, both courses led to the same end. The foundation that the development of the township afforded was too weak to bear the structure of the nation.

It may be asked why the City-State did not develop new organs to meet its new conditions and its increasing

* Tacitus, "Annals," xi., 24.

† Mommsen's "Hist. of Rome," vol. iii., p. 393.

bulk. The men of that day had no experience of a national government, and their traditional beliefs were, as I have already said, inconsistent with any such form. This answer, although it is true, is hardly complete. Everything must have a beginning, and parliamentary institutions were not less strange in the time of Henry III. than they were in the time of the Gracchi. Some explanation, therefore, is wanted to account for the rise of representation in the one case, and for its absence in the other. I think that, in addition to these obstacles, other conditions were absent in Rome, without which national representation could never have existed. Men's minds had not been educated to that point. The custom of Rome recognized Contract only in certain special forms. It knew nothing whatever of Agency. In the time of the later republic, these great branches * of law were still undeveloped. If the ideas of agreement and of representation were not familiar to men's minds in private affairs, it was not likely that they should have been applied to public business. When, after many centuries of training, the notions of the consensual contract and of general agency had been thoroughly established, when the special sanctity of a particular place was no longer felt and the holy auspices were no longer taken, and when political business assumed the form of money dealings with the king, the conditions for political representations were fulfilled.

The growth of Territorial Sovereignty.

§ 5. The City-State was not truly territorial. In the examples I have cited, there is no substitution of a territorial for a personal relation. They only show that vicinity was sometimes accepted as a ground of admission to an association, the basis of which was, and

* Mr. Poste's "Gaius," p. 433.

continued to be, personal. Men were not fellow-citizens because they lived in the same country. They might, however, for that reason be adopted into the State. They then became worshippers of the great goddess, Athenê Polias, or, as the case might be, of Jupiter Capitolinus and of Father Quirinus. But that change which made vicinity, and not either kindred or religion, the basis of political relations, belongs to a comparatively recent date. "Territorial sovereignty," says Sir Henry Maine,*—"the view which connects sovereignty with the possession of a limited portion of the earth's surface—was distinctly an offshoot, though a tardy one, of feudalism." An inquiry into the development of this principle is outside my present limits. I can only notice, in the briefest manner, some of the most salient among the forces which led to its establishment. I conceive that one of them was the gradual dissolution of the Gentile ties. When, from causes which I shall presently consider, the clan broke down, the only connection that was left for the clansmen was neighbourhood. It was a force with which they were already familiar, and it formed the natural and the easiest substitute for the old social bond. But the principle of community was, at that time, not merely weakened: it was brought into competition with an energetic and formidable rival. From various causes, of which some at least are on the surface, after the events known as the "Invasion of the Barbarians," a considerable inequality of wealth, and especially of landed property, became apparent in the greater part of Western Europe. Both the Teutons and the Kelts, as I have in a former chapter observed, were familiar with the practice of Commendation. Military colonies, too, with special forms of tenure, had, for the purposes of defence,

* "Ancient Law," p. 106.

been long settled on the marches under the Empire. The central government was paralyzed, and incapable of protecting life and property. From this concurrence of conditions, feudalism naturally sprung; and, with the aid of lawyers trained in the jurisprudence of Rome, was gradually consolidated into a system. Various motives,* in these favourable circumstances, led to action. Sometimes, as in the establishment by Chlotaire † of the Hundred, in place of the old Vigiliæ, there was the feeling that a customary institution was hopelessly inefficient, and a deliberate attempt at reform took place. Sometimes a powerful lord, or a king like Harald Harfager, compelled his poorer free neighbours, or even the adjacent clans, to become *gafol-geldas,* that is, to acknowledge themselves to be his men and to pay him tribute. Again, as the kingdom was developed, and the responsibilities of the Crown exceeded its means, the king became anxious to establish, at the least possible expense, some kind of local government. Like King Henry VIII. with Lord Kildare, he entertained the well-founded belief that the government of the local magnate, bad as it might be, was better than no government at all. To this cause was due, in our own country, the repeated legislation that every man should have a lord; and the term lord was understood to indicate a wealthy landed proprietor. A further influence may be traced in the altered position of a chief of a clan, who, whether by conquest or otherwise, had been accepted as the lord of an adjoining people. He could not be their chief: he did not pretend to be their master. If he was their lord, he was in a different relation to them from that in which he stood to his own kin. In cases of dispute between his new subjects and his old, an embar-

* See Robertson's "Scotland under her Early Kings," vol. i., pp. 81, 164; vol. ii., pp. 265, 299, 334.

† Canciani, Leg. Barb., ii., 19.

rassing conflict of duties might arise. Uniformity of relation was plainly desirable. But the strangers could not, and perhaps would not, be admitted as members of the old clan. Difficulties, too, might arise in the formation of a new complex nation. There remained but one solution of the problem. The kinsmen might become homagers, and the kindred tie be changed into that of commendation. Thus, as Professor Stubbs* has observed, "the rapid consolidation of the Danish with the Angle and Saxon population involved the necessity of the uniform tie between them and the king: the Danes became the king's men and entered into the public peace; the native English could not be left in a less close connection with their king. The commendation of the one involved the tightening of the cords that united the latter to their native ruler. Something of the same kind must have taken place as each of the heptarchic kingdoms fell under West Saxon rule, but the principle is most strongly brought out in connection with the Danish submission."

This extension of the royal authority, at a time when a common royalty was established over different tribes, was the cause of the uniformity of modern law. As the '*Jus Honorarium*' superseded the '*Jus Quiritium*,' so, among the Teutonic races, the '*Amt-recht*' superseded the old '*Folk-recht*;' and became the '*Jus Civile*' in its full sense, or the national law of the community. There were, as I shall have occasion presently to notice, a great variety of Peaces in every community. There was the Peace of the Church and the Peace of the Folk, the Peace of the Town and the Peace of every Household. But as the king was usually more powerful than any other person in the community, the King's Peace was more efficient than any other

* "Const. Hist.," vol. i., p. 176.

peace. It followed that the king's courts, in like manner, established their superiority. Whether better justice was there administered,* or the local courts were abused for purposes of extortion, a distinct movement of suitors to the king's courts set in, and could not be restrained. But uniformity of court means uniformity of rule. The rise of the common law, therefore—that is, of the common customs of the realm, is due to the extended jurisdiction of the *curia regis.* The process was facilitated by the general similarity which the customs of the several divisions of the country presented. There was no fundamental difference between the customs of the English and of the Danes and of the Normans. They were readily fused into one people beneath the pressure of the king's court. But the case was far otherwise with those who lived under the law of the Romans and those who lived under the law of the Franks or of the Visigoths.† There was a much wider difference between the Frank, the Alemannian, and the Lombard, than there was between the men of Mercia and of Wessex and of the Danelagh. Hence the process of integration was both more speedy and more complete in England than it was either on the Continent or in the other portions of the British Isles. The people were more homogeneous, and the royal courts were more active in England than they were elsewhere.

Sir Henry Maine ‡ justly remarks that the derivation of territorial sovereignty from feudalism "might have been expected *à priori,* for it was feudalism which, for the first time, linked personal duties and by consequence personal rights to the ownership of land." There is little difficulty in tracing the political sequence. But it is less easy to

* See Professor Stubbs's "Const. Hist.," vol. i., p. 393.

† *Ib.*, vol. i., p. 197.

‡ "Ancient Law," p. 107.

establish the first step, that by which men come to regard mere vicinity as a source of duty. Yet, from what I have already said, the course of thought may be traced. The unfree population furnished a precedent. They had certain duties and certain rights towards their lord, by reason of their occupation of his land. The practice of commendation, or rather the extension of that practice, naturally gave rise, in a different class of persons, to similar relations. The alodist who commended himself and took back his land as a fief, passed into a position in some respects resembling that of a Læt. The inducements to make such a sacrifice were, as they must necessarily have been, strong. The old community had broken down. It religious basis had disappeared. Its organization was inadequate to provide for the needs of those troubled times that followed the disappearance of the Roman Peace. The clan was gone, and the empire was gone, and the modern kingdom was, at the most, immature. The only secular means, then, by which at that time society could be to some extent held together, was the extension of the relation of lord and vassal. Such was the firm and universal conviction of the men of those days. To them, such a relation seemed * to be the only alternative with anarchy. By it, and by it alone, so far as their experience extended, could order be maintained and property secured. It was the only form of government which, in practice, they thought of adopting. It supplied the one ideal of society which their imaginations were able to conceive. The old order had passed away; a new and vigorous growth had supplied its place. To men who knew what anarchy was, and by how slender a partition they were divided from it, the new order seemed so beautiful and so strong that they thought it must last

* See "The Government of England," p. 301.

for ever. But change is the law of life. The new order, in its turn, became old, and from its decay a higher form of political life arose. In what various ways this form, too, has been modified, we can now, at least, partly see. What will be the outcome of its changes no man can tell. But of this we may be well assured, that the tendency, so far as it is not counteracted or retarded by our own conduct, is towards a still higher stage of social evolution.

The doctrines of Allegiance and Territoriality.

§ 6. It is a long step from the reforms of Kleisthenes and of Servius Tullius, or even from the decrees of Chlotaire, to the law of national character under Queen Victoria. Yet, in this case, as in so many others, the continuity of legal history is unbroken. The subject of National Character is so rarely discussed, that I venture to deviate a little from my subject, and to make upon it a few observations. Our law very plainly recognizes both the personal and the local elements. The natural-born and the naturalized subjects of the Queen owe to her an allegiance very different from that of Regnicoles, or persons who happen to reside, whether temporarily or otherwise, in her dominions. For the former, Her Majesty may legislate, in whatever part of the world they may be. They are amenable to her laws, whether their acts are done within her dominions, or on the high seas, or in any foreign country; although, of course, in the absence of treaty, British law cannot be enforced against a British subject within the dominions of another sovereign. An English subject, for example, who lives in Brazil, where slavery is lawful, and traffics in slaves there, is safe so long as he remains in Brazil; but as soon as he is found upon the seas, or British ground, he may be arrested for felony. For strangers the Queen may legislate * when they

* See "Reg. *v.* Keyn, L.R., 2 Exch. Div.," p. 161, per Cockburn, L.C.J. Also, 32 H. VIII., c. 16, s. 9.

are within her dominions, or are on board a British ship, or are on board a foreign ship which is within any of Her Majesty's ports or harbours; but not further or otherwise. That is, the Queen's legislative power is personal as regards her own subjects, but territorial as regards foreigners. Under the present custom of Europe, the possession of some territory is essential to the idea of a State; and within that territory each State has —except as to sovereign princes, their ambassadors and their forces—absolute jurisdiction. But the national character goes beyond the territory, and gives rise to a distinct status. The immediate origin of the difference between allegiance and territorial jurisdiction is feudal; but its remote pedigree must be traced to a much more distant period.

Whatever its claims to antiquity may be, this distinction has given rise to one of the most notable political inventions of modern times—the self-governing colonies of England. The basis of that remarkable relation is that the Imperial Parliament has supreme legislative authority in the colony; but that the Colonial Parliament has, in and for the colony, a concurrent, though subordinate, power. There is also the understanding, most important, yet still merely an understanding, that the authority of the Imperial Parliament will be exercised only in exceptional cases, or in cases where legislation is required for the whole Empire. The reason of the difference is, that the legislation of the Imperial Parliament is personal, and reaches all Her Majesty's subjects wherever they may be, and consequently the lands which they inhabit; and that the power delegated to the Colonial Legislature is, by the terms of the grant, limited to its own territory. The Colonial Legislature may, with some slight reservations, "make laws on all subjects whatsoever;" but these laws, except where special authority is given, must be "in and for" the colony. Thus the Imperial law that applies to the colony is in force there because the colonists are Her Majesty's subjects. The Colonial law is also in force, but its local limits are clearly defined. When the two laws clash, the Colonial law gives way, because the tie of allegiance is older and closer than the tie of neighbourhood.

So too, when, under the laws of a colony, a foreigner has been naturalized, he becomes thenceforth a subject of the Queen as against the world. The national character is not local but personal. The consequences that follow the assumption of that character in each portion of the Empire are, indeed, determined by the laws of that portion. But as between nations, nationality does not admit of degrees. The Queen owes as much protection to a Maori, or to a Chinaman of Hong Kong, as she does to the citizen who, like his father before him, was never beyond the sound of Bow Bells. "Had Don Pacifico," says Sir Alexander Cockburn,* "been naturalized at Gibraltar instead of having been born there, he would not have been the less entitled to British protection."

* "Nationality," p. 38.

CHAPTER XVII.

LAW AND CUSTOM.

§ 1. THE notion of law is now sufficiently understood. The analysis of the great analytical jurists is generally accepted; and it is only necessary that I should, so far as my present purpose requires, briefly recapitulate the result of their investigations. Law, then, is a species of command or signification of desire. This species has three leading characteristics. First, the command prescribes a course of conduct, and not an isolated act of forbearance; and that, not in one person or a few persons, but in all the members of a certain class. Secondly, the command implies its enforcement by means, in the last resort, of the physical force which the person who issues the command can bring to bear. Thirdly, the command proceeds from the governing body; or, as it is usually called, the sovereign; or, as I prefer to designate it, the political organ of the community. It is this last circumstance that distinguishes law from the commands of a House Father, or from the rules of voluntary associations. The commands of a Trades Union, or of a Ribbon Lodge, have every one of the other characteristics of a law. They are general commands of a determinate superior to determinate inferiors, imposing duties and enforced by sanctions. But they are not law in our sense of the term; on the contrary, some of them are opposed to, and condemned by, law. Law *par excellence* is State-law—that is, it is the enforceable command of the

The nature of Law.

State, addressed either to its subjects generally, or to some defined classes of them.

I shall, perhaps, best explain what law is, if I briefly notice some examples of what law is not. Besides those notions which I have mentioned, law involves a further meaning. The enforceable command implies obedience; and where the power is great and the sanction adequate, that obedience is proportionately prompt and complete. It is, therefore, a result, not invariable indeed, but very usual, of this command of the State, that it produces a regularity of conduct in conformity to its precepts. But it does not follow that every regularity, either in nature or in human conduct, is the consequence of a command, much less of the command of a particular authority. Nevertheless, the term law has been extended to the sequences of nature; and this metaphor seems likely to absorb the original signification of the term. Two circumstances have probably led to this extension. First, the order of physical causation resembles the uniformity of conduct which an accepted law brings with it. Second, there was a tacit reference to that Supreme Will whose word even the winds and the waves obey. It is not needless to repeat, even though it be for the thousandth time, the distinction between a true law and this metaphorical use of the term. A law of nature, as it is called, is a statement of an invariable unconditional uniformity of sequence. In it there is no room for obedience, since there is no room for will. If the facts do not correspond with the alleged law, the law, in the absence of any disturbing force by which the phenomena can be explained, is not broken, but vanishes. The statement of uniformity was inexact, and there never was such a law of nature; there was only a blunder in the assumption of its existence. But a true law does not cease to be a law, however frequent or serious the breaches of it may be.

A single contradictory instance, clearly proved and unexplained, is fatal to any general proposition of uniformity. But a command of the State remains a command of the State, although little respect be shown to its authority, and although the force that gives effect to it be weak.

Again, even in human conduct, it is not every uniformity that is law. If it be so called, the word law is used in an ambiguous sense, denoting either uniformity in general, or a uniformity produced by a particular cause. The command of the State is not the only cause of the uniformity of men's conduct, or even its principal or its earliest cause. Men often act in a particular manner because they have always acted in that manner. This habitual practice is called custom. Since custom and law thus agree in being rules of conduct, they have, necessarily, certain points of resemblance. But these resemblances relate to the effects, not to the causes. Between themselves, indeed, the differences are clearly marked. Custom neither is, nor implies, a command in the strict sense of the term. It does not create a duty in any particular person. It does not enforce any duty by any definite sanction. In law, everything is definite; in custom, everything is indefinite. In the case of a custom, every person thinks, or acts, or forbears in a particular way; and every person expects that every other person will, in the like circumstances, think, and act, and forbear in a similar manner; and every person has a very bad opinion of any other person that thinks, acts, or forbears otherwise than according to the regulation pattern. In place of the precise commands of a political superior, there are the vague expectations of indefinite persons. In place of the prompt and sharp sanction of the law, there is the dim and indistinct influence of public opinion. Thus, custom is much more nearly related to a law of nature than to a true law. It implies a uniformity of sequence; but between the extent to which a sequence is uniform and the extent to which a command is obeyed, there is no room for comparison.

The nature of Custom.

§ 2. Law, then, denotes the enforceable general commands of the State. The absence of law, consequently, denotes the absence of such commands. But it must not be assumed that the absence of such commands necessarily implies disorder. The State is not the only possible condition of human society. It is, I think, the main error of the analytical jurists, that they, in effect, admit no intermediate condition between law and anarchy. The latter term is always dyslogistic, and denotes not simply the absence of law, but such an absence as destroys social stability. The great thinkers to whom I refer were doubtless right upon their own premises. They accepted the condition of society in which they lived as an ultimate fact. In a society which is organized politically, the line is probably very narrow between actual anarchy and the mere absence of law. But it is not all human societies that are organized politically. Large societies have lived, and are now living, happily, under an organization quite different from that of the State. "Here in India," says Mr. Lyall,* "can still be seen primitive sets of people who never came under the arbitrary despotism of a single man, and among whom no written law has ever been made since the making of the world. Yet these people are not loose, incoherent assemblages of savages; but are very ancient societies, restrained and stringently directed by custom and usages, by rules and rites irresistible." To the like effect another recent observer † remarks, "The Turcomans are a curious example of a people among whom the State does not exist. There is no body

* "Fort. Review," No. 121, N.S., p. 121.

† Mr. MacGahan's "Campaigning on the Oxus," p. 350.

politic, no recognized authority, no supreme power, no higher tribunal than public opinion. Their headmen, it is true, have a kind of nominal authority to settle disputes, but they have no power to enforce decisions. These the litigants can accept, or fight out their quarrel just as they please. And yet they have such well-defined notions of right and wrong as between themselves, and public opinion is so strong in enforcing these notions, that there are rarely dissensions or quarrels amongst them."

The force which, in such societies, assumes that place as a rule of conduct which law fills among modern nations is custom. I have already described the difference between custom and law, and may therefore assume that the terms are far from being equipollent. There is custom which is not law, and there is law which is not custom. By what process the two are combined I shall presently inquire. Why different communities have different customs, and what is the cause of the great power of custom, are questions which I cannot undertake to treat. The answer to the former question must be sought for in the diversities of the history of each people. The latter question, although an immemorial common-place, has scarcely yet received all the treatment that it deserves. Undoubtedly, use doth breed a habit in a man; and the mere repetition of an act or of a forbearance tends, from whatever cause, to generate an inclination towards that act or forbearance for its own sake, and without regard to the motives on which it originally depended. Nor is it difficult to understand how, in the course of time, so strong a web of association and of sentiment is formed, that few even think of breaking it. I offer no opinion upon the tendency of these acquired associations to become hereditary. But custom, in the sense in which I now use the term, relates to masses of men, and is to a great extent confirmed and perpetuated by their reciprocal influence. Men approve that which they themselves do, and which they have during all their lives seen others do. The uncultured intellect is averse to suspend its judgment, and, consequently, men usually disapprove that which is unfamiliar and strange. This disapprobation is especially marked when the innovation is not merely a novelty, but is directly hostile to their received views. The approbation, or the disapprobation, of those among whom he lives can never be wholly indifferent to any human being. Thus the force of public opinion exercises, in favour of an established custom, an influence which, in the absence of any great counteracting sentiment, is almost if not altogether irresistible.

I need not illustrate either the power of custom or its variety. The former is sufficiently shown in our daily life. The recognition of the latter requires but a moment's reflection. In the course of a few generations, men can be trained to think or to feel almost anything that is not beyond the limits of their nature. When King Darius asked * the Callatian Indians what he should give them if they would consent to burn their fathers on their decease, and not to eat them, they "exclaimed aloud, and bade him forbear such language." Orientals look † with horror and loathing upon the European system of a single wife. Practices to us the most revolting, are, to those who follow these practices, innocent and laudable. So true is it in our day, no less than in the time of Herodotus,‡ that "custom is king over all." But it is remarkable, how odious a custom which has been outgrown appears, when the descendants of those who once followed

* Herodotus, iii., 38.

† See Mr. Spencer's "Sociology," vol. i., p. 635, and the authorities there cited.

‡ *νόμος πάντων βασιλέει, ubi supra.*

it observe it in other people. It has been remarked that a man is never so severe in his condemnation as when he censures some inclination which he once followed, but which he has succeeded in bringing under restraint. Some similar tendency seems to exist in national life. I have already noticed the probable connection between our aversion to horseflesh and the Odin-worship of our forefathers. Mr. Lyall,* in his animated description, drawn apparently from the life, of an Indian inquiry respecting a cattle-lifting difficulty, notices the "slight shudder" that runs through the high-caste Hindu officials who record the candid statement of the Bheel headman, and his business-like proposal to pay the proper blood-money for the Brahman that he and his companions shot. The feelings of these officers were probably nearly akin to those of Sir John Davies,† when he denounced the horrible nature of the Irish customs, and their practice of commuting all offences by an eric or fine. "Therefore, when Sir William Fitz-Williams (being Lord-Deputy) told Maguyre that he was to send a sheriff into Fermanagh, being lately before made a county, 'Your sheriff (said Maguyre) shall be welcome to me, but let me know his eric (or the price of his head) beforehand; that, if my people cut if off, I may cut the eric upon the country.'" Yet the ancestors of the Brahmans and the ancestors of Sir William Fitz-Williams undoubtedly practised, and at no very distant date, the custom which Maguyre proposed to observe. So, too, the English judges in Ireland did not measure their language, when, early in the reign of James I., they decided ‡ against the customs of Tanistry and Gavelkind. These customs were held to be inconvenient and unreasonable: they were

* "Fort. Rev.," No. 121, N.S., p. 104.
† "Hist. Tracts," p. 126.
‡ Sir John Davies's Reports, p. 40.

inconsistent with that just and honourable law of England which His Majesty, by extending his royal protection to all Irishmen, had by implication introduced. They admitted of no permanent estate in the land, without which there could be no good government; and the interest under them amounted at most to a "transitory and scambling possession." Yet these unlucky customs were only an older form of that Kentish Gavelkind which the judges were careful to distinguish; and their origin was much more ancient than that of the just and honourable law, which, in an evil hour,* and to the great miscarriage of justice, was substituted for them.

The other illustration that I propose to offer relates to the wide diffusion of custom. Men, or at least bodies of men, never habitually act from mere unregulated caprice. They may have no laws in the proper sense of the term, but even in the most unpromising circumstances their conduct is governed by very stringent usages. It is not easy to conceive men apparently more lawless, that is, less dependent upon the will of others, than the wandering tribes of the Asian deserts. Whatever may be the internal organization of each tribe, the tribe itself is the conventional emblem of all that is unfettered and free. Yet, on a nearer approach, it is found that these tribes are by no means exempt from control, but live under well-established customs. Each member of a tribe, of course, obeys his tribal rules; and the various tribes, as among themselves, conform to their immemorial usages. On this subject Mr. MacGahan † thus writes. He is describing the annual migrations of the Kirghiz, a people who roam from the Oxus to the Syr:—

"To anybody unacquainted with their habits of life, there

* See Professor Richey's "Lectures on the History of Ireland" (second series), p. 455.

† "Campaigning on the Oxus," p. 50.

does not seem to be the slightest system in their movements. They have a system, nevertheless. Every tribe and every aul follows, year after year, exactly the same itinerary; pursuing the same paths, stopping at the same wells, as their ancestors did a thousand years ago; and thus many auls, whose inhabitants winter together, are hundreds of miles apart in the summer. The regularity and exactitude of their movements is such that you can predict to a day where, in a circuit of several hundred miles, any aul will be at any season of the year. A map of the desert, showing all the routes of the different auls, if it could be made, would present a network of paths meeting, crossing, intersecting each other in every conceivable direction; forming, apparently, a most inextricable entanglement and confusion. Yet no aul ever mistakes its own way, or allows another to trespass upon its itinerary. One aul may at any point cross the path of another, but it is not allowed to proceed for any distance upon it. Any deviation of an aul or tribe from the path which their ancestors have trodden is a cause for war; and, in fact, nearly all the internecine struggles among the Kirghiz have resulted from the encroachment of some tribe, not upon the pasture grounds, as might be supposed, but upon the itinerary of another. . . .

"I took occasion now to ask my friend why his people did not stay on the same spot, instead of continually wandering from place to place? 'The pasture,' he said, 'was not sufficient in one place to sustain their flocks and herds.' 'But why do those who live on the Syr in the winter not stay there in the summer, where the pasture is good, instead of wandering off into the desert, where it is thin and scarce?' I ask. 'Because other auls come; and if they all stayed, they would soon eat it all bare.' 'But why do not the other auls stay at home on the Amu and the Irghiz, instead of coming?' 'Because other auls come there too,' he replied. 'But why do they not all stay at home?' 'Well, our fathers never did so, and why should not we do as they have always done?' he replied. And I suppose this is as near the true reason of their migration as any other."

The nature of Customary Law.

§ 3. Sir Henry Maine * has expressed his opinion that "all of Austin's remarks on customary law seem comparatively unfruitful." I cannot concur in this opinion. Mr. Austin's object was to explain the nature of customary law, and not to trace the origin or the history of custom. He has, accordingly, pointed out that custom is one thing, and that law is another thing. He has proved, in opposition to an opinion once very prevalent, that custom is not law *consensu utentium*, or by any inherent property. He has shown that the transmutation of custom into law takes place only by the recognition of competent authority, and by the extension of the custom of the sovereign's sanction. Subject to some remarks that I shall presently have to make as to the process of transmutation, I think that this explanation is correct. Nor is its value diminished because it throws no light upon an entirely different subject. The difficulty which presses Sir Henry Maine, arises, if I may venture to say so, from his failure to appreciate the broad distinction between law and custom. It is true that, as he observes,† Runjeet Singh ruled extensive territories in the Punjab, and never made a law in his life. But there was no law in Runjeet Singh's dominions. His subjects, or rather his tributaries, lived according to their respective customs, and merely paid tribute to what was practically a foreign power. I have already shown that the tax-taking empires, according to Sir Henry Maine's judicious distinction, are not States at all. It is only when we come to legislating empires, or

* "Early Hist. of Inst.," p. 392.

† *Ib.*, p. 380.

rather when we come to the Empire of Rome, that the question as to the relation of custom and of law arises. That relation, as Mr. Austin has stated it, is easily understood. Custom becomes law when, and only when, it is adopted by the State, and is enforced by its sanction. Thus, custom furnishes both the motive and the material for law, but is not of itself law. The fact that a custom exists, supplies to the State a reason for bringing that custom, whether for the purpose of supporting or of modifying it, within the range of its authority. Further, when the State desires to legislate upon any subject, it naturally takes into its consideration the customs under which its subjects have previously lived. To these customs, or to some of them, the State, whatever may be its motive, extends its sanction; that is, it commands that the customs shall be observed under penalty of its displeasure. Thereupon and thereby that which was merely custom is transmuted into positive law.

On one portion of this subject, indeed, I venture to dissent from the great authority of Mr. Austin. He has shown that custom becomes law when it is sanctioned by the State; but his description of the mode in which that sanction is given is questionable. The process, as he represents it, is twofold—first, the judges, of their own mere motion, give effect to customs; second, the State, which has the power to control the judges' conduct, tacitly acquiesces in this proceeding. Both these propositions seem to me erroneous. No motive is suggested why the judges should, against the duty of their office, habitually act upon unauthorized customs. A solitary instance of the kind might be explained by some individual peculiarity; but no personal eccentricity can account for the persistence in such a course of a succession of great magistrates during many generations. The judges, too, do not claim for themselves any legislative powers. On the contrary, they always repudiate any such pretension. They profess not to make law, but to explain the law as they find it. Part of the law they find in the general customs of the country. It is a much less violent, and certainly a more charitable explanation, to suppose that the judges administer these customs because they believe them to have, in some manner, become established law, than to suppose that a succession of able and upright men have audaciously usurped a power of legislation which was never given to them, and habitually exercise this usurped power, the existence of which they hypocritically deny.

The doctrine of the tacit acquiescence of the State is expressed in the maxim—"What the State permits, it commands;" that is, since the State has the power of preventing, at its pleasure, any act or forbearance, its omission to exercise that power is equivalent to its consent. Sir Henry Maine,* although he has said much to discredit the maxim, remarks that it is of vital importance to the system of the analytical jurists; and adds, that "the theory is perfectly defensible as a theory, but its practical value, and the degree in which it approximates to truth, differ greatly in different ages and countries."

These concessions seem to me too great. For my part, I do not admit any such maxim. I do not believe that it is needed to remove any difficulty in jurisprudence. I think that the condition on which it is professedly founded exists only in certain advanced stages of political development. I think that its application is inconsistent with the history of law, and especially with the fundamental principles of our own constitution. It was invented by the analytical jurists to assist them in explaining, not the nature or even

* "Early Hist. of Inst.," p. 364.

the origin of customary law, but the process by which custom, without apparent legislation, becomes law. I hope presently to show that the supposed anomaly does not, in fact, exist; and that, therefore, the maxim may be dismissed with the imaginary difficulty which it was created to solve. But it is in itself untenable. It rests upon the unfounded assumption that the State precedes society, or is at least external to it, and above it. But as the State is historically of comparatively recent formation, there must have been, and in fact there was, a large part of men's conduct which was not ruled by State law, and which the State did not, for many ages, pretend either to prohibit or to direct. Nor is this all. The foundation of the rule is said to be the irresistible power of the State, not necessarily exerted, but capable of being exerted. In other words, the rule postulates the existence of a strong central government. Such a government is of very modern growth. The beginnings of the State were feeble. It was not competent for the State to change any custom merely because it disapproved of it. If Solon or Rothar had been asked whether he considered that this maxim applied to his Athenians or to his Lombards, he would probably have replied that, so far from commanding what he permitted, he was fortunate in being permitted to command. The history of early law is full of traces which show that, even in the administration of justice, it was only by slow degrees that the State could establish its authority. No custom in the archaic world was more firmly settled or more widely diffused than that of the blood-feud. There was no custom against which the State, even when appearing to accept it, maintained so unceasing an opposition. It is idle to say that the State either permitted or commanded a rule which existed for centuries before the State existed, and which it was always labouring ineffectually to modify or to repress.

Even in a highly developed political society, the maxim is not true. The silence of the State may be evidence of its consent, but not of its command. Between the two ideas there is a wide distinction. It makes no inconsiderable difference to a people whether they may do whatever is not forbidden, or only that which is expressly commanded. Our whole system of personal and political liberty rests upon the two principles—that individual freedom of action is the rule, and that the interference of the State is the exception. In these circumstances, it cannot be fairly said that the State because it permits—that is, does not prevent—thereby commands the enjoyment of any personal or proprietary right. Its silence does not create any duty of enjoyment. The law merely leaves the owner alone, and requires from all other persons a similar forbearance. The owner is free to enjoy his right, or to abstain from doing so. The law neither directly nor by implication commands him to eat, drink, and be merry. It merely prevents any other person from molesting him, whether his humour be to be merry or to be sad. Further, the practical application of this maxim becomes occasionally highly preplexing. Sometimes the law, avowedly and in express terms, adopts an existing custom. A few years since, an Act of Parliament provided that the custom known as the tenant-right of Ulster should be observed as law, both in that province and in the rest of Ireland. But the custom thus recognized had existed for centuries before the time of Mr. Gladstone. Since, therefore, the custom existed, the law must have permitted it; and since the law permitted the custom, the law, if this maxim be true, must have commanded the custom. Consequently, the custom must have been always law; and there was no difference in the state of the law in this particular before 1870 and after that date—which were news, indeed.

§ 4. I think that the true explanation of customary law is, that the customs of the community have, as a whole, been adopted by the legislature; and that their extent, their meaning, and their relation, as well to each other as to other parts of the law, are determined in the usual way by the courts. I include, of course, in the terms legislature and courts, that body which, when differentiated, is developed into separate legislative and judicial organs, whatever may at different times, or in different communities, have been its title or its structure. There is nothing anomalous or exceptional in customary law. Like all other law, it is made by the legislator, and it is administered by the judges. Men did indeed follow these rules of conduct long before they heard either of law, or of legislators, or of courts. But when these agencies come into existence, they exercise a new and very notable influence upon pre-existing customs. These customs are adopted by the State; and, after they have been ascertained by its proper officers, are enforced not merely by public opinion, but by the collective force of the community. In this view, judges do not contrive how they may stealthily introduce into their practice some favourite usage; but they evolve order first out of vague and often inconsistent customs, and next out of the conflict of these customs, when they have been defined, with the positive legislation of the State. This view depends upon a question of fact. If the legislature at any time, or in any country, have adopted in general terms the existing customs of the people, or any considerable portions of them, the burthen of proof rests with those who maintain the affirmation. I accept the necessity, and proceed to state such historical evidence as I am able to offer in support of my contention.

How Custom becomes Law.

Most of the so-called barbarian codes which have come down to us—the Salic law, the laws of the Ripuarians and of the Burgundians, the laws of the Welsh, the Brehon laws—recite an examination of existing customs, and their embodiment as amended in the code. Sometimes they add the sanction, whether the command of the King or the admonition of the Church or both, by which obedience to the rules thus promulgated shall be enforced. Thus we are told * that Howel the Good, the son of Cadell, Prince of all Cymru, seeing the Cymry perverting the laws, summoned to him, to the White House on the Tav, the wisest among the people. After a careful revision of the ancient laws, they promulgated the laws which they decided to establish; "and Howel sanctioned them with his authority, and strictly commanded them to be diligently observed." It may be broadly stated that these "*Leges Barbarorum*" are merely digests, more or less complete, of the customs of the several tribes. By far the greater part of them relate to personal injuries, and regulate the amount for which the feuds thence resulting may be composed. They have thus no true sanction or penalty of disobedience inflicted by the central government. They are merely the customs of arbitration. It was not until a later period that the royal power attained sufficient strength to enforce, by its officers, its commands. In other words, the nations lived according to their respective customs, and wrongs were redressed in the customary manner by the party interested therein. Law—that is, the enforceable command of the King—could not, and did not, arise until the kingly office was firmly established. I shall have occasion, in a subsequent chapter, to discuss the growth of Civil Jurisdiction. For my present purpose, it will be sufficient to examine the history of our two great legal examples, the law of Rome and the law of England.

* "Laws of Wales," vol. i., p. 3.

At Rome, under the old constitution, the curule magistrates, and among them the Prætor, exercised by their edicts a certain delegated power of legislation. They were, within their several spheres, the organs of the popular will, elected by the people for a certain term and for certain purposes. During that time, and within those purposes, they severally exercised the whole power of the State. It was their practice to issue, at the commencement of their year of office, a statement of the principles upon which they proposed to act. When, by the creation of the Præturate, the judicial business was separated from the ordinary business of administration, the Prætorian edict acquired a special importance. It was by this agency that the great development of Roman law in the later Republic took place. But Cicero * informs us that the Prætor declared that which he found established by usage: he gave to usage the form and character of real law.

The case, however, that has for us both the greatest interest and the greatest importance, is that of the common law of England. I know that to many persons I shall seem to maintain an unseemly, perhaps an unpatriotic, paradox, when I contend that that venerable body of customs derives its legal strength from the authority of the legislature. Every English lawyer boasts that his common law owes nothing to Act of Parliament. It was only by very slow degrees that the legal mind came to admit the idea that a statute was stronger than a rule of common law. In its literal sense, this independence of parliament is unquestionably true. The name parliament was first used in England in the time of Richard I. The institution with which, under that name, we are familiar, is at least a century, perhaps nearly two centuries, later. But long before the

* See Long's "Cicero," vol. i., p. 163.

reign of Richard, the common law was recognized and enforced. The common law, therefore, is not the creature of parliament. But it does not follow that the common law does not depend upon the legislative organ of the nation, whatever it may have been, from which parliament was gradually developed. It cannot be denied that the good customs of the country were, not by one king but by many kings, recognized, accepted, and enforced. Thus, the laws of King Cnut* declare—"This is the first that I will: that just laws be established, and every unjust law carefully suppressed; and that every injustice be weeded out and rooted up with all possible diligence from this country. And let God's justice be exalted; and henceforth let every man, both poor and rich, be esteemed worthy of folk-right, and let just dooms be doomed to him." This enactment presupposes an existing standard of right to which the king required his subjects to conform. So, too, Professor Stubbs† observes:—"Offences against the law (*i. e.*, as I conceive, against the custom) become offences against the king, and a crime of disobedience a crime of contempt to be expiated by a special sort of fine, the *ofer-hyrnesse*, to the outraged majesty of the law-giver and judge. The first mention of the *ofer-hyrnesse* occurs in the laws of Edward the Elder: at the era, accordingly, at which the change of idea seems to have become permanent." The same idea of a pre-existing custom, and of the royal recognition and enforcement of that custom, is expressed in the laws of the Conqueror. I translate the following section from one‡ of his charters:—"William, King of the English, Duke of the Normans, to all his men, French and English, greeting: We command, especially, above all things, that one God

* "Anc. Laws of England," vol. i., p. 377. See also for Alfred, p. 59.

† "Const. Hist.," vol. i., p. 183.

‡ "Anc. Laws and Inst. of England," vol. i., p. 490.

be worshipped through the whole of our realm; that one faith of Christ be kept ever inviolate; that peace, and security, and concord, judgment and justice between English and Normans, Franks and Britons of Wales and Cornwall, Picts and Scots of Albany, likewise between French and islanders, provinces, and countries, which pertain to the crown and dignity, defence, and observance, and honour of our realm, and between all our subjects through the whole monarchy of the realm of Britain, be firmly and inviolably observed, so that no person may incur forfeiture to another in any respect, upon pain of our full forfeiture."

In the reign of the first Plantagenet, as the country grew and its business increased, a special organization was by act of the legislature created for the administration of justice; that is, for the enforcement by the king's authority of the good customs of the country. Such customs so enforced became common law, and the special organ created for its administration was the judicial bench. This, I conceive, is the position which the judges have always claimed for themselves, and which their commission defines. The judges of the present day are commanded, as their predecessors have always been commanded, "to do what to justice appertains according to the laws and customs of England." That is, they are required to guide their official conduct by three rules—first, by the statute law; second, by the customs of England, that is the common law, or recognized local customs; third, by the principles of natural justice, which, as well as custom, is thus expressly recognized as part of our legal system. This is the answer to the attack of Bentham upon "Judge-made law." Judge-made law, apart from the interpretation of statutes, means nothing more than the administration by the proper officers of the general customs of the kingdom. So far is it from being the authorized work of the judges, that it is the direct work of the people themselves. That which formerly was vague, the judges reduce to certainty. That which formerly was followed as usage, the judges, with the aid of the strong arm of the Executive, enforce as law.

This process of the intentional conversion of custom into law by the act of the legislature is still in force among ourselves. Mr. Justice Markby * observes, that "wherever the legislature of this country has defined the special duties of the courts in India in reference to natives, it is to the law and *usages* of Hindus and Mohammedans, and not to the law alone, that they are directed to conform." A still more recent example is the Irish Land Act, to which I have already referred. That Act provided that the custom of the Ulster tenant-right should be law; and left to the judges the task of ascertaining the extent of the custom, and of applying it when it was ascertained. So, in an earlier year of Her Majesty's reign, † a number of mining customs in Derbyshire were collected, and converted into law. A similar process is described by Blackstone. Writing of offences against the law of nations, he concludes his account with these words:—"These are the principal cases in which the statute law of England interposed to aid and enforce the law of nations as a part of the common law, by inflicting an adequate punishment upon offences against that universal law, committed by private persons." The law of nations is only the custom of nations; and, as against private offenders, this custom had no operation until it was armed with the sanction of the law, in the first instance by the aid of the common law, and subsequently by the more effective assistance of Parliament.

Some consequences of this theory.

§ 5. This account of the genesis of customary law explains several important facts. In the first place, it coincides

* "Elements of Law," p. 34.

† See 14 and 15 Vict. c. 94, § 16.

with and confirms the view which the English judges have always taken of their position. They have at all times invariably declared that it is their province not to make law, but to administer it. They are the officers of the State; and the duty of their office is the administration of the law which the State has adopted, or from time to time enacts. Part of this law is found in the customs of the country; and these customs it is the business of the judge to ascertain, define, and co-ordinate. What, in their description of their province, the judges have not thought it necessary to state, was the proof that these customs had been at some time formally acknowledged and adopted by the State. They have always assumed this fact as the basis of their position; and, as a dispute upon such a point could not and did not arise in practice, they did not concern themselves with a matter which seemed to be of merely speculative interest. There has been no usurpation on the part of the judges, and no interference by them with the powers of the legislature. It is true that the judicial powers are large and important. It is true, also, that the change of vague and floating custom into precise and rigorous law has often produced amongst us, as amongst other people, serious and unexpected changes. On some occasions, perhaps, judges may have been, to some extent, influenced in their decisions by their views of what the public convenience required. But the customary law which governs the courts is neither caprice nor mystery. It is the immemorial usage of the community, or the application to new cases of secondary principles deduced from that usage, which the State has accepted and has undertaken to enforce by its paramount authority.

Again, Mr. Austin, although he speaks of judiciary law in terms very different from those which Bentham employed, fails to perceive the process by which the custom becomes law. He speaks * of the "childish fiction employed by our judges that judiciary law is not made by them, but is a miraculous something, existing, I suppose, from eternity, and merely declared from time to time by the judges." He insists, as I understand him, that the judges have by law a sort of concurrent legislative power; and he blames † Lord Eldon, not because he exercised that power, but because he exercised it badly; because, when he might have amended the law, he left it worse than he found it. Certainly, Lord Eldon never claimed, or even conceived that he possessed, any such power. Certainly, if any judge now ventured to disregard any precedent ‡ on the ground only that he disagreed with it, his judgment would be promptly reversed. Whether the judges ought to have any such power, is another question; but the hypothesis that they do possess it has much more pretension to be styled a fiction than that which Mr. Austin condemns. His difficulty, of course, arose from his acceptance of the State as an ultimate fact. On the assumption that the State and the commands of the State were the original and the only bonds of society, and that men never did live and never could have lived in any orderly manner under any other conditions than those of political government, Mr. Austin's view of the fictitious character of the judges' theory is not unreasonable. But when it is understood that men lived according to their customs long before these customs were touched by the State, that the State commenced its control by undertaking to enforce these customs, and that it was only at a late period that it ventured gradually to alter them, it may well be believed that in professing to expound only and to

* "Lectures on Jurisprudence," vol. ii., p. 655.

† *Ib.*, p. 668.

‡ See Chapman *v.* Monmouthshire Railway and Canal Company, 27 L. J., Exch., 101.

develop, not to make, the law, the judges employed no legal fiction, but simply stated the very truth.

There is a peculiarity in the structure of modern law, which is of greater practical interest than the speculations of jurists, however eminent. For this peculiarity, the view in support of which I am contending, and, as I think, that view alone, furnishes an explanation. It is remarkable that in all mdoern law there is no distinct statement of men's general duties. It might reasonably be expected that such a record, in plain and unambiguous terms, would be found in the very front of every national system of law. Yet, as Mr. Justice Markby* observes, there is no country in which we have, on official authority, a complete catalogue of duties. The law invariably takes the shape of penalty. It does not command its subjects to do certain acts, or to observe certain forbearances. What it says is, that if any person does, or forbears to do, such and such acts, he shall undergo such and such a punishment. There is no direct command; and the primary object of the legislator's regard is that which really is subsidiary—the sanction. The duty is always assumed to be known; and its definition must be extracted from the penalty annexed to its violation. This arrangement is certainly neither the most obvious nor the most convenient. Why, then, has it been universally adopted? The answer, as I think, is that the law merely enforced the customs that it found. It assumed that every person was already familiar with these customs; and the sanction or penalty was the part of the transaction with which it was specially concerned. Hence, there is no law which directly prescribes absolute and general duties. So little noted are these duties, that even Mr. Austin can find in his classification no definite place for them, and does not

* "Elements of Law," p. 74.

seem to think the omission material. They must be gathered, as best they may, from the Law relating to Crimes and Punishments. When a code is prepared, the first step in the work will, I conceive, be the extrication of these duties from their present obscurity. There will be then promulgated a plain and precise statement, first, of what—having regard to the motive and the state of mind, as well as to the act and its consequences—the State requires its subjects to do and to avoid; and, next, of the penalties with which it will visit each degree of disobedience. The cause of the present anomaly is altogether historical. It proceeds from the universal priority of custom to law, and from the universal adoption and modification of that custom by the State.

Reciprocal influence of Law and Custom.

§ 6. Legal customs differ from customary law. As the latter is law which has risen on the basis of custom, so the former are customs which, although exceptional in their character, are permitted to exist by the favour of law, and under its protection. Where, as in England, the national integration has been complete, general customs are, as I have said, taken up into the legal system, and soon become almost exclusively known by the name of law. Some local customs are strong enough to maintain their ground, and to obtain a limited recognition. Such customs are in derogation of the Common Law, and are consequently not regarded with much judicial favour. They retain the name of custom, which thus becomes contrasted with that of law. Law, in this sense, means recognized general customs. Custom, in this sense, means recognized particular customs. Thus, the rule of Primogeniture is a rule of Common Law; but the rules of Gavelkind or of Borough English are the customs of Kent or of London. Such customs, however, are now merely survivals;

and, as they must have existed since time beyond legal memory, they are but old-world fashions with little practical interest. The shape which modern custom takes is different, and deserves a passing notice. It appears mainly in contracts. Custom no longer founds a general rule of law binding upon all persons who come within its operation. In the greater freedom of modern society, men, in most of the ordinary transactions of life, make their own laws. As in former times the State adopted and enforced preceding customs of general extent, so in modern times the State adopts and enforces the arrangements by which men undertake to regulate their future conduct. The primary rule of law, the major premiss, so to speak, in all matters relating to contracts, is in effect a command of the State, that, subject to certain exceptions, every agreement duly made between any two persons not incompetent to contract shall, as between the parties and their representatives, be deemed to have the force of law. But men's agreements need to be interpreted; and a reasonable interpretation notices the ordinary course of business in which the parties were engaged. Sometimes this course of business is identified with a particular form of transaction, and so becomes a part or necessary incident of it. Thus, the contract arising out of a bill of exchange involves no small amount of interpretation, and the law regards as essential to the instrument that it recognizes under that title the three days of grace after the nominal date of payment. These are among the customs of merchants of which the law takes notice, and they show that the material relations of custom and of law are still in operation. The influence of custom is still felt in law, but it operates now by way of interpretation, and not as formerly by way of direct command.

The old Horatian exclamation, "Quid vanæ sine moribus

leges proficiunt," contains an important, though perhaps an unintended truth; yet it is one which needs to be distinguished. The connection of law and of custom arises in various circumstances. Sometimes the law is introduced to suppress or alter the custom; sometimes to enforce it. Sometimes the authority is external, as in the case of foreign conquest, or where a strong central government controls a recalcitrant portion of its own community. Sometimes the law is the genuine expression of the legislative organ; but, whether from error or accident, is inconsistent with the habits and the wishes of the bulk of the people. Sometimes, again, it is invoked to give effect to the wishes of the majority, and to enforce the good customs of the country against the innovating few. In the first class of cases, the question is one of the strength and activity of the government. There is a struggle, the duration and the consequences of which depend upon the relative strength of the opposing parties, and the energy with which that strength is exerted. If, however, the State choose to incur the necessary cost, which may sometimes amount to the actual extirpation of its opponents, the law usually triumphs; and the custom either disappears or is modified so as to meet the requirements of the case. "There is no middle course," says Mr. Hallam,* "in dealing with religious sectaries, between the persecution that exterminates and the toleration that satisfies. They were wise in their generation, the Loaisas and the Valdes of Spain, who kindled the fires of the Inquisition, and quenched the rising spirit of Protestantism in the blood of a Seso and a Cazalla." When, on the other hand, the law is not imposed from without, the case seems to be that of a failure on the part of the political organ to perform its proper functions.

* "Const. Hist.," vol. i., p. 204.

Just as some particular House of Commons may fail to express truly the national will, so the entire legislative organ is for the time not in accord with the national sentiment. In these circumstances, the law inevitably gives way. Sometimes it is in due course repealed. Sometimes it is simply disregarded. If the law refuse its assistance to arrangements which the public find it convenient or agreeable to make, the arrangement will be made and observed without that assistance. The deficiency of the law finds its compensation in the increased activity of public opinion. If the law command something to be done which public opinion holds to be unfit to be done, a passive resistance, which is most difficult to overcome, is set up. Judges become preternaturally astute. Juries absolutely decline to be bound by the evidence. Justices are reluctant to commit. Witnesses are reluctant to appear, and when they do appear, to tell all they know. Even the police are less keen than usual in their search. If a conviction be by chance secured, the culprit is not lowered in public estimation. A very practical check is thus placed upon any excess of inconvenient legislation. On the other hand, when both law and custom coincide, the result is altogether irresistible. Yet it needs but little reflection to understand* how much more of the security and the comfort of our daily life we owe to the action of custom than to the protection of law.

There is another relation of custom and law that claims attention. Frequently, the aid of the law is invoked to enforce and support some custom which previously had been followed without any legal sanction. It matters not from what motive this aid is sought or given. The actual fact produces results that were not foreseen, and that are often unwelcome. The effect of the operation is that the

* See Hallam, "Middle Ages," vol. iii., p. 158.

custom becomes a true law. Evidence of its existence is given; the fact thus established is recorded, and the sanction of the State is added to it. The practice is thus no longer observed as a custom: it depends upon authority, and is obeyed as law. Both in its substance and in its sanction it ceases to be vague, and becomes precise. It can no longer be applied according to what a loose public opinion regards as the merits of each particular case. It becomes inexorable, not respecting persons, and not regarding consequences. It acts not by a common condition of thought, but by the influence of an external force. Further, from the very nature of the case, the proposition affirming the custom is always too broadly stated. It does not comprise the exceptions and the limitations which were present to the minds of the customaries, although they did not know how to formulate them. It has, too, no elasticity—no power of gradually modifying itself to meet any alteration in circumstances. Hence, in place of custom there sometimes arises a law which neither the people expected nor the legislature intended. Serious changes in men's rights and duties take place, without any desire on the part either of those who bring about the change or of those who are affected by it. Such a result is inevitable; but those who feel the inconvenience and do not understand its cause, always blame the law and its administrators. The most conspicuous instance of such a process is that which, under British rule, is still going on in India. On this subject, I need only refer to the very able discussion in the first three lectures of Sir Henry Maine's "Village Communities." In that country, the great subject of complaint has been our courts of justice. Even the very worst of these courts probably administered purer and better justice than the native mind ever dreamt of; and the officers charged with the duty have been, as a class, conscientious and competent men. But even in the hands of skilled judges, the change must have been complete, and the transition, as such transitions always are, painful and often exasperating. "The truth is," says Sir Henry Maine,* "that the written and customary law of such a society as the English found in India, is not of a nature to bear the strict *criteria* applied by English lawyers. The rule is so vague as to seem capable of almost any interpretation; and the construction which, in those days, an English lawyer would place upon it, would almost certainly be coloured by associations collected from English practice." Thus the loose corporate tenure in the Hindu village communities acquired, in the hands of English lawyers, the character of individual right. But this right brought with it the power of dissolving partnership, and the liability of his share in the joint property for the owner's debts. Hence it is said † that "the partition of inheritances and execution for debt levied on land are destroying the communities." Yet, this result was certainly not intended. The remedy for the difficulty is systematic legislation; and that remedy, fortunately for India, is now in course of skilful application.

But when we appreciate these influences, a light begins to glimmer upon some perplexing things that occurred in our own history at a time when no such remedy was available as the Indian code of Queen Victoria. We may remember the earnest demands of our forefathers from their Norman kings for the "good laws of King Edward." No such laws were ever found; and no new legislation was forced upon the English. On the contrary, King William granted to his new subjects their respective rights and customs; and even, it is said, abandoned, at their request, his project of establish-

* "Vill. Com.," p. 37.

† *Ib.*, p. 113; see also p. 73.

ing uniformity of law throughout his kingdom. I cannot doubt that Mr. Hallam's explanation * is correct, and that the demand for King Edward's law was merely an expression of dissatisfaction with the Norman administration. Such, too, but upon a greater scale and in a more aggravated form, was the history of the disappearance of the Keltic society in the British Isles. I cannot venture here to open the troublous pages of Irish and of Gaelic history. But I incline strongly to the belief that, when the facts are fairly stated, the historian of the Keltic people will be found in some officer who had worked in the Punjab or in Oudh. Another illustration of the influence of law upon custom, and of the rigidity which the consequent rule acquires, occurs in the history of Equity. This was a sort of discretionary power in the Crown to supplement, in certain circumstances, the law, and to prevent the commission of substantial wrong under the colour of strict justice. It was thus in the nature of a custom which gradually was brought under systematic administration. In course of time, Equity became as inflexible as law. "It is shocking but it is the law," has more than once been the exclamation † of great judges. The rule had stiffened, and the result was unexpected and undesired; but still it was the law. The defect was not in the men under whose hands the rule had grown, but in the nature of the materials. Parliament alone was competent to amend the law; and it is somewhat hard to blame Lord Eldon, as Mr. Austin ‡ blames him, for not assuming those legislative functions which Bentham accuses him of having wickedly usurped.

* "Middle Ages," p. 321, *note*.

† See Doe *v.* Pott, "Douglas' Reports, 722."

‡ "Jurisprudence," p. 668.

CHAPTER XVIII.

THE LAW AND CUSTOM OF PROPERTY.

§ 1. Few questions have more fully engaged the attention of philosophical writers than the origin of Property. It is from no want of respect to the eminent men who have in different ages proposed their respective theories on this subject that I decline to consider their views. These views were, in the absence of any positive evidence, formed upon conjectures as to what men, with modes of thought such as were familiar to the writers, would, if they had been placed in certain imaginary circumstances, have probably done. In such an inquiry, the greater the ingenuity of the theorist the farther he is likely to stray. But if we are content to take man as our evidence discloses him to us, we shall find along with him, always and everywhere, the presence of property. The forms of property vary considerably, but the fact of its existence is constant. Men have always taken possession of such natural agents as are susceptible of appropriation; have used them for their own purposes to any extent and during any time that they thought fit; have prevented other persons from interfering with them; and have acknowledged the corresponding claims of their companions who were in similar circumstances. Prominent among the natural agents that have been thus appropriated, because, although apparently simple, it really includes a multitude of physical forces, is land. The right of property in land has been denied for reasons which, in their

Universality of Property.

legitimate conclusions, extend to almost every kind of commodity, and tend to annihilate all separate national existence. The same argument which is used to prove that individual property in land is unjust, would also, if it were true, prove that no nation can have any exclusive right in its territory. If the land of England be, in the sense in which communist writers use the expression, the gift of God, that gift is not made to Englishmen, but to mankind. If, therefore, an individual Englishman cannot claim property in it, no number of Englishmen, whether separately or collectively, can urge any such claim. If land be incapable of appropriation, that incapacity must exist not only between members of the same communities, but between different communities. Yet, whatever may be the casuistry of the subject, no such incapacity has ever been, in fact, admitted. In all ages, and even in the lowest and rudest forms of society, the common property of the clan or tribe is rigorously defined. The boundaries of Australian tribe lands are as carefully marked out as the boundaries of any English gentleman's estate. A black-fellow would die rather than commit a trespass, and has much less scruple in killing a man than within the boundaries of another tribe killing a kangaroo. Even as between kindred communities in India, the rights of property are rigorously enforced. "The grazing ground of each village," says Sir George Campbell,* "is common to all; but the division between the grazing grounds of different villages is very jealously maintained, and any uncertain or undecided boundary leads to very bloody affrays." I need only refer to the sacred character which, in early times, the landmark always maintained, and the guilt which attached to its removal. The spirits of the

* "Modern India," p. 88.

Kin, like the spirits of the House, watched over their consecrated boundaries. No stranger—that is, no person who did not participate in the worship of that Kin—could possess any part of those lands, or derive any benefit from them.

§ 2. Sir H. S. Maine, a writer whose opinions on this subject are based upon a knowledge of facts far beyond the command of his predecessors, finds himself, in dealing * with the early history of property, confronted by the question, "Why do men respect other men's property?" He points out that this question coincides with the other question, "Why did men live under the system of the Family?" He thinks that the problem is insoluble: at all events, that jurisprudence has no answer for it. I agree that the origin of property is connected with the origin of the Family, or, as I have called it, the Household; and that, consequently, the explanation of the one ought to furnish the explanation of the other. But I venture to think that Sir Henry Maine underrates the resources of the science of which he is so distinguished a student, and that historical jurisprudence is not silent in the presence of this great problem. If Sir Henry Maine had not, in common with most English jurists, slighted the theory of ancestral worship, which M. de Coulanges had advocated with such power and clearness, he would not, I think, have so readily abandoned this part of his inquiry.

The origin of Aryan Property.

If it be true that the question as to the origin of property coincides with the question as to the origin of the Household, the answer that I must make to the former question is plain. As the Household depended upon the House Spirit, so the respect for another's property was due

* "Ancient Law," p. 270.

to the respect for the spirits that guarded that property. Of the institution of property, as well as of every other archaic institution, religion, as it was then understood, was the basis. I do not mean that property so depended upon House-worship that when the latter failed the former must fail also. I only contend that the habit or sentiment of respect for property was generated by the system of the Household; and that it acquired under that system sufficient strength to stand alone when the originating force was withdrawn. In other words, property is a custom; in civilized States that custom has been adopted and enforced by law; and the origin of this custom thus legalized is House-worship.

In proof of this contention, I must claim all that I have in the preceding pages urged respecting the origin of the Household. If the two questions coincide, the answer to the one involves the answer to the other; and in accounting for the Household, we have also accounted for property. But I must specially refer to that part of these inquiries in which the House Spirit appears as the guardian of the property of his Household. The Lares have, indeed, long abandoned their watch, yet the belief has not even yet wholly vanished from the world. Men still live, with whom the security of property is maintained—not by their own strong hand, or by the majesty of the law, but by spiritual terrors only. A recent traveller in Asia * thus writes:—"The place of our encampment (near Kohut, south of Peshawur) was a ziarat, called Turkumul, round the burial-ground of which the whole country seemed to have piled their grain. In troublesome times, when a man is fain to quit his native village until the return of order, he prefers trusting his valuables to the sacred guardianship of such a place rather than to his weak and failing brother.

* Wood's "Journey to the Source of the Oxus," p. 86.

I inquired of Agha Maheide if such was really the case, and whether thieves would not be induced to violate the repository from the certainty of being able to do so with impunity. The old man put the forefinger of his right hand to his lips, and looked at me, exclaiming, 'God forbid! bad as men are, they are not yet so utterly profligate.' . . . A stronger instance cannot be shown of the firm hold superstition has over the human mind. Here we find it overcoming the worst passions and the most confirmed habits of depraved men." So, too, among uncultured people, if an offence against property has been committed, the remedy that is sought, apart from actual violence, is spiritual. Among the nomads of Central Asia, if a horse be stolen, the owner seeks to recover his property by fixing a spear in the grave of the father of the suspected thief. This proceeding is understood to be equivalent to a complaint to the deceased House Father against his son. If the suspicion be well-founded, the horse is found the next morning tied to the spear. It is said that this strange remedy rarely fails. Mr. Tylor * mentions a remarkable case, in which a Brahman cut off his mother's head with the old woman's consent, and at her earnest request. The object of this deed was that her spirit might punish a neighbour who had repudiated some small debt which he owed to the Household. Again, in the remarkable custom of sitting '*dharna*,' which once existed in Ireland, and has within the last few years been prohibited by the penal code in India, and of which, perhaps, traces may be found in the Twelve Tables, the same principle may be observed. The implied threat was that the spirit would avenge the wrongs done to it in the flesh.

Not only is the affirmative proposition true, that, where

* "Primitive Culture," vol. ii., p. 103.

a community of religion existed, respect for property was also found: the corresponding negative is equally true; where no special relation existed, all respect for property was wanting. It was only those who worshipped the same gods, or who had made some specific agreement, that had any scruples about each other's goods. Beyond these limits they acknowledged no moral duty of forbearance. Piracy * was not held in any disesteem by the early Greeks. It was, indeed, regarded as a recognized and respectable vocation. Even in the time of the fathers of Æschylus and of Herodotus, "undistinguishing plunder at sea, committed by Greek ships against ships not Greek, seems not to have been held discreditable." Herodotus tells † how Dionysius of Phocæa, after the failure of the Ionic revolt, went with three ships of war to Sicily, and there established himself as a professed pirate, "not plundering any of the Greeks, but the Carthaginians and Tyrrhenians." Among these Tyrrhenians similar rules ‡ prevailed; and so, too, among the Iberians. But many years after the time of Herodotus, when Attic philosophy and Attic culture were universally admired, the old maxim remained in full force—that among all Greeks § there was eternal war with foreigners. In the earliest treaty between Rome and Carthage, it is stipulated that, within certain prescribed limits, the Romans shall neither plunder nor trade nor colonize. In the absence of any treaty, the three operations were equally natural, and might with equal reason be expected. The rule of the matured Roman law is very remarkable. It is stated, in the "Digest," ‖ that those nations with whom no specific relation of friend-

* See Grote, "Hist. of Greece," vol. ii., p. 122, and the authorities there cited.

† vi., 17.

‡ "Diod. Sic.," v., 34.

§ Livy, xxxi., 29.

‖ xlix., 15, 5.

ship existed were not indeed enemies, but that if any Roman chattel should be found in their territory it became their property; and a Roman freeman, in the like circumstances, became their slave. Of course, Roman citizens had analogous rights over foreign persons and things found within the boundaries of Rome. Nor was this a mere case of violence. The Roman law distinctly recognized such a capture as lawful. To the Roman citizen so seized, the principle of *postliminium* applied as fully as if he had been made prisoner in a regular war. Of the Germans, Cæsar * tells that robberies, if they were committed outside the territories of their own community, were not regarded with any disfavour. It was, indeed, supposed that such operations were a manly and useful exercise for young men. Nearer home were the Caterans and the Vikings,† with their creaghs by land and their sumorlidas by sea. "Highway robbery," says Mr. Hallam,‡ "was from the earliest times a sort of national crime." Even at the present day, among uncultured men, the same feeling may be traced. A traveller,§ whom I have already cited, speaking of one of the many soldiers of fortune whose swords have made kingdoms more or less lasting in Central Asia, observes—"Murad Beg, the Usbeg, maintains a well ordered domestic government, and a course of rapine over his neighbours, over the whole upper waters of the Oxus, from the frontiers of China to the river that runs through Balkh. Punishment for highway robbery, if the highway be in their own country — for that makes a wonderful difference—is death."

I may thus state my contention. The sentiment of religion

* "De Bell. Gall.," vi., 23.
† See Robertson, "Early Kings," vol. i., p. 259.
‡ "Middle Ages," vol. iii., p. 167.
§ Wood's "Journey to the Source of the Oxus," p. 140.

is a force which, even at this day, exists, and is adequate to produce the supposed effect. A similar force was in operation in archaic society, and did there—at least in those cases with which we are acquainted — produce similar results. The explanation also fulfils the condition that it should account not only for the origin of property, but also for the origin of the Household. Further, in cases where the sentiment of religion did not exist—that is, between strangers, who were not connected by any community of worship—the respect for property was not present. The sentiment of justice, when once it had been generated, grew, or failed to grow, according to the circumstances in which it was placed. In some cases it was stunted; in more favourable conditions it attained a fuller development There are, at this day, people with whom justice is limited to those of their own country, or their own community, or their own creed, or their own colour. But there are those, too, who hold that right is not confined to blood, or race, or creed, or country; and who look for the coming of the time when there shall, at length, be realized in practice that lesson of universal benevolence—so hard to be understood by its first hearers, so hard to be accepted by subsequent generations—which was given in answer to the question once asked by a certain young man—"And who is my neighbour?"

Jus Civile and Jus Honorarium.

§ 3. In a former chapter I endeavoured to show that in early times property assumed two forms—the one, corporate; the other, individual. Corporate property did not include all the property of every member of the corporation, but meant only the property, strictly speaking, of the corporation, and the natural produce of that property. There was thus a clear distinction between inherited property and acquired property. It was to the former, and not to the latter, that the rules of the Household and of the Kin applied. In the inherited property, other parties beside the House Father were interested. The dealings with it were, therefore, restricted by the customary rules. In the acquired property, no person save its owner had any concern. Consequently, no custom limited him in its disposition. In archaic society, however, there was little room for acquisitions; and any such property must have generally sunk, in the course of two or three generations, into the mass of hereditary property. It was to the hereditary property that the earliest law of property, in the strict sense, applied. Law was, as I have said, the extension of a particular sanction to custom; but the subject of the custom was the inheritance, not the acquests. This law, too, was, from the nature of the case, not general, but was the privilege of those persons who were members of the State. The early law of property was thus limited to one particular class of property and to one particular class of persons. '*Dominium ex jure Quiritium*' meant ownership of the property of the Household, which ownership Roman citizens, and none others, could enjoy.

Two causes, therefore, must have been in operation to modify the customary law. Persons claimed to exercise the rights of ownership, or some of those rights, who were not members of the State. Even as regards members of the State, the law did not include the whole extent of proprietary rights. For the outsider in all cases, for the citizen in the case of his acquisitions, there was no legal recognition. But as the State grew, its natural tendency was to enlarge its jurisdiction. Some provision for both these classes became necessary. The necessity became urgent, when new forms of interests and new classes of persons arose which could by no pretence be brought within the limits of any custom then existing.

We can thus perceive the relation between the two systems of the law of property which co-existed at Rome. The elder system, or '*Jus Civile,*' was the custom of the clans sanctioned by the State for the benefit of the people of Quirinus. The younger system, or '*Jus Honorarium,*' was the law which, by the judicial officers of the State, was gradually established to regulate the acquired rights of Roman citizens, and the rights, whether acquired or inherited, of those residents at Rome who were not citizens. The former was contained in the Twelve Tables and in the Statutes, and in the learning affecting them. The latter was found in the Edicts of the Prætors, and sometimes of other high officials. The two systems were parallel and distinct. As to ownership, as to the mode of acquisition, as to remedy, as to conveyance, as to succession, as to contract, each had its own provisions. The Quirite had the dominion or full ownership of his inherited property; he acquired any additional property by the act of any member of his Household, and not of any other person; he sought redress for any injury in respect of his property by '*vindicatio,*' a special name for the '*Legis Actio Sacramenti.*' He conveyed his interest by mancipation. On his death, the property descended to his agnates: his contracts regarding it were made by sponsion. The non-Quirite, or the Quirite who was dealing with novel kinds of property, had need of all those rights, but he could not obtain them under the old law. By degrees a new law, under the direction of the Prætor, formed itself. The place of dominion was, in certain circumstances, taken by possession. Agency or representation *per liberam personam*—that is, by a person not a member of the Household—was slowly, and step by step, established.* The possession was enforced not by a

* See Mr. Poste's "Gaius," p. 432.

'*Legis Actio*,' but by an interdict, or, as we, I think, should call it, a prerogative * writ. Instead of mancipation, with its bronze and balance, simple delivery sufficed to pass the property. In cases of intestacy, the cognates, not the agnates, were the successors. Contracts were held to be binding, even though the mystic word, '*spondeo*,' which no lips save those of a Quirite might utter, had not been spoken. Thus the two bodies of law, applying each to different subjects, continued to co-exist so long as the distinction between their subjects prevailed. But as the clan waned, the property of the clan became of less and less importance. New interests grew with the growth of an advancing community, and strangers constantly flocked in ever-increasing numbers to great and wealthy and conquering Rome. The simpler methods, too, of the edictal law were found to be more convenient than the rigorous formality of the archaic customs. And so, from all these causes, without any positive repeal, the '*Jus Civile*' died a natural though lingering death, and the law of the Prætors reigned in its stead.

Jus Civile was the Customary Law of the Property of the Household.

§ 4. There is no doubt either as to the existence of these two systems of law, or as to their relative antiquity. The correspondence † of the two series of terms that I have mentioned, may also be now accepted. But I must add a few words in support of the further view that I have ventured to propose—namely, that the '*Jus Civile*' was the customary law of the old corporate form of property. In the first place, the Roman lawyers describe the succession of children in terms that imply ownership by a corporation, and that corporation the Household. In the case of '*Sui heredes*,' that is, lineal descendants, "we

* See Mr. Poste's "Gaius," p. 622.

† See *Ib.*, p. 28.

have," says the "Digest," * "a still more striking instance of an unbroken continuity of dominion, for there appears to be no vesting of new property by descent, but the heir is deemed to have been previously proprietor, even during the lifetime of the father. Hence the names, *Filius familias* and *Pater familias,* implying a similar legal relation to the patrimony, though one is parent and the other child. Therefore, the death of the parent occasions no acquisition of new property by descent, but only an increased freedom in the administration of already existing property." In the next place, the succession of the agnates is, as I have said, that form of succession which is characteristic of the Household. The '*Sui heredes,*' the Agnati, the Gentiles—such was the earliest order of succession; such was the order of the '*Jus Civile;*' and such was the order which the Prætor and the statute law continually endeavoured to modify. The distinction may also, I think, be observed in the mode of conveyance. One of the divisions of things in Roman law was that of '*Res Mancipi*' and '*Res nec Mancipi.*' To the former class, which consisted of certain specified objects, a particular form of conveyance, that by the bronze and the balance, was appropriated. The latter class included all other objects, and these residual objects were transferred by simple delivery. The '*Res Mancipi*' were—land in Italy; rustic servitudes therein, that is, rights of way and of water-courses, but not of lights; persons, whether slaves or free; tame animals employed for draught or carriage, as oxen, horses, mules, or asses. The difficulty in this matter has been to account for the selection of these particular objects. Various explanations † have been offered. Some writers say that these objects were those which were alone known

* "Dig." 38, 2, 11. The translation is that of Mr. Poste, p. 234.

† See Mr. Poste's "Gaius," p. 172. Mr. Hunter's "Roman Law," p. 114.

to the Romans. Others regard them as the ordinary booty of a predatory tribe. Others contend that '*Res Mancipi*' are of a wasting nature; or that they all are specific, and are contrasted with things sold by number, measure, or weight. Dr. Arnold * conjectured that the distinction was a privilege of the plebeian landowners. It is clear that the division does not rest upon any logical principle; and the inference, therefore, is that its origin was historical. The third class, for example, does not include all tame animals, or all animals that were used in draught or carriage; for Gaius expressly excludes both the smaller domestic animals, and also elephants and camels. Of the explanations I have mentioned, all except the first are avowedly mere guesses in the absence of anything better. As to the first, it might be difficult to prove that the '*Res Mancipi*' were the only or even the principal articles of value known to the early Romans. But they constituted, I think, the necessary property, or '*χρήματα*' of a Household. Their first division includes land and servitudes, respecting which two points have to be observed. First, the land must be in Italian soil, as distinguished from the Provincial soil, which appears at a much later period of legal history. But 'dominion,' that is 'ownership' '*ex jure Quiritium,*' was confined to land in Italy; and thus there is a connection between dominion and mancipation. Secondly, the servitudes were those known as "*prædiorum rusticorum, non urbanorum;*" that is, they included rights of way, of water-course, and the like—easements likely to arise in a village community, but not those which belong to a crowded city. The second and the third divisions of the '*Res Mancipi,*' are in effect the "*Familia Pecuniave*" of the Twelve Tables; that is, the persons

* "Hist. of Rome," vol. i., p. 172, *note*.

who are in the House Father's hand, and the cattle or stock which were necessary for working the land of the Household. Thus the mancipation was the form of conveyance for the Household estate. The meaning of the difference was not that favour, as Sir Henry Maine * suggests, was shown to one class of objects rather than to another; but that, of the two great classes, each came under a different rule. The fundamental division of things in the Roman law † was into things that are in our patrimony, and things that are not in our patrimony. The Household property, or *patrimonium*, passed according to the custom of the community. By the side of this patrimony, another kind of property grew up, which was outside the patrimony, and so was not subject to the customs. For this latter kind of property—as to its conveyance, its protection, and its devolution—new methods were necessarily invented. The conveyance by mancipation and the descent by agnation went together, '*Jure Civili;*' just as the conveyance by delivery and the descent by cognation were alike parts of the '*Jus Gentium.*'

Historical origin of Jus Honorarium.

§ 5. This remarkable change in the Roman legal system appears to be due to two leading events. These events were the extension of the '*Ager Publicus*,' or land of the community, and the increase of immigration. With each new conquest, the land of the conquered community became a part of the territory of the Roman people. Sometimes this land, or part of it, was re-granted to its former owners on terms more or less favourable. Sometimes it was held by Roman citizens. In all cases, however, the dominion or ownership was vested in the State. Where the occupation was by citizens, the tenure had two characteristics. None

* "Ancient Law," p. 274.

† "Gaius," vol. ii., p. 1.

but a Roman citizen, that is, a member of the *Populus Romanus*, could, in the absence of an express grant, have any interest in land belonging to the Roman State. As against the State, the occupancy of its citizen was merely permissive. He was strictly a tenant-at-will. His holding was, in the language of the Roman lawyers, "precarious," that is, upon his request to the owner, and with that owner's leave. On the determination of the landlord's will, the tenancy came to an end; but until such determination, the tenant had—as against all other citizens and *a fortiori* as against strangers—a complete title. But he was not the owner; and he could not, therefore, obtain any redress from those customary remedies which had been devised to meet injuries to ownership alone. He could not declare, in the terms of the '*Legis Actio Sacramenti*,' that the land was his '*ex jure Quiritium*.' The pleasure of the State in his favour, however, continued; and there was no reason why it should not continue for an indefinite time. The longer the duration of the tenancy, the greater was the expectation that it would not be disturbed. Thus a new form of property was brought into existence; and this form was, by reason of its novelty, outside the provisions of the law. It was only reasonable that the State's officers should lend their assistance to secure the State's tenants. Accordingly, the Prætor granted an interdict, or, as we should say, an injunction, forbidding the party to whom it was addressed to disturb the possession of the occupier. Where the circumstances required it, this order assumed a positive form, and commanded the trespasser to restore the possession from which the complainant had been wrongfully ousted. This form of occupation—so familiar to British Colonists, and so strange to the inhabitants of long-settled countries—was technically called '*possessio*;' and the occupation thus guaranteed by interdict became, as I have said, a form of property practically equivalent to 'dominion,' or ownership. This form of property, if it had not the benefit of the '*Jus Civile*,' was free from its restraints. It was the creature of the Prætorian jurisdiction, and the Prætor was therefore able to mould its incidents at his discretion. Partly from its more rapid rate of increase, partly from its superior convenience, it superseded its older rival. It was the only kind of ownership that was possible in the Provinces. In Italy, when, after the Social War, full citizenship was granted to all Italians; and when, as the result of a series of land acts, the State had gradually parted with all its wide domains, 'dominion' was, in effect, established as the ordinary rule. But, outside Italy, 'dominion' was entirely unknown. The '*Solum Provinciale*' was vested in the Roman people, and all interests in it were only '*Possessiones*.' These possessions, when the distinction between Italy and the Provinces was abolished, and the expressions Roman citizen and subject of Cæsar became in substance equivalent, grew into true ownership, but retained the incidents which had marked their origin. Even in Italy the advantages of the Prætorian rules, especially in the conveyance of land, were appreciated. When a mancipation failed, or had not been executed after the contract of sale had been completed, the Prætor, by means of his '*Bonorum possessio*,' gave relief. He put the real owner into possession, and let usucapion do the rest. Gradually the mancipation fell into disuse, and, by the legislation of Justinian, was finally abolished. "Thus," as Mr. Hunter* observes, "in the time of the Twelve Tables, there is but one form of ownership (*dominium ex jure Quiritium*); in the time of Justinian, there is but one form of ownership (*dominium*): but the ownership of Justinian

* "Roman Law," p. 216.

is an institution that is separated from the Quiritarian ownership by a wide gulf—a gulf as wide, and of precisely the same character, as that which lies generally between the narrow and provincial system of the early Romans, and the liberal and magnificent jurisprudence bequeathed by the Roman Empire to mankind."

I cannot think that the great discovery, for such it was, of Niebuhr and of Savigny, respecting the historical origin of possession, has been shaken, or is at all doubtful. But I do not contend that their explanation covers the whole of the present question. That explanation relates only to land; and the Prætorian jurisdiction extended not to land only, but also to movables. The rise of this latter branch of the '*Jus Honorarium*' must be sought in the requirements, not of a particular class of citizens, but of outsiders. This aspect of the question has been ably discussed by Mr. Hunter * in his recent work on Roman Law; although, with the natural enthusiasm of the advocate of a neglected truth, he presses, as I venture to think, his theory somewhat too far. It is unnecessary for his purpose to prove that Savigny was wrong. There is ample room for both the Possessor and the Peregrinus. It is certain that from the earliest times there was a considerable foreign, that is, non-Roman, population at Rome; that these foreigners had no share in the '*Jus Quiritium;*' and that they were obliged to live under the protection of a Roman citizen as their *Patronus.* With the growth of the city and the extension of its power, the numbers of these foreigners increased. In the earlier days of the Republic, most of these persons were Italians, men generally of the same blood as the Romans, and having, as it would now be said, a common nationality. Over these men and their dealings the Prætor

* p. 205, *et seq.*

was appointed to preside, and it was his policy to extend to them proprietary rights. He appears to have effected this object by the usual fiction called a '*utilis actio*;' that is, he in effect permitted proceedings to be taken in the same way as they would have been taken if both the parties were Roman citizens; and he disallowed the objection that one of them was a foreigner. There were, however, cases in which this course could not be adopted; and it is probable that the form of interdict known as "*Utrubi*," which related exclusively to movables, was introduced for the protection of aliens.

Whether the jurisdiction over the '*Possessores*' or the jurisdiction over the '*Peregrini*' was the older, is a question on which there is no distinct information, and which is not, I think, particularly important. The two probably reacted upon each other, and the more frequent exercise of his functions must have tended to strengthen the Prætor's authority. It is remarkable that, at Athens,* the Polemarch exercised, in the case of aliens, powers similar to those of the Prætor Peregrinus at Rome; and yet at Athens there was nothing analogous to the '*Jus Honorarium*.' To say that this difference is due to the superior legal genius of the Roman people, is a solution much more easy than satisfactory. To arrive at the truth, the slower and more laborious method must be pursued, of tracing the difference in the conditions of the two countries. Two of these differences I may, in passing, notice. One is, that Athens does not appear to have held any extensive public estates like those of Rome. The territory of Attica itself was small and poor; and the Empire of Athens was, in its origin, merely tax-taking. Long before it could pass into the Roman type, although not

* Hermann's "Grecian Antiquities," p. 275.

before its tendency in that direction was apparent, that Empire was checked by external force. The other difference was the relative shortness of the period of Athenian development. From the Persian invasion to the time of Philip of Macedon—from the battle of Salamis to the battle of Chæronea—less than a century and a half intervene. The rise and the fall of the Athenian Empire were comprised in half of that period. But more than six times the duration of the Athenian Empire elapsed between the publication of the Twelve Tables and the full consolidation, under the Cæsars, of the Roman State; and the interval of a thousand years separates the legislation of Justinian from the legislation of the Decemviri. Even with all the help of the great precedent of the Roman law, fourteen centuries have not exhausted the power of growth and of development in England.

CHAPTER XIX.

THE RISE OF CIVIL JURISDICTION.

Law originally limited to direct interests of the State.

§ 1. I HAVE said that law is a command of the State; and that the State is only one, and that a comparatively late, form of social development. Our forefathers lived together—as in some cases other men now live together—when there was no State, and consequently no law. That which then regulated their conduct was custom. I have shown how custom and law coalesced, but there are some parts of the process that deserve special attention. Law was originally distinct from custom, was later than custom, and for a long time was weaker than custom. All these circumstances have impressed their mark upon the early history of law.

The State was distinct from the clan, had a different organization from it, and pursued different objects. It follows that it had different interests, and issued different commands. The leading cause of political association was, probably, the necessity of defence against a common enemy. It certainly has been under the pressure of external dangers that the principal combinations within historical times have been made. But men, when they co-operated for external purposes, never intended to abandon their internal arrangements. It was not to the State that, in their daily life, men looked for the protection of their property, or the security of their persons. They acknowledged, indeed, a certain allegiance, and showed a certain deference to the State; but their first duty was to their own class. The State, therefore, attended primarily to its own interests, and issued, in relation to them, its own commands. It was, practically, only one of a number of analogous associations. It accordingly made its own rules, and punished all its disobedient members, just as the clans did in the like cases. But it did not presume to interfere with the private rights of any of its citizens, or with the customary remedies by which these citizens redressed their wrongs. Nor did the State, in its rudimentary form, present that complex system of related powers with which, in its higher development, we are familiar. There was then no distinction, or, at the most, only a faint distinction, between the legislature, the judiciary, and the executive. The undifferentiated body politic contrived to perform such functions as were needful to it. So, too, the clan lived, according to its customs, its corporate life; and the first founders of political society, when it co-existed with clan society, could not have forcseen the future of the association which they established.

I have said that the State dealt exclusively with its own affairs. It punished the person who betrayed its secrets to the enemy; or who, whether in the field or by less open aid, took part against his country. But it did not interfere in the private quarrels of its citizens. Every man took care of his own property and his own household; and every hand guarded its own head. If any injury were done to any person, he retaliated, or made reprisals, or otherwise sought redress, as custom prescribed. The State cared for none of these things. Yet there were certain matters which, although they were of a private nature, directly affected the well-being of the State. If the Gentile *sacra* were not performed, the anger of the offended spirits might not be limited to the culprit, but might extend to the whole community. The first interference of the State seems to have been directed towards these rites. It was careful to inquire* whether candidates for its offices, among other qualifications, had fulfilled their duties to the Household and the Gentile gods. It laid down the rule, "*Perpetua Sacra sunto.*" It did not pretend to perform or to regulate these ceremonies. It only insisted that those persons whose duty it was to attend to them should perform that duty. This superintendence naturally devolved upon the head of the State. In course of time, special officers were created to watch over the ever-increasing rites, and a large body of pontifical law was gradually formed. So, too, when any new worship was introduced, or when any sorcerer or magician practised his mysterious arts, the whole force of the community was directed to repress the common enemy, and the State did not hesitate to repel a danger that seemed to threaten as well itself as all its subjects.

The State arbitrates in private disputes.

§ 2. It would, of course, have been an easy task to prove that the State was interested in the quiet and the good order of its citizens. But in its earlier days the State had no thought of such refinements. It accepted the facts as they existed. Even if it had the desire, it certainly had not the power to undertake the duties of police or the general administration of justice. Neither its resources nor its organization were adapted for any such purpose. Yet no State could be insensible to the advantages of what we call good government, or to the evils which, even in the most favourable circumstances, the blood-feud and self-redress imply. Nor, on the other hand, are men slow to appreciate the benefits of a just and firm system of law. But archaic men knew nothing of the greatest-happiness principle; and if they had known it, they would not have accepted it. As

* Wachsmuth, "Hist. Ant.," vol. i., p. 385.

the full-grown State is scarcely recognizable in its rudimentary form, so the history of the growth of law discloses an embryonic condition entirely unlike that to which we are accustomed.

Our best starting point is, I think, that description of the present Kirghiz which I have already cited. We are told that the Kirghiz have no central government; that, in their quarrels, their Elders have some sort of authority; that it rests entirely with the parties themselves whether they will be bound by the opinion of the Elders, since there is no means of enforcing it; and that, somehow, these opinions are seldom resisted, and that serious difficulties rarely arise. This description, which relates to a rude non-Aryan race of the present day, may well have been true of our archaic fathers. Out of some such condition of society as that which still prevails in the countries which were the cradle of our race, our great system of law originally sprung. The earliest juridical record represents * a dispute between two men on a question of fact, and the issue coming on for trial before the Elders in the presence of the assembled people. Two men, the poet tells, were disputing respecting the blood-money of a man who had been slain; the one alleged that he had paid it, and the other altogether denied its receipt. In the oldest legal formula, the '*Legis Actio Sacramenti*' of the Roman law, all the proceedings † carefully simulate the casual interference of some third party in a dispute on a question of ownership. Of our own early law, I will only observe that it is full of contrivances for getting the parties to accept, as it were, its jurisdiction. It seems to have felt that, if it had the opportunity, it could speak as one having authority; but the opportunity could only be given by the consent of both

* "Iliad," xviii., 497-507. † "Gaius," iv., 13-17.

parties to its interference. If a prisoner refused to plead, the court had no authority to try him; and a severe course of treatment, which subsequently degenerated into a horrible torture, was used to extort the required consent. It was not until a very late period that the legislature ventured to construe persistent silence into a plea of not guilty. It is, I think, generally admitted that jurisdiction was originally founded in consent. In the Homeric precedent, the Elders, like the Kirghiz old men, appear to have some sort of authority. Every clan, too, and even every Household had a tribunal of its own. It is not unreasonable to suppose that a similar rudimentary authority, undefined perhaps, and sanctioned by custom and public opinion rather than by any legal force, existed in the society which we call a State. Something more than a metaphor was intended when the king was called the Father of his people. But whether as having a sort of right, or whether as being the most influential person in the community, the arbitration of the king * or other Fürst was often invoked or accepted. It is at this point that the earliest approach to a sanction is found. A sum is staked to abide the decision. In the Homeric precedent, two talents of gold lie in the midst, "to give to him whoso should speak justice most righteously." These words may refer either to the litigants or the judges. To speak justice may mean either to plead a cause or to pronounce a judgment. I observe that Mr. Grote adopts the former and Sir Henry Maine the latter view, in each case without remark. For my part, I hesitate to accept a meaning which implies such a singular competitive examination in judicial ability as that which assigns the two talents to the most popular judge; and the

* See a curious case in Mallet's "Northern Antiquities," p. 337.

more so as the question raised—that of payment or non-payment—did not admit of the display of much ingenuity. The magnitude of the sum, too, even when allowance has been made for the exaggeration of poetry, seems to suggest that it was, or at least that it included, the blood-money for some person of rank, rather than that it was a fee for judicial services. In the account which Gaius gives of the '*sacramentum*,' a sum, although of a much more reasonable amount than two talents of gold, is staked by each party. The successful party recovers his money; the deposit of the unsuccessful party goes to the State. The stake varied according to the value of the matter in dispute. There is no positive information as to the object of this stake. Sir Henry Maine* suggests that it was an expedient to gain, by the help of a bet, time for angry passions to become cool. To me it seems that the stake was intended to be a security that the parties would abide by the decision of the tribunal. In either case, it is not difficult to understand how the deposit could serve as a check upon unjust litigation, and still less difficult to recognize in it the oldest form of the fees of court. But whatever may have been its origin, numerous advantages followed from it. The parties stayed their hands. They gave a material guarantee for their readiness to accept the decision of the arbitrator, and to acquiesce in that decision. The arbitrator was enabled to proceed at once with his office, and to give directions for the immediate custody of the object in dispute. The sum deposited was also a guarantee that the dispute was neither frivolous nor vexatious. It was available either for costs, or for the remuneration of the judge, or for the benefit of the State whose officer had used its influence to determine the controversy. There was a tradition at

* "Early Hist. of Inst.," p. 259.

Rome that originally such moneys were applied to religious purposes, and that the first arbitrators were the Pontifices. If this tradition were true, it would point to the king as the original arbitrator, and to the tendency of justice to pass to the officer who succeeded to the religious functions of royalty. But a differentiation must have commenced at an early period. Certainly, the deposit in the '*Legis Actio Sacramenti*' went to the treasury; and, shortly after the time of the Twelve Tables, a modified form (*condictio*) of that action was adopted. This form was used in all cases arising out of obligations, and in effect rendered the deposit available for the payment of costs. Except so far as I have thus stated, court fees and costs do not seem to have been known to the Roman law. In medieval law, before the complete integration of the State, the administration of justice was regarded as a lucrative incident of property. The Lord's Court was not unnaturally made at first self-supporting, and then profitable. With the development of the State, court fees, although they were not abolished, no longer formed part of judicial remuneration. It is noteworthy that in the English system costs come by statute, and not by common law. Perhaps the reason was that, in the Roman law, costs were not paid as such, but were included in the ordinary form of action provided by the mutual stipulations—that is, in substance, by the wagers—of the parties.

The State regulates private remedies.

§ 3. One of the most striking differences between the modern and the archaic conception of law is found in the motives for the interference of the State. To us the State appears to perform its natural functions in enforcing civil rights, in punishing and repressing crime, in securing to every man his own, and in so dealing with offenders that peaceful men may live undisturbed. No such aspect of the functions of the State presented itself to the archaic man. He did not consider that the State was concerned in dealing with cases of violence or of fraud. These were matters not of public but of individual concern, or at most required the interference of the kin. But he could understand that the State, if its mediation were invited, should interpose its influence to protect a person who had got into trouble, or rather to mitigate his punishment. A man who had committed what we should call a crime thereby forfeited his property, or his liberty, or even his life, to the party whom he had wronged. It was much if the State could effect a reconciliation; and persuade the injured man to forego his resentment, and to accept reasonable satisfaction. In the case of blood revenge, for example, it was the recognized duty of the next of kin to kill the homicide, or some of his clan. This vengeance might, however, be commuted for a money payment. The "Iliad"* makes distinct mention both of the duty of vengeance and of the customary acceptance of the compensation. But it also shows that the avenger of blood was under no compulsion to forego his feud. Public opinion was, doubtless, in favour of his acceptance of a proper compromise; but if he refused, his refusal could only be regarded as the harsh exercise of an undoubted right. Thus the position of the archaic State was not that of a modern government dealing with its subjects, but that of a friendly nation interposing its good offices between two belligerents. When one citizen had injured another, custom allowed, and in certain circumstances required, the injured person, or his next of kin, to obtain redress by making reprisals, or to take vengeance by inflicting similar injuries, upon the wrongdoer or his clan. In these reprisals, or this revenge, he was

* ix., 632-636.

supported not only by public opinion but by the active assistance of his clansmen. It was not the business of any third party to interfere in the dispute. But by the intervention of common friends amends might be offered and accepted, and the quarrel might be composed. In the emphatic words of the old English maxim, a man must either "buy off the spear or bear it." The State by its chief or other officer acted the part of common friend. It of necessity accepted the facts as it found them. It recognized the existence of the custom of self-redress as older and stronger than its own power. It had to depend for success not upon force but upon influence. In order to induce the injured party to accept mediation, the terms offered to him must be nearly as good as those which he might reasonably expect to obtain by his own hand or by the assistance of his friends. It was not until the State was far advanced towards maturity, until its political organs were developed, until the means of at once exerting in any given direction the whole public force were perfected, and until long habits of deference had rendered obedience to its commands almost a second nature, that it was enabled to claim exclusive authority both in setting up a standard of duty, and in determining all matters of dispute, and giving effect to its decisions.

It was evidently the policy of the State to check those bloody quarrels which continually deprived it of the services of its most active and warlike citizens. The method by which it sought to attain this object was by making the best terms it could for the wrong-doer. Accordingly, it proceeded to determine the amount payable by the offender for every injury to life, limb, or reputation. It is a conspicuous mark of the comparatively early maturity of the Roman State,*

* Mommsen, "Hist. of Rome," vol. i., p. 158.

that there is in Roman law no trace, or at most the faintest trace, of this system. But in the Teutonic peoples, and also among the Kelts, the learning of the wer-geld, or the Eric*—that is the man-price—formed the largest portion of their law. The '*Leges Barbarorum*' are full of the most minute provisions on the subject. They contain elaborate tariffs of the damages payable according to the rank of the offender for every kind of injury done to every part of the body, or to the reputation, or to the Household, of persons of every degree. They give directions to what persons the money shall be paid, in what shares, and according to what order of succession. They provide, with equal care, as to the parties upon whom the burthen is to fall. They regulate the modes of proof by which the fact of the offence is established or is refuted. But if the guilty person be ascertained, and if the proper wer-geld be not paid, the State does not further interfere. It does not take upon itself the duty of punishment. It merely leaves the offender to the mercy of the injured party; or, at the most, allows the sum to be recovered as an ordinary debt.

We are not without information as to the standard which the archaic legislator applied as the measure of damages. It was not the amount of injury that was sustained, much less the amount likely to prevent the recurrence of the offence. It was simply the lowest sum that, upon the whole, it was likely that the aggrieved party would accept. On this point, King Rothar, in his "Laws of the Langobards,"† speaks very plainly. He gives the relatives of the slain their election between their customary vengeance and a wer-geld fixed by law and recoverable before the public tribunals. He says that he fixes a high price in order to induce plaintiffs to forego their right of feud.

* Fear=man, aic=price.

† c. 74. "Canciani," vol. i., p. 69.

The passage seems to imply that if he could, the King would gladly have abolished the system of retributory violence. Absurd as such legislation now seems, it was undoubtedly a great gain that men should be content to submit their vengeance to rule; to admit legal proof, however rude; to accept a compensation instead of blood, and to allow the amount of compensation to be ascertained by law, and not left to the heated passions of the parties interested.

I have taken the wer-geld as the example, at once the most important and the most striking, of this regulative action of the State. But the wer-geld is only a single case of a general principle. As the State interfered by way of arbitration in all cases of disputed rights, so it interfered by way of regulation in all cases of remedies, or, as they are sometimes called, rights arising *ex delicto*. Thus in Roman law, whence, as I have said, the wer-geld had long disappeared, there are many examples of self-redress. If a man had sustained from another any serious personal injury, he was entitled to demand an eye for an eye, and a tooth for a tooth. I have already observed * that the nearest agnate was the person to whom the duty of exacting this vengeance pertained. If a man owed another man money, the creditor laid hands on him, and threw him into his own prison. If a man took possession of another's property, the party injured expelled the trespasser from the land, or took from him the goods, with or without violence, as the case might be. In certain cases he seized the goods of the offender † by way of reprisal. If a man were found stealing another's goods at night, or if being so found in the day time he defended himself with a weapon, the owner might

* *Supra*, p. 135.

† It is noteworthy that in International law reprisal is still a recognized method of redress, and that it is not only consistent with a state of peace but depends on that state. "Repressaliis locum non esse nisi in pace.' See Sir Travers Twiss' "Law of Nations," vol. ii., p. 28.

kill the thief. Where a man's goods were stolen, if he suspected that they were in another man's house, he might enter and search that house in a certain specified manner, without any search warrant or other authority. If he then and there found the stolen goods, he might proceed as if the thief had been taken *flagrante delicto*. If a man were found in adultery, or in unlawful intercourse with an unmarried woman *in manu*, his life was at the disposal of the injured husband or House Father. Gradually, however, the law succeeded in establishing, at least as an alternative for these extreme rights, a system of pecuniary commutation; and the measure of damages was, as in the case of the wer-geld, the state of mind of the injured party, when his right of self-redress accrued. Both in its arbitration, however, and in its legislation, the interference of the State, as I have already said, was voluntary. No person was entitled to call upon the State or its officers so to interfere. No person was compelled to submit to the State's decision. That decision depended for its effect upon the deference with which the decision of the tribunal was regarded. The State endeavoured to promote a reconciliation, but its power was limited to making on behalf of one party an offer of terms which the other party was at liberty to accept or to reject. The person aggrieved had his election to accept the compensation, or to pursue the feud. If he chose the latter alternative, he did but exercise his undoubted right, and he was not guilty of any offence against the State in declining to accept its services. In such circumstances, when all attempts at an arrangement had failed, it was still possible for the State, if it could do no more, to regulate the conditions of the feud. It might require notice of the intended attack to be given. It might direct that hostilities should be suspended during certain seasons. It might forbid certain places from being made the scenes of strife. It might even appoint a time and place and weapons, at and with which, under the superintendence of its own officers, the parties should fight out their quarrel to the end. When some sixty years ago the Justices of the King's Bench were, by a law long disused, required to preside officially upon an appeal of murder at a duel between two champions armed with staves, the public morality of the day was shocked, and Parliament hastened to repeal a rule which society had outgrown. Yet the judicial combat, and the numerous restrictions as to time, place, and circumstance under which a feud might be pursued, were in their day notable advances in the history of law. Thus a wrong done was originally resented by the injured party, without limit and without restraint, to the full extent of his power and of his anger. The effect of his resentment extended both to the wrongdoer himself and to his kindred. At an early period limiting customs were introduced. First it was held that the punishment ought to equal but not to exceed the offence. Second it was held that a pecuniary satisfaction might, and ought to be accepted in full satisfaction for the damage. Thus both the *Lex talionis* and the wer-geld were restrictive and not vindictive proceedings. When the State was established, it interposed to mitigate the quarrels of its citizens, to induce them to accept compensation and to regulate, if it could not prevent, their violence. But it rested with the parties themselves to accept or to refuse this interference. Even if they did accept it, they were entitled * at any time before the conclusion of the proceedings, to withdraw their submission, and to have recourse to the final arbitrement of the sword. Gradually, however, the power of the State became established. The blood-feud, as I shall presently show, was

* See Dr. Dasent, "Burnt Njal," vol. i., p. 140.

limited to the guilty individual; and his kin, unless they chose actively to interfere, were exempted. Disobedience to the law was deemed to be an offence against the King. The process of the court was rendered effectual. Its orders became compulsory. Self-redress was rigorously limited, not only in extent, but in time, place, and circumstance. At length the party wronged was forbidden to do more than to complain. To take the law into a man's own hands became a serious offence, and in the graver kinds of cases the damage done to the individual was merged in the offence committed against the majesty of the State.

The State enforces rights.

§ 4. Such voluntary action as that I have described, even where it had become habitual, would not now be regarded as law. It fails in one essential element of true law—the sanction. It is only a transition, or first step, towards law, in the proper sense of the term. Between the proceeding in which a plaintiff dragged his opponent, with twisted neck, before the chief of the State, praying him to direct an arbitration between them, and then, on being assured of his right, kept his prisoner to work in chains as his slave, and the proceeding in which the regular officers of the State assumed exclusive jurisdiction in all matters connected with litigation, from the first summons to the final execution, there is a wide interval. If we desire to learn how that interval was bridged over, how the advice of the State was turned into its commands, how out of mere custom true law was established, we must look to the history of Rome. It was in Rome, of all the ancient world, that the State attained its highest development; it was in Rome that distinct legal organs assumed a definite form; and it was in Rome that the great function of law was exercised with transcendent success. From the history of civil jurisdiction in Rome can best be learned the ever-growing authority of the State, and the slow degrees by which its supremacy was established.

The original form of civil proceedings in Rome presupposes, as I have already said, a dispute, attended with, or at least threatening, violence between two parties, and the unpremeditated interference of the Prætor. The next step is, that one of the parties forces the other to come before the Prætor. Then the law requires that, before violence is used, a demand to proceed into court shall be made; and that witnesses shall be present to testify to the refusal of this demand. Then the Prætor treats a refusal to come into court as a wrong, for which he will give a remedy by action. Ultimately, and not until the time of Diocletian—perhaps not sooner than the time of Justinian—the State undertook to summon, by its own authority, the defendant, and to compel his attendance, in obedience to its order.

When the parties appeared before the Prætor, the object of that officer was to effect an arbitration. There is a tradition * that in early days the kings in person interposed to effect a mutual understanding, and this tradition we may probably accept. But in historical times the Prætor did not personally arbitrate; he regulated the arbitration. He heard the dispute so far as to ascertain the fact in issue; he directed that an arbitration should take place, and that the parties should agree upon a *Judex;* he instructed the Judex so accepted as to the facts in dispute, and the law applicable to those facts; and he caused him, subject to these instructions, to hear and determine the case. Thus the first step in the interference of the State after the appearance of the parties, was to compel an arbitration. At what time, or in what circumstances this step was originally taken, there is no information. But, although a trial was thus in the

* Cicero, "De Republica," v., 2.

nature of a compulsory reference, it was only a reference. The Judex was a private citizen selected by the litigants to deal with that particular dispute. His appointment was sanctioned by the State; and his proceedings within certain limits were regulated by the State. Still, he was merely an arbitrator selected by the parties *pro hac vice*, and deriving his authority from their consent; and not an official exercising apart from their concurrence the delegated power of the State. A marked distinction was always maintained between proceedings before a Prætor and those before a Judex, or, as they were technically termed, proceedings *in jure* and *in judicio*. Two curious consequences of this difference materially affected the practice of the law. One was that, while the Prætor could only sit upon certain days which were determined by the religious usages of the State, the Judex, who was not an officer or representative of the State, might sit upon any day. The other was that the exact commencement of a suit—a date which, for practical purposes, it was sometimes necessary to ascertain—was the appointment of the Judex, that is, the beginning of the arbitration. All proceedings before the Prætor were merely preliminary. The true suit was the arbitration of the dispute between the parties by the Judex of their own choice. It was not until the time of Diocletian—three hundred years after our era—that the State, as a consequence, doubtless, of the great centralizing changes effected by that Emperor, undertook by its own officers the determination of civil causes.

Again, when the Judex had pronounced his decision, it was not the officers of the State that enforced it. The successful party himself* proceeded to act upon it. His remedy was in all cases against, not the property, but the

* Mr. Hunter, "Roman Law," p. 811.

person of the debtor. In later times the finding of the Judex was the ground for a new action, which appears to have served the double purpose of giving to the Prætor an opportunity to inquire whether the Judex had properly followed his directions, and also of notifying, as it were, to the State, the arrest of one of its citizens. But the arrest was first made by the plaintiff, and not by the State; and the defendant was detained in the custody, not of an official, but of the opposite party; and he was finally, if judgment went against him, turned over, not to the sheriff, but to the plaintiff. In other words, the State, if the proceedings already taken were found to be regular, declined to interfere between the wrong-doer and the injured party. At the time, apparently, of Sulla * this mode of execution on a judgment debt was abolished, and imprisonment in a public prison took the place of private slavery. By degrees, as personal rights became disentangled from the corporate property of the Household, means, which I shall presently notice, were adopted, of reaching the property of the debtor as well as his person. Finally in the time of the Emperor Antoninus Pius, judgment debts were enforced by the seizure and sale of the debtor's goods by public officers. Two great changes were thus completed. The property, and not the person, became available for debt. The payment of the debt was enforced, not by the creditor, but by the State.

So, too, in cases of disputed ownership, the original remedy was, simply to seize the property, whether it was land or chattel, and to drive away the aggressor. If the property could not be found, the obvious resource was to make reprisals, and to seize in its turn some property of the reiver. Out of these seizures, whether recapturing or

* Mr. Hunter, "Roman Law," p. 875.

retaliatory, an action grew. The form of that action was a wager as to the ownership; and the decision of the Judex was, that the successful claimant had won his wager. The victor thereupon proceeded to take possession of his property; but to obtain that possession he had to depend upon his own exertions, and not upon any assistance from the State. The Court had made no order respecting the property, although it had recognized his right to it; and if such an order had been made, there was no sheriff or other executive officer to carry it into effect. If he ejected his opponent, he was entitled to plead in answer to a charge of violent dispossession the badness of his opponent's original possession. If, however, he failed to eject him, the State did not provide any remedy. At length, towards the close of the fourth century, by a constitution of the Emperors Valentinian Theodosius and Arcadius, it was provided that the violent dispossessor, if he were the rightful owner, should forfeit the property to the person dispossessed; and if he were not the rightful owner that he should restore the possession and forfeit the value of the property. "This Constitution," says Mr. Poste,* "may be regarded as the final blow struck by the Roman legislator at the archaic form of remedial procedure, private violence and self-redress." Thenceforward, the State decided directly the question of ownership, and gave possession †—*manu militari*—with the strong hand to the party whose claim it had acknowledged.

§ 5. There is another principle which, in Western Europe, has been widely influential in creating the civil jurisdiction of the State. This principle is warranty. The State, or its representative, guarantees a general protection

The State warrants protection.

* "Gaius," p. 466.
† "Dig." vi., 1, 68.

to a particular person; and if he is injured, it resents the injury as a contempt of itself. This principle was unknown in Rome. In the early days of the Republic, clientage was in effect, an example of it; and there are examples of the public faith being pledged to a variety of persons. These latter transactions, however, relate mainly to foreigners; and in domestic affairs, the tendencies of urban life were not, as I have said, favourable to clientage. But after the Empire had ceased to protect, and before the kings of the Teutonic settlers had consolidated their power, the practice of Commendation became of the very essence of society. It was, indeed, a mere development of the Household. The House Father not only ruled but protected those who were in his *Mund*. Every injury done to them was an injury done to him. At first, those persons who were in a man's *Mund* were the immediate members of his Household—his wife, his children, his servants, and the stranger who was within his gates. When settlements were made among an inferior population, the rule of the Household was naturally extended to the outdoor dependents, or Læts. Then the Household extended itself by the admission of the free-born or even noble retainers, who shared, by a sort of quasi-adoption, the fortunes whether good or evil of their chief.

It was not a great step to apply these principles to persons who desired the protection that a powerful chief could alone afford. A man might surrender his land to another, and receive it again, in whole or in part, upon certain terms, and thus become a better sort of Læt; or he might be admitted by the chief of some clan as a clansman, or at least to the rights of favour and of protection which the clansmen enjoyed; or he might form a personal obligation with a great man, with reciprocal covenants of fidelity and protection. Such transactions would, of course, be evidenced by deeds executed in the usual manner. Thus the homager, although he continued to reside in his own home, would stand in the same relation to the lord as if he lived in the lord's house; and the lord guaranteed him protection against all the world. It followed that the homager ceased to be a free member of the community, and depended upon the commands of his lord. It was at the hands of his lord—that is, in his lord's court, according to the usages of the magnified Household—that he could claim, or could receive justice. If he did any wrong, it was to his lord that he answered it. If he sustained any wrong, it was to his lord that he complained. The lord, in effect, represented his men in all their external relations. Thus, every free man might grant to another his peace; but the value of such a grant, like the value of a promissory note at the present day, varied with the ability of the grantor. It was an object of paramount importance with our early kings to encourage commendation. All men were required to seek out a lord, and damages for breaches of peace were assessed according to the rank of the person whose peace had been broken. About the beginning of the tenth century, offences against the law were regarded as contempts of the king, and were punished accordingly.* Finally, William the Conqueror declared that all persons within the realm were within his peace;† and from the time, as it seems, of Henry II., a similar proclamation was made upon every coronation. In the reign of John, offences committed in the interregnum‡—that is, the period between the death of the king and the coronation of his successor—were unpunishable in the king's courts. I do not know the precise time at which the maxim which denies an inter-

* Professor Stubbs's "Const. Hist.," vol. i., p. 183.

† See Hallam's "Middle Ages," vol. ii., p. 427.

‡ Palgrave's "English Commonwealth," vol. i., p. 285.

regnum was established; but this doctrine was well settled * in the time of Henry VI. Thus, *the* peace of which we still speak means the Queen's peace; and that peace now includes all Her Majesty's subjects. In the presence of that great protection, all other grants of peace have become superfluous, and have long been discontinued. Even the Crown's special grants are read as subject to the more general grant, and are not allowed to contradict it. And so, notwithstanding some local resistance and complaints, the royal courts have claimed, and have by degrees enforced, their exclusive control, not only in matters involving a direct breach of the peace, but in all cases between any of Her Majesty's subjects.

Analogies in the history of International Law.

§ 6. These views seem both to give and to receive illustration from the history of international law. It has often been observed, and it is indeed abundantly obvious, that the greater part of international law is not law, in the proper sense of the term. It is not a command. It does not proceed from any definite political organ. It has no sanction. Subject to the exception that I shall presently notice, it is merely the customs which regulate the intercourse of independent political communities. When rational beings come into contact, if they can preserve their independence, they unavoidably, as it seems, adopt certain rules of conduct in their mutual dealings. It is not less inevitable that these rules should, by repeated use, acquire a constantly increasing influence. There is, indeed, nothing to enforce their observance, except the danger of quarrel and the force of general opinion. Nor do any means other than an appeal to arms exist of determining disputes, save some sort of friendly arbitration. As these agencies enable

* See 7 Rep., 10 *b*, Calvin's case.

societies of men to hold together without any stronger cement, so, in the case of the society of States, custom and its vague supports have not been wholly inadequate. How great a portion of the so-called law of nature and of nations comes under this description, every person may easily judge by merely recalling to mind the titles of the principal chapters in the works of any publicist. These international customs tend to regulate the violence that they cannot control, and to place certain limits upon the exercise of political self-redress. From the archaic "*Væ Victis*" to the rules of war as they are now observed by civilized nations, there is a wide step. The interval is bridged by customs insensibly modified from generation to generation as the moral sense of the world becomes more cultured, and always tending to mitigate the evils of war, to define its limits, and, if it be possible, to restrain its commencement. Between the history of private war and the history of public war, it would be no difficult task to trace some striking resemblances.

There is, however, amid these vague customs and usages of States, one portion of true law. The Customs of the Sea have been accepted by all the nations of Europe as a portion of their respective municipal laws; and this customary law is administered in each country by a duly authorized tribunal. By the comity of nations the decision of every Court of Admiralty is, so long as it administers the common customary law and as its *bona fides* is not disputed, accepted by every other nation. Such decision, nevertheless, is really a determination of municipal law, enforced by the Executive of the country in which it is given, whether such enforcement be or be not regarded as a ground for complaint by the Government whose subject is thereby affected.

A comparison of the law as administered in Courts of

Admiralty with the so-called laws of war by land, furnishes a notable illustration of the influence of law upon custom. Under the hands of a court the Customs of the Sea, once as shifting as its sands, become fixed and definite, sometimes, too, with the results neither foreseen nor welcome. "Of the two codes," says Professor Bernard,* "the one made by generals and the other made by judges, the latter is the harshest; the latter shows the least concern for those private rights which are the offspring and peculiar charge of the law. Private property which is sacred on dry land is lawful booty at sea; private industry and commerce are the objects against which naval hostilities are principally carried on." No explanations of the commentators on international law are less satisfactory than those which relate to the difference to which the above passage alludes. But the difficulty vanishes when it is understood that the laws of war upon land are mere customs which by simple disuse become obsolete, and thus are readily changed with the changes in the minds of men. But the laws of maritime warfare are true laws, and, therefore, admit of no such easy change. They depend upon principles which have been exactly determined by a long line of great judges, and to which, until they are altered by competent authority, the successors of these judges are bound to conform.

* "Oxford Essays," 1856, p. 120.

CHAPTER XX.

THE DECADENCE OF THE CLAN.

§ 1. In comparing the modern form of society with its archaic form, two differences, at the very outset, present themselves. The foundation of the two forms is dissimilar, and their history is distinct. Neither in origin nor in structure are they alike. The unit of modern society is the individual; the unit of archaic society is the Household. Modern society is not simply the natural development of archaic society. It is not by any process of internal change that the genealogic clan has become the State. The primitive social type was complete in itself. It had its own nature, and its own evolution. But the final result of that evolution is not the present political organization of Western Europe. The constitutional government of Queen Victoria is not, and probably could not be, the direct descendant of a genealogic clan. Yet, that such clans and the associations formed upon the model of them were antecedent forms of society to our own form, and consequently had their influence in moulding it, there is, I think, no room for doubt. The question remains, What were the steps of that transition—what was the additional force of which, acting upon the simple clan, our present State is the resultant—what the graft upon the old wild stock that has produced the fruit of modern civilization?

State action tends to Gentile Disintegration.

This influence is found in the State. That form of association which, under the name of the State, I have endeavoured to describe—itself one of those forms of society which was originally constructed upon the model of the Household type—has included, has altered, and in favourable conditions has assimilated, both the old clan system, and also, although more slowly, the system of the Household. Ultimately, in the ordinary course of its own development it has substituted a political relation for the old bond of union. As the new system increased in vigour and activity, the old system gradually dwindled, and at length fell into complete decay. Thus, without any formal change, the old dead corporate system was almost insensibly replaced by that living force which recognizes the full freedom of individual action. I have, therefore, to show that the State does in fact produce these changes, and to describe the mode in which these changes have occurred. The former contention requires little elaboration. It is patent that the individual is the unit of modern society. So entirely is this the case, that it requires no inconsiderable mental effort to realize the existence of a different state of things. Modern society is emphatically political society. It implies great aggregates of individuals living together under a central government, whatever may be its origin and its form. Of this government, they recognize the authority and they obey the commands. Their common bond of union is that they are fellow-subjects of the same sovereign. Each man is accountable for his conduct to the law, and to the law only. Within the limits of the law, he may act, or forbear to act, as he pleases; may gain and may spend; may accumulate property, and may alienate it for such interest as the law allows, either during his life or upon his death, without any regard to any kinsmen or other persons, and merely at his own will and pleasure. He has to answer for his own conduct only, or for the conduct of those persons who are under his direct control; and he is under no legal obligation for any misdoings of his brother, or of his uncle. No such powers or immunities existed, or could exist, in the clan system. They are absolutely inconsistent wth the Gentile relation. In the records of former clan societies, in the description of such clan societies as still exist, they are conspicuous by their absence. If they be introduced into a clan, that clan forthwith commences to break up. In such circumstances, men live no longer by custom, but by law; that is, they live under conditions differing, it may be for good or it may be for evil, but certainly differing, and that too always in the direction of individual rights, from those which in the archaic society prevailed. On the other hand, these powers and immunities are directly produced by the action of the State, whether judicial or legislative. In the proportion, too, that a State advances towards perfection, it removes, except so far as its own requirements and the limiting rights of others demand, all impediments from the action of the individual. Thus the freedom of individual action is found in the State, and is not found elsewhere. Its intensity is concomitant with the development of the State. If it be introduced into a clan, it tends, as I have said, to disintegrate that clan.

The State performs Gentile Functions.

§ 2. Assuming the State to have been fully established and its authority recognized, the question arises, what effect, if any, whether intentional or unintentional, the exercise of that authority produced upon the clans. On this subject the evidence mainly comes from Athens and from Rome. In India there was no State. In Western Europe the changes may have been due, and in many cases certainly were due, to the action of the highly-developed Roman law upon the customs of the Teutons and of the Kelts. But at Rome, and to some extent, though much less distinctly, at Athens, the course of events may be dimly discerned, by which, in the earliest cases of their conflict, the rules of immemorial custom gave way to law. Apart from their *sacra*, the principal secular ties among clansmen were their community in land; their duties of mutual responsibility, assistance, and redress; and their rights of mutual succession. The first of these ties was necessarily dissolved by the formation of the State. The clan land merged into the public land. After the establishment of the State, there was no trace of *Ager gentilis*, except the common tomb, as distinct from the *Ager publicus*. Further, a *Synoikismos*, or integration of clans, implied the rights of intermarriage, of common arable land, and of common pasturage. As to the second of these ties, that of personal solidarity, if I may so call it, the matter is less clear. I have said that at Rome, from the earliest known time, the State superseded all other forms of protection. It is to the "*fides Quiritium*," and not of any other association, that the injured citizen appeals for help. It is the State and not the kin that punishes the homicide. Traces, indeed, of the customary duty long lingered. At Athens, the law required the next of kin to a murdered man to prosecute the murderer. At Rome, the next of kin had the duty of inflicting the retaliation in cases short of death. His clansmen, too, assisted, with their sympathy and moral support, an offender whose guilt they were unable to deny. Public sentiment received a violent shock when, on the trial of M. Manlius Capitolinus,* his brothers did not appear with him in mourning in the usual way. This event, perhaps, marks at Rome the supremacy of the political connection. Its very success renders it difficult to trace the manner in which the State obtained its victory. There is no

* Livy, vi., 20.

distinct evidence upon the subject, and we must be content with such hints as words and analogies suggest.

The Latin word for murder is '*paricidium*.' This word, the oldest form of which is written as I have spelled it, is usually supposed to mean the killing of a father. Neither its form nor its meaning supports this explanation. The derivatives of *pater* take the form of *patr*, not of *par*. The word was never limited to the murder of a father. Towards the end of the Republic, the offence of paricide is defined by law * as the killing of certain specified near relatives, including cousins. Although the statute in question goes on to include relatives by affinity and others, it suggests the traces of the old Familia, or Mæg. Again, one of the oldest meanings of '*paricidium*' is the murder of a citizen. The etymological meaning of the word is the killing of a '*par*,' or equal. But '*pares*,' like the Greek 'Ομôιοι,† and the 'peer' of Feudal Law, seems to have meant members of the same Household or other association. At the Persian Court the words ὁμοῖοι and συγγενεῖς were synonymously used to express a compliment similar to that conveyed by Her Majesty when she addresses an earl as her right well beloved cousin and counsellor. The definition of 'peers,' in our old law books, is persons who hold by the same tenure. Since the death of a kinsman and the death of a citizen are thus expressed by the same term, it is not rash to conjecture that, in a new relation, the same word was used to express the same fact; and that all citizens were regarded as kinsmen. That is, the nature of the original political union was to establish between all its members—at least, to a certain extent—the same relations as those which, by custom, subsisted between members of the same House-

* "Lex Pompeia de Paricidiis," B.C. 52. "Dig.," xlviii., 9, 1.

† *ουδὲ πατὴρ πάιδεσσιν ὁμοΐιος ὀυδέ τι παῖδες*
ουδε ξεῖνος ξεινοδόκῳ καὶ ἑτᾶιρος ἑταίρῳ.—*Hesiod*, Opp. Di., 182.

hold or gens. This view is, I think, confirmed by the earliest description of '*paricidium.*' The terms of the old law* upon the subject, attributed to King Numa Pompilius, have been preserved. "If a person wilfully murder a free man, he shall be deemed a paricide." These words imply that paricide was already a known offence; and that this offence was extended to the killing of any free man—that is, of any Roman citizen. Thus the State regarded all its citizens as members of a common clan; and, as a clan in the like case would have done, punished, in its own tribunal and by a direct personal infliction, the slaughter of one of its members by another member. From this action of the State several consequences naturally followed. First, there was no blood-feud. The State was the avenger of blood; and its command, like that of the *Pater familias* in his domestic tribunal, was a sufficient authority for the execution of an offending member. Second, there was, for the same reason, no commutation or war-geld. Such an arrangement was a substitute for the feud; and if there were no feud, there could be no commutation. Third, the State avenged its citizen, whether he was, or whether he was not, subject to the '*Jus Privatum,*' that is to say, whether he was *sui juris* or a son *in manu.* But this rule does not apply to the lawful exercise of the acknowledged power of the *Pater familias.* Lastly, as the State dealt with its citizens individually, and not in Households or in clans, even while it recognized such associations, its punishment fell upon the offender alone, and not upon any person connected with him.

In England,† the joint liability of the kin continued, at all events, up to the Conquest. The old rule is stated very

* Si quis hominem liberum dolo sciens morti duit, paricida esto.—*Festus.*

† See Kemble's "Saxons in England," vol. i., pp. 261-277.

concisely in the laws of Edward the Confessor—"Let amends be made to the kin, or let their war be borne." Many attempts were made to control this custom. Alfred, while he seeks to regulate it, acknowledges in the plainest terms the general rule. The most vigorous effort at repression seems to be found in the laws of King Edmund about the middle of the tenth century. The king, with the counsel of his witan, recites that "both I and all of us hold in horror the unrighteous and manifold fightings that exist among ourselves." He then proceeds to enact that if any man slay another he is to bear the feud himself, unless within a year his friends assist him to pay the full *wer*. But if his kindred forsake him and will not pay for him, all the kindreds are to be *unfáh*, exempt from the feud, except the offender himself. If, however, any kinsman subsequently harbour the offender, such kinsman thereby makes himself a party to the feud. It is probable that this enactment meant a total foris-familiation, or dismission of the offender from the Mæg. It certainly failed to put an end to private war. But in all these attempts at reform the presence of the sanction is noteworthy. It consists in what was technically called "rearing the king's mund;" that is, in setting up his protection. The form of this process appears in the law of King Edmund, which I have just cited. "But if any of the other kindred take vengeance upon any man save the actual perpetrator, let him be foe to the king and all his friends, and forfeit all that he has." Two circumstances thus tended to break down the liability of the kin, and consequently, so far as that liability was its cause, of private war. One was the gradual substitution of the neighbourhood for the clan, of the *neah búr* for the *neah mæg*. The other was the increase of the king's power, and the consequent increase in the value of the king's peace. Private war, indeed, was tolerated to a later period * in our legal history than perhaps is usually supposed; but the recognition of men's single responsibility must, I think, have been effected with the full establishment of the royal power. It also deserves notice, that, when the royal authority was weak, it spontaneously reverted to the practice of collective responsibility. Thus, after the energetic attempt of King Edmund that I have mentioned, Æthelred,† the ill-advised, sought to secure the peace which he could not maintain, by enacting "that if a breach of peace be committed within a town, let the inhabitants of the town go in person and take the murderers, alive or dead, or their nearest of kin, head for head." So late as the year 1581,‡ the Scottish legislature, in dealing with certain troublesome Highlanders, made a whole clan answerable for the misdeeds of its individual members; and in another statute, shortly afterwards, the chief of each tribe was made responsible for all the offences of the surname. It may, therefore, be affirmed that the State union tends to supersede the Gentile union, both as regards common property and as regards guaranteed protection. I have, therefore, only to consider the right of mutual succession, or, rather, of ultimate reversion.

I have already noticed the old Roman rule of succession. In case of intestacy, the succession went first to the lineal descendants; failing them, to the next agnate; failing him, to the Gentiles. This rule excluded not only all relatives through the female line, but even all

* "It was said by Lowther that if Hugh and Henry be both one side in time of war, and during that period Henry enfeoff Hugh of his land, the feoffment is good; for the reason that, although it be a time of war as between the opposite parties, yet, nevertheless, to those who are on one side it is sufficiently time of peace—which is false."—*Year Book*, 20 and 21, Ed. I., p. 156.

† See Kemble, *ubi supra*, p. 264.

‡ See "Fraser's Magazine," April, 1878, p. 480.

those '*Sui heredes*,' such as an emancipated son, who had passed beyond the limits of the Household. It is noteworthy that the earliest construction of the words of the Twelve Tables was highly favourable to the gens, at the expense not only of these outside relatives, but of the agnates. The words '*Proximus Agnatus*' were construed strictly, and were held to describe a person, not a class. If, therefore, the '*Proximus Agnatus*' declined to accept the succession, or died before he had intimated his acceptance of it, the agnate next to him did not take his place, but the right of the Gentiles became at once vested. It is also remarkable that the Prætor, when he admitted the cognates and the emancipated children, never gave the agnates any relief from the effects of this harsh interpretation. But at some period, of which the date is not known, the Prætor by his edict established a new system of succession. He could not, indeed, make an heir,* nor could he directly unmake an heir. But by an ingenious fiction he introduced various new classes of heirs in such a manner as practically to render inoperative the Gentile rights. His method was to give to the persons he favoured the goods of the deceased; and to maintain them in such possession for a year, or in the case of land for two years, at the end of which time the Roman customary law operated to give the possessor the full legal ownership. The parties who were the objects of the Prætorian favour were, first, the '*Sui heredes*' who had quitted the Household, and next the cognates generally. Thus, although the old customary law was unaltered, the rights of the Gentiles rarely in fact accrued, and in course of time died out from disuse. Such a change was, by its nature, gradual; and its date, therefore, cannot be precisely fixed. An attempt, how-

* "Gaius," iii., 32.

ever, may be made to approximate to it. Gaius* speaks of the '*Jus Gentilicium*' as having become, in his day, a matter of mere antiquarian interest. On the other hand, in the second Punic war,† their clansmen desired, in accordance with their Gentile duty, to ransom the prisoners who had been taken by Hannibal, and the Senate forbade them to do so. This case is remarkable, both because it proves the continuance of the clan duty to so late a period, and because it shows that the State did not hesitate, even on so tender a point, to control the action of the clan. From a case mentioned by Cicero,‡ it appears that in his time the entire subject of Gentile rights was discussed in the courts. Unfortunately, he gives us no information upon the matter, except that the case arose upon a disputed succession to the son of a freedman. The tone of the whole passage seems to indicate that the question was one of old law, and was not of frequent occurrence in ordinary practice. If, as Niebuhr § thinks, the judgment were given against the Gentile claim, the decision would doubtless have accelerated the tendency which we are considering. To me it seems that the legislation of Augustus marks the final catastrophe of the gens. By the '*Lex Julia*' ||—that is, the great statute or collection of acts known as the '*Lex Papia et Poppæa*'—vacant inheritances went to the people; in other words, the State was established as the ultimate reversioner, in place of the clan. Thus, although the law of the Twelve Tables was not in terms repealed, the rights of the Gentiles finally disappeared. They had no claim so long as there were any cognates; and under the new law, when the cognates failed, the State interposed. In name, the '*Jus Gentilicium*'

* iii., 17.

† See Niebuhr's "Hist. of Rome," vol. i., p. 317.

‡ "De Oratore," i., 39.

§ "Hist. of Rome," vol. i., p. 321.

|| "Ulp. Reg.," xxviii., 7. "Gaius," ii., 150.

remained; but nothing was left upon which it could operate.

The changes which, at Rome, were produced by the edict of the Prætor, were effected at Athens by direct legislation. I have said that, in the latter State, the rule of succession was substantially the same as that in Rome, and, indeed, in all Aryan communities. First came the children; then the near agnatic kin, including always the first and usually the second cousin; thirdly, the clan. But after the Peloponnesian war, the cognates succeeded in establishing their claim, even though the ultimate reversion of the State was not asserted as it was in Imperial Rome. The text of the Athenian law, which takes as its commencement the famous archonate of Eukleides, is still preserved in one of the private orations * of Demosthenes. In effect it directs the succession, on failure of children, in the following order:—1. To brothers and their sons *per stirpes;* 2. To relatives up to the degree of second-cousin by the father's side, preferring the male line; 3. To relatives on the mother's side up to the like degree; 4. To the nearest of kin on the father's side. There is here a process similar to that of Rome, namely, the relaxation of the old rule by the introduction of a new class of relatives, not representing, as the old principle required, the spirit of the founder; and the consequent reduction to a minimum of the chances of Gentile succession. On the whole, then, it appears that the clans gave way as the State advanced; that the last secular bond of Gentile union was the right of succession; and that the right of succession was gradually undermined by the authority of the officers of the State, or by its positive command.

An answer can now, I think, be given to a question that

* Against Makartatos.

presents itself on the threshold of Roman law. It was, undoubtedly, as Mr. Poste observes,* "the policy of the Prætors," to encourage the cognates at the expense of the agnates. But why should the Prætors have adopted this policy, and why should they so persistently have pursued it? The Prætor changed from year to year, and the new Prætor was not bound by the edict of his predecessor. Yet, for generation after generation, the edicts continued to evade the customary law, and to secure the succession of the cognates. Some writers tell us of natural love and affection; but, in the first place, these feelings permitted the establishment of the system which they are assumed to have overthrown, and so cannot have been inconsistent with it; and, in the second place, it was upon the remoter and not upon the more immediate relatives that the Prætor's change principally operated. Nor can the change be attributed to the extension of Stoic principles, for it had commenced before the Romans had even heard of the philosophy of the Porch; and that philosophy, although it furnished a theory for an existing practice, could not, and did not, originate the practice. Nor will Mr. Poste's † suggestion suffice, that the '*possessio bonorum*' sprang from that wrongful *possessio* (*pro possessore*) which, as Gaius ‡ tells, was originally given to secure the uninterrupted performance of the Household *sacra*. This theory, at most, serves to explain the method which the Prætor adopted, but does not account for his motive in habitually converting the possession of certain persons excluded by customary law into actual ownership. Nor will any of these explanations account for the Prætor's indifference to the moral claims of the second agnate. But when it is remembered that the Prætor was the officer of the State, and was bound to

* "Gaius," p. 314. † "Gaius," p. 191. ‡ ii., 15.

promote its interest, and that the agnatic brotherhood was a rival very near the throne, an intelligible principle for his conduct can be discerned. It is, indeed, probable that the rule of cognate succession, like all the '*Jus Prætorium*,' had its origin outside the Household; but there was naturally a large class to whom its extension was acceptable, and a sound public policy pointed in the same direction.

Transition from Corporate to Individual Ownership.

§ 3. The Household was much more compatible with political authority than the clan. It, consequently, long survived the full ascendency of the State; and it left, at least in Roman law, deep traces of its influence. The principle of universal succession, the principle that no acquisition could be made by means of a stranger, the consequent retardation of the natural growth of agency, and the whole doctrine of the *Patria Potestas*, are all due to the original conception of the Household as a corporation. Yet this corporate Household was inconsistent with full social and political development, and slowly and gradually broke asunder. Its disintegration was caused, not by any single influence, but by the concurrent effect of various causes. The process may be described in general terms as an alteration in the position of the *Pater familias*. In one direction his powers were greatly extended; in another direction they were greatly abridged. On the one side the State gradually discharged the trusts upon which the *Pater familias* held his property, and, consequently, the restrictions upon his enjoyment of it. On the other side it strictly limited the exercise of his authority over the persons of his Household. Thus, the history of individual property and the history of personal liberty coincide. Both of them resulted from the disintegration of the Household. The House-master stood forth secure in his property, but shorn of his power. The dependent emerged from the ruins, penniless, but free.

"The partition of inheritances,* and execution for debt levied on land, are destroying the communities—this is the formula heard, nowadays, everywhere in India." The like forces were in more or less active operation in Rome at the time of the Twelve Tables. Those Tables recognized the partition of inheritances, the sale of the property of the Household, and the power of testation. As to the partition of inheritances, we have already seen that the principle was recognized by custom, and was indeed essential, at least within certain limits, to the growth of archaic society. But it was a serious matter to establish a new Household, with its peculiar *sacra*, for the continued maintenance of which provision must have been made. The process of separation was probably, therefore, slow and difficult, and required the consent of all parties concerned. The interference of the State gave precision to the vague customary duties. The rule was established, that no person could be retained in a partnership against his will. A process, which was at least comparatively prompt, was devised for ascertaining the amount of each partner's share, and of winding up the affairs of the partnership. So, too, actions were given for the partition of individual property, and for the settlement of boundaries. Little is known of these proceedings; but they belong to the older period of the history of Roman law, and it is not unreasonable to suppose that their tendency was similar to that which we know that similar measures produce in other countries at the present time.

The sale of the Household estate was a grave matter. Originally, as I have said, it was probably prohibited, or perhaps I should rather say unheard of. It was then

* Sir H. S. Maine's "Village Communities," p. 113.

allowed with the consent of the community, who, as the ultimate heirs, had a direct interest in such a transaction. Gradually, as the exigencies of social life grew urgent, it was considered that such sales might be made in cases of extreme necessity, or, as in India, of failure in business. In Ireland there appears to have been a special tribunal, whose duty it was to decide upon the existence of the alleged necessity. The tomb was excepted from the sale, and, if it were possible, the hearth. Still the sale would be effected, but only in a particular form and with the consents of specified persons. This customary mode of sale was, in Roman law, called mancipation, or, from the ceremonies used in it, sale by the bronze and balance. The transaction was attested by five witnesses, who may have been, or have represented, the parties whose consent was required. The authority of the State furnished a simpler and perhaps a safer method. This method,* which was one of the Roman '*Legis Actiones*,' or forms of procedure recognized by the Twelve Tables, was styled "*In Jure Cessio*." It was, in effect, a collusive action before the Prætor, who, upon the defendant admitting the claim, adjudged the property to the plaintiff. At a later period, when the consent of the five witnesses was reduced to a form, the mancipation became practically the easier process, and superseded in its turn the fictitious surrender. But the assistance of the State had done its work, and alienation had become habitual and comparatively easy. With regard to the power of testation, there is a distinction to which I have previously adverted, and which it is important to note. A testament was at one time a means for continuing the universal succession; at another time it was a means of distributing the testator's property. In the language of

* "Gaius," ii., 24.

Roman law, it was either a method of appointing a '*Heres*' or universal successor; or it was a method of providing for the payment of legacies or charges on the property. How the one object was related to the other, or by what steps the modern will was developed, I must, since I am not writing the history of law, resist the temptation to discuss. That which is material for my present purpose is, that the will is distinctly the creature of the State. The true will is found only at Rome, or, if anywhere else, at Athens; that is, it is found in those countries, and at that period of their history where and when the State was developed; and it is not found in any Aryan community while it remained in the clan system. But Solon's will was a clear innovation by legislative authority upon clan custom. As to the Roman will, it is enough to cite the words of the "Digest" *—"*Testamenti factio non privati sed publici juris est.*" There is, however, another aspect of this power. In matters of succession, we are so accustomed to look to the powers of the decedent, or to the gain of the successor, that we forget that that successor has not only rights, but duties. It must be remembered that, by the custom, a *Filius familias,* or other person *in manu,*† could not, if he were required to act, refuse to be his father's heir, and that it might be very disadvantageous to him to be so. The heir was the universal successor—that is, he succeeded to all the liabilities, as well as to all the rights of his ancestor. If, therefore, the estate were insolvent, he succeeded to what the Roman lawyers emphatically called "*damnosa hereditas.*" His liabilities were not confined to the assets that he received, but he was bound to pay all the debts ‡ of the deceased, even if there were no assets at all. The reason was, that the *Familia,* or property of the Household, belonged to a corporation; that

* xxviii., 1, 3.

† "Gaius," ii., 157.

‡ "Dig.," xxxviii., 1, 3.

the corporation was bound by the acts of its *Pater*, or manager for the time being; that the successor was a member of the corporation, either indicated for that office by custom, with or without the sanction of law, or appointed, by virtue of a power conferred on him by law to make such nomination, by the late *Pater;* that, as such member of the corporation, all his acquisitions while he was *in manu* formed part of the common fund; and that he took the property as he found it, subject to all the proceedings of his predecessor. Such was the rule of immemorial custom; and this custom was accepted and enforced by law. But Gaius * states that "the Prætor permits them (*i.e.* the *heredes necessarii*) to abstain from the succession, so that the goods of the parent may rather be sold." There is no information as to the time when the Prætor first introduced this "*beneficium abstinendi*," as it was called. Whatever may have been its date, it marks another distinct step in the disintegration, by the operation of law, of the archaic Household.

There is a peculiarity in archaic procedure which has been often noticed. The remedy against a debtor † was always personal. A creditor could seize his defaulting debtor, imprison him, and treat him as a slave; but he could not enter his house or sell a foot of his land. The reason of this apparent anomaly is sufficiently clear. The land belonged to the Household, not to the individual debtor; and a sale of the holy hearth and its belongings could not take place without grave injury to the *sacra.* The State, indeed, might, for its own debts, and then for the most part by way of punishment, sell out a citizen; but in a transaction between party and party, neither custom nor law sanctioned so extreme a course. At first the

* ii., 158.

† See Mr. Hunter's "Roman Law," p. 73, and the authorities there collected.

Prætor ventured to interpose his authority when, by the conduct of the debtor, the ordinary remedy against him was not available. If, without appointing any person to act on his behalf, the debtor left the jurisdiction, or if he hid, the Prætor had recourse to his favourite mode of operation through the Possession. He gave the creditor possession of the defendant's goods, subject to such conditions as the justice of the case required; and in due time possession ripened into ownership. It is noteworthy that, although he thus assisted the creditor, the Prætor never ventured to interfere on behalf of the debtor. The first attempt to introduce the modern principle of insolvency—not merely to substitute a remedy against the goods for a remedy against the person, but to close the whole transaction by applying, so far as they would go, the existing assets to liquidate the existing debts—was due to the great Julius. It is probable that Augustus carried into effect the unfinished policy of the Dictator. Ultimately, under Antoninus Pius, judgment debts were enforced directly by the seizure and sale of the debtor's goods by public officials.

Limitation of the House Father's Power.

§ 4. The influence of the State upon the authority of the House Father over the members of his Household need not detain us long. No State is likely to permit to any person the uncontrolled power of life and death over its subjects. Thus, in India, as I have said, the British Government never even listened to the claims of the natives to exercise their paternal power. In early times, the assertion of the supremacy of the State, even within the sacred precinct, was necessarily gradual and slow. It was in Rome that the paternal power longest survived; and it was in Rome that the authority of the State was most vigorous and complete. It will therefore suffice if I briefly narrate the principal events in the history of Roman Family Law.

With regard to wives, although cases, even under the Empire, occurred where the husband acted as a domestic judge, yet, in the later periods of Roman history, there are no examples of any severity of marital discipline. This circumstance may be explained by the fact that wives were rarely married so as to come within their husbands' *manus*. Mainly from considerations affecting the property of the wife, the old religious marriage had fallen into disuse. Under the method which took its place, means were found to prevent the usual power from attaching to the spouses. The wife remained in the Household of her birth, under the *manus* of her *Pater familias* or other agnate, and thus was not amenable to her husband's jurisdiction. In these circumstances, the remedy for any domestic misconduct was divorce, a remedy which was obtained as easily as the marriage itself was effected. The marriage tie was, indeed, looser at Rome, towards the fall of the Republic, than it has been in almost any other Aryan community. It was against this merely nominal marriage, if so transient a connection deserve at all the name, that a violent reaction set in under Christianity; and it is probable that a desire to revert to the old confarreal form had a material effect upon the teachings of the early Church. However this may be, this change must have seriously modified the archaic Household. One of its principal members was gone. The 'Uxor' of late days, the mere 'woman in the House,'* could never, in a religious aspect, have filled the place of the *Mater familias*.

The earliest limitation of the power of the father over the children is contained in the Twelve Tables. It is there

* See Fick, "Wörterbuch," p. 23.

provided, that "if the father sell his son three times, the son shall be free from the father." From a passage in Gaius,* it has been inferred that the census, which took place every five years, freed all persons thus sold, except those who were surrendered in satisfaction of damage done by them, and those who for purposes of emancipation were the subjects of a fictitious sale. In this view,† the effect of the enactment would be to limit the father's power of sale to a maximum term of fifteen years. There is, however, no definite information on the subject. We only know that, except in the case of infants immediately after birth, the power of selling, giving, or pledging children was taken away by Diocletian and his successors; and that the power of surrender in lieu of payment of damages had become obsolete before the time of Justinian, and was by him formally abolished. As to the power of life and death, Alexander Severus provided, that the magistrate should hear the father's complaint, and if the son were found guilty, should execute upon him the sentence which the father demanded. Constantine included within the meaning of the law relating to paricide, the killing by a father of his son; a case which, in the first Statute of Paricide,‡ three hundred and seventy years before, had been carefully omitted. About half a century after the law of Constantine, by a constitution of Valentinian Valens and Gratian, the old power of exposing children was taken away; and the duty of every parent to rear his offspring was declared.

The law extended its protection to slaves, probably because the necessity was more urgent, at an earlier period than it did to sons. In this case, also,§ it was under the Emperors that the improvement began. A '*Lex*

* i., 140. † See Mr. Poste's "Gaius," p. 116.

‡ "Lex Pompeia de Paricidiis," B.C. 52.

§ See the authorities collected in Mr. Poste's "Gaius," p. 63.

Petronia' of uncertain date, but probably in the reign of Augustus, forbade the exposure of a slave to wild beasts without the permission of a magistrate, and restricted such permission to the case of slaves guilty of some grave offence. Claudius forbade the killing or the exposure of sick slaves. Hadrian forbade the mutilation of a slave, and took away the power of killing him without a judicial sentence. Antoninus Pius protected slaves against cruelty and personal violation. Finally, Justinian prohibited any severity to slaves, either excessive in degree or for any cause not recognized by law.

§ 5. Milton, in his description of the terror and dismay which, on the eve of the Nativity, were spread among the powers of darkness, notices,* though casually and as of small account, the Lares moaning with their midnight plaint upon the holy hearth. Good cause, indeed, had the Lar to moan; and yet his importance in the new warfare, obscure as he seemed, was far beyond that of those more pretentious deities of whom the poet sings. Ever since that memorable night there has been between the Lar and the Church a war without parley and without truce. In the East the Lar to this day obstinately maintains his ground. In the West he has been remorselessly hunted down. I need not repeat the evidence, which in an earlier chapter I have offered, to show the war of extermination which the Church carried on against the Household worship, and its general success. But this worship was the foundation of archaic society; and when the old beliefs were thus destroyed, the social superstructure could no longer stand. Nor was this all. The precepts on which the Church daily insisted were antagonistic to the most cherished principles of the clan

The disintegrating influence of Christianity.

* "Hymn of the Nativity," xxi.

The God of the Christians was no mere Gentile deity, who confined his favours to his own people. The dream of the Hellenic poet had assumed a definite shape, and the description of the Pantheistic Zeus was applied in a sense which its author would hardly have regarded as possible. All men were alleged to be of one blood, 'for we are his offspring.' So long as this view was confined to mere theory, little regard was paid to it. But it was a hard thing for a Eupatrid to sympathize with a deity who was no respecter of persons, and in whose eyes a slave might be of equal or greater worth than a man who, like Hekatæos, reckoned sixteen ancestors, and the seventeenth was a god. To the clansman, blood-revenge was the most imperative of duties; and the resentment of injuries was a sacred obligation. How, then, could he forgive his enemies, and pray for those that despitefully used him? Further, the whole theory and practice of Christianity implied the recognition of the individual man, and the value of the single human soul. It involved rights and duties which could not be subordinated to the commands of the House Father. It did not merely ignore the Gentile relations, or introduce a tendency to disobedience into the Household; it was directly antagonistic to them. No Christian man could make the daily offerings to the Lar, or take part in his Gentile sacred rites. He therefore ceased to be a member of his Household and of his Gens; and his rights and duties were limited to the members of his new association. So strong was the old feeling that, within that society, and subject to its rules, the principles of Gentile organization were sometimes applied. But there must always have been fundamental differences between a Christian Church and a true clan.

In those cases where the Roman law had disintegrated the archaic society, Christianity supplied a pressing want.

The State had taken the place of the clan. But in the State there was no place for women or for children or for slaves. From these classes the protection of the Lar was practically withdrawn, and the protection of the State was not yet granted to them. It was natural, therefore, that they should welcome a religion which gave to them not only protection, but a social position and consideration much beyond anything to which they could otherwise aspire. Perhaps these considerations may account for the fact which has often been noticed, that it was in towns* that Christianity was most successful; and that it was in the remote country districts, in the Pagi and among the Heathmen, with the Pagans and the Heathen, that its advance was slowest. No allowance for rustic stupidity, or for the keener intelligence of city life, will entirely explain these facts. Other religions have made rapid progress in country districts. Nor is the acceptance of Christianity a purely intellectual process. In every great religious change some event must have shaken public confidence in the old system before men are prepared to accept the new. That event had occurred in the towns, but was slow in reaching the country. It was the breaking up of the old clan system by the exercise of the Proconsular jurisdiction. The Lycian Orontes had long poured down its turbid flood into the Tiber; and even among Romans of pure descent, the Gentile organization, as I have said, had been in effect abandoned. The '*Edictum Provinciale*' had made its way to every great town in the empire, and that edict meant true law. Where that great solvent had been applied, the Christian Church found a ready field for its operations. In every Household many were eager to accept its teachings; few cared much to oppose them. Opposition

* See Dr. Smith's "Gibbon," vol. iii., pp. 422, 426.

the Church had, indeed, to meet * in the public worship, in the classes that were dependent on that worship, and in the countless minor difficulties which arose from the extent to which the old religion permeated every form of ancient life. These, however, were difficulties that might be overcome, and were very different from the stolid *vis inertiæ* of the worship of the Lar. In the depths of the country districts the old Household organization held its course, careless of the changes above its head, and safe in its obscurity from the lictors of the Proconsul, and the subtilties of the advocates. There, too, the old kindly system of domestic servitude continued; and the want of change was not so keenly felt as it was in towns, or in those parts of the country where the system of the slave-gang had been established.

It is material to distinguish between the principles of the Christian religion and that great organization which is known as the Christian Church. Both were powerful social forces, but they operated in different modes. I have hinted at some of the effects of the former. Of the latter I can now but very briefly speak. In the troubled times that followed the long decay of the Roman Empire, the Church was the sure refuge of every form of literature, and of peaceful art. Churchmen were the confidential advisers of the Kings of the Barbarians, because their class had, and for a long time continued to have, a monopoly of culture. But these ecclesiastics were trained in the Roman law, and their administration, under this influence, tended both to strengthen royalty and to disintegrate the clans. Further, the Church itself required, for its own purposes, the assistance which the Roman law alone could give. The Church depended for its income upon the gifts of the pious. It

* See Professor Blunt's "Hist. of the Christian Church during the First Three Centuries," p. 149, *et seq.*

would naturally look with much disfavour upon any claim made by the next agnate, on the ground that the property given or promised or bequeathed by the pious *Pater familias* belonged not to him, but to his Household. The Imperial Jurisprudence, the highest result at that time of the trained intellect, and the object of enduring reverence alike to Roman and to Barbarian, contained principles which exactly met their difficulties. Accordingly, in dealing with those people among whom the archaic customs prevailed, the legal ecclesiastics* gave to some of the later principles of Roman law a powerful impulse. Under their hands the contract, the trust, the will, and consequently the separate ownership, were gradually introduced. Without these agencies the endowments of the Church could not be secured. With their assistance the whole Gentile system of property, and all that depended on that system, were sooner or later doomed to fall.

One great portion, then, of the influence of the Church as an agent in European civilization has been indirect. That influence has been exercised, not in the capacity of Church, but because churchmen were also lawyers and men of affairs. In other words, the Church was the medium through which the Roman law was brought to bear on the clans. To this circumstance is, in a great measure, due the difference between the political results of Mohammedanism and of Christianity. Both these creeds, after their first success, presented themselves to their converts not merely as a religion but as a system of law. Wherever they extended, they destroyed or modified the old clan relations. But, in the case of Mohammedanism, the law was an essential part of the creed, and that law was based on the narrow and inconvenient rules of the Koran. This foundation secured the permanence of the system, but it also repressed its

* See Sir H. S. Maine, "Early Hist. of Inst.," pp. 56, 104.

natural growth. In the case of Christianity, the law was no part of its creed; it was, indeed, foreign, and even hostile, to its Jewish antecedents. But the creed accidentally became the means of carrying a legal system with it, and that system was the matured wisdom of the Imperial code. Thus, the Mohammedan law was itself the product of a lower culture, and was inconsistent with progress. The law which accompanied the Christian Church was one of the greatest efforts of the human mind, and admitted of indefinite improvement. Further, where the Church did not take with it the Roman law, its results were different. The primitive Keltic Church adapted itself to the clan system, and seems not to have materially affected the structure of its society. But no Clan Church, if I may use the expression, has ever been able to maintain itself in competition with the definite organization and the vigorous impulses of the Churches that were founded on the model of the Empire.

The rise of the Modern Nation.

§ 6. The modern nation is thus of comparatively recent date. The rise and growth of each nation forms the proper subject of its own special history. But whatever variation these nations may severally present, they have all a common ancestry. M. Guizot * pointed out that there are three great factors in European civilization, and that these are the customs of the Barbarians, the Christian Church, and the Empire of Rome. This analysis may be expanded, and worked out in detail; and as our knowledge of each separate element increases, their reciprocal influence will also be better understood. The general proposition, however, appears to be indisputable. M. Guizot complains † of the difficulty attendant upon any detailed examination of the extinct customs of the Barbarians. Since he delivered his famous lectures, materials not then available have been collected;

* "Civilization in Europe," Lecture II. † *Ib.*, vol. i., p. 39.

and the preceding pages attempt, in some slight degree, to supply the deficiency which he lamented. His expression, "the customs of the Barbarians," must be taken to include the principles of commendation and of neighbourhood. But it must not be forgotten that these principles could not of themselves have produced the results to which they have so largely contributed. They needed the magnificent precedent of the Empire and the accumulated experience of the jurists. Nor could the latter influence have been practically available without the assistance of the Church, and the services of those learned officials whom the Church, and the Church alone, was then able to provide. Thus the Empire furnished the law, and the Church furnished the lawyers, by which, and by whom, the customs of the Barbarians were insensibly changed; and both the Empire and the Church presented that high organization, and that spectacle of centralized activity, which made so deep an impression upon the Barbarian mind. We justly count among those victories which changed the destinies of the world the defeat of Varus; and, to the Teutonic mind, the Hermanschlacht ranks with Marathon. But Teutons though we be, we are equally bound to rejoice in the great victories that Caius Marius won over our ancestors at Aquæ Sextiæ, and on the Raudine Plain. If Herman saved Northern Europe from becoming Romanized, and so preserved one main element of our civilization, so Marius, the precursor of the Cæsars, rendered possible the Empire. It was Imperial law and Imperial tradition, and not those of the Republic, that shaped the history of modern Europe. It was the consulate of Constantine, and not the consulate of the Scipios, that seemed to the Barbarian chiefs* the

* Writing of Theodosius, the Gothic historian says:—"Factus est consul ordinarius quod summum bonum primumque in mundo decus edicitur."—*Jourandes de Reb. Get.*, c. 57.

summit of human ambition and the highest crown of earthly glory. It was the law of Justinian, and not the law of Cicero, that—more effectually than, in its day, even Hellenic culture had done—took captive its rude conquerors. It was the centralized Church, and not the isolated churches of the several tribes, that administered that law and built up the modern kingship. It is idle to speculate upon what, in totally different circumstances, might have happened; but it is not too much to assert that, if the Teutonic clans, two thousand years ago, had settled, after their usual fashion, in Italy, modern civilization might never have arisen; and that, if it had arisen, its course would certainly have taken a different direction.

Few subjects have caused to historical students more difficulty than the division of history. The old division into ancient, mediæval, and modern, has long been abandoned. The division was hopelessly indistinct, for no person could tell where the one ended and the other began. Further, no mere chronological arrangement is sufficient to indicate the social changes which true history must describe. The time depends on the changes of structure, not the changes of structure upon the time. Hence every attempt to draw the line between ancient and modern history has been, and must be, unsuccessful. The ordinary division, which was certainly incorrect, was at the extinction of the Empire of the West. Dr. Arnold, with greater historic insight, drew the line at the coronation of Charlemagne. Mr. Freeman would, I think, accept this division. Mr. Hallam, for at least Byzantine history, selected the reign of Heraclius. "That prince," he observes,* "may be said to have stood on the verge of both hemispheres of time, whose youth was crowned with the last victories over the successors of Artaxerxes,

* "Middle Ages," vol. ii., p. 112.

and whose age was clouded by the first calamities of Mohammedan invasion." Mommsen* has proposed a new and original division. He wishes to divide history, not by years, but by locality. In his view, history is the history of civilization on the Mediterranean, and the history of civilization on the ocean. But a true division of any organism ought to rest upon some characteristic of structure, and not upon any accident either of time or of place. To me it seems that Aryan history includes both the history of Gentile society among the members of the Aryan race, and the history of political society. The Clan and the State are its two leading features. Gentile history is the history of the Clan. Political history is the history of the State.

* "Hist. of Rome," vol. i., p. 4.

INDEX.

Of the books specified, the following are the editions to which reference is made in this work :—

Austin's Lectures on Jurisprudence, 1869.

Cobden Club Essays—Systems of Land Tenure, 1870.

Grote's History of Greece—
Vols. i. and ii., 1849.
Vols. iii. and iv., 1851.

Hallam's Middle Ages, 1853.

Macaulay's History of England—
Vols. iii. and iv., 1855.

Maine's Village Communities, 1876.

Mommsen's History of Rome—
Vols. i. and ii., 1862.
Vol. iii., 1863.
Vol. iv., 1866.

Max Müller's Lectures on the Science of Language—
First series, 1861.

Poste's Gaius, 1875.

Rawlinson's Herodotus, 1862.

Mr. Lyall is cited as the author of an article in the "Edinburgh Review," on the authority of Sir H. S. Maine, in his article in the second volume of "The Nineteenth Century."

Richard Clay & Sons, Limited,
London & Bungay.

www.ingramcontent.com/pod-product-compliance
Lightning Source LLC
LaVergne TN
LVHW102007210926
848483LV00009B/117
* 9 7 8 1 5 8 4 7 7 1 2 4 1 *